THE COMPLETE ENCYCLOPEDIA OF
CHEESE

THE COMPLETE ENCYCLOPEDIA OF

CHEESE

CHRISTIAN CALLEC

REBO
PUBLISHERS

© 2002 Rebo International b.v., Lisse, The Netherlands

This 2nd edition printed in 2007

Text and photographs: Christian Callec
Translation by: Stephen Challacombe
Production and editing: TextCase, Groningen, The Netherlands
Layout: Michèle Thurnim
Cover design: Minkowsky Graphics, Enkhuizen, The Netherlands
Typesetting: de Zrij, Utrecht, The Netherlands

ISBN: 978-90-366-1599-0

Contents

Introduction 7

History of cheese 9

    How is cheese made? 12

    Types of cheese 23

    Cheese tasting 26

    Storing cheese 28

    Hints for buying cheese 30

    Serving cheese 33

    Cooking with cheese 35

North, West, and Central Europe 39

    Iceland 39

    Norway 39

    Sweden 40

    Finland 42

    Denmark 45

    Great Britain and Ireland 51

    The Netherlands 69

    Belgium 85

    Germany 92

    Switzerland 98

    Austria 104

Eastern Europe 107

    Poland 107

    Slovakia 107

    Czech Republic 108

    Hungary 108

South-East Europe 109

    The Balkans 109

    Greece 110

    Turkey 115

    Cyprus 116

South and South-west Europe 117

    The Iberian Peninsula 117

    Italy 138

    France 155

Middle East and Africa 209

    North Africa 211

    South Africa 212

Asia 213

    Afghanistan, Pakistan, Nepal, Mongolia, and Tibet 213

    India 214

The Far-East **215**

    China 215

    Japan 215

Oceania **217**

    New Zealand 217

    Australia 218

America **223**

    Canada 223

    The USA 223

    Central America 227

    South America 228

Recipes with cheese **229**

A final word **241**

Acknowledgements **242**

Suggested further reading **243**

Index **245**

Introduction

Cheese is an extraordinarily exciting subject, not just because of the tremendous variety of cheese there is but because of the great cultural differences surrounding when cheese is eaten and with what. The Dutch like thin slices of cheese on their bread for breakfast or lunch, or eat small pieces of cheese in the evening with a glass of wine. In countries such as Italy, France, and Spain, but also in Britain, cheese is seen as an enjoyable conclusion to a meal, perhaps with an extra special wine or glass of port. In Scandinavia many tourists will be surprised how the locals dunk their cheese in a large mug of steaming hot coffee. In France the children like semi-mature Camembert in the afternoon spread with strawberry jam. The Americans are renowned for their pizzas generously topped with cheese. In some of the more remote mountain areas of France, Spain, and Italy people nonchalantly brush away maggots or the little worms one can find in mature cheese before enjoying very ripe cheese...

The character of the different cheeses is tremendously varied. Cheese can be creamy, buttery, rich and fully-flavoured, or mild. Yet again it might be sharp to the taste, dry, salty, and crumbly. The aroma can vary from slightly

Feta and fruit, delicacies since time immemorial

mouldy to the extreme smell of sweaty-feet, and the rind can be coarse and inedible or thin and soft. Cheese is inextricably linked with the history of humankind. Cheese is made from milk and from the time thousands of years ago that humans started to keep goats, sheep, cattle, and horses, they also made cheese. Cheese is a link with our primitive beginnings, when humans led a nomadic style of life. Cheese is made virtually everywhere in the world. For some countries cheese is even one of the most important staple foods.

The making of cheese today is less romantic. Large companies have taken over cheese making from the small cheesemakers. Now while there are some excellent large-scale cheese factories I still have great nostalgia for the time when each dairy or individual made its own cheese and the seasons determined which cheese would be eaten. But it is not too late to learn to enjoy old-fashioned style cheeses. Increasing numbers of people are enjoying and learning to value these superb and often unique cheeses. They are the icing on the cake of the dairy industry.

In many countries there are numerous different types of cheese with countless local varieties. There can even be differences in taste within the same village, depending on the quality of the grass. There are also branded products that have a life of their own and cannot be compared with other cheeses. It is simply impossible to include every cheese in the world in this one book but this encyclopedia does describe the most important cheeses from every cheese-producing country.

History of cheese

Ancient times

Early writings identify the Middle East as the birthplace of cheese, bread, and wine. It is probable that the first cheeses were discovered by accident by nomadic tribes in Southern Asia and the Middle East. Humans discovered a very long time ago that the milk from mammals – goats, sheep, cows, horses, and even camels – contains a high level of nutrients. The milk was drunk fresh at that time. When some warriors poured the milk into leather bags in order to quench their thirst on their journey they discovered something strange about the milk: the thick fluid milk turned into a pale thin liquid with thick clumps of white curd. The leather bags were made from the stomachs of young animals and probably still contained curdling enzymes. The sun and the movement of the galloping horse did the rest. Quickly people began to value these clumps of curd as a pleasing addition to the daily intake of protein and the whey still slaked their thirst.

Many historians date the early domestication of goats and sheep to around 10,000 BC. Cattle were domesticated some time later. There are numerous traces of cheese found in ancient civilisations. The earliest of these finds of ancient Mesopotamia, dating from around 6,000 BC according to archaeologists, were found in present-day Iraq among other places. Sumerians kept their cheese in narrow elongated jugs around 4,000 BC. The ancient Greeks refer to cheese in their myths and the Old Testament of the Bible refers to cheese as a welcome source of food and as a gift at 1 Samuel 17–18 and 2 Samuel 17–19 and elsewhere. Numerous wall paintings testify to the knowledge of cheesemaking in ancient Egypt where cheeses were suspended in leather bags so that they could drain. It was clear even at this time that there were two directions to take in making cheese: some products resulted from fermentation of the milk as in the case of yoghurt, kefir, and kumis; others from souring milk, causing separation of the curd and whey. This whey was then scooped into perforated earthenware bowls or captured in large coarsely-woven muslin cloths. The use of perforated earthenware continues to this day in India for making panir and in France for hand-made production of Camembert in Normandy and also Crottin de Chavignol.

The Romans

It was the Romans who perfected the process of making cheese. They were able to influence the maturing process of cheese in their large houses with many rooms. Moisture, warmth, and above all draft, together with smoke from the oven, washing of the cheese, and addition of herbs were all factors that led to a great diversity in types and tastes. Different types of milk were also used: from sheep, cows, and goats were the main types but mare's and ass's milk were also used. These latter two types of milk are only used in cheesemaking these days in certain Asian countries and in Russia. The kumis (fermented liquor also known as kumiss or koumiss) from Russia is made from fermented mare's milk and is around 3% proof alcohol.

The renowned Roman gastronome and culinary author Columella edited an extensive guide for cheesemakers around 50 AD. Romans were then using *coagulum*, a rennet that originated in the fourth stomach of a young goat or lamb. Columella also explained why the use of salt was essential: for drying and preserving cheese and making it suitable to be transported. Roman cheesemaking knowledge spread to the corners of their empire with their legions who were billeted throughout Europe where they took cheeses for provisioning their troops. After their period of active service the soldiers and officers were rewarded with their own parcel of land in one of the Roman provinces. In turn the Romans taught the local populace how to make cheese. Many words for cheese originate from the Latin *caseus*. The English *cheese* can be traced back through the Saxon languages to Old English cese or cyse, via old Saxon kasi, old high German

Cantal, already prized in Roman times

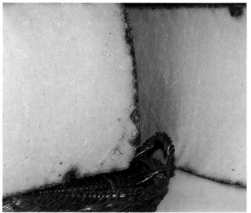

9

chasi or *kasi*. Modern German is käse, Dutch is *kaas*, and Spanish and Portuguese use *queso* and *queijo*. French and Italian words for cheese on the other hand are derived from the Greek *formos* – the form of basket in which the cheese was drained – given rise to *fromage* and *formaggio*. In many parts of Italy though the word *cacio* is also used for cheese.

Surprisingly there are few reports of cheese-making from the areas outside the extensive Roman empire. In Asia for instance milk was used as an offering but the value of milk and cheese to their population was not appreciated. The Chinese too had no tradition of making cheese. Oxen were used in the paddy fields but there was no interest whatever in cow's milk. America too appears to have been devoid of milk or cheese before the arrival of the first pioneers. After the fall of the Roman empire around 410 AD knowledge of cheesemaking was disseminated by sea and along the rivers. The cheesemakers in the fertile valleys mainly made their cheeses from cow's milk while those up in the hills and mountains relied upon goats and sheep.

Ancient maturing cellars in the Auvergne

The Middle Ages

Many of our present cheeses were already establishing themselves by the Middle Ages. In Italy Gorgonzola was created in 879, Grana in 1200, and Parmesan in 1579. The French had famous cheeses such as Roquefort (created in 1070) and Cantal (prized by the Romans) from early times. Dutch cheeses quickly gained popularity because their soaking in brine meant they lost little moisture and therefore little weight as they matured. Trade in Dutch cheese was very successful. Gouda cheese dates from 1697. Swiss cheese too such as Emmental became very popular.

This was partly due to the fact that during the turbulent times of mass movements of refugees,

Rustic scene in Appenzel, Switzerland

daily life was drastically disturbed in Central and Southern Europe. Only the people who lived high up in the mountains lived relatively safely and were able to carry on farming. Hence Swiss cheesemaking continued to develop while others were happy to be able to get something to eat between battles and invasions.

Once the Barbarian onslaught had passed people started once more to make cheese throughout Europe. In comparison to the lands of the north those in Central and Southern Europe preferred to make soft cheeses with longer times to maturity.

From the Renaissance to the Industrial Revolution

During the Renaissance the nobility in the royal courts of Europe determined that eating of cheese was unhealthy and barbaric. Fortunately the people took no notice of them (including the monks who improved the quality of their cheeses and developed new varieties). Cheddar was already famous in England by the sixteenth century and Gloucester in the seventeenth. Stilton is first officially reported in 1785. Camembert followed on from Brie as a prized delicacy (from 1791). The great Industrial Revolution took place in the nineteenth century and this did not leave the world of cheesemaking undisturbed. Increasingly more and more farmers stopped making their own cheese and took their milk to large-scale co-operatives. These were rapidly modernised and the dairy industry grew rapidly but its growth was explosive following World War II. A major stimulus for this process was the great expansion of the towns and cities.

Cheesemaking increasingly became science based with increased research. Scientists such as Louis Pasteur had already demonstrated the effect of micro-organisms in fermentation processes such as that of cheese. Although Pasteur himself did not directly engage in research with cheese, his close colleague Metchnikoff did and it was Pasteur who gave his name to the short heating of milk to eliminate dangerous bacteria. After pasteurisation a pure culture is added to the milk to restart the process.

Craftsmanship: cutting cheese

Modern times

Pasteur's discoveries had an enormous influence upon the dairy industry. There are both great proponents and detractors of pasteurisation of cheese.

Through increasingly stricter hygiene measures together with rules governing the marketing of cheese the European Commission has attempted to remove any risk for consumers but this has made it extremely difficult for small-scale craft cheesemakers to stay in business. Currently there is an enormous growth of branded cheeses that originate either from huge dairy concerns

or combinations of dairy co-operatives that are a little nearer in scale to the individual hand-made cheese producer.

In part because of tragic consequences resulting from untreated cheeses (listeriosis), the future for the independent craft cheesemakers looks rather bleak. Their disappearance though would be a great loss to civilisation. The master cheese-maker who cuts his cheese with great care forms an irreplaceable link with our ancestors.

Successful product of the modern dairy industry

How is cheese made?

The way a cheese is made depends on the geographic area and even from cheese to cheese. Before we delve into cheesemaking though we first need to consider the basis of all cheese: milk.

Good milk is the basis of all cheese

Milk

Good cheese needs good milk as its basis. Good cheese was never made from poor milk, even though the most advanced dairy technology is capable of making tasteless cheese by the addition of enzymes and other artificial aids.

Milking herds

In the Western world we predominantly eat cheese made from milk from cows, goats, and sheep but a good many other animals also provide milk that is used in cheesemaking.

Milk, specially for the little ones

CAMELS AND DROMEDARIES

Both the single hump Bactrian camel (*Camelus ferus*) and two hump Arabian camel (*Camelus dromedarius*, usually known as a dromedary) are capable of drinking large volumes of water at one go (up to 26 gallons/100 litres) and are then able to live without drinking for several months. These animals are used for transport in desert areas and are also slain for their meat. The hides are used to make coats and bags. Camel milk is also important and is drunk and made into cheese by various nomadic groups.
The amount of milk produced per animal is quite low and the animals can only be milked after their second year.
The first year milk is reserved for the calves. Camel milk is richer in fat and much sweeter than cow's milk.

MARE AND ASS MILK

Mares and asses are rarely milked these days but their milk is high in lactose but low in fat and is only ever used to produce soft cheeses and yoghurt-like products such as the kumis of the Far East. Horse's milk is extremely healthy, closely resembles natural human mother's milk and contains many essential polyunsaturated fatty acids and proteins, minerals, and vitamins, including vitamin C. Mare's milk is good for the circulation and very nourishing. The best milk is produced by the Haflinger horses found in Southern Tyrol.

REINDEER

Reindeer are only found naturally in very cold climates e.g. Canada and Lapland (northern Finland/Sweden/Norway/Russia). Many herds of reindeer have been domesticated for their meat and milk. The milk output from a reindeer is extremely low but it is high in fat and proteins which is useful for long journeys through ice and snow.

WATER BUFFALO, YAK, ZEBU

Buffalo, water buffalo, yak, and zebu are different forms of Asiatic oxen. Buffalo and water buffalo are ideally suited to hotter regions and are found throughout Asia from India to China and from Indonesia to the Philippines but also in the Middle East, the Balkans, and even Southern Italy. Increasing numbers of buffalo are now being found grazing in other parts of Europe. Most of these new arrivals come from Italy where their milk is used for the famous tasty soft cheese Mozzarella di Bufala. Buffalo are being encountered more commonly now to in France and more recently even in The Netherlands.
Buffalo milk is fat and contains slightly more lactose than cow's milk. After cows the buffalo is the largest volume milk producer.
Yaks are a heavily built primitive form of ox that is generally kept in the uplands of central Asia

(above 6,500 ft/2,000 m and up to 13,000 ft/4,000 m). The yak is a valuable beast of burden in mountain regions and its milk contains more fat than cow's milk and slightly more protein.
Zebus are a humped ox, domesticated in India, that live at lower altitude in tropical and warm climates. They are found throughout Asia and Africa.

COWS

All cows and other ruminants such as the various forms of oxen originated from the primitive oxen that roamed Europe, Asia, and Africa long ago. There is a considerable variety in types of cow and although all of them produce milk, many are kept for their meat, hide, and horn rather than their milk. The different breeds of cow have varying levels of milk production. A Salers from the Auvergne in France gives less

Swiss Braunvieh

Salers cows

milk and meat – with Friesians or Limousins for a slight drop in quality but much higher yields. The resulting progeny of black and white cattle with caramel brown are also aesthetically less pleasing. Unfortunately this is a common situation. Many traditional cheeses are similarly threatened with oblivion in the near future. A number of breeds are renowned world-wide for their high milk yield such as the red spotted cows of Normandy, the Jersey and Guernsey breeds, black and white Friesian, the Holstein, and Swiss Braunvieh (brown cow).
Cow's milk is slightly sweet with a mild taste and smooth texture. The colour and taste vary depending on the breed of cow but also on what its forage has been.

Cows come in many shapes and sizes

milk than the equally French in origin Limousin or the ubiquitous black and white Friesian.
Unfortunately many old breeds are disappearing under economic pressure to produce both quality and quantity. This is why red spotted Swiss cows graze the slopes of the Aubrac between the Auvergne and Aveyron after efforts with Holsteins proved unsatisfactory. The original breed from this region has vanished. In the Auvergne they are increasingly crossing their Salers cattle – that produce excellent quality

SHEEP

Those who keep sheep do so mainly for their wool and meat. The keeping of sheep for milking is a cottage industry compared with dairy cows. Sheep do have the advantage though of being able to graze less hospitable pastures in mountains and on high plateaux and also in fairly arid regions. One of the most important differences between cows and sheep is that

Sheep only produce milk for a short time

Goats live inside during winter

sheep can only be milked for a short period each year and the yield is quite low. Sheep's milk is only marginally richer in lactose than cow's milk but significantly richer in protein and fat. The milk has a mild but sweeter taste than cow's milk with a stronger aroma. It also has smooth texture. The smell of sheep's milk is reminiscent of mutton fat or wool and the taste also depends on where the sheep have grazed. In some mountain regions sheep's milk has a distinctive nutty taste that is imparted into the better cheeses made from sheep milk.

Manchego sheep

GOATS

In some parts of the world herds of goats are kept for their meat but they are kept more

commonly for the cheese made from their milk. Goats can be kept almost anywhere, having very few demands, like sheep. They are therefore found in many desert-like areas and also at higher altitudes – areas in which cows would not survive very long. The quality of goat's milk is directly related to the quality of their forage. Where they have ample good forage their yield also improves. One breed of goat that is recognised as of high quality is the Saaner from Switzerland and the brown Alpine goat. There is quite an art to making goat's-milk cheese. Those made under less than ideal conditions of hygiene often smell of stale bock beer – very unpleasant. This is partly due to the susceptibility of the fats in goat's milk to tainting, requiring considerable care. If goat's milk is properly handled it produces a fresh-tasting pleasing cheese with vegetal undertones.

Healthy goats produce delicious milk

Forage

Everyone can perhaps appreciate that milk from animals that graze pastures of grass, wild flowers, clover, and wild herbs as their daily forage tastes quite different from milk from stock that is fed inside on manufactured concentrates,

carrots and other root vegetables, hay, and silage. Cows grazing natural pasture may perhaps produce less milk than others kept under cover and fed an artificial diet with its vitamins, antibiotics, and dietary supplements but the quality of their milk and hence their cheese will be far better. There is even a difference between low-lying pasture in valleys that on the higher slopes. A Salers cow in Cantal yields creamy milk with slightly herbal and bitter undertones (alpine wild flowers, especially gentian). A Swiss cow in the Emmental on the other hand produces a fuller, more rounded milk with a slightly sweet taste (fresh alpine grass and alpine flowers). The soil too even has an effect on the taste of the grass and thus of the milk. Finally the seasons and weather conditions also influence the flavour of milk.

Pasteurised or not

The subject of pasteurisation or not of milk for cheesemaking is highly controversial. Cheese has been made since early times with untreated milk. These cheeses were locally made in the neighbourhood where the animals were milked and were always fine and healthy. The advent of industrialisation and growing demand plus financial considerations led to milk being transported greater distances to dairies. Milk might only be collected from the farmer once in three to four days and hence the quality of the milk could no longer be guaranteed. The discoveries of Pasteur and others mean that milk and other foods can be briefly heated to 72°C (161.6°F) in a process known as pasteurisation for which the dairy industry is eternally grateful. Small independent cheesemakers though with their heart in their work always prefer to use milk that has not been treated.

Everyone agrees that good cheese can only be made with good milk but the question of what is 'good' is debatable. With all due respect to the large dairy concerns I have always found that

the quality of a cheese is in inverse proportion to the yield of the animals. The less milk a cow produces the more concentrated and full of flavour the cheese will be. High yields always produce milk of lower quality with a higher proportion of water and a less flavour.

The question then is whether good milk needs to be pasteurised. Pasteurisation is ideal for the large-scale dairy industry for which production volume is of greater importance than taste and authenticity. They often collect milk from a large and varied area which is mixed together and chilled.

Milk quickly changes its texture under these circumstances. Under such situations it is certainly safer to pasteurise this milk to remove all risk of infection. The problem is that by eliminating all the potentially harmful bacteria and micro-organisms beneficial bacteria and organisms are also destroyed which give milk is characteristic taste. This 'kills' both the milk and its cheese. The strength of the dairy industry is that they then impart artificial additives to bring life back to the milk and the results of this can be excellent. The intrinsic charm though of non treated cheese will never be approximated by such mass-produced cheeses.

Cheeses from untreated milk often possess a local character, generally of necessity. Those living high up in the mountains cannot easily take their milk to a large dairy within twenty-four hours and therefore they need to make their

Leidam cheese from a master cheesemaker

cheese locally. This enables the cheese to retain its own identity and roots. These cheeses bear the stamp of their area, village, animals, and soil. The Italian writer Italo Calvino once wrote: "Behind every cheese there is a meadow of a different colour green beneath a different sky." Although a few pasteurised cheeses obtain reasonably high standards, it is the untreated ones that connoisseurs regard as the true cheeses.

Each year countless small dairy concerns that do not meet the strict new hygiene regime disappear, usually for lack of money. Some of these businesses were indeed decrepit and inefficient but survival is difficult too for many well-equipped small businesses. Fortunately increasing numbers of cheese lovers appear to be valuing untreated cheese, offering a glimmer of hope for the future.

Listeriosis

People have certainly been cautious about untreated cheese since there was an explosion of listeriosis, a serious illness that can lead to death. The disease is caused by the *Listeria monocytogenes* bacterium. This pathogen is not solely found in cheese that has not been treated – as certain of the large dairy concerns would have you believe – but can also be found in other foodstuffs and even in pasteurised milk and cheese.

This has been proven a number of times in Canada and the USA. The infection can occur in the factory through lack of adequate hygiene but it also occurs in shops from cross infection or storage/distribution at too high a temperature. The consumer often can be partly to blame in relation to these latter causes.

There is little risk involved with untreated goat cheese because this naturally protects against Listeria with its lacto-peroxidase. This has been proven from extensive research in Spain. This is extremely fortunate because no pasteurised goat's-milk cheese comes anywhere near the

Genuine Cabécou from Rocamadour

flavour of genuine Crottin, Picodin, or Cabécou. These pathogens do not develop rapidly either in hard farm cheeses made from either untreated sheep or cow's milk because the moisture content of them is too low and cheeses with a high level of salt are virtually at no risk to Listeria.

The only reason then for pasteurisation is for general hygiene but if the milk is handled properly within twenty-four hours and the cheese is properly stored then such cheese poses no greater risk for health than pasteurised cheese.

Delicious French goat's-milk cheeses

The constituents of milk

Fat

Fat in milk consists of a great variety of different molecules and perhaps the most important component in milk for cheesemaking. It helps determine the aroma, taste, and texture of the cheese. Cheese made from skimmed milk has a much milder taste and is more neutral than with full cream milk.

Protein

There are two main forms of protein in milk. Casein in soluble form is known as caseinogen which starts to coagulate as it comes in contact with lactic acid. The addition of rennet furthers the coagulation process and the caseinogen turns into casein. The other protein, albumin remains in fluid form in the whey and can only be turned into a solid through ultra-fine filtration or by heating. You can see this happen when you heat milk and leave it to stand so that a thin layer of albumin protein forms on the surface, producing the 'skin' that many people detest.

Enzymes

Enzymes are proteins that act as catalysts for certain biochemical reactions such as fermentation or decay. A number of natural enzymes are present in milk that were sucked out of the udders together with the milk. Lipase, protease, and lactase help to turn fat, protein, and lactose into new components.

These three enzymes are systematically added with rennet to pasteurised milk but also to milk that has not been treated if it does not naturally have sufficient of them. These enzymes ensure the conversion of fat, casein, and lactose during the maturing process into fragrant and tasty constituents.

Vitamins

Milk is rich in vitamins. Some of these are soluble in water such as the vitamin B complex and C while the others are only soluble in fat, such as A, D, E, and K. Vitamins too also act as catalysts during the process of maturing.

Lactose

Lactose or milk sugar provides rennet with the energy to produce lactic acid. Only a small part of the lactose is used in the process with the remainder being removed with the whey. In Scandinavia an unusual cheese is made by heating the whey, leading to coagulation forming a curd which is very high in lactose. This Gjetost cheese resembles a bar of soap or a giant toffee, has an aroma and flavour of coffee caramel and is eaten in wafer thin slices on bread for breakfast. Children adore it. Most countries either discard the whey unused, or it goes for use in the pharmaceutical industry or to add to animal feed.

Trace elements

Milk also contains small amounts of salts and trace elements including calcium, magnesium, phosphor, and iron. These substances mainly originate from the animal's feed. The greater the presence of trace elements in the soil where the animal grazes the greater will be their concentration in its milk.

The process of cheesemaking

The process of cheesemaking is partially biochemical (through rennet or other souring agent) and partially mechanical and physical (such as cutting, stirring, and pressing). The milk is first checked for quality when it arrives and then, depending on whether it is to be pasteurised or not, either slightly heated to 15–40°C (59–104°F) or for pasteurisation briefly heated to 72°C (161.6°F) for 20–30 seconds and then cooled to 15–40°C (59–104°F).

Coagulation

To make cheese the whey (liquid part of the milk) is separated from the curd (solid part). If milk is left long enough it will turn sour on its own and this separation will take place naturally. To speed up this process and control it, rennet, yeast, or lactic acid is added to the milk. These days the process is often started by adding *Lactococcus lactis* bacteria which turns the milk sour.

For cheeses that are to be eaten young and drained without salting or pressing, such as fresh cottage cheese and quark a starting culture can be used of remnants of immature cheese or yoghurt. The coagulation process is fairly slow (around 48 hours) at a temperature around 20°C (68°F). With pasteurised milk the beneficial bacteria that were removed during the heating need to be replaced with a pure culture of bacteria and enzymes which will impart taste to the cheese. This culture gives results ranging from reasonable to good but never attains the levels of taste that the natural presence of the beneficial bacteria in the milk provide.

Rennet

For cheese that is to be salted and pressed into shape rennet is added. Rennet consists of a pair of enzymes (chymotrypsin and pepsin) that originate in the stomachs of young mammals. These enable the young suckling animals to separate their mother's milk into a fluid that is naturally passed through the body and solid matter comprising proteins and fats that can be absorbed.

This discovery was made a very long time ago, perhaps when a Bedouin shepherd stored milk in a lamb's stomach. Rennet is a very good aid for cheesemakers. The harder the cheese is to be the greater amount of rennet that is added. The coagulation temperature with rennet is often higher than with cottage cheese (30–40°C/ 86–104°F) but the coagulation time for hard cheeses is reduced by this.

Increasing numbers of vegetarians will not eat cheese that is produced using rennet but fortunately they can opt for the vegetarian cheeses increasingly now available (especially in the United Kingdom and Ireland). The coagulation process for these cheeses is got under way using moulds that originate from plants, such as the sap from sweet woodruff. Mass-produced cheese uses synthesised chymotrypsin for all cheeses (even for non vegetarians) because of a shortage of the natural thing.

Curd

Once the whey has been separated the mechanical or physical part of cheesemaking begins. The cheesemaker needs to capture the curd in this phase. For cheese such as cottage cheese which will drain themselves the curd is hardly worked at all.

For other cheeses the curd is cut with special knives into large blocks or small pieces, depending on the type of cheese. The purpose of cutting the curd is to release the whey still present but the cheesemaker has to do this with care to prevent too much of the valuable constituents of the milk being lost.

Straining

A mass of curd is quickly acquired and this is then captured in a large cloth. For quark, cottage cheese, or Serac from the Alps the curd is left to

The curd is cut small...

Slicing the curd by hand...

...smaller...

drain in the cloth or in a strainer. For some cheeses such as the famous cheeses of France with white downy covering (Brie, Camembert, Coulommiers), the curd is strained with a special scoop and then placed directly into perforated moulds and the process is repeated. This type of cheese is recognised by the notification "moulé à la mouche".

Stirring

Not every type of cheese is immediately pressed in large or small forms after cutting. This is only done for soft and creamy cheeses. Various other cheeses now undergo a further two procedures. Stirring is intended to separate yet further whey from the curd in order to make it more dense.

The knives are turned around for the stirring process

Heating

This additional treatment is used for large alpine type hard cheeses (Gruyère, Emmental, Beaufort, Raclette). By heating the separated milk (whey and curd) the curd becomes elastic and this is furthered by stirring. With certain Italian cheeses the strained curd is then stretched until it forms threads and is then kneaded again.

Salting

Cottage cheese and also some goat's-milk cheeses and certain cheeses with a white downy covering (Chaource) or red bacterial rind (Langres) are not salted after they have been pressed into their moulds but other cheeses are. The cheese can be washed with or soaked in brine.

The curd becomes more dense

Warming the curd with hot water

The whey is removed

Collecting the curd

Collecting the curd

Collecting the curd

Curd, the purpose of it all

Maturing

Once the cheese has been moulded successfully into shape it can be left to mature. The process to this point will have taken two to three days. The maturing process depends on both the type of cheese and its size. The long road during

Curd is formed into shape...

Excess whey is forced out

...and lightly pressed

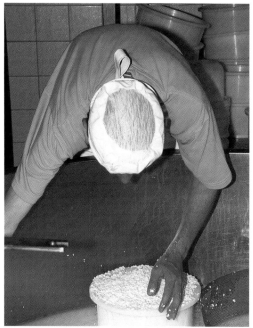

Lid on, ready for pressing

which the cheese acquires its eventual texture, aroma, and taste starts after salting/soaking in brine and the final draining of the cheese. Not every cheese is allowed to mature. Cottage cheese, quark, and similar types of cheese are immediately packed after being drained. Some cheeses are packed in a bath of whey (Mozzarella, Feta). The French term *faiselle* for this type of cheese is wholly inappropriate since this refers to the basket in which cheese is strained. More accurate would be *fromage en faiselle*. These types of cheese still contain around eighty per cent water. Fresh goat's-milk cheese is matured for a short period up to two weeks. It contains about seventy-five per cent water at the end of this time. A longer period of maturing leads to drier cheese e.g. Crottin and Chavignol. Creamy cheeses such as the majority of those with a white downy coating are matured

on average for six weeks after which they contain sixty per cent moisture. The smaller red bacteria cheeses are matured slightly longer at around ten weeks after which they contain just fifty per cent moisture. The larger red bacteria cheeses and hard pressed cheeses may be matured for up to three months and then contain

Young cheese being pressed

The cheeses are turned

Ready for salting

Herb cheeses are also salted

The cheeses get a protective layer

Maturing in a cold room

about forty-five per cent water. Larger pressed cheeses that were not heated are matured for up to six months and are then slightly drier. Finally there are the very large cheeses that are pressed and made from heated milk that are often matured for more than one year. These then contain only about thirty per cent moisture.

During maturing salt is absorbed throughout the cheese and the rind is formed. The proteins in the cheese, in particular casein, are converted by the natural yeast or added yeast and bacteria and this increases the flavour. Lactose and fats are also altered by enzymes with a further contribution to the taste. The creation of the flavour is initiated by the rennet and subsequently taken over by yeast and bacteria. Cheeses made by natural processes with milk that is not pasteurised acquire their individual taste and character in this way.

Goat's-milk cheese

The famous goat's-milk cheeses are a different story. During their maturing specific bacteria convert lactose which releases gas that cannot escape. This leads to the well-known 'air bubbles' in the cheese.

Moulds

A whole series of factors play a role of course in the maturing process. Depending on the temperature and humidity of the cellars in which cheese is matured various moulds can form. With soft cheeses this will generally be a white downy covering on the rind. This can occur naturally or as is usually the case in factory made cheese by human intervention. Blue cheeses acquire blue or green moulds inside the cheese. These internal moulds are usually formed through human action and are introduced by injecting the cheese. Some modern factory-made cheeses such as Cambazola have both a white mould on the rind and blue mould inside.

Bacteria

Soft or slightly hard cheeses sometimes have a red rind formed by bacteria. This results from frequent washing of the cheese with wine, cider or other substance. The dissolution of the proteins is speeded up by red-orange corynebacteria. This gives the cheese its specific aroma (some say stink) but also a superb taste. Examples are Munster, Limburger, Herve, and Maroilles.

Other moulds

Harmless moulds often form a downy covering on the crust on semi-hard cheeses such as St-

Fresh cheese

Nectaire. These grey to orange moulds impart a nutty aroma to the cheese that is highly regarded by connoisseurs. The rind from such cheese is generally not consumed.

Types of cheese

There are many different types of cheese and it is virtually impossible to separate them all into different categories. This why books have several different ways of dividing them.

Categorising by type of milk

This is probably the easiest way to categorise a cheese. Cheese is made from milk produced by cows, goats, or sheep, or even a mixture of these. We are not considering ass, mare, lama, camel, or other types of milk here.
Cheeses are also made from pasteurised and unpasteurised milk.

Categorising by hardness

The hardness of a cheese in mainly a question of the type of cheese that has been made but cheeses generally become harder with age as the moisture content drops. The lower the moisture content in a cheese, the harder it is. Hardness is also related to the amount of fat that a cheese contains. Cheese is further categorised into fresh, soft, semi-hard, and hard.

Fresh cheese

These cheeses are very high in moisture and are intended for early consumption without further maturing. Examples are cottage cheese, quark, fromage frais, cream cheese.

Soft cheese

Soft cheese is matured for a short time. They are so creamy that they may even be spreadable. Examples are Camembert, Brie, Coulommiers, Neufchâtel.

Semi-hard cheese

This type of cheese is firm but can be cut easily. If pressed these cheeses also feel slightly elastic. Examples are Roquefort, Stilton, Edam, Gouda.

Hard cheese

These are hard cheeses with a firm curd that often cannot be sliced without crumbling. Most of these cheeses are grated or ground for use in cooking. Examples are Cheddar, Emmental, Parmesan, Sbrinz.

Soft cheese

Semi-hard cheese

Hard cheese

Categorising by sharpness or fat content

Terms such as low fat cheese are frequently used by supermarkets. A specialist cheese shop will be able to advise you clearly about the fat content of cheese because this takes a little understanding. A cheese indicated as minimum 48 per cent fat may well contain significantly less, depending on the amount of moisture in the cheese because the fat content is measured against the dry matter of the cheese. This explains why weight for weight a Dutch Gouda is better than cheddar for someone who likes a firm cheese and is trying to reduce their fat intake. Both cheeses may have similar percentage fat in their dry matter but a Gouda contains almost 50 per cent moisture. In many countries in Europe cheese is clearly marked at point of sale according to its fat content (as a percentage of its dry matter) but this can be as misleading as many of the other fat claims you will find in food stores. Both supermarkets and a cheese shop can be very helpful in the matter of taste of a cheese with varying schemes marking cheeses from extremely mild to very strong with points or stars. Many supermarkets have leaflets explaining their taste marking system or display it at their delicatessen counter. Almost all shops will allow you to sample cheese before you buy.

A low fat cheese? This 'light' cheese contains more than 30 per cent fat but unless you know its moisture content it is difficult to determine if this is better for you than another apparently fattier cheese that may in reality contain less fat

Categorising by appearance

Cheeses are categorised by appearance in France. This method is much easier for the professionals and lovers of cheese than others. Not just the external appearance of the cheese but the whole cheese is assessed. The categories are as follows.

Fresh cheese (pâtes frâiches)

These fresh cheeses have no rind and appear to have come straight from the straining process. The category applies to all fresh cheeses such as *fromage frais* or *fromage blanc* and includes Petit-Suisse.

Soft cheese with white downy rind (pâtes molles à croûte fleurie)

This includes cheeses for which less rennet was used, the curd only cut lightly and of which the rind has a light downy covering of penicillin. Examples: Camembert de Normandie, Brie de Meaux, Brie de Meluns, Coulommiers, Chaource.

Soft cheese with white downy coating

Soft cheese with washed rind (pâtes molles à croûte lavée)

These soft cheeses with an orange-red rind – sometimes additionally coloured with annatto (*roucou* in French), a harmless colouring – emit a strong aroma as they mature which not everyone appreciates and some describe as a stink. The taste of this type of cheese though is superb. The rind of the cheese is extensively washed many times e.g. with white wine and Marc de Bourgogne (Epoisses and Langres), beer (Rollot), or just with brine, making the rind smooth and sometimes lustrous. The red bacteria concentrate on the outside of the cheese. Examples: Munster, Maroilles, Herve, Livarot.

Blue-veined cheese (pâtes persillées)

The French term *persillé* (sprinkled with parsley) is a euphemism for blue or green mould but it also has another meaning for the French. They term a piece of meat that is interspersed with fat, that provides additional flavour and tenderness (and disappears during cooking) as persillé. After salting, the cheese is drained and then injected with long probes with cultures of *Penicillium roqueforti* or *Penicillium gorgonzolai*.

This culture will spread throughout the cheese to produce attractive blue or green veins. These cheeses mature from inside. Examples: Roquefort, Bleu d'Auvergne, Fourme d'Ambert, Stilton, Gorgonzola.

Blue-veined cheese

Pressed, non heated cheese (pâtes presées non cuites)

These cheeses are fairly dense but still soft to the touch. The curd for these cheeses is lightly cut and well stirred but without heating.

These cheeses are elastic but retain a fairly high level of moisture. During maturing (*affinage*) of

Soft cheese with washed rind

three to six months these cheeses acquire their flavour, hardness, and inedible rind. Some of these cheeses – that have mainly matured in damp cellars – have also acquired a layer of grey to orange mould on the outside which gives them a distinctive nutty aroma. Examples: St-Nectaire, Morbier, Cantal, Salers, Cheddar, Caerphilly.

Pressed but not heated cheese

Pressed and heated cheese (pâtes presées cuites)

These cheeses are the densest and largest cheeses. They differentiate themselves from other cheeses not just by cutting the curd in large blocks with extensive stirring but also by heating the curd as high as 55°C (131°F) so that the cheese drains more quickly. Such cheeses need a long time to mature (up to two years). These are cheeses for keeping. Examples: Comté, Beaufort, Parmesan, Pecorino.

Pressed and heated cheese

Other types

The French system of categorising cheeses would be perfect but for the fact that like other systems it is not complete. Some cheeses do not fit into the categories above.

• **Mozzarella** is in reality a fresh cheese but is then prepared in the manner of a pressed and heated cheese.

• **Goat's-milk cheeses** are all on their own. Depending on the way in which they are made they might fall into any of the categories above. There are very fresh goat's-milk cheeses, slightly matured ones with a natural rind or coating of wax, others with a white downy coating (e.g. Bougon), but also pressed cheeses with a white down or a washed rind.

• **Whey cheeses**, such as Mysost with which the whey has been condensed.

• **Albumin cheeses**, with which they whey has been boiled. The protein still present in the whey coagulates to form curd. Some of these cheeses are known as 're-cooked' cheese (*pâtes recuites*, *ricotta* etc.). Examples: ricotta, Brocciu, Serac.

• **Melted cheese** is created by heating one or more pressed cheeses (usually of lower quality) until they melt and then adding salt and butter. These cheeses are sold both with and without added aromatic substances. These by-products of the cheese industry are not dealt with further in this book with the exception of Cancoillotte that is made from adding butter to melted Metton (a type of albumin cheese). This is a very popular cheese in France.

Cheese tasting

Most consumers compare cheeses according to their 'creaminess' or the strength or mildness of their taste. Sharp-tasting cheeses, especially

Tapping and looking: getting acquainted

those with very strong aromas, tend to be off-putting to those inexperienced in cheese. It is a great pity if you take this stance towards cheese because it has much more to offer than cream and a simple taste. Cheese can put all your senses to good use.

The sound of cheese

What does the cheese sound like? Try it yourself; tap a blunt object against the outside of an Edam, Gouda, Gruyère, or Emmental. The sounds are quite different. A cheese expert can tell you whether there are hollows in a cheese by tapping it and even whether they are well distributed throughout the cheese. The greater the number of air bubbles in a cheese the more hollow it sounds. Cheese without internal hollows sounds dull.

The appearance

The shape and size of a cheese give some clues to its origin, how it was made, its age and such like. Look at the rind. Does the cheese have one? Is it a natural rind or one created by wax or even plastic? Is the rind coated in white down or with a grey or orange mould? Has the rind been washed, is it dry, or moist?
Touch also plays a minor role in assessing cheese. Try this test: with the tips of the fingers touch the soft downy rind of an untreated Camembert de Normandie, the moist rind of a young fresh goat's-milk cheese, the rough rind of a farm-made St-Nectaire, the smooth rind of a Gouda cheese, and finally the often sticky rind of a red bacteria cheese.
Look at the inside of the cheese too where it has been cut. Note the difference between smooth almost elastic Swiss cheese and the soft and supple creamy cheese of a well-matured Camembert or Brie.
The texture of the cheese is also extremely interesting. Note the differences between the almost melting texture of a ripe white downy or red bacteria cheese and the firm but granular texture of a dry goat's-milk cheese. And compare the almost virginal cut of a creamy mature cheddar, Cantal, or Salers with one of the veined blue cheeses. There is a difference in texture too between blue cheeses. Blue-veined cow's milk cheeses are usually more elastic than those made from sheep's milk such as Roquefort.
Some cheeses have acquired their texture and appearance through additives. A typical example is Sage Derby which is often taken for blue-veined cheese because of its attractive green-veined exterior. This effect though is created by the addition of finely-chopped sage to the curd. There are other cheeses to which herbs are added such as the Dutch branded Subenhara or

Examine the cut surface

traditional cheeses from Northern France such as Dauphin or Boulette d'Avesnes which is made from less delicious Maroilles to which herbs have been added.

The aroma of cheese

Some people just regard cheese as a soft tasty filling for a sandwich or as chunks on the end of cocktail sticks. It is preferred for these everyday and party cheeses not to have a strong aroma because this would make the role of the cheese too important. People who use cheese as an inconsequential adjunct to their life are not true cheese lovers. A true cheese lover prefers real cheese made on a farm or in a huge dairy but with both taste and aroma.
Farmhouse cheese has a natural aroma which varies from mild, fresh, and milky to strong, herbal, and even downright smelly. It is unlikely that you will ever encounter a truly smelly cheese that is a product of a big diary concern but they do make strong-tasting cheeses. The taste is created in part by adding enzymes or flavourings such as peppers, garlic, onion, herbs, or even potato peelings. The addition of these

Sampling with a special probe

Much can be detected from a cheese's aroma

ingredients also gives the cheese a definite aroma. Four basic aromas are recognised in the cheese world: fresh to acidic, fatty to rancid, sharp to burning, and fragrant to smelly. Young goat's-milk cheese for example has a fresh acidic aroma that becomes more sharp with animal overtones as it matures. Sheep's-milk cheeses often smell of mutton fat becoming increasingly rancid with age. Many cheeses have a slightly musty smell like an old cellar but others are nutty. Red bacteria cheeses have a strong smell of the gas that is discharged by the breakdown of the proteins in the washed rind. An immature Camembert smells of mushrooms, faintly fungal but more mature ones tend towards ammonia. Connoisseurs can detect from the aroma alone whether a cheese is made with milk from cows, goats, or sheep.

The taste

Our powers of taste are relatively poor and certainly much worse than most people realise. Our mouth and tongue can only really detect four basic differences in taste: sweet, sour, bitter, and salty. We can also assess the texture of a

Try before you buy

cheese with our mouths but that is an end of the matter. Observations such as herbal, fruity, fungal, and so on do not arise through our mouths but through our sense of smell. For this reason it is important not to chew or swallow cheese too quickly but to thoughtfully analyse it in your mouth. This allows the cheese to release its taste and its aroma. These are detected by the taste buds on your tongue and in your mouth and by the scenting receptor at the back of your mouth. The aromatic molecules that are released in the form of gas as cheese melts in our mouths are mainly responsible for our impression of taste. Try it for yourself: sample a small bite of one of your favourite farmhouse cheeses in the usual way and then do so again with your nose pinched shut. The tasty cheese will suddenly have lost much of its delight.

Conclusion

Cheese is a fine product that can excite all the senses if your are open to its possibilities. Chewing a piece of cheese should be an innermost moment, a sort of love affair between the cheese and you. Note how people take great trouble in choosing their cheese from markets in Southern Europe. Supermarkets will generally not allow you to tap the cheese, touch it, or sniff it but most these days allow you to taste a little before you buy where cheese is sold by weight at a delicatessen counter. It is fine to buy pre-packed cheese for a packed lunch or quick snack of cheese on toast, or if the cheese is destined for a pizza topping or as an ingredient in a pasta sauce. On the other hand if you really want to fully enjoy cheese then go to a specialist cheese shop which will have more time for you and be much better informed. Cheese is simply another commodity at the supermarket but it is the sole purpose of the specialist shop. Most cheese shops are run and staffed by the owners themselves, who are usually enthusiasts for cheese. Supermarkets offer an increasingly interesting selection of cheeses and often provide good information about their cheeses available from the delicatessen counter but the staff would not recognise the difference between a Camembert or a Brie or a Caerphilly from a Wensleydale but for the labels. Do not forget that cheese is a living product and that its condition changes rapidly after purchase. The manner in which and length of time a cheese is stored has a direct bearing on those changes in the cheese. Check the condition of cheese regularly.

Storing cheese

Cheese is a food that needs to be stored in cool to chilled conditions. If the chill chain is broken by you then the cheese will start to deteriorate quickly in common with many other foods. Some cheese though, such as the large cheeses of the Swiss Alps or the small rock-hard dried cheese of e.g. Corsica can happily be kept at room temperature. Most cheese though needs to be stored in cool conditions.

The enemies of cheese

DRYING OUT
Cheese needs to be well packed to prevent it drying out. Anyone with a good dark cellar that stays around 10–12°C (50–53.6°F) with humidity of 90 per cent can keep cheese in optimum conditions. The best manner to keep cheese is on untreated wood that is regularly cleaned with vinegar and water. These clean and disinfect and the vinegar quickly evaporates, leaving no trace of itself. You can also lay fresh straw each time on the plank but bear in mind you should not keep cheese close to wine because the wine will eventually absorb the aroma and taste of the cheese. If you do not have a cellar then you will need to keep cheese in a refrigerator. Provided each cheese is individually well packed (since each cheese has its own aroma) most cheeses can be kept in the least cold part of the fridge.

Straw helps to control humidity

Storage on wooden planks

EXTREME COLD
Do not store cheese at a temperature that is too cold because cold air has a drying effect. Cold also slows down the process of a cheese maturing. Check the temperature of you refrigerator. According to their manufacturers the top part is also the coldest which is why salad drawers are placed at the bottom but measurements often show that the top shelf is the least cold while the temperature in the salad tray is far too cold to keep salad and vegetables in. It is often advised to keep cheese in the salad tray but if the average temperature of your refrigerator is 4°C (39.2°F) then the salad tray is often around 0°C (32°F). This is far too cold for keeping cheese.

Find a place in your refrigerator with a temperature of 7–10°C (44.6–50°F). Your cheese will reward you.

HEAT
Dry cheeses can cope better with high temperatures than creamy or fresh ones. Long-term warmth is never good for any cheese with a high moisture content and can actually be dangerous, especially if a few *Listeria* pathogens were already present in your cheese before it left the shop. The deadly bacteria multiply rapidly at temperatures above 10°C (50°F). Dry cheeses are less troubled by this problem because bacteria like moist conditions.
Heat is not only dangerous but makes cheese less pleasing in both appearance and taste. Hard cheeses start to sweat and quickly become rancid while soft ones become very clinging and quickly run after you if you do not watch out...In the case of cheeses that are normally rather smelly the result of too much heat does not bear thinking about.

COVERED STORAGE
Cheese is a living product – or at least the real ones are – which need to breathe. They cannot do this if packed away in plastic or even in a cheese dish with a cover. Today there are plastic cheese storage covers with adjustable ventilation which also controls humidity. Earthenware or wooden cheese dishes with ventilation holes are far better though.

Packing cheese

The specialist cheese retailer knows the importance of the way cheese is packed, providing a sort of second skin. In the supermarket on the other hand cheese will simply be packed in plastic or polythene which makes it impossible for the cheese to live. This hardly matters of course for a lifeless mass-produced cheese but is important for a hand-crafted one. Vacuum packing or wrapping in plastic is not a problem if the wrapping is merely used to get the cheese home and not as a means of keeping the cheese. In this case remove the original packing as soon as you get home and repack it in special cheese paper or use greaseproof paper or breathable cooking foil. Ordinary aluminium foil can also be used if you cut a slice off the same cheese each day and there are special aluminium foils with a paper liner which are more suitable for cheese. This latter material is intended for storing cheese but is best used for short-term storage rather than keeping a cheese which is to be further matured. Whichever material you use to wrap cheese in change it frequently.

Special cheeses, special care

Storage requirements are not the same for every type of cheese. Hard cheeses do not need as much care as others, some of which require special consideration. The temperature needs to be kept low for fresh cheeses because their appeal is in their freshness. Put another way, one actually seeks to halt the maturing process with this type of cheese by keeping it chilled. This applies to all fresh cheese (cottage cheese, quark etc.). Buy only when required, take them home immediately, and store in the coldest part of your refrigerator.

Soft and semi-hard cheeses are stored at a slightly higher temperature with hard cheeses being able to withstand the higher temperatures in a fridge or a cool cellar. This enables these cheeses to continue maturing whereas if they were chilled the process would be halted with consequences for their taste.

Many cheeses have a dry rind and the art of keeping them is to try to keep this rind as dry as possible while at the same time preventing the cheese itself from drying out. If the rind becomes too moist this encourages the growth of mould and bacteria which is not beneficial for this type of cheese.

Turn the cheese regularly to enable air to get at the rind in order to keep it dry. This can also be achieved by washing with brine (but this is not something you can do yourself at home but work for a specialist). You can give the cheese a good brushing with a cheese brush or wipe it dry with a clean and dry muslin cloth (which is the easiest approach for you to use at home). Many dairy-producing countries find this turning and

drying a much too labour intensive activity and so they protect their hard and semi-hard cheeses with a layer of paraffin or a synthetic wax coating to reduce the risk of bacteria and mould. Paraffin wax is a natural product and much better than synthetic wax because it breathes, allowing cheese to continue maturing and gas created during that process to be vented. Synthetic wax forms a plastic and impervious coating and should therefore only be used for cheese that is virtually mature.

Cheeses such as Camembert and Brie (white down), Maroilles, Munster, Livaror, or Limburg (red bacterial rind) acquire an important part of their character from the fungal or bacterial growth on the surface of the cheese. These cheeses must not be kept at too cool a temperature and also not kept too dry.

Hints for buying cheese

Buy from the specialist retailer

Most towns have at least one specialist cheese retailer or delicatessen which pays special attention to cheese. Although supermarkets too now offer a wide selection of cheeses sold by weight and an opportunity to taste before you buy they are unable to match the cheese specialist in the knowledge they possess and are happy to pass on to you, their customer. Most cheese specialists are also enthusiasts for cheese who will happily answer your questions and try to obtain special cheeses for you.

Consider the season

Cheese is a living product which is heavily influenced by nature. Mass-produced cheeses can be made all year round and have the same taste winter, spring, summer, and autumn. Genuine hand-made farmhouse cheese not only lives but like humans has its good and bad times. Certain cheeses are only available during a few months of the year. Learn to eat cheese when it is at its best in terms of taste and character.

WINTER
It's dreadful out: snow, wind, frost...the cattle is all indoors in the warm, there is no fresh grass left for them to eat, only hay or all too often cattle cake. The winter milk is less rich than that of spring and summer and cheese made from this milk is not so filled with flavour. At this time real cheese lovers select a cheese that was made earlier in the spring through to autumn, depending on the length of time the cheese needs to mature. The most popular are the hard cheeses such as those from Switzerland, the French Jura or Savoie that taste superb by an open fire. There are exceptions of course like the wonderful cheeses with aromas of nuts, resin, and pine needles that you can enjoy with your friends during long winter evenings, such as Vacherin du Mont d'Or.

Buy from a specialist cheese shop

SPRING
Spring-time is feast-time. New life springs up everywhere and there is new grass in the meadows.
Once the first sun appears the cows are turned out onto the new grass and their milk from the tender, juicy grass is very tasty, which can best be tasted in fresh cheeses, especially with untreated goat's-milk cheeses.

Untreated goat's-milk cheese is especially tasty in spring and summer

SUMMER
Sun ripens everything and in the dark cellars cheese made in spring is just reaching full maturity. Now is especially a time for those cheeses with a white downy crust such as Camembert,

Vacherin du Mont d'Or is a true winter cheese

Brie, and Coulommiers but also for soft farm-house cheeses like St-Nectaire.

St-Nectaire for summer and autumn

AUTUMN
Summer's warmth ebbs away, grass that was parched and burnt out by the summer sun gets new life.

After mowing there is fresh young grass that the cattle enjoy. Cheese kept in cool dark cellars during summer is now reaching its ideal texture and taste and blue sheep's-milk cheeses are at their most creamy and aromatic.

Not all cheese is seasonal. Large cheeses such as Cantal, Salers, Laguiole, Beaufort, Comté, and Abondance taste rich and full provided they were made when the grass was at its best.

Sheep's-milk cheese for autumn and winter

Learn to recognise real cheese

Many of the manufacturers of mass-produced cheeses recognise that consumers appreciate a 'story behind their cheese' and incorporate this in their marketing. Cheese that is devoid of any character is presented as if it is a product of the farmhouse or a specific region. Genuine farm-house cheeses live up to their name and have no need to create stories which are solely created to sell nondescript commodities to the consumer. Genuine regional or specific location cheeses indicate their origins on the label, are well documented by various bodies around the world, and have protection for their names that denote their origin (where those had not already been grossly abused e.g. Cheddar). Make a good note of descriptions such as 'farmhouse cheese', fromage fermier', 'boerenkaas', and 'Apellation d'Origine Protégée (protected name of origin) such as the French AC, Spanish DO, Italian DOC etc. Pay good attention to indications about pasteurisation or use of untreated milk such as the French 'au lait cru'. The Northern European cheesemakers such as those of the United Kingdom and The Netherlands did not protect the names of local cheeses early enough so that by the time all the different national legis-lation was brought into line within the European Community it was decided that famous cheeses such as English Cheddar and Dutch Gouda could be made by large plants entirely remote from these areas. It is entirely normal to find New Zealand Cheddar and Irish Cheddar in the shops. The big producers took advantage of the name but did not want to be restricted to making these cheeses only in a defined area.

Ring the changes

Do not always stick to the same pattern of cheese buying. What do you buy for a party? Eternal Brie – as creamy as possible – or one of those factory-made cheese rolls with herbs in, or pineapple, ginger, sun-dried tomato; who cares as long as it is tasty on a wafer or thin bit of toast? Most people buy the same cheese year in year out so that they never learn about the countless other cheeses. Visit the cheese special-ist and let him or her help you make your choice. These people know which cheese is most suit-

Vary your choice

able for every possible occasion or use. In this way you may bring entirely different cheeses home and pleasantly surprise your guests.

Be daring

Admittedly anyone who has never experienced anything other than very creamy factory Brie or rubbery mass-produced cheese will probably turn their nose up at a strange-looking or unusual smelling cheese. Yet behind the mouldy exterior of a Pouligny-St-Pierre is a delicious, fresh and fruity goat's-milk cheese and beneath the smelly, sticky, moist crust of an Epoisses is a creamy soft cheese with an amenable fully-flavoured taste. Try to push back the boundaries of your taste in cheeses.

Serving cheese

What is your main reason for buying cheese? For breakfast, lunch, a picnic, high-tea, evening meal, or with a glass of something after dinner? Certain cheeses are more suitable for a given moment than others. Hence a fresh creamy cheese with herbs and garlic is perfect for a picnic but too overpowering for breakfast or as conclusion to a heavy meal. Young Dutch cheese is fine for breakfast (it's what it is made for) on a cracker or at lunch but can be rather lost at the end of dinner. Some cheeses such as the more mature Dutch cheeses and Brie or Camembert are actually fine at any time of day. In Holland they eat their *belegen* (mature) Gouda thinly sliced for breakfast or perked up with jam, marmalade, or syrup to share with a late evening glass of genever or Dutch gin.

The cheeseboard

Cheese can be served in many different ways. Although many people eat cheese for breakfast or lunch the cheeseboard remains a treat for the eye and a culinary delight. A cheeseboard can be made as extensive as you wish or feature just a single whole cheese. Not a Gruyère or Emmental of course but a Camembert de Normandie or Brie de Meaux or Meluns that are perfect with French bread. At the end of a somewhat rustic meal you might choose to end with cheese. Hollow out the upper part of a Stilton and mix the hollowed out cheese well with some tawny port. Return this mixture to the hole in the cheese and chill well. Serve with stewed pears with nuts and some tawny port of course. There are other variants on this idea with the various French blue cheeses such as Fourme d'Ambert with good French liqueurs. A wonderful experience for winter time is for you and your guests

to jointly spoon out the creamy and exceedingly tasty Vacherin du Mont d'Or. This is simply divine! A cheeseboard usually consists of a collection of different cheeses. Although a selection of five different blue cheeses served with delicious sweet white wine such as Sauternes, Loupiac, Barsac, or Cadillac will please many, the majority find this insufficiently varied. The best choice then is probably a varied assortment and an ideal selection contains at least one cheese of each type: semi-hard, hard, blue-veined, plus goat's-milk and sheep's-milk cheeses, white downy crusted, and those with a red bacterial rind. Choose cheese that is in season and if possible from the same area as the wine although it can be particular fun to have a 'Tour de France' on the cheeseboard or whatever other national cheeses you fancy. In this case the wine choice will need to be a compromise to place the main emphasis on the cheese.

Slicing cheese

At parties cheese is often sliced – intentionally or out of ignorance – in a selfish manner. The consistency of hand-made craftsman cheeses is not uniform and generally the centre of the cheese is the creamiest and most tasty. With blue cheeses the middle is also where the greatest concentration of blue veining is found.

Two important points need to be born in mind when cutting a portion of cheese: the cheese itself and the other guests. Cutting diagonally across a wedge shaped piece of cheese shows lack of respect for others. Out of consideration for your fellow guests and the cheese everyone should each slice a portion from the rind to the centre. In this way everybody has the same mixture of tastiest cheese and rind and the cheese itself retains a reasonable appearance.

Another important matter is that a separate knife should be used for each cheese. The freshness of a young goat's-milk cheese is not improved by the more rustic aromas of a mature Munster.

Use a different knife for each cheese

Cheese, wine, and bread

Many books refer to the perfect marriage between wine and cheese but for the marriage to really work a suitable piece of bread is also needed (as witness?). The judicious combination of the right bread with the ideal cheese and the perfect wine for them both can remain in the memory for a very long time.

CHEESE AND BREAD
The moment cheese is mentioned the eternal image of the Frenchman with his French stick under his arm comes to mind but there is much more to bread – even in France – than the French *baton*. Although a freshly-baked French *baton* is tasty, or for that matter *focaccia*, *ciabatta*, or Turkish bread, with cheese that can be spread or fresh cottage cheese it can be beaten easily by the combination of a great hand-made farmhouse cheese and freshly-baked cottage loaf or sourdough bread. Virtually every type of cheese is great with sourdough bread.

In Alsace and Germany the combination of the red bacterial cheeses and cumin is a by-word. To complete the combination you could choose cumin bread.

Is your cheese strong in taste? Then try a delicious creamy currant loaf for a surprisingly refreshing combination. With fresh goat's-milk cheeses or other fresh cheese (e.g. cottage cheese) you can create a contrast by choosing a multigrain loaf. Rye bread or a combination of rye and wheat is excellent with cheeses like Brie and Camembert.

Cheese, wine, and ...bread

Finally with an extensive cheeseboard of a country-style buffet with various types of cheese why not also offer a choice of different types of bread. Try perhaps nut bread, currant, sultana, or date loaf etc.

WINE AND CHEESE
Perhaps no other combination of comestibles is as regularly lauded as that of wine and cheese. If you slurp a little plonk and then follow it with a small chunk of cheese the taste of the very *ordinaire* wine is immediately enhanced.

Unfortunately there is a lot of confusion surrounding wine and cheese. There are almost countless different sorts of cheese and even more different wines. Not every wine is suitable to be drunk with every cheese. Red wine is frequently served with cheese but this is not always the best choice.

Many serve red wine with cheese at the end of a meal because many people do not like to mix red and white wine but much more for the purely economic reason that the red wine was already open. If you or your guests really prefer red wine – which is absolutely no sin – then choose cheese that is best with red wine. A young fresh sheep's-milk cheese like the Corsican Brocciu or a Pouligny-St-Pierre from the Loire go well with either red wine or a fresh white or rosé. There are no set rules for the right combinations of wines and cheeses but experience has shown that the fuller the flavour of the cheese the more full-bodied and robust the wine needs to be. Young fresh goat's-milk cheeses demand a fresh light wine like a Sauvignon Blanc from the Loire.

Delicate downy white crusted cheeses require a lighter red than the more robust flavoured Camembert or Brie that is made from untreated milk. There are also certain cheeses that really are not suitable for eating with wine or can be very unpleasant with the choice of the wrong wine. For example if you are uncertain about whether one of the red bacteria rind cheeses will

Irish cheddar with a pint of Guinness or other dark beers

combine well with a particular red wine then remove the rind and only eat the inner part of the cheese. This helps to avoid disappointment or worse.

A number of very strong cheeses such as Boulette d'Avesnes or Dauphin made from rejected Maroilles are additionally flavoured with peppers and a natural red colouring and really do not taste at all pleasing with wine. You can try a very sturdy red or spicy white but these cheeses work better with a bitter brown ale or even a glass of French gin. Other cheeses like Dutch Edam and Gouda are fine with wine but not with beer.

Belgian cheeses made in Trappist monasteries are far better eaten with Belgian beer, not least of which of course Belgian Trappist monastery-brewed beer.

Generally it is fun discovering which cheeses and which wines combine well. Well-known French combinations include Munster with Gewürztraminer (Alsace), Beaufort with Arbois Jaune from the Jura or a fine Chignin from Savoie, Bleu d'Auvergne with a Gamay from St-Pourçain or a Châteaugay (Auvergne), Bleu de Bresse with a Mâcon red, Chèvre de Corse with a white Patrimonio, Comté with a Château Châlon, Crottin de Chavignol with a Sancerre (from Chavignol or elsewhere), Époisses with perhaps a Savigny (Burgundy), Ossau-Iraty with an Irouléguy, Laruns with a Jurançon, Pélardon with a Blanquette de Bellegarde, Reblochon with a Gamay or a Chignin-Bergeron from Savoie, Rigotte de Condrieu with a Condrieu, Ste-Maure with a white Cheverny Romorantin or a Cheverny Gamay, St-Nectaire with a Côtes d'Auvergne, Selles-sur-Cher with a Côteaux de l'Aubance, a Cheverny-Romarantin, or a Cheverny Gamay, Valençay with a white Haut-Poitou or a Gamay from Valençay or Haut-Poitou. There are of course many more.

Spanish sheep's-milk cheese and red Navarra

Unfortunately many cheeses – and certainly not the lowest quality ones – do not come from wine areas. But if you look you will find surprising combinations among the local cheeses and local tipples. Mention was made earlier of the monastic beers of Belgium and the cheeses of Northern France with beer or even French gin but there are many other combinations of course. One delightful marriage is of a ripe Camembert de Normandie with a glass of the local cider. Close your eyes and you can imagine a delightful rural landscape.

If you are not afraid of strong taste combinations then try the local Livaror red bacteria cheese with a glass of Calvados. It is an unforgettable experience.

Delicious with a glass of whisky

Cooking with cheese

Cheese is versatile. It can be eaten on its own but is also widely used in cooking. Certain dishes owe their entire character to cheese, such as cheese fondue or *raclette*. What can be done with which cheeses?

Cheese dishes can be quite simple from the simple cheese and chutney sandwich or Welsh rarebit (cheese on toast). Cheese can be incorporated into dishes as chunks or grated, can be part of delightful salad, used as a topping in slices (and then browned under the grill) and...whatever your preference.

Cheese in soup

Some countries put cheese into certain soups. Soft cheese such as Tomme (in France) or Toma (in Italy) is sliced thinly and placed on croutons on the bottom of a deep bowl. Hot thickened soup e.g. vegetable is then gently poured into the bowl. Instead of slices of young cheese you could use a grated Swiss cheese. Another possibility is to place thick slices of farmhouse bread that are copiously covered with cheese in the bottom of an oven-proof dish and to cover this with soup. Place the entire mixture under the grill to brown (*gratin*). For this dish the soup must not cover the slices of bread. An extremely well known example of a soup *au gratin* is French onion soup to which grated Gruyère, Comté, Beaufort, or Cantal is added. But did you know that a really ripe Camembert with the its crust removed is ideal for a *gratin* topping to soups such as onion soup?

Instead of putting the cheese on croutons or slices of bread and then pouring hot soup over the top you can also grate cheese into the soup or into the bottom of a soup tureen before adding the soup. Home-made vegetable soup can be turned into something quite special with a little grated Gruyère, Comté, Beaufort, Cantal, Emmental, or even Parmesan. With the more robust type of vegetable soup you might even experiment with other cheeses such as blue cheeses.

Cheese snacks

A slice of white bread, a slice of Gruyère, a slightly thicker slice of York ham, some pepper, perhaps a touch of Dijon mustard on top, then a second slice of bread, briefly in the sandwich toaster and you have a French *croque monsieur* that surely beats the average toasted cheese sandwich.

You could of course use Cheddar or Gouda, or Fontina instead of Gruyère. An everyday snack in many English pubs and across the Channel in Northern France since the tunnel is cheese on toast or Welsh rarebit to give it its proper name. Take two slices of toast and cover them with a mixture of melted Cheddar, beer, flour, and mustard. Put the whole lot under the grill and season with a little ground paprika and cayenne pepper. If you want a greater bite to the dish then add some Worcester sauce either to the mixture or on the end result before serving. The Italians have a version of their own with Mozzarella coated with bread-crumbs and sprinkled with Fresh Italian herbs that makes a tasty and nutritious lunch.

Other ideas for cheese snacks include the Tex-Mex burritos and tacos of Mexico and Texas or the sunny baguettes, panini, or ciabatta filled with tomatoes, onion, cheese, peppers, and salami. In the hot southern parts of Europe they always use cheeses such as Fontina or Taleggio. Very dainty snacks can be made for parties or receptions that are more imaginative than the chunks of cheese with a bit of pineapple, ginger, or glacé cherry or a grape or olive on a cocktail stick. Very tasty *canapés* can be made with delicate pieces of toast or small wafers covered with Roquefort or another blue cheese, fresh goat's-milk cheese, or soft cheese with herbs. These can be made with or without ham or smoked salmon.

Hors d'oeuvres and lunch dishes with cheese

Every type and taste of cheese can be incorporated readily in salads of either minimalist simplicity or rustic earthiness. An example of the latter is the use of Alsace *knackwurst* with cheese (*salade Alsacienne au gruyère et au cervelat*). For a more refined salad try *Salade de Crottin de Chavignol chaud* consisting of a mixed salad and Crottin goat's-milk cheese browned under the grill.

One of the easiest salads to prepare is the Italian *tricolore salata* with fresh ripe tomatoes, fresh basil, slices of Mozzarella di Bufala, some olive oil from Tuscany and balsamic vinegar. Just season to taste with salt and pepper – it's done! The secret of this salad is largely the quality of its ingredients.

Another marvellous salad is made with curly lettuce, croutons, chunks of Bleu d'Auvergne, with a little raw ham from the Auvergne if you like and walnuts: *Salade Auvergnoise*. Some more suggestions: chicory salad with Swiss cheese, pear salad with Roquefort, grilled peppers with grilled Halloumi, peppers with Fontina, Greek Choriatiki salad with genuine Feta, potato salad with Cantal.

In addition to salads their are numerous other starters that can be prepared using cheese such as omelettes with fresh goat's-milk cheese or grated Swiss cheese, *oeufs Florentine* (Florentine eggs: toast, spinach, bechamel sauce, still soft 'hard-boiled' eggs, grated cheese placed under the grill), all manner of flans or quiches

Pasta can also be extended with cheese

with cheese, soufflés, cheese vol-au-vents made from flaky or choux pastry filled with fish or shellfish (e.g. scallops) and mushrooms – cover with white sauce or bechamel sauce and grated cheese before placing in the oven to brown the topping.

Mozzarella is used throughout the world as pizza topping and virtually every *pizzeria* features a four cheese pizza (*pizza al quattro formaggi*) with cheeses such as Bel Paese, Mozzarella, Pecorino, and Gorgonzola.

Main and side dishes with cheese

The best-known main dishes with cheese of course are the various *au gratin* concoctions in which pasta, sliced potato, mashed potato, polenta, rice, or vegetables are covered with a layer of cheese which is then browned under a grill or in the oven. Is there anyone who does not know of moussaka? Another classic is *gratin dauphinois*.

There is much more you can do with cheese though than use it as topping for *gratin* dishes. Wonderful sauces can be made with cheese as a basis to add flavour to meat, pastry, and vegetables. A sauce made with soft cheese is delicious with poultry, veal, or pork. For beef it is better to choose a blue cheese.

Cheese can also be used as a stuffing for meat, usually in combination with slices of raw or cooked ham. A wonderful combination of cheese and meat is fillet steak with those surprising Italian fried rice balls that have a heart of melted Mozzarella. Cheese can also be added to a dish to make it more tasty without further

Swiss green cheese is delicious with pasta

cooking such as the addition of grated Parmesan on top of pasta or risotto. Less well-known by many is the combination of cheese with fish. Try a delicious trout or salmon at least once with slices of Cantal or Comté.

Fondue, raclette, tartiflette and pela

These traditional dishes from the French and Swiss Alps have become pretty well-known throughout much of the world, or at least *fondue* and *raclette* have. *Tartiflette* and *pela* are currently catching the first two up. Pela is the more traditional version of tartiflette with the usurper prepared from layers of potato, onion, bacon, or raw ham that are cooked in the oven with melted Reblochon. *Pela* is prepared in a saucepan with the same ingredients (with or without bacon or raw ham).

Raclette is the name of a dish not of a cheese although you may often find the cheese used for this dish named as *Raclette*. The full name of this alpine dish of France and Switzerland is *racelette à fromage*. Traditionally cheese is placed on a stick but these days a special tool is used, toasting the cheese by holding it close to a

Cheese fondue, an international classic

Classic oven-baked chicory with cheese and ham

fire (or these days special table-top electric heaters). When the outer layer of cheese melts it is scraped off and traditionally eaten with potatoes boiled in their jackets, gherkins, and pickled onions. The term *raclette* literally means 'a scraping'.

Fondue is tasty but most of all it is a sociable and cosy get-together with family and friends. There is a wide variety of fondue choice. The best known are:

- Traditional Swiss fondue (with 50% Gruyère, 50% Emmental, dry white wine and kirsch)
- Traditional French fondue (with 50% Comté, 50% Beaufort or 33% Comté, 33% French Emmental, and 33% Beaufort)
- Swiss Gruyère fondue served with apple schnapps in place of kirsch
- Half-and-half Swiss fondue (50% Gruyère, 50% Vacherin Fribourgeois)
- Valais fondue using local cheese and often with plum schnapps instead of kirsch
- Neuchâtel fondue (33% Gruyère, 33% Emmental, and 33% Vacherin Fribourgeois)
- Vacherin made solely with Vacherin Fribourgeois and water instead of wine
- Appenzel cheese fondue from eastern Switzerland with cider, apple schnapps and a little lemon juice
- Swiss tomato and cheese fondue with same ingredients as the traditional Valais recipe but with 25 ml (1½ tablespoons) of tomato *coulis* (tomato cooked to a runny purée) per person extended with a little white wine; this fondue is served with firm potatoes cooked in their jackets rather than bread
- French Vacherin (50% Vacherin du Mont d'Or, 50% Beaufort, dry white wine and kirsch)
- Parisian bistro style fondue (with strong Gruyère, dry white wine, and a good dash of Madeira)
- French fondue with morellos (50% Comté, 50% French Emmental, dry white wine and chopped morellos (sour cherries)

The method of 'cooking' for fondue is very straightforward. Take an earthenware dish (*caquelon*) and rub with a clove of garlic sliced through its middle and gently warm the liquid to be used (white wine, apple juice). Then the chosen cheese is slowly melted while constantly stirring.

If necessary bind the mixture with cornflour or potato flour and flavour with a dash of spirits (e.g. schnapps) or Madeira, salt, and freshly-ground pepper. The earthenware *caquelon* is kept warm on a small heat lamp. Your guests take turns to dip pieces of bread (or in some cases potato) into the mixture.

Desserts and pastries with cheese

When cheese is mentioned in the same breath as desserts people generally think of Mascarpone, ricotta, or fromage frais, perhaps with fresh fruit but there are many other ways to use cheese for a dessert.

Cheese-cake has spread far and wide from the USA and Britain with enormous diversity of combinations and *tiramisu* from Italy has also conquered widely with its combination of sponge fingers, coffee or cocoa extract, Marsala (or other liqueur, rum, or brandy), eggs, and chocolate topping for a refreshing desserts. The French make small cream cheese hearts from fresh cheese and cream (*crèmets or coeurs à la crème*) that are traditionally served with a fresh *coulis* of red summer fruits.

Cheese can be a sweet in its own right such as thin slices of Pyrenean sheep's-milk cheese with a blob of black cherry preserve, Herve, or better still Belgian Remoudou cheese with syrup from Liege, Roquefort with fresh pears and walnuts, gorgonzola with poached peach...much is possible with cheese.

Cheese with fruit is simple and delicious

Cheese can be a delicious and stylish dessert

North, West, and Central Europe

Iceland

Iceland is a country full of contrasts with a climate strangely influenced by glaciers and geysers. Only a very small part of the area of this land mass is suitable for any form of agriculture. A proportionately high number of animals are kept on the small green strip of land between the sea and the high mountains. Once it was mainly sheep's-milk cheeses that were made in Iceland such as Skyr but unfortunately many of the sheep have given way to cows which produce more milk from the same piece of ground. Iceland's dairy industry today is dynamic but it mainly produces copies of cheeses from elsewhere, and not just Scandinavia.

SKYR

Skyr is a fresh cheese originally made from sheep's milk but now from cow's milk. It resembles a thick quark and is mainly used for culinary purposes. Stiffly beaten with milk and lots of sugar it makes a favourite treat for Icelandic children.

Norway

Norway is a large and very elongated country with only a very small part available for grazing animals on thin strips of land along the coast. The rest of the country consists of immense forests, tundra, inhospitable rocky plateaux, mountains, and towns. Norway did not really establish its own cheese industry in the past, relying mainly on fishing and trading fish in return for other foods, including cheese. Some of that cheese was imported was from Leiden in the provinces of Holland in part of what is today The Netherlands and from the seventeenth century on the Norwegians started to make their own version of this cheese. Besides this Nökkelost cheese, as it is called, they started to make other cheeses, some of which have centuries of local tradition behind them. The best-known of these are Gammelost, Mysost, Gjetost, Jarlsberg, and Ridder. There are also plenty of modern but less interesting cheeses now made in Norway such as Brie, Camembert, Gouda, Edam, Emmental, Tilsit, and a number of blue cheeses.

GAMMELOST

Gammelost means 'old cheese' in Norwegian. This really is a cheese to be stored for the cold months of winter and it has a long history behind it. Genuine Gammelost is made from goat's milk and has a fairly crude external appearance. The colour of this cylindrical cheese is greenish to dark brown at the sides. The weight varies from 6 lb 8 oz (3 kg) for an immature cheese to 4 lb 6 oz (2 kg) for a really mature example. The exterior of this cheese is pitted with lots of cracks in the rind. Immature cheese has a smooth texture and is mild tasting while mature ones are rock hard and very strong. The strong taste is created by adding fungal cultures which often manage to find their way inside the cheese. This was once a coincidental occurrence resulting from less than hygienic cellars but today the process is controlled from beginning to end to ensure it occurs. Blue veins are often found in the otherwise predominantly yellow-brown cheese. This unusual cheese has an additional advantage for those trying to watch their weight: it contains only 5% fat. The strong and somewhat herbal taste is not really suitable for combining with wine and certainly not lighter ones such as Beaujolais as is sometimes recommended. A strong winter beer such as Trippel or some aquavit (*eau-e-vie*) or Dutch genever is far more appropriate.

GEITOST/GEJTOST/GJETOST

It seems to be difficult deciding which spelling is correct for this cheese. The name is pronounced 'Yight-ost'. In any even this cheese is made from *geitmjøst* or goat's milk and we have chosen the most frequently occurring spelling of 'Geitost'. This *ekte Geitost* or genuine Geitost is still made from goat's milk but many imitations are made from a blend of goat's and cow's milk. Geitost is an exceptional cheese that is produced by heating whey so that the proteins in the whey coagulate. It resembles a bar of soap, and is semi-hard and the colour of caramel. The aroma is

Geitost

also unusual and reminiscent of a soft caramel toffee with a hint of goat's-milk. If at all possible the taste is even more unusual with suggestions of caramel toffee, goat, salty nuances, a hint of eel or other smoked fish. Norwegian children adore this cheese and eat it very thinly sliced on their bread or a cracker for breakfast. Wine is not appropriate for this cheese. It is a true breakfast cheese which the Norwegians dunk in a steaming cup of tea or large beaker of milky coffee.

JARLSBERG

Jarlsberg cheese is enjoying a revival. It was previously very popular in the Middle Ages but fell into virtual oblivion for a very long time. This old Norwegian variant of an Emmental cheese was rediscovered in the middle of the twentieth century, and not just in Norway. Americans have also become very keen on it. The cheese resembles a mini Emmental of about 22 lb (10 kg). The cheese has strikingly large air bubbles and is quite soft. Jarslberg is produced from rich summer milk from the higher pastures. It is an extremely pleasing cheese that is ideal on bread but also useful in the kitchen or on a cheeseboard. The taste is creamy and milder than the Swiss Emmental, also less nutty, but certainly sweeter. The mild taste makes this cheese an ideal combination with wine, beer, or aquavit. Choose a fresh white e.g. from Alsace, the Jura, Savoie, or from Switzerland for the best contrast.

MYSOST

Geitost was once exclusively made from goat's milk but today such cheeses are produced from a blend of goat's milk and cow's milk or solely with cow's milk. The cheeses are differentiated as follows: real Geitost made from 100% goat's milk, Geitost from a blend of both types of milk, and Mytost made with just cow's milk. Mytost is just as sweet a cheese as both of the Geitost cheeses but slightly milder in taste, with a hint of whey. This is a breakfast cheese that combines well with tea or milk coffee.

NÖKKELOST

The story behind Nökkelost is directly linked to a very old Dutch cheese made by the farmers around Leiden. The cheese was imprinted with the keys from the town's coat of arms as a sign of quality. The hard Dutch cheese with a very low level of fat travels well and its taste was strong enough to appeal to the Scandinavians and so ship loads of Leiden cheese were imported into Norway. In the seventeenth century the Norwegians started to make an identical cheese themselves, right down to the keys of the Leiden coat of arms and this is also where the Norwegian name for this cheese springs: *nökkel* means 'key' in Norse. Nökkelost is a semi-hard cheese in the shape of a flat wagon wheel of 11 lb or 26 lb 7 oz (5 or 12 kg). The maturing time is three months and just like Dutch Leiden cheese Nökkelost has cumin seed added. The strong taste and aroma of cumin goes well with a full-bodied white wine such as Pinot Gris d'Alsace, a Gewürztraminer from Alsace or Germany or a southern Tramini from Hungary.

RIDDER

Ridder is the best of all the modern Norwegian cheeses. It is a very successful copy of St-Paulin except that it is much creamier. This orange cheese with form of a squat wagon wheel or cylinder weighs 3 lb 5 oz–6 lb 10 oz (1.5–3 kg). Maturing time is three months. The 'creator' of Ridder, Sven Fenelius, comes from Sweden. He cannot have expected his cheese to be so successful. The cheese is very creamy and reminiscent of farm butter with mellow undertones. Do not leave it in its packaging too long because the cheese suffers as you will quickly smell when tasting. This makes the cheese quite strong and it develops an unpleasant smell. Drink a delicious glass of pinot noir with this cheese e.g. a Burgundy or Swiss wine.

Sweden

Sweden is much larger than Norway and has more agricultural land, although the north of the country is mainly forest and agriculture is concentrated in the south where the climate is more moderate. Sweden imported cheese for a long time just like Norway and the major imports were of Dutch cheese. Yet Sweden did make its own cheese in the Middle Ages, mainly prepared from sheep's-milk. The north of the country is where the extremely rare reindeer-milk cheese or *Lapparnas* is made. Today this cheese is made in very small quantity and because the yield of reindeer milk is so low you will never encounter this cheese outside Lapland. Sweden has several cheeses of a regional character. Cheeses such as Prästost hark back to an era when the village pastor kept himself on a patch of land belonging to the church. Home-made cheeses or *Hushållsost* are named after the

Sweden has many regional cheeses and brands

area where they are made. The best-known is Gräddost. These cheeses are quite young and mild tasting. One real Swedish speciality is Sveciaost that is produced in several forms and tastes from mild to strong. A similar but larger cheese is Västerbottenost. Aromatic Kryddost is comparable with a Norwegian and Leiden 'key' cheese, with cumin and cloves. There are also a number of 'Scandinavian' cheeses produced in Sweden such as Riddarost, Mesost, and Getost. Finally many modern cheeses are also made in Sweden that are copies of international cheeses. If you are presented with a cheeseboard in Sweden you will not be disappointed. The Swedish people are mad about cheese and eat on average 33 lb (15 kg) per person each year.

ADELOST
Adelost is a blue-veined cow's milk cheese that resembles Bleu d'Auvergne. This cheese has a fine ivory coloured 'curd' with delightful blue-grey veins. The rind is often lightly covered with mould. The aroma is mild, the taste is creamy, slightly salty, and strong. Maturing time is 2–3 months, fat content 50%. Drink a slightly sweet white wine such as a Rosette or Côtes de Montravel or even sweeter white such as a Saussignac or Haut-Montravel with this cheese. Other wines you could choose include a German or Austrian Spätlese or Auslese. Those who prefer red wine should choose a full-bodied one from South-western France such as Cahors, Madiran, Gaillac, or Marmandais.

GEITOST
Geitost is a goat's milk version of Norwegian Mytost/Geitost (see Norway).

GRADDOST
This is probably Sweden's most popular cheese. It is a modern semi-hard cheese made with cow's milk, weight about 2 lb 3 oz (1kg).
It closely resembles Havarti and it is creamy, mild in taste, and you may often detect a smoky aroma as though the cheese has been smoked over beech wood. The cheese also has a slightly bitter after-

Graddost

taste. Fat content is 60%. You can eat this cheese with either fresh white wines e.g. Alsace, dry Mosel, Jura, Trentino bianco or light reds, preferable made from Gamay e.g. Touraine, Beaujolais, of Swiss Gamay.

GREVEOST
Some regard this cheese, which is also known simply as Grevé, as Sweden's best. Others find it a poor copy of a Swiss Emmental. Grevéost is a large wagon wheel of a cheese weighing 26 lb 7 oz–30 lb 14 oz (12–14 kg). The cow's milk cheese with large air bubbles in it is soft, creamy (fat content 45%) and sweet, with a slightly nutty taste. Despite its maturing time of ten months this cheese did not really excite me. It has too little character for that. Despite this it is a fine cheese for the table to eat as chunks or grated. Drink a fresh white wine from Alsace, Germany, Austria, Switzerland, or Northern Italy with this cheese or a light Gamay red from the Jura, Savoie, or Switzerland.

Grevéost

HERRGARDSOST
A literal translation of the name of this cheese is 'knight's house cheese'. The cheese does have certain nobility and comes in the form of a wagon wheel of 26 lb 7 oz–44 lb (12–20 kg). The cheese takes at least seven months to mature. This traditional cow's milk cheese with small air bubbles in is often coated with yellow wax. While Grevéost is a poor imitation of Emmental, Herrgardsost is a successful version of Swiss Gruyère. The cheese itself is creamy, supple and soft, the taste is mild and creamy (45% fat), fresh and slightly salty. There is also a 30% fat version.
This cheese demands a fresh white wine such as the Swiss Fendant or a Savoie, preferably a Crépy or an Chignin-Bergeron.

HUSHÅLLSOST
The traditional semi-hard cheese is made from cow's milk. This is a fairly old cheese that was originally made at home by housewives, hence its

name of "household cheese." Today this cheese is factory made. The 11 lb (5kg) cheese is like a rather flat cylinder. Inside the cheese is slightly ivory coloured and has small air bubbles. It tastes creamy and is also delightfully fresh. Maturing time is 1–3 months, fat content 45%. This is a tasty cheese for lunch with freshly-basked farmhouse bread but it is also suitable for use with *gratin* dishes. Serve with mild-mannered white from the Loire of Alsace.

Hushållsost

MESOST
Mesost is the Swedish version of Mysost (See Norway). This is a traditional cheese made by heating the whey of cow's milk. In this way the albumin proteins in the whey coagulate. They contain a lot of lactose which can be readily detected. This cheese looks like a large toffee and both smells and tastes of caramel, is creamy tasty too but with a slightly bitter undertone. This cheese contains only 20% fat. No wine really suits this cheese. Mesost is very much a breakfast cheese that is drunk with a large cup of coffee with whipped milk.

PRÅTOST
A traditional semi-hard cheese that originally came from meadows belonging to the church in the sixteenth century. The village pastor was paid in milk at the time and his wife made cheese from it which was then sold at the local market. Today these cheeses are all made in large industrial-scale dairies and they weigh 26 lb 6 oz–33 lb (12–15 kg) being shaped like a wagon wheel. The fat content is 45%. The inner cheese is light to darker ivory in colour with small irregular air bubbles. This cheese is mild and fresh when young but stronger with age. The fresh sweet nuances in its flavour are characteristic of this cheese together with fruitiness and strength in the taste and milky aroma.

Each region has its own Prätost and there are rare varieties which have the rind regularly washed

with liquor e.g. whisky. Serve a white wine with this cheese such as a Rias Baixas from Galicia in Spain but a Touraine Gamay is also a good accompaniment.

Prätost

SVECIAOST
Svecia is the Latin for Sweden. This is a fairly modern cheese that is produced in a range of types and tastes which are in reality successful copies of Dutch Gouda and Edam. They are sold plain or aromatically spiced with cloves, cumin, or caraway seeds, varying in age from very young to very mature. The younger examples have a fresh taste that become stronger with age. The fat content varies between 30 and 45%. The plain varieties can be grated for use in *gratin* dishes.
Drink a fine glass of red Bordeaux or Bergerac with the non aromatic cheeses but for the spiced types a glass of aromatic Gewürztraminer from Alsace is a better choice.

VÄSTENBOTTENOST
This traditional cheese from Western Bothnia has existed for more than a hundred years. It is a cow's milk cheese made in wagon wheels of about 44 lb (20 kg).
The cheese is matured for eighteen months and it has a somewhat granular texture with a pleasing fruity taste. It is worth adding to a cheeseboard for the contrast it brings and can be used grated or sliced in *gratin* dishes.
Serve this cheese with a more full-bodied red wine such as an Italian Ghemme or Gattinara.

Finland

Finland is renowned for its superb landscape with thousands of lakes. The northern tundra is bare, cold, and inhospitable.
Milking herds are predominantly in the fertile south where they have to compete with extensive urbanisation because there is little space for agri-

culture and stock rearing. Cheese has been made in Finland since the Middle Ages similar to that of surrounding countries. A number of Swedish cheesemakers established themselves in Finland in the second half of the nineteenth century and this led to a change in Finnish cheese habits. After World War II the Finnish dairy industry grew significantly, mainly through the stimulus from the ultra-modern Valio dairy co-operative. Today Finland exports a large volume of Swiss-type cheese, especially to the USA. In addition to excellent imitations of cheeses such as Swiss, e.g.

Valio Emmental

Emmental etc., French Camembert and Brie, Italian Mozzarella, Greek Feta, and Dutch Gouda,

Finland also has a number of its own cheeses with individual character.

FINLANDIA SWISS
This is the export-quality Emmental-like cheese that is mainly encountered in the USA. These cheeses are partially made with skimmed cow's milk and otherwise in the manner of all other industrially processed versions of Emmental. Apart from the origin of the milk the other important difference between Finnish and genuine Emmental is that all the milk for the Finnish cheeses is pasteurised.
The entire production takes place under extremely hygienic conditions and the cheese is made in large volume by a fully-automated process. It is fine for cheese on toast or sandwiches but does

Finlandia Swiss

Assortment of Finnish cheeses including Camembert, Emmental, Turunmaa, Ilves, and Luostari

not compare with real Swiss cheese. Serve with a glass of Swiss white wine or a white from Alsace, the Jura, or Savoie.

JUUSTOLEIPÄ
This is the most tasty and most popular Finnish cheese without any shadow of a doubt. This speciality cheese from the centre and north of the country (the Laps are especially fond of this cheese) was once only available on a limited scale but it is now made throughout the country on an industrial scale. The Laps used reindeer milk for this cheese but cow's milk is much more common-place these days. From a distance this cheese looks like a giant matzo – the Jewish cracker. Perhaps coincidentally Juustoleipä roughly means 'cheese bread' in Finnish.

The young cheese is heated over a fire so that the exterior blisters and changes colour. Once the cheese is cooled it is left for several days before being ready to eat. The taste of the inner cheese is mild and creamy with a more mature taste from the caramelised rind. The Fins eat Juustoleipä as a dessert with jam or wild berries from Lapland but redcurrant or blackcurrant jam is just as good. This cheese is also delicious on salads and ideal for a cheeseboard. The Fins happily eat this cheese for breakfast when they dunk large chunks of the cheese in big mugs of steaming coffee. Drink either a fresh white or a fairly tannin-free red wine with this cheese.

Juustoleipä

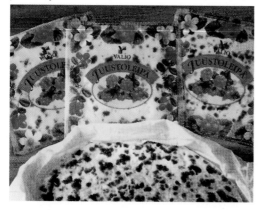

KOTIJUUSTO
This is a very unusual cheese made from cow's milk, buttermilk, eggs, and salt. Although this cheese is now widely mass-produced it is also easy to make yourself, try it!

3 eggs
1 litre (approx. 2 pints) buttermilk
3 litres (approx. 6 pints) milk
salt

Beat the egg with the buttermilk. Heat the milk and as it comes to the boil stir in the mixture of egg

and buttermilk. Turn off the heat but allow the pan to remain on the hob until the whey and curd have separated. Use a sieve or cheesecloth and skim the curd with a slotted spoon. Add a little salt from time to time.

Cover the sieve or cloth with a lid. Once the mixture has drained somewhat place it in a refrigerator and serve the following day on toast.

Serve this cheese with a fresh Sauvignon Blanc from the Loire, Sylvaner from Alsace, a dry German or Italian white.

Kotijuusto

LAPPI
This is another mass-produced cheese sold in long rectangular blocks. This cheese is very popular in the USA. Its great success has much to do with its low price, the absence of any character or taste, and its great versatility for use in cooking.

In fact this cheese can be used with anything but is much better as an ingredient of the food than at the end of the meal. The cheese is so neutral you can drink what you like with it.

Lappi

MUNAJUUSTO
ILVES
Munajuusto is an exceptional farm cheese made with cow's milk or reindeer milk that is eaten

young before maturing. Raw eggs are added to the milk at the beginning of the process and the cheese is then gently pressed. The fresh cheese, which has the shape of a squat cone, is then heated and takes on a golden-yellow colour more reminiscent of egg custard than cheese.

The Fins adore this cheese and in the long winter evenings they huddle around their fireplaces to toast pieces of it. The taste of this cheese is a good one: fresh and mild and the cheese is granular in texture.

Munajuusto is also served as a dessert with jam, red fruit, and whipped cream. The cheese is delicious in salads or as part of a cheeseboard. The mass-produced version is known as Ilves (lynx) which refers to the stripes and spots on the cheese. You can drink whatever you choose with this cheese: white or none too tannic red wine, beer, or even a glass of hard liquor.

Ilves

TURUNMAA

This is the Finnish version of the Danish Cream Havarti (see Denmark) and it originally came from around Turku. Scholars have traced the origins of this cheese back to at least the sixteenth century so this is a traditional cheese. It is sold as a medium-sized wagon wheel or cut and pre-packed. As everywhere the factory made cheese has less

Turunmaa

flavour than the small-scale farm versions, which are creamier, with a fuller taste that includes a slightly piquant freshly acidic finish. This cheese needs to mature for at least seven weeks. The cheese is eaten on bread or at the end of a meal. Turunmaa is often used in *gratin* dishes, other baked savouries, quiches, and also salads.

Serve a tasty Pinot Blanc from Alsace or an Italian Alto-Adige Pinot Bianco with this cheese.

Denmark

Although Denmark is the smallest of the Scandinavian countries (43,000 km^2) it is the most important in terms of cheese. The comparatively mild climate and level pasture land has much to do with this. Denmark's history of cheese-production goes back to before the time of Christ. Originally it was sheep's-milk and goat's-milk cheeses that were made with the cows coming much later.

The Vikings came in contact with many other cultures and hence cheeses during their expeditions of conquest and pillage. Of course they could only bring back hard cheeses to their native land from their travels.

A great passion for cheese developed in Denmark in the Middle Ages and this had much to do with the monasteries. Because the monks ate little or no meat they sought a protein rich replacement for meat and cheese proved an excellent substitute. The monks developed new techniques for making cheese such as the coagulating of milk with plant extracts that contained the same enzymes as animal derived rennet. Cheese was regarded as a status symbol for a long time on the various Danish islands and considerable prowess as a cheesemaker could be displayed by producing the largest cheeses possible. The recipes for these cheeses mainly came from elsewhere such as the neighbouring lands of Germany and the Low Countries, who made cheeses most able to travel. The Danes also quickly learned to make Swiss-type cheeses.

Three of these foreign-inspired Danish cheeses had become well-known outside Denmark well before the twentieth century: Havarti, Tybo, and Samsø. Anyone now searching for a true original Danish cheese should try the fresh cheese from the island of Funen, whether home-made or not, to which the Danes often add caraway seed and smoke over a fire of stinging nettles. This is delicious on rye bread with some raw vegetables and finely chopped chives.

Very dynamic dairy industry

Although virtually every Danish farm has made cheese for centuries the country's present strength as a dairy producer is of comparatively recent origin. The Danes can thank one woman, Hanne

Nielsen, a farmer with guts, who took the cheese world by storm from her farm at Havarti and passed her knowledge on to other Danish women cheesemakers. Nielsen was also the first woman member of the elite Danish *Landhulsholdnings-selskabet* (agricultural society). She was never permitted to take part of course in any of the more serious discussions because regardless of their competence women were not admitted to these. Regardless of this Hanne Nielsen and her followers established the basis of the Danish dairy industry. During her extensive travels she learned how the best-known cheese countries made their products. She experimented with Norwegian goat's-milk cheeses, Dutch Gouda, English Cheddar,

Danish Camembert

French Roquefort, Camembert, German Tilsitter, and Swiss Emmental. The cheeses from the Havarti farm quickly became famous, especially after it became known that the Danish royal family were among Nielsen's satisfied customers. In the late nineteenth century the establishment of ever-greater dairy co-operatives totally changed the scene in Denmark.

In part as a result of poor results in other sectors such as grain, farmers started to concentrate on dairy and meat production. Denmark established

Danish Brie

good markets for its products in the United Kingdom and the USA and the growth of the dairy industry was now unstoppable. In the twentieth century the Danes had enormous successes with various types of Feta, Mozzarella, and Danish blue.

Flexible, good quality and value, and safe

Currently Denmark is one of the top five dairy producing countries in the world. Perhaps the most striking strength of the Danish dairy industry is that it remains extremely flexible and eager to meet all the needs of its customers. In countries such as the USA Danish cheese is not just appreciated for its mild taste and good value but also for its hygienic guarantees.

From the cows' fodder to the final cheese everything is strictly and systematically controlled to prevent any form of pathogen. Extreme measures are undertaken during the making of Danish cheese. Danish standards of hygiene during milking have become the norm in other western European countries. Before the cows are milked – twice per day – their udders are thoroughly disinfected.

The milk is pumped by a closed pipe network directly to cool storage (maximum 6°C/42.8°F). After milking the pipes and all the milking equipment are thoroughly cleaned and disinfected. Since 1972 one co-operative, MD Foods has had its hands on 90% of the Danish dairy market. The

Danish blue and white mould cheeses

largest independent cheese company is Tholstrup Cheese, known for its Blue Castello and other cheeses.

DANISH BLUE

Hanne Nielsen caused a sensation back in 1874 with her imitation Roquefort with which she won a medal at an exhibition in London. This blue-veined Danish cheese was only made sporadically until World War I. The breakthrough occurred after the war in 1927 when a certain Marius Boel rediscovered the cheese. The name Danish Blue is not legally protected but Danblu is. If you see Danblu on the pack you are certain of a good cheese.

This cheese, which was recognised by the European Commission with protected origin status, is sold in small cylinders of 6 lb 9 oz (3 kg) or rectangular blocks of 4 lb 6 oz (2 kg). The outside of this cheese is fairly sticky, white to ivory coloured, with patches of grey or brown mould here and there. The inside is white to ivory with well distributed dark blue veins and irregular eyes. The creamy 50% plus fat cheese is easily sliced. The cheese is quite strong and salty with a fresh acidic taste.

The Danblu 60% plus is creamier and milder. Danablu is made by numerous producers and sold in Europe and the USA under a number of different brand names. Because of the ease with which this cheese can be sliced Danblu can readily be used for pizzas, quiches, and oven dishes.

The fairly strong and salty taste of this cheese makes it difficult to combine with wine, either sweet white or full-bodied red. A glass of Danish aquavit or genever is more successful.

DANBO

Open any Danish refrigerator and you are guaranteed to find a piece of Danbo cheese in it. This is the Danes favourite cheese. This wagon wheel cheese of 13 lb 3 oz (6 kg) is semi hard and made of cow's milk. The dry rind is coated in a thin layer of red or yellow wax. The majority of Danbo cheese is consumed in the domestic market so you will rarely encounter Danbo outside Denmark. The colour of the cheese is white to ivory and the texture is smooth and elastic with a number of modest air bubbles. This cheese is mild in taste and creamy (45% fat). In reality Danbo is part of the Samsø family of cheeses. There is also a version with caraway seeds. Drink a glass of lager beer, aquavit, genever, or a light fruity white or red wine with this cheese. With the caraway seed version try a northern Italian Pinot Grigio.

Danbo

DANISH FETA

Danish Feta was the subject of a major row between the cheese-producing nations of Europe for a long time. Greeks regarded Feta as a typical Greek product that required protection. Although the European court at first agreed with this viewpoint it was later decided that the name 'feta' could not be protected because the cheese had been made all around the Mediterranean for scores of years and that the restriction was difficult to apply in countries such as Denmark and The Netherlands.

The Greek name actually only mean 'slice' and it was deemed impossible to define a specific geographic area for this cheese. This was hard for the Greeks but brought relief for the rest of the cheese world – especially to the Danes.

Danish Feta is produced in two different qualities: the crumbly ivory-coloured one of coarse texture with many small or medium-sized 'eyes', and the soft, white, smooth feta that is creamy and can be spread. This type is widely sold in plastic containers in the Middle East. The other type is generally more popular in Europe.

One common complaint about Danish Feta is that it is too salty. A tip: buy the cheese ahead of time and soak it the night before use in a bowl of water. Replace the water in the morning and by the

Danablu

Danish coarse-texture Feta

Danish fine-texture Feta

blue-veined cheeses. These cheese are exported in numerous different varieties under brands such as Rosenborg and Høng (both of MD Foods) and of course Blue Castello of Tholstrup Cheese. A number of these Danish cheeses are also now made under licence in the USA (e.g. Saga Blue). This is a surprisingly creamy (70% fat) cheese combined with a piquant taste with the slight saltiness of Danish cheeses.

With its extra creamy and slightly piquant nature this cheese demands a somewhat more full-bodied wine with well-matured notes. Some people might choose a sweet white from the south-west of France (e.g. Jurançon, Loupiac, Barsac, Monbazillac etc.) but personally I advise against these because the result may be too heavy and there are wines that are better suited. Try instead an Australian Semillon or a smooth Chardonnay that is not too strongly oaked (vanilla), e.g. Australian or South African. Those who prefer red might choose a light Australian or South African shiraz/syrah.

evening you will have a much milder cheese. The use of the cheese (in a salad, snack, starter, vol-au-vent, or in an oven-baked dish etc.) and the other ingredients used have a bearing on the choice of wine.

DANISH FONTINA
You will rarely encounter this cheese outside of Denmark, except in the USA where it is very popular. Danish Fontina is a pale yellow cheese, semi-hard in texture, with a mild, almost sweet taste. It is made from semi-skimmed cow's milk and is sold in large wheels of 17 lb 9 oz–39 lb 9 oz (8–18 kg), protected by a thin layer of red paraffin wax. Danish Fontina is an ideal cheese for pasta and oven dishes, sandwiches, and toasted sandwiches. Because this cheese is so commonly used in cooking the choice of wine is dependent upon the other ingredients used. If used on a cheeseboard then select a soft fruity wine such as a simple red or white French or Italian country wine (*vins de pays*).

DANISH MOZZARELLA
You are unlikely to see Danish Mozzarella too often in shops but you have probably eaten it on pizzas for example. You may also have encountered this cheese ready-grated as pizza topping in the supermarket.
Ready-made pasta meals, including lasagne, available as convenience meals also often used this Danish Mozzarella. This mild Mozzarella is also available in blocks, with or without herbs, for use in salads or with a drink.
Because this cheese is mainly used in cooking you will need to choose the wine against the balance of ingredients. Consumed with a drink though it is mild enough to be eaten with any type of drink.

Danish blue and white mould cheeses

Alongside the well-known Danish Camembert and Brie the Danes also make a number of other blue and white mould cheeses with the characteristics of Brie or Camembert combined with those of

Other Danish blue mould cheeses

ELBO
Rectangular variant of Danbo with coating of red paraffin wax.

Danish Mozzarella

ESROM

This cheese is quite widely distributed but unfortunately it is generally eaten too young. Also and quite unfairly known as the Danish 'Port Salut', Esrom is sold in flattened rectangular blocks of about 3 lb 5 oz (1.5 kg). These are usually packed in aluminium foil but sometimes also in yellow wax. This is a 'monk's cheese' of the type once made in Europe before cheesemaking became an industrial process. Monks often exchanged their cheese for other goods they themselves could not make and this enabled more people to enjoy these delicious products.

So it was in Denmark in 1935 when a long forgotten recipe for a cheese made by the monks of Esrom was rediscovered. At that time Port Salut was still made by the monks of the monastery of Entrammes and tasted superb, unlike today's industrially compromised version. Because Esrom had similarities with Port Salut it gained its nickname of Danish Port Salut in the 1950s but this is now quite inappropriate. Esrom has far more to offer than the industrially-produced French cheese. The rind of this cow's milk cheese is pale yellow, sticky, moist, and fragrant in the case of a mature example. Immature cheeses are creamy and mild in taste, almost buttery (fat content 45–60%). Inside the cheese is supple and has a pale white to ivory colour with many 'eyes'.

Young Esrom

With more mature examples the aroma and taste are much stronger. This is because the rind is washed (red bacteria cheese). Esrom is the favourite cheese of true cheese lovers among the Danes, preferring a full-flavoured cheese. Eaten young Esrom is ideal for breakfast, sliced for the famous *smørrebrød* together with raw vegetables and a shallot.

When mature this cheese is also a worthy addition to any cheeseboard. There are also versions flavoured with garlic, onion, caraway seed, and herbs. In common with Danblu cheeses, Esrom enjoys the shield of European Commission protected origin status.

Esrom combines the creaminess of a ripe Mascar-

Mature Esrom

pone with the full flavour of an immature Limburg cheese. Mellow fruity Italian wines combine well with this cheese: Pinot Bianco from Alto-Adige or Pinot Grigio with more mature cheese, and for those who prefer red with cheese a fruity Valpolicella, Bardolino, or Alto-Adige are fine. An excellent alternative is French wines made from gamay.

FONTAL
This is a more mature version of Danish Fontina with greater aroma and taste.
Drink a fruity red or white Italian wine e.g. Alto-Adige or Friuli-Venzia-Giulia.

DANISH CHEDDAR
This is a fine imitation of an industrial quality Cheddar that is used in convenience foods and as ready-grated cheese for use with e.g. pizza. Danish Cheddar is rarely sold as whole or block cheese directly to consumers.

FYNBO
This cheese from the island of Fynbo is a smaller version of Danbo but milder in taste with a smoother texture and fewer air bubbles.

HAVARTI
This traditional Danish cheese acquires its name from the famous farm of Hanne Nielsen, the nineteenth century cheesemaker.
The semi-hard cheese without a rind is sold in blocks or cylinders of varying dimensions and weights. The lower fat varieties are often coated in

yellow wax, the 60% plus cheeses with red wax. Both types are rindless, fairly white to ivory inside, with many small and irregular 'eyes'. The texture of this cheese is supple, elastic, and creamy while the taste is extremely mild with a hint of freshness. Unfortunately good Havarti is seldom allowed to mature so the cheese sold does not have the fuller flavour of a mature one.

A mature example is well worth sampling. Havarti slices easily or cuts into chunks and is a first class cheese for cooking with.

With a young Havarti drink a fairly light wine e.g. a Gamay or Pinot Blanc. With more mature cheese try a Beaujolais-Villages or even a Brouilly.

MOLBO

Yet another variant of Danbo, on this occasion originating from the Mols region.

Danish Havarti

SAMSØ

In deference to their customers abroad the Danes now generally write the name of this cheese as Samsoe. This cheese is often compared with Swiss Emmental.

The original Samsø was certainly intended to be a copy of an Emmental but since that time this Danish cheese has acquired a life of its own. The

Samsø

original enormous wheels of cheese have now been replaced as a result of mass-production by large discs or blocks of 35 lb 3 oz–44 lb (16–20 kg). In shops you will encounter smaller packs of about 10 lb (4.5 kg).

The dry rind is often coated with a layer of yellow wax. The colour of this 45% plus cheese is pale ivory with a few quite small air bubbles. This is a very mild cheese that is not as dry as a Swiss one, making more like a Cantal or a cheddar. As the cheese ages it acquires additional aroma and taste with the slightly hint of nuttiness in the aroma of the young cheese being replaced by more of a wet walnut smell.

Samsø is an ideal cheese for those who generally find the taste of cheese overpowering, especially for with a drink or as a snack in sandwiches, toasted sandwiches, salads, or used for *gratin* dishes. You can drink what you fancy with this cheese such as a simple *vin de pays* or an Alsace Pinot Blanc.

TYBO

Similar to a Fynbo but this cheese is smoother in texture with fewer air bubbles.

Danish herbal cheese (Flødeoste)

Danish melting cheeses

Other Danish cheeses

Denmark also makes a number of classic cheese for both the domestic and export markets such as Danish Halloumi flavoured with mint, various herbal cheeses with garlic, dill, paprika, chilli, caraway seeds etc. and many cream cheeses with and without herbs and spices, fruit, liqueurs, nuts, and of course many different spreading cheeses.

Great Britain and Ireland

Green pastures and stirring history

The verdant landscape of the British Isles and Ireland as seen in picture postcards looks like a paradise for ruminants and other grazing animals. It is not surprising then that so many famous cheeses originate from here – especially the creamy firm types for which these islands are renowned. It is surprising though that cheese production has long been regarded as a by-product of making cream and butter.

In the British islands most of the cheese is not the very creamy type, more hard or semi-hard cheeses with a great deal of flavour. The English word cheese originates from the Latin *caseus* via the Anglo-Saxon *cese* and *cyse*.

Extensive assortment of British cheeses

Historians consider that it is likely during prehistoric times that fresh cheeses were made (especially in Scotland) although if this is so it must have been sporadic. Archaeological finds in Britain include perforated earthenware bowls of about 2000 BC which were probably used for draining fresh cheese.

Nevertheless it was the Romans who developed cheesemaking in Britain and Ireland. Although pride many deny it there is a strong possibility the origins of Britain's distinctive cheeses came as recipes with the Roman legions. The ancient large cheeses of the Auvergne were highly regarded by the Romans because they kept well and could be transported easily making them ideal for soldiers' rations. Coincidentally (or not) many British cheeses closely resemble those of Cantal and Salers.

The Auvergne cheeses are also made in the same manner as British cheeses. Could Cantal be the forefather of the famous cheddar? To a non British mind this is not impossible.

From monastery to the industrial revolution

The expansion of Christianity and the evangelical drive associated with it also created something of a revolution. Monks (predominantly Cistercians from Burgundy) travelled throughout Europe, taking their knowledge of cheesemaking with them.

In the Middle Ages Scotland and England had a flourishing trade in cheese far beyond their own borders. Because the British Empire became later so powerful and extended, British cheeses spread to the colonies. Britain's dairy herd was hit by disaster though in 1860. Cattle died by the tens of thousands as a result of a disease epidemic. Britain's own dairy production was hit severely and Britain started to import cheese from her colonies and former colonies.

The Americans took great advantage of this with their Cheddar-type cheeses. The British cheesemakers decided to put an end to this and united in order to produce their specific cheeses on a larger scale once the herd was rebuilt. The first large-scale creameries and dairies were established around 1870.

Bloody wars

World War I was a tremendous blow for the British dairy industry: it lost markets, lost certainty, and lost so much of their workforce that it finished off many businesses.

Recovery after the war was difficult and after an unfortunate and over-zealous start the Milk Marketing Board was set-up in 1933 to bring some necessary structure to the industry. The plans were quickly shelved as a result of World War II. Because land was needed for food production many individual cheesemakers and large-scale creameries were sacrificed. Cheese production was standardised and cheese was increasingly sold much less mature.

Since the 1950s a clear distinction has grown in Britain between the cheeses made with great care and properly matured (for an expanding market of people who appreciate such cheese) and the mass-produced cheese with short period of maturing. There are proponents for both types of cheese.

Stranglehold of European regulation

Unfortunately the European regulations for the production of fresh products are often so strict (and not always justifiably so) that it has become increasingly difficult for the smaller scale cheese-maker to make their cheese in a traditional hand-crafted manner.

It will be an appalling shame if the faceless Eurocrats succeed in having all English cheeses eventually end up as elongated catering blocks, all with the same Identikit taste. Almost no-one on the European mainland knows that Britain has more than 300 craft-made cheeses. This is unfor-

British cheese deserves better

tunate for many of these cheeses deserve much better recognition. There are many more delicious cheeses than Cheddar or Stilton, as tasty as these cheeses are.

It is absolutely deplorable that the combination of small-scale production and lack of any proper collective marketing policy for these cheeses means that only the mass-produced cheeses are exported.

The English, Welsh, Scottish, and Irish cheeses deserve much better than this.

Cheddar and cheddarisation

Many British cheeses are made in a similar manner. The differences between them have more to do with the different origins of the milk, the breed of cow, the quality of the grass etc. than the method of preparation with the exception of differ-

ences in the degree of acidity, temperature, and heating time. These cheesemaking processes are very similar to the large cylindrical cheeses of the Auvergne. In Britain this process is named after their national pride: Cheddar.

Cheddarisation

The traditional process for making Cheddar heats full cream milk to 73°C (163.4°F) which is then allowed to cool to 30°C (86°F). Rennet is added and the mixture is well stirred. After about 45 minutes the young curd is firm enough to be cut by large knives into small blocks, which helps the separation process.

The curd and whey are heated to 39°C (102.2°F) and stirred continuously. The small pieces of curd then shed more whey and the acidity is increased. Once the desired level is achieved the whey is allowed to drain out. The why is then cut into large blocks and regularly turned during the space of two hours which causes the acidity in the cheese to increase further and the cheese becomes drier. The large blocks are then ground and salted. The young salted mass of cheese is then scooped into large cylindrical cheese moulds covered with cheesecloth.

The moulds are pressed in order to force further whey from the cheese over the course of about two to three days during which time the cheese is regularly turned and the cloths changed. After pressing the cheese is removed from the mould and wrapped in a protective cloth and coated with paraffin wax. The cheese is left to develop further in a maturing room where the temperature and humidity is controlled to enable the characteristic taste to develop.

With mass-produced cheese these physically demanding activities are replaced by machines but otherwise the process is much the same except that much larger volumes of milk are dealt with to make much more cheese. One fundamental difference with factory cheeses is that they are not cylindrical but huge rectangular blocks and the cheese

Cheesemaker Leon Fowney making his Llangloffan

is no longer wrapped in cloth and protected with paraffin wax but immediately vacuum packed in thick polythene. The choice of rectangular form is partly for ease of stacking for storage and transport but also to do away with the problems and economics associated with the rind (weight loss, time loss in cutting). These factory made cheeses have a good taste but cannot approach a genuine hand-made farmhouse cheese. Yet the factory cheese often costs more!

English cheeses

APPLEWOOD

These fairly small cheeses used to be smoked over a fire of apple wood and then coated with ground paprika. These days the factory-made version is not smoked but has smoke aromas added to the curd. The taste is of a mild cheddar with a slightly smoky undertone. This cheese is coated in a protective layer of wax. Serve a simple but not too light red Spanish wine with this cheese, with the old-fashioned taste of wood.

BASING

Basing is a modern organic hard farmhouse cheese from Kent without a strong goat's-milk taste. It is

Applewood

a light and fresh cheese with a certain piquancy with a moist but crumbly texture that becomes creamier with age. Fat content: 45%.
Drink a fresh Sauvignon Blanc with this cheese.

BATH

A popular modern farmhouse cheese made from untreated cow's milk. This square white mould cheese from the county of Avon is mild tasting with salty undertones when young and is slightly granular. When more mature this cheese develops stronger aromas reminiscent of mushrooms, hay, hot milk, and dandelions. Like most white mould cheeses Bath matures for three to four weeks. Drink a glass of cider with it or a fresh fruity white or red wine such as a Pinot Noir or Gamay.

BEENLEIGH BLUE

A modern farmhouse cheese made from untreated milk from organically fed flocks of sheep in Devon. This cylindrical, blue-veined sheep's-milk cheese is very much a seasonal product and is not available in spring. The rind is rough and sticky and becomes covered in colourful colonies of moulds.
The curd of the cheese is white, moist, and slightly crumbly and it is well-marked with blue-green veining of mould. The initial taste is fairly strong but the finish is creamy and almost sweet with hints of mushroom and nut. Beenleigh Blue is matured for at least five to ten months and has fat content of 45–50%.
The English like to drink sweet cider with this cheese. On the continent the preference might be more for a sweet wine from the south-west of France e.g. Jurançon moelleux or a Rivesaltes, Maury, or even port.

Port and English cheese

BERKSWELL

A modern farmhouse cheese made from untreated sheep's-milk originating from organically fed flocks in the West Midlands. The rind is somewhat red in colour and bears traces of the mould in which the cheese was pressed. After four months maturing the rind is hard and rough and the cheese smells sweaty. A wonderful cheese for the lover of somewhat hard and strong tasting sheep's-milk cheese but not suitable for beginners. Fat content is 48%. A full-bodied but slightly sweet white Jurançon or robust Irouléguy or Madiran red – both from the south-west of France – are good combinations with this cheese.

BLUE VINNEY

Legendary blue-veined cow's milk cheese made in Dorset. Although the cheese is widely spoken of and written about it is actually extremely rare. Maturing time is three to five months and fat content is 40%.

BOSWORTH

Another modern farmhouse cheese, this time of untreated goat's milk from Staffordshire. This cheese is small and round with a soft rind coated in downy white mould. The cheese itself is firm. The taste is mild, almost sweet, with hints of nut in the background. Sometimes this cheese is packed in chestnut leaves and called *Bosworth Leaf*. This version is reminiscent of the French Banon and it has a creamy texture and almost sweet nutty taste. Maturing time is three to four weeks, fat content is 45%.

Drink smoother whites with this goat's-milk cheese e.g. white Rhône, Provence, or Languedoc.

BUFFALO

A very popular modern cheese from Hereford and Worcester, made from untreated buffalo milk. This is in no respects a Mozzarella look-alike. Instead this is a hard cheese with a thin but very hard crust that has a mild taste and aroma of nuts.

Choose a smooth white or red wine of personal preference to drink with this cheese.

BUTTON/INNES

A fresh cheese made from goat's milk that is very soft with an extremely refined and complex taste with notes of fresh citrus fruits, almonds, and honey.

There are several different versions of this cheese, plain or covered with ground pepper, nuts, of herbs. Fat content is 45%. Drink a delicious and honest mild fresh white with this cheese, such as a Sauvignon Blanc from the Loire.

BUXTON BLUE

Modern blue-veined cheese of cow's milk, made in Derbyshire. This cheese is slightly sweaty and herbal in taste. Maturing time is three months. Fat content is 45%. Ideal for use in cooking or on toast. Drink a mild-mannered dry or semi-dry white wine with this cheese.

CAPRICORN GOAT

A first-class goat's-milk cheese from Somerset, cylindrical or rectangular, fairly soft with a creamy taste. If you keep this cheese a bit longer it becomes stronger in taste and creamier with hints of nuts in the finish. Fat content is only 26%.

Drink a delicious fresh and fruity white wine or a young fruity light red with little tannin e.g. Gamay.

CERNEY

This Gloucestershire goat's-milk cheese is sold in the well-known pyramid form, covered with a coating of ash. The name comes from the picturesque Cotswold village where the cheese is made. This is a mild-tasting cheese with a very pleasing latent freshness, due to the use of untreated milk. Maturing time is seven to ten days. Fat content is 43%.

Serve a fresh Sauvignon Blanc from the Loire with this cheese.

CHEDDAR

Although the name suggest it, the origins of this cheese were not the Cheddar Gorge but the nearby Mendip Hills, also in Somerset. English Cheddar is famous at home and abroad and its renown spreads back to the sixteenth century. Genuine farmhouse Cheddar is still made in England's West Country while other modern Cheddar is mass-produced world-wide. West Country peasant farmers took their cheese know-how with them when they emigrated to the colonies such as America (now the USA), Canada, Australia, New Zealand, and South Africa. It is therefore no surprise that these very countries also make excellent Cheddar cheese. The name 'Cheddar' is not protected in common with 'Brie' and 'Camembert' and can be made anywhere.

There are many varieties of Cheddar from very ghostly white to dark yellow (and even sometimes orange) and from mild to very mature. Farmhouse Cheddar made by hand or to a small scale is never orange but also never ghostly white, more usually a soft ivory colour.

Traditional Cheddar is sold in large cylinders of 13⅞–15¾ in (35–40 cm) in height with a weight of about 61 lb 9 oz (28 kg). The craft-made cheeses

Mass-produced cheddar in its typical form

Real farmhouse Cheddar

vary widely in both weight and dimensions but within the area indicated. The mild varieties are sold after maturing for three to five months but for a really tasty English cheddar it needs to mature for at least five months. The best cheese is matured for nine months to a year and even two to three years when they acquire a much stronger taste. Fat content is 45–48%.

All manner of attractive names are given to certain mass-produced Cheddar to suggest quality or even specific origins but many of these are factory made from milk drawn from diverse regions that is mixed together.

For certainty of a hand-made farmhouse Cheddar buy one cut (by a wire) from a large cylinder with a cloth embedded in the rind.

CHEDDAR WITH PORT

A trendy recent arrival with a hint of port and addition of colouring.

Small Cheddars make good Christmas gifts

Cheddar with Guinness

Cheddar with port

CHEDDAR WITH PORT AND STILTON

Yet another trendy cheese, this time with layers of Stilton. Looks good as part of a buffet but otherwise this is nothing special. Cheddar tastes good with a glass of red or white wine but also with a fruity port or a delicious glass of dry English cider

Cheddar with port and Stilton

(e.g. Strongbow). A little Guinness is sometimes added to Cheddar during its production. With this speciality drink either Guinness or another Irish or English stout or porter (dark strong beer).

CHESHIRE

Reputedly the oldest known English cheese but probably the closest member of the family of Auvergne cheeses. This cheese was in existence as a locally-produced cheese from Cheshire during the reign of Queen Elizabeth in the sixteenth century. Although originally only produced in the county of Cheshire this cheese is now made both industrially and by craft means throughout England and Wales. The traditional Cheshire cheese acquired its characteristic fresh acidity and salty taste from the mineral-rich soil of Cheshire in north-west England where there are extensive salt mines. There are three types of Cheshire cheese. The Red Cheshire is coloured with *annato*, a natural colouring derived from South American berries. Originally these cheeses were coloured with other natural colourings such as carotene from carrot juice or saffron. White Cheshire is matured in common with the red variety for at least six weeks. White and red varieties are both moist with a fat content of 48% and they have a granular texture which becomes more crumbly as the cheese matures. The taste is well-developed but mild with a hint of saltiness. Blue Cheshire was until recently a typical farmhouse cheese that is much creamier than the white and red varieties with irregular blue veining in the cheese. Unfortunately this cheese is no longer made.

Serve a well-matured Burgundy Chardonnay or equally mature red Bordeaux or Burgundy wine with Cheshire.

COQUETDALE

A hard traditional cheese from Northumberland with a round shape that is similar to a Belgian Passendaele, Wijnendaele, and Chimay. The thin rind is often coated with soft mould. The cheese is supple and soft, with a full but mild taste that is almost sweet at first but salty in its finish. Maturing time is ten weeks and fat content 55%.

You can drink any good wine with this cheese or even a glass of sherry.

CORNISH PEPPER

A less well-known cheese from Cornwall that is well worth discovering. This is a cheese for real lovers of a bite that is here provided by crushed peppercorns. The cheese is creamy and moist, contrasting well with the spiciness of the peppercorns. This cheese is also available in other varieties of taste such as garlic and other herbs/spices. Fat content is 45%.

Serve a glass of beer, a genever, or a more sturdy *vins de pays* with this cheese.

CORNISH YARG

A fairly unusual cheese with a wrapping of stinging nettles from Cornwall. Its appearance is similar to Caerphilly but the taste is quite different, much fresher and more spicy. With extra maturing the freshness is lost and the taste more strongly spicy with pepper in the finish. Perfect as a cooking cheese but much tastier eaten on its own or forming part of a cheeseboard. Maturing time six to eight weeks and fat content 57%.

Serve a good quality white or red wine with this cheese.

COTHERSTONE

This hard cheese from Durham is made according to a traditional recipe from untreated cow's milk. The taste is very fresh when young (at least two weeks) and more pronounced after a few more weeks (up to ten) maturing. Fat content is 45%. Drink a fresh white or red with this cheese, a Belgian white beer, or glass of ale.

COVERDALE

Modern well-made factory-produced cheese from North Yorkshire with a pale yellow rind. he curd is firm but the taste is mild, almost

Cheese-board of English cheeses. A taste apart!

buttery. Maturing time is four to five weeks. Wonderful with any type of wine but preferably with a mellow fruity white.

CRANDALE
See Wensleydale.

CURWORTHY ⊛
A hard farmhouse cheese made from untreated cow's milk in Devon. After three to four months maturing the cheese is soft and supple inside and creamy, almost buttery in taste. The cheese is coated with paraffin wax. Fat content is 48%.
Ideal with a beer but also with more full-bodied white wines.

DERBY
Genuine Derby cheese is difficult to find. Its colour is a pale ivory, the texture of the cheese is moist but crumbly but fairly firm due to four to six weeks of maturing. The taste is mild and refined. The difference between Derby and Cheddar is mainly the buttery undertones of Derby cheese. Fat content is 45%. Delicious with fruit such as apples, pears, and grapes.

SAGE DERBY
This was once a traditional Christmas cheese. This cheese is now available throughout the year everywhere and is mainly mass-produced. During cheesemaking finely chopped sage is added to the curd which creates a green marbling in the cheese which is usually of a regular nature although the colour can vary in intensity. Today sage is not used for the mass-produced version of this cheese but chlorophyll, the natural green colouring of plants, available from sap of the cheapest green plants available in quantity. At present spinach juice is mainly used. Sage Derby takes longer to mature than an ordinary Derby, being three to four months.

DEVON BLUE
Blue veined cheese of heated cow's milk from Devon. It is creamy and strongly spiced with

Sage Derby

DOUBLE GLOUCESTER
The pronunciation of 'Gloucester' gives trouble even to native speakers of English who are not British. It is *glosster*. Two different sizes of cheese were once made in Gloucestershire: single and double (twice as big). Today the single Gloucester has virtually disappeared and Double Gloucester is everywhere.
Single Gloucester was made from skimmed milk and was intended for early consumption while Double on the other hand is made from full-cream milk for longer maturing. The *annato* coloured Double Gloucester has a full but mild flavour that is very creamy. The traditional farmhouse cheeses are still made with untreated milk and these have a stronger taste than the factory made examples. Fat content is 48%.
This cheese is good with a glass of English ale. For those who prefer wine, choose a medium dry German white or mellow red.

DOUBLE WORCESTER
Like Gloucester, Worcester too is a pronunciation tease for non British speakers of English. It is *wuster*. This cheese is really a smaller Double Gloucester made nearby in Worcestershire (*wustersher*). Full of flavour with a hint of citrus fruit. Matured for five to seven months. There is also an Old Worcester variant of this cheese. For advice on wine see Double Gloucester.

DUDDLESWELL ⊛
A fairly popular hard sheep's-milk cheese from East Sussex that is made with untreated milk. Duddeswell is fairly crumbly in texture and has a slightly sweet taste, reminiscent of hay and nuts. Fat content 45%.
A delicious not too dry white or a full and fruity red go superbly with this cheese

EMLETT
A modern untreated sheep's-milk cheese from Avon. The small round cheese is soft and white with brown-orange flecks. The texture is firm but creamy. With additional maturing the cheese becomes more creamy and the taste becomes stronger. A mature Emlett typically develops aromas of fresh baker's yeast and a fairly down-to-earth taste with fresh undertones.
Drink a fairly strong white or red wine with this cheese, preferably from south-west France.

EXMOOR BLUE ⊛
A blue cheese in various sizes and different tastes made from mixed herd milk from Somerset, i.e. a mixture of cow's, goat's, and sheep's milk. The same cheese is also known as Somerset Blue. This cheese has a much stronger taste than Stilton. Drink a medium dry white wine or amontillado sherry with this cheese.

FINN

The only triple cream cheese I am aware of from England. Finn is mild with latent freshness, particularly in the initial taste, with creamy taste and undertones of mushrooms. Matured for two to four weeks with a fat content of 75%!
Drink a mildly sweet German white that is freshly acidic with this cheese.

FIVE COUNTIES

A modern cheese that is attractive in appearance, made from layers of five different coloured Cheddar-type cheeses: including Derby, Double Gloucester, and Cheshire. A sampling of different English cheeses at one go! The central layer is of a ghostly white and salty Cheshire.

Five Counties

Drink a fruity white or red wine with this blend of cheeses.

GLENPHILLY

A modern cheese from the Cheddar family. After the cheese has initially matured a dash of eight-year-old Scotch whisky is added to the finely ground curd before it is pressed in its mould. The small cheeses are coated with black wax that contrasts well with the fairly light curd of this

Glenphilly, with a dash of Scotch

cheese. The cheese is not strongly tasting and the whisky is not readily obvious unless you allow the cheese to mature further. Actually a glass of whisky or a malt beer are good combinations with this cheese but for those preferring wine choose a mildly sweet German white.

GLOUCESTER (GOAT'S-MILK)

Semi hard goat's-milk cheese that is matured for at least two months for the single versions and six months for the double variety. The double is much stronger in taste.
Serve Sauvignon Blanc with Single Gloucester (goat's-milk cheese) and a more full-bodied white with the Double variety e.g. Rhône.

GOLDEN CROSS

An English version of the French Ste-Maure, a delicious soft goat's-milk cheese from East Sussex that can be eaten young but deserves a longer period to mature. The taste of the mature cheese is a mixture of fresh and bitter hints against a full and creamy background. Matured for four to six weeks.
Drink a pleasing white from Alsace or the Loire with this cheese.

HARBOURNE BLUE

A very popular cheese from Devon made with untreated goat's-milk. This round cheese combines the mild sweet taste of goat's milk with the slightly more robust and spicy taste of blue mould as no other cheese does. Matured for three to five months. Fat content is 48%.
Drink a good quality medium dry German or French white wine with this cheese.

HEREFORD HOP

A fairly recent revival of an old traditional English cheese that is soft, fresh, and mild in taste to salty and also almost buttery. The cheese has some similarity with Caerphilly but with the addition of roasted hops. This gives the cheese a slightly fermented aroma of beer that makes it very popular in English pubs. Fat content is 45%.
Delicious with a good glass of English bitter but also with a fresh white wine from Alsace.

HUNTSMAN

Some know this cheese as the 'E' cheese because of the form of the alternate three layers of orange Double Gloucester and two of Blue Stilton.
Given the mild taste of both cheeses a sultry Australian, South American, or South African red is an excellent choice as accompaniment but choose wines not high in tannin.

LANCASHIRE

This is a smaller and younger local variant of the Cheddar type of cheese that originates from Lancashire. When sold young they are called Creamy Lancashire and are pale in colour, fresh and mild tasting with a slightly crumbly texture.

The natural rind is thin but very hard and bears traces of the cloth in which the cheese was wrapped. Older cheeses are matured for two months when they are darker in colour, firmer, and stronger tasting. Farmhouse Lancashire is now quite rare and most Lancashire cheese is factory made. Fat content is 45%.

The choice of wine depends on what the cheese is combined with. If eaten on its own or part of a cheeseboard then a medium dry white such as an Australian Semillon or either a light fruity red (low in tannin) or specifically a well matured Bordeaux or Burgundy red.

MALVERN

Craftsmanlike dry sheep's-milk cheese made from untreated milk. This cheese is hard but has a mild taste somewhat resembling *semi-curado* (semi-mature) Manchego cheese. Maturing time is two to three months.

With young cheese serve a full-bodied but mellow white Rhône wine or a more powerful tasting red e.g. a Tempranillo.

MENALLACK FARMHOUSE

A cheese from Cornwall that deserves much greater recognition. Its small following is not due to the quality of this cheese but the limited production. Menallack Farmhouse is made from untreated cow's milk and can be eaten either after a couple of months or when more mature. Young cheese is soft with a creamy taste. When mature the cheese is naturally harder and stronger tasting. It is an ideal cheese to cook with. Fat content is 45%.

Huntsman cheese with 'E' form layers

Drink a delicious glass of either white or red to personal preference.

MENDIP

A firm cheese made from untreated goat's milk that is matured for two to eight weeks. The curd is creamy yellow with small irregular 'eyes'. A freshly acidic and fruity cheese.

Drink a fresh and fruity white such as a sauvignon blanc from the Loire with this cheese.

OLDE YORK

In complete contrast to expectation created by the name this is a modern sheep's-milk cheese that most closely resembles Greek Feta, although sold in the round Turkish form. The curd is very moist and creamy with a definite fresh acidic taste and a mild to sweet finish. Maturing time is ten to twenty-two days. Fat content is 45%. Delicious in salads or *gratin* dishes.

The choice of accompanying wine depends on the other ingredients.

OXFORD BLUE

A fairly recent alternative to Blue Stilton. A creamy cheese that is more spicy than Stilton. Maturing time is two to four months. Is sold in a packing of silver foil. Fat content is 30%.

For accompanying drinks see Stilton.

RED LEICESTER

Another of those English place names to trip up unwary Americans. It is *lester*. Leicester cheese is another offspring from the Cheddar family, made in large wheels instead of cylinders like most other traditional Cheddar types. The red-orange rind is often covered with a thin powdery mould. The colour of the inner cheese is red-orange, achieved by adding *annato*.

Leicester cheese is matured for at least twelve weeks but the cheese fully develops its characteristic taste after nine months to a year. Young cheese has a fairly granular texture and is mild in taste. Mature cheese develops a nutty flavour. Fat content is 48%.

The foregoing is true of the traditionally made Red Leicester but these days almost all this cheese is made in catering slabs for ease of slicing. The traditional flat wheels of 12 in (30 cm) in depth and 20 in (50 cm) diameter and weighing about 48 lb 6 oz (22 kg) are increasingly rare. Yet another great cheese to ingloriously disappear.

Although Leicester is a good cooking cheese (especially for Welsh rarebit), it is ideal on its own or accompanied by an amontillado or palo cortado sherry or a glass of good beer. I once saw a pair of elderly English gentlemen secretly take portions of Leicester from the bag to eat with their red Burgundy: and why ever not?

SHROPSHIRE BLUE

A modern blue cheese that was originally from Inverness in Scotland but is now regarded as a typical English cheese. In reality, this cheese that has a history of not more than thirty years, is a variant of Stilton.

The only difference is a stronger colour through the addition of *annato*, a brighter blue vein, and a stronger but cruder taste.

Serve this cheese ideally at the end of a meal with a delicious glass of port, Malvasia, or sweet sherry. In England some advise a fino sherry but personal I would not expose the delicate fino to the crude force of this cheese.

Shropshire Blue

SOMERSET BRIE

Extremely popular English version of the world famous cheese originally from Brie, south-west of Limoges. Unlike the many French and non-French copies of the genuine article this soft English cheese is close in quality to the very best Brie. This fantastic cheese also has the same refined aroma of mushrooms and straw, the same firm creaminess, the same undertones of nuts and mushrooms. Any difference is minimal and perhaps lies in the longer and richer finish of top quality Brie. Nevertheless this is a gorgeous cheese! Maturing time is six weeks. Fat content is 50%.

I find the most delicious combination with a Brie type cheese is a white sparkling wine, preferably 100% Chardonnay. For those who prefer red choose a lighter Pinot Noir that is low in tannin.

STILTON

Stilton is the queen of English cheeses. Not only is Blue Stilton from Nottinghamshire the reference cheese for Britain it is also one of the best cheeses in the world.

Stilton is a protected origin cheese that may only be produced in Nottinghamshire, Derbyshire, and Leicestershire (not Cambridgeshire where the village of Stilton is located). The name Stilton is derived from the first known reference to this cheese in the diaries of eighteenth century travellers who were served the cheese at the Bell Inn in the village of Stilton. The cheese quickly gained popularity among travellers en route between

Stilton, queen of cheeses

London and York. The recipe was from the housewife Elizabeth Scrabrow who improved a local cheese known as Quenby. The cheese was never made in the village of Stilton itself, its role was merely as an outlet for the surplus production of this cheese made by Mrs Scarbrow. Her secret was the mixing of the cream from morning milking with the full-cream milk from the following morning. This resulted in the characteristic rich creaminess of Stilton.

The cylindrical cheese has a fairly coarse and irregular pale brown rind. The cheeses are about $7\frac{7}{8}$–9 in (20–23 cm) deep and wide, weighing 15 lb 6 oz–17 lb 9 lb (7–8 kg). Very occasionally very special jubilee Stiltons are made to commemorate a special anniversary. Then mammoth Stiltons are made weighing up to 66 lb (30 kg). The cheese is ivory coloured, smooth and creamy, with well

Stilton: one of the best cheeses of the world

distributed veins of blue mould. The holes through which the cheese was injected to ensure even veining can be seen in the rind surrounding the cheese. The taste is creamy, rich, complex, and less salty or bitter than other blue cheeses. The creaminess rules with these 55% fat cheeses. Unfortunately the magnificent traditional Stilton made from untreated milk has disappeared from the market completely.

WHITE STILTON
White Stilton is nothing more than an immature 'Blue' Stilton that has not yet acquired its blue

Cheddar with white Stilton and herbs

veining. The white variety is a mild and fresh tasting cheese that is moister than more mature examples. White stilton is also flavoured with herbs and combined with Cheddar and fruit such as apricots are often added to immature white varieties of stilton.

The control over the origin is unfortunately much stronger than the control over quality of the varied Stiltons and it is all too common to find cheap examples of the cheese lacking in quality such as irregular veining, absence of them entirely, much too dry in texture, and being sold much too early. The 'Blue' Stilton is traditionally accompanied by one or more glasses of vintage port. Provided both

the Stilton and port are good you will not be disappointed. Why opt for a different combination? Why change a winning team?

Well stored Stilton is creamy and moist

Some cheese merchants, restaurateurs, and wine merchants continue an old tradition: they remove the top of an old Stilton and scoop part of the cheese out and turn a bottle of port upside down in the hole. What a waste of both cheese and port!

Stilton and port: a winning team

The origin of this dreadful custom in reality is that a cheese might be too big for a family or restaurant and hence dried out. Cheap port was added to enable the cheese to be used for longer. This is not a means of improving the cheese but a method of avoiding wastage of a cheese.

If you enjoy Stilton and wish to benefit from its fully-matured flavour then serve it at room temperature. On the other hand if you prefer a milder taste then keep the cheese chilled until it is served.

STINKING BISHOP

The name alone probably keeps this cheese from many tables but this is unfortunate because this is a very interesting cheese that has much in common with a Alsace or Munster cheese. This wonderful cow's milk cheese has a washed rind that is very aromatic – fragrant when ripe in spite of the name. The *Stinking Bishop* is actually a liqueur made from a local variety of pear which is used to wash the rind of this cheese. Maturing time is six to eight weeks and the fat content is 48%.

A strong tasting wine is needed as accompaniment to this strong tasting cheese such as a Pinot Gris or Gewürztraminer from Alsace.

SUSSEX SLIPCOTE

An old traditional sheep's-milk cheese that is generally sold as a round cheese. Very soft in texture this cheese has a mild, almost sweet taste. There are also varieties with herbs, garlic, or peppercorns. Fat content is 45%.

Drink a medium dry or mellow dry white wine with this cheese.

SWALEDALE

This modern hard farmhouse cheese from North Yorkshire is made of both cow's and sheep's milk and 'pickled' prior to storing in damp cellars to mature.

The outside of the cheese becomes covered with a protective layer of grey mould. The taste of this cheese is similar to Wensleydale but is moister and softer. There are also varieties with different flavourings added. Fat content is 48%.

Swaledale combines well with a glass of beer, a fresh white, or a young fruity Gamay or Pinot Noir.

TICKLEMORE

Thick disc of a cheese with the very unusual pattern of the cheese mould on the hard grey rind. The taste of this cheese made with untreated goat's milk is freshly acidic with aromas of nuts and mushrooms. Maturing time is two to three months. Drink a fresh white wine with this cheese, from the Loire or Haut-Poitou.

TYMSBORO

The soft modern farmhouse cheese from Avon is made from untreated goat's milk. The natural rind of this pyramid-shaped cheese is covered with a mixture of ash and downy white mould. The curd is firm and very fresh tasting with a soft herbal finish. Maturing time is two to four weeks. Any good Sauvignon Blanc from France to New Zealand combines well with this cheese.

TYNING

An excellent and successful local variant of Italian Pecorino, made from untreated sheep's milk.

Drink a strong-tasting white or red wine or even a glass of fortified wine with this cheese.

VULSCOMBE

A fairly recently developed farmhouse cheese from Devon made from untreated goat's milk. A very special cheese in which coagulation is not started by addition of any form of rennet but solely through the lactic acid in the milk.

A fresh cheese produced in an elegant domed form, sometimes covered with crushed peppercorns and/or bay leaves. There are varieties with different flavourings such as garlic, herbs, spices, and pepper.

Drink a fresh white with this cheese, e.g. a Savoie or Swiss wine.

WATERLOO

Semi-hard cheese of cow's milk with a very mellow taste that is mild to sweet, becoming stronger with longer maturing. Fat content is 45%.

Almost and red or white wine is suitable to drink with this cheese.

WENSLEYDALE

An English cheese that deserves much greater recognition. Once this cheese was made of sheep's milk in the same way as many other French monk's cheeses. The origins of Wensleydale cheese would appear to be in France, especially as it was first made in England by Cistercian monks who came to England with William the Conqueror.

After the hasty withdrawal by the successors of those Cistercians in the fifteenth century, ahead of the troops of Henry VIII, local farmers found the recipe for this cheese. After a period of time the farmers changed the sheep's milk for cow's milk as elsewhere in the country.

Wensleydale is generally sold not earlier than before three weeks maturing when it is very pale, quite firm, but crumbly, with a mild, even slightly sweet taste and a simply gorgeous finish with an aftertaste that is reminiscent of a thin layer of honey on freshly toasted white bread. Fat content is 45%.

Blue Wensleydale is sold more mature than ordinary Wensleydale (six months) with blue veins of mould. The texture is smoother and the taste is creamier. Once all Wensleydale cheeses turned blue with age.

Choose a juicy white wine that is not so very fresh tasting as accompaniment for Wensleydale eaten from a cheeseboard e.g. a Chardonnay. A light red, glass of beer, or farm cider are equally good companions with this cheese.

WENSLEYDALE WITH CRANBERRIES
A trendy and fresh variety of Wensleydale flavoured with cranberries or cranberry juice and coloured.

Crandale: Wensleydale with cranberries

WIGMORE
Modern farmhouse cheese from Berkshire made from untreated sheep's milk. A very surprising cheese with a brown-orange rind created from washing that has a white mould coating. The curd of this cheese is firm and fatty and almost sweet in taste with notes of caramel, nuts, and lamb fat. Drink a full-bodied Pinot Gris from Alsace with this sturdy cheese.

WINDSOR RED
This cheese seems very odd in appearance with its irregular marbling of white Cheddar turned light red by being drenched in elderberry wine.

Windsor Red

YORKSHIRE BLUE   ✿
Traditional blue farmhouse cheese made in North Yorkshire from pasteurised sheep's milk. This cheese tastes somewhat like a Wensleydale when young but become stronger and creamier with maturing over eight to ten weeks. Fat content is 48%.

Cheeses from Wales

Before World War II Caerphilly made with untreated milk was a very famous cheese with a very individual taste. After the war though with the introduction of the destructive forces of standardisation and pasteurisation with milk coming from ever wider catchment areas Caerphilly lost much of its individuality, making it yet another variant of Cheddar. Fortunately in the past decades a revival has taken place in Welsh cheese, in part through the arrival of Italian and Dutch immigrants. Things are now going well for Welsh cheese.

CAERPHILLY
This cheese has its origins in the once thriving coal mining community of South Wales, centred on the small town of Caerphilly. Caerphilly cheese was popular with the miners because it provided them with a source of moist nourishment in the heat they encountered 'down the pit' and the cheese sliced easily for the sandwiches for their lunch boxes. The cheese itself had a hard enough rind for them to grasp in blackened hands and the size and shape of the cheese enabled them to nibble away at the cheese between the rind before throwing the rind away. A complete lunch could be created by wrapping young Caerphilly in blanched cabbage leaves with the addition of some bread.
Caerphilly is a semi-hard cheese that is matured for at least two to three weeks with a somewhat crumbly texture though moist. The taste is mild but slightly salty with freshness. Genuine farmhouse Caerphilly is sold as a wheel of about 8 lb 13 oz–9 lb 14 oz (4–4.5 kg) slightly more than (7.5 cm) 2 in deep with a diameter of 12 in (30 cm). These farmhouse cheeses are matured for at least three months rather than weeks which makes the taste creamier and more pronounced, indeed buttery. British people often eat Caerphilly with high tea, on toast, or in sandwiches, sometimes with the addition of celery. On the continent this cheese is more likely to be accompanied by a glass of white or red wine according to preference. Try a young Zinfandel, Primitivo, or Tempranillo that has not been aged in wood.

CELTIC PROMISE   ✿
A wheel-shaped modern farmhouse cheese made from cow's milk with a thin soft orange rind created by washing and a soft and supple inner cheese that is very aromatic, full of flavour, and quite spicy. Maturing time is about eight weeks.
You could drink a delicious glass of beer with this but a fine Pinot Gris or Gewürztraminer from Alsace is a better choice. It is a matter of what you have in house.

LLANGLOFFAN FARMHOUSE
The extremely considerate Leon Downey is one of the most active craft cheesemakers in Britain let alone Wales. His Llangloffan Farmhouse cheese is a classic among the best British cheeses. The cheese is a wheel of 4 in (10 cm) thickness and 12 in (30 cm) in diameter that weighs about 9 lb 14 oz (4.5 kg) and is semi hard with a natural rind. The cheese itself is fairly dry yet creamy and slightly crumbly with a full flavour that includes intense creaminess to the extent of buttery undertones and hints of grass. The milk comes from their own cows grazed on organically managed pasture, which makes for creamier milk. The output is quite small but this cheese is worth tracking down. Maturing time is two to six months. Fat content is 45%. Drink a full-bodied white (dry or medium dry) with this extremely creamy cheese.

Leon Downey tests his Llangloffan cheese

PANT YS GAWN
A modern fresh farmhouse goat's-milk cheese that has become popular in Britain recently in quite a short period of time. In addition to the soft and creamy plain variety there are also flavoured versions with crushed peppercorns, herbs, garlic, etc. Serve a fresh and fruity white wine with this cheese.

PENBRYN
A farmhouse cheese somewhat like a Dutch Gouda that comes from organically managed agriculture and herds. This is perhaps what traditional Gouda once tasted like before almost everything was pasteurised and sterilised out of existence. This cheese is full of flavour with fruitiness, grass, and hints of nuts, with a sweet buttery finish. Maturing time is two months.
A glass of a good beer, a genever, or white or red wine are all perfect accompaniments for this cheese.

PENCARREG
A small Brie-type cheese made from untreated cow's milk from organic farming that is made by modern methods. The cheese smells of hay and mushrooms and tastes slightly bitter, creamy, and sweet. Maturing time is two to eight weeks.
Drink either a full-bodied Chardonnay or young red Burgundy with this creamy cheese.

TEIFI
(Pronounced *tyfi*). A very successful Welsh variant made with untreated milk of the traditional farmhouse Gouda cheese. The one year old variety is of superb quality.
Whatever you drink with this cheese – beer, genever, glass of white, red, or fortified wine – it will always be delicious.

TYN GRUG
A creamy Welsh variety of Cheddar with a nod in the direction of Switzerland. This cheese is made from untreated milk from cows that graze freely in the mountains of mid Wales on entirely organic pasture. The natural rind bears marks of the cheesecloth. The cheese itself is firm, initially fresh, then rich, creamy, and slightly sweet with a spicy, even peppery finish. This cheese is available in two sizes: 16 lb 8 oz–19 lb 13 oz (7.5–9 kg) and 33 lb–39 lb oz (15–18 kg).
This cheese is delicious on its own or with fruit, nuts, or grapes and makes an excellent addition to a cheeseboard. Any noble drink is an accompaniment for Tyn Grug.

Scottish cheeses

Only small areas of Scotland are suitable for cattle husbandry and hence despite the fairly large size of the country it has relatively few cheeses. The very best of the craft cheeses solely bear the indication of protected origin status but the future of such cheeses is threatened by the strangling regulations of the European Commission, which are applied more rigorously in Britain than anywhere

Is this the future for Scottish cheese?

else. How long can these cheeses continue to be made by hand in the craft manner and from untreated milk?

BISHOP KENNEDY

Surprising and very well made modern cheese from untreated cow's milk. The rind is liberally washed with Scotch whisky during maturing which gives this cheese a very individual character. The young cheese is velvet smooth but after several weeks maturing the taste and aroma become much stronger and sharper. Fat content is 45%.

A glass of Pinot Gris or Gewürztraminer from Alsace are good accompaniments with this cheese provided it is not over mature.

BONCHESTER

This is one of the British cheeses that does have protected origin status, but for how long? Recent reports about the state of craft-made Scottish cheese are alarming so we are keeping our fingers crossed for them. This cheese is a classic example of what wonderful things man can make with good untreated milk from magnificent Jersey cows. The rind on this cheese, which resembles a Camembert, is covered with white mould that at first is downy and unmarked but after several weeks of maturing this takes on a brown colouring. The soft ivory-coloured inner cheese is full and creamy, almost buttery, with sweet undertones. Maturing time is four to eight weeks. Fat content is 48%.

Drink a fine Chardonnay of character, a fresh young Pinot Noir or Gamay, or a well-matured Bordeaux or Burgundy with this cheese.

CABOC

This is a fairly unusual farmhouse cheese made from untreated cow's milk that is enriched with additional cream. The almost buttery cheese is rolled in a mixture of roasted oatmeal that imparts additional flavours of nuts and years. Maturing time is just five days. Fat content is 69%.

Try a fino sherry, a glass of a smooth blended Scotch, or a malt beer with this surprising cheese.

CAIRNSMORE

A modern hard farmhouse cheese made from untreated sheep's milk. The rind of the small cylindrical Cairnsmore cheese is often covered with an extremely varied culture of downy moulds. Through the nine months of maturing Cairnsmore acquires typical sheep's-milk cheese notes of caramel, wool, mutton fat, and nuts, all crowned by a somewhat sweet and creamy finish. Available in small quantity only from April to October.

Serve a tasty white or red wine from south-west France.

CROWDIE/GRUTH

English speakers call this cheese Crowdie while the Gaelic tongues prefer Gruth. This traditional fresh farmhouse cheese is made from skimmed milk. The cream is retained for adding to scones. This cheese is freshly acidic and creamy tasting and is often used as a breakfast cheese, in cooking, or as a snack.

DUNLOP

A traditional semi-hard farmhouse cheese made from untreated cow's milk. The name of this cheese that is shared with a well-known brand of tyres does not refer to the fairly elastic consistency of this cheese but the town of Dunlop where both the cheese and the tyres originated. The taste is mild and buttery with an initial sweetness that is replaced with a fresh acidity in the finish. A glass of port or amontillado sherry is a suitable companion for this cheese.

GOWRIE

Modern hard farmhouse cheese that lies between a Cheddar and a Dunlop.

ISLE OF MULL

Excellent local variety (untreated milk) of Cheddar-type cheese that is paler in colour and more powerful and spicy in taste.

LANARK BLUE

One of the few remaining craft-made traditional Scottish cheeses. This blue mould cheese made with untreated milk can be regarded as a relative of Roquefort but its texture is less creamy and the taste less sharp. There is also Lanark Blue made from pasteurised milk. Drink a full-bodied and richly sweet from wine Bergerac or Bordeaux.

ORKNEY EXTRA MATURE CHEDDAR

A very successful Scottish island variety of the English Cheddar that is of excellent quality for a mass-produced cheese. Orkney is fully-flavoured with creaminess and nuts. Maturing time is at least one year. Fat content is 50%. Choose a glass of good port or sherry with this cheese.

ST. ANDREWS

A round or rectangular modern version of a Trappist monastery cheese with a ribbed orange rind created through washing. The cheese itself is fairly elastic and exhibits some small 'eyes'. The taste is freshly acidic with undertones of yeast.

A delicious glass of beer, a sultry malt scotch, or a young Pinot Gris from Alsace are good combinations with this cheese.

Irish cheeses

Strange as it may seem but the Irish have never really developed a great love for cheese. Although they probably have the most luxuriant, verdant, and finest pastures of the British Isles and produce a great deal of milk and butter they have never been much interested in cheese and neither the arrival of the Celts or the later monks managed to change this. In the twentieth century the northern provinces of Ulster exported copies of cheeses popular across the water in the rest of the United Kingdom such as Cheddar and Red Leicester but that was it. Fortunately things have changed, in

Irish Red Leicester

part due to the arrival of some Dutch immigrants in Eire and the work of Kerrygold. Modern Irish

Celtic influence is everywhere

cheeses manage to convey the magical mythology and melancholy of the Celts.

ARDRAHAN

This cow's milk farmhouse cheese cannot be compared with any other. The washed rind protects a dark yellow inner cheese that is firm and dense with small 'eyes'. The taste is fresh and somewhat down-to-earth but supported with both butter and nuts. This is very much a cheese to chew at during a long walk along the misty coasts of Ireland. A pint of Guinness perhaps, or a shot of Irish Whiskey?

CASHEL BLUE

This is one of the very best cheeses from the entire British Isles. It is a blue cheese made from

untreated cow's milk with a very creamy taste and texture. About 5 in (13 cm) deep and 6 in (15 cm) in diameter, weighing about 4 lb 6 oz (2 kg), this cheese closely resembles gorgonzola dolcelatte. There is also a version of this cheese for vegetarians. Drink a mellow medium dry white wine with it.

COOLEA

This farmhouse cheese is made from untreated cow's milk and closely resembles an old-fashioned farmhouse-made delicious Gouda which is perhaps no surprise in view of the fact that it is made by a Dutch couple. An excellent cheese in every respect available as both young or mature cheese of either three months or one year old.
Drink a glass of lager or Pilsener beer or a white or red wine with this cheese.

Cooleeney

Ardrahan

COOLEENEY

Camembert like cheese made from untreated cow's milk. The taste is full of flavour with typically hints of mushrooms. The moisture content appears somewhat higher than a true Camembert so that the cheese can spontaneously reach the other side of the table when fully mature. Maturing time is four to eight weeks and fat content is 45%.

A glass of a good farm cider is delicious with this cheese but a white beer or even a young fruity red wine go well with it too.

CROGHAN

This soft goat's-milk cheese made with untreated milk is also made by Dutch immigrants. This is a cheese with bite that is full of flavour with hints of nuts and spices. This cheese is only available from

Doolin

spring until Christmas. Drink a beer with a strong taste or a genever with this cheese but you might also try a fresh but full-bodied white wine.

DOOLIN

My first acquaintance with this modern hard Irish cheese made of cow's milk was anything but convincing. I found it deadly dull but I discovered later that this is because it is exported to the continent when far from mature so that it has precious little taste. Do not bother with the two months old Young Doolin but choose instead a Mature Doolin that has a much fuller and fruitier flavour or Vintage Doolin with its rich and complex taste of fresh butter. Fat content is 45%. Serve beer, cider, wine, or port with this cheese. The more mature the cheese the stronger the taste of the drink.

DUBLINER

A natural cheese of the Cheddar type that is matured for one year when it has a full and well-rounded flavour, lightly spiced and dense yet slightly crumbly in texture. A Kerrygold product (see also Kerrygold). Matured for one year; fat content is 45%. Serve beer, port, or well-rounded white or red with this cheese.

DURRUS

This cheese of untreated cow's milk resembles somewhat a Tomme. It is full in flavour, creamy, nutty, fresh and sweet with a bit of down-to-earth taste – in other words superb! Fat content is 45%. The ideal accompaniment for this cheese can be a beer, a genever, an excellent white wine from the mountains of France, Switzerland, or Italy, and an open hearth fire.

GABRIEL

A hard farmhouse cheese with Swiss style made from untreated cow's milk. The enormous wheels of 15 lb 6 oz–66 lb (7–30 kg) are slowly matured in the mild climate of West Cork. There are two varieties of this cheese, one of which is at least 99 lb (45 kg)! Drink a glass of fresh white wine from the mountains or a light fruity red e.g. Gamay or Pinot Noir.

GUBBEEN

A wheel of a cheese of just 2lb 3 oz–3 lb 5 oz (1–1.5 kg) that was once made of untreated cow's milk. This cheese with its washed rind has clearly taken the French St-Nectaire as its example and the better ones at that. This cheese is full of flavour, initially fresh with distinct notes of

Dubliner

Dubliner

mushrooms and undertones of a dusty cellar which make this not a suitable cheese for inexperienced tastes but ideal for cheese lovers. Drink a rather

Gubbeen

expressive white or red with this cheese such as a Côtes d'Auvergne, Savoie, or even a Arbois.

IRISH CHEDDAR

Irish Cheddar is sold throughout the world, often in small attractive packs but also as large whole (round) cheeses, catering size blocks, or ready-sliced. Much of this cheese bears the Kerrygold brand that is the trade mark of the Irish dairy organisation. You may also encounter small individual Cheddars and vintage Cheddar under

Kerrygold Cheddar

different names. The Irish also make a number of speciality cheeses based on Cheddar with e.g. porter beer (e.g. Guinness or Murphy stout) added.

IRISH VINTAGE CHEDDAR

Irish vintage Cheddar is at least one year old and it has a rich, well-rounded taste. It is a firm cheese but has a soft and creamy texture that is ideal for a cheeseboard.
Drink a glass of beer or port with this cheese. If you prefer wine then choose a full-bodied white or red.

KERRYGOLD

Kerrygold is the brand name of the Irish dairy industry organisation and not a cheese variety. Through the use of a national brand identity with strict quality control Ireland is able to export high quality products throughout the world.
The Kerrygold name is a guarantee of good basic quality of both the original cows, their milk, the natural cheesemaking processes, and of purity and hygiene.
This latter quality is specifically important for the Irish exports to the USA. The cheese, and also butter, milk, and dried milk are produced by members of the Kerrygold co-operative which is controlled by the Irish state dairy industry organisation. See also Dubliner and Irish Cheddar.

Porter Cheddar

Irish vintage Cheddar

MILLEENS

A superb cheese made from untreated cow's milk in County Cork. This is a soft cheese with a full-flavoured taste that is somewhat reminiscent of a first class Brie de Coulommiers but also because of its washed rind of a Reblochon or a soft Trappist monastery cheese. Maturing time is four to ten weeks and fat content is 45%.

Drink a glass of first-class Chardonnay or a mellow Pinot Noir from Burgundy, Alsace, or the Côtes de Youl with this cheese.

MINE-GABHAR

A very popular and superbly made soft to semi-hard cheese made from untreated goat's milk from organic farms. This cheese is reminiscent of the best French goat's-milk cheeses from the Loire.

Serve a fresh Sauvignon Blanc or a delicious red with this cheese from e.g. St-Pourçain, the Forez, Lyonnais, or Beaujolais.

ORLA

A semi-soft to semi-hard untreated sheep's-milk cheese from organic farms around County Cork.

Drink a glass of a good red wine with this cheese such as those of the south-west of France (Irouléguy, Tursan, Madiran), or a white from the same region that is none too dry.

ST. KILLIAN

Another Camembert like cheese made from pasteurised cow's milk that is very popular in Ireland. It is creamy and buttery with the usual mushroom overtones. Drink cider, Chardonnay, Gamay, or Pinot Noir with this.

BLUE RATHGORE

A rare goat's-milk blue cheese. Drink a white that is not too dry with this cheese such as a Côteaux de l'Aubance or a good German or Austrian medium dry (e.g. slightly sweet) white wine.

The Netherlands

The Netherlands advertises itself as the world's number two cheese country. This claim is clearly based on the volume of exports rather than the quality of the cheese or its diversity. Travels abroad are rather revealing to the Dutch when it comes to the opinion of other nationalities to their cheese. Remarks such as: "Tasteless, only any good for toasted sandwiches, or for cooking with" are far from complimentary and in truth these voices are right about my native country's cheese because none of them have ever had the opportunity to taste a genuine craft-made and properly matured genuine traditional Gouda that has been made with much care and devotion. Give them some really good Dutch Gouda and you will see the look of surprise on their face. I have never understood that The Netherlands can import the most unknown of goat's-milk cheeses from the Savoie

Being well-known does not always guarantee quality

Belegen kaas – mature Dutch cheese

Overjarige or year plus crumbly Dutch cheese

Extra belegen kaas – extra mature Dutch cheese

Oude kaas – old Dutch cheese

Fat content in dry matter

A cheese consists of dry matter and moisture and the moisture content is a variable because as the cheese becomes older it looses moisture and hence becomes drier. A Gouda cheese at four weeks for instance has 60% dry matter and 40% moisture, making these the minimum values for this cheese. As the cheese matures the percentage of dry matter will increase in proportion to the overall weight of the cheese. Dry matter consists of proteins, fats, calcium, sodium, and vitamins. The determination of the fat content of a Dutch cheese is always on the basis of the proportion of fat in the dry matter. A Gouda cheese rated as 48 + has 48% fat in the overall 60% weight of the cheese at a young age that is dry matter.

This actually means that the fat represents only 29% fat (48% of 60%) or 29 grams per 100 grams of the young cheese. The percentage of fat/dry matter does not change but the percentage of fat to the overall weight of the cheese increases during maturing. The indication 48+ is therefore the minimum fat percentage to dry matter of a Gouda cheese.

Strict control

The Dutch cheese mark (Nederlandse Kaasmerk) is a guarantee of the quality of a cheese. The round disc is formed from the casein laid on the cheese during cheesemaking and subsequently pressed into the cheese. After the cheese is dipped in brine the mark becomes integral with the rind. The small disc also bears the name of the type of cheese, the fat content, the country of origin, and two codes that enable the production area and producer to be traced.

Generally any cheese that does not satisfy the strict checks at the end of the maturing process is removed from sale. Such cheese does not get a seal of approval. Cheese has to meet certain standards in respect of health issues, fat, moisture, salt content and also a number of other characteristics. The rind of a Gouda cheese must be 'clean, smooth, fully closed, and of an even yellow colour' while shape must be as 'round as a wagon wheel' and the consistency of the cheese itself must be 'sufficiently firm and sliceable' with any air bubbles or 'eyes' evenly distributed.

Fine then but what about the taste? This is tested when the cheese has matured. The keurmeesters or tasters first tap the cheese to ascertain if it has matured properly before extracting samples from

Tasting and checking cheese is not just men's work

the cheese with special probes to check for taste, colour, and aroma.

Numerous types and tastes of Dutch cheese

Although the Dutch cheesemakers largely produce the two main types of cheese (Edam and Gouda), rather like the domination of Cheddar and Stilton in Britain there are countless varieties on a theme: less salt, less fat, full-cream milk or skimmed milk, with or without herbs and spices or other additions, young or really old, from salty pastures or lush clay ground, really traditional old Dutch or with a nod towards foreign styles of cheese. In other words there is enormous variety on a basic theme. In the context of this book I do not make comparisons between different brands but I do actually refer to certain brand names.

Blue mould cheeses

Less well-known and mainly produced for export. The Dutch blue mould cheeses are well worth discovering.

BLAUWE BASTIAANSE (BASTIAANSE BLUE)
A cheese from the province of North Brabant that is popular among caterers from the Molenschot cheese farm. Bastian's Blue resembles a wheel with bulbous sides. The taste is quite individual to this cheese: creamy and initially mild then slightly sharp from the blue mould. Drink a fresh sweet white with this cheese from Germany or the Loire.

BLUEFORT
Cow's milk cheese made by Coberco of Meppel. The hexagonal shape of this approx. 8 lb 13 oz (4 kg) cheese is attractive but also a blessing for the purchaser who always wants to slice perfect wedges. Bluefort has a fat content of 60% of dry matter (38% overall) and is at least five weeks old when sold to shops but can be matured for a further two months. The cheese is very creamy and mild, although given a sharpness by the blue mould. Delicious as a snack with a drink with a glass of genever or other drinks but also suitable for incorporation in hot and cold dishes.

Bluefort

DELFTS BLAUW (BLUE DELFT)
Probably the best known and most popular of all the Dutch blue cheeses. Blue Delft is made from organically produced milk using Gouda cream cheese as its basis (60–65+). A superb cheese.
Drink a fresh sweet white wine from the Loire e.g. Côteaux de l'Aubance or a Côteaux du Layon.

Delfts Blauw or Blue Delft

FARM CHEESE

For taste you will always be better off with farm cheese known as *Boerenkaas*. It does not matter whether the milk is from cows, goats, or sheep for with the farm cheese maker it is taste that matters most. The milk is not pasteurised for farm cheese and the farmers use their own milk which changes its taste during the course of the year. Spring milk has an entirely different taste than winter milk and the fat content can also vary. With mass-produced cheese the milk is always first homogenised so that it always tastes the same. The taste of a farm cheese is therefore much closer to nature and much closer to the taste of the milk itself. No enormous machines are used for farm cheese, instead processes are carried out by hand with considerable devotion to the task. There is a tremendous variety of farm cheese from Gouda through to goat's-milk and sheep's-milk cheese. There is no such thing as farm Edam cheese although numerous farms do make an Edam-type cheese that may not be sold as Edam.

The queens of Dutch farm cheeses are undoubtedly the Beemster and Stolwijker cheeses that are much fuller and richer in flavour than most farm cheeses. They are made from untreated full-cream milk that imparts the rich taste and makes the cheese much creamier. The smell and taste are much more aromatic than the majority of factory-made cheeses. The richness of farm cheese and

Dutch farm cheese (Boerenkaas)

slightly sweet taste enables these farm cheeses to combine with almost any type of wine, beer, or even spirits.

DORUVAEL

Despite the apparently Flemish nature of the name, this cheese is wholly Dutch. This is a strong tasting creamy and smooth cheese that belongs to the family of cheeses with red bacterial rinds. This cheese has a greater strength of flavour than a Port Salut or even a Kernheim and is reminiscent of old Dutch cheeses that have unfortunately disappeared, such as Barsselle. The name is not derived from some ancient place name but is a local farmer's protest at the dairy policy in The Netherlands. Those in the know can find an abbreviation of his protest in the name.

Edam (Edammer)

From the fourteenth to the eighteenth century Edam cheese was probably the most popular cheese in the world, and certainly in far flung colonies of the Dutch. Because the cheese matured well and could be eaten to a ripe old age it was ideal as provisions for long voyages and for distant communities. Less favourable voices suggested the cheese was perfect replacement for cannonballs. It is certainly true that a fully mature Edam can withstand a great deal and also that these cheeses are indeed shaped liked cannonballs. The name Edam (the Dutch *Edammer* means from or of Edam) does not relate to where this cheese is made but the port from which it was shipped.

Present-day Edam is nothing like the cheese the Dutch pioneers and colonists knew. Since the nineteenth century this cheese is no longer made with full-cream milk but with semi-skimmed milk. The fat content of an Edam is less than that of a Gouda: 40% of the dry matter (40+ minimum) compared with 48% for Gouda cheese. The stronger tasting farm-made Edam cheese has also disappeared from the scene and been replaced with many different softer mass-produced versions. Most Edam is made to a weight of approx. 3 lb 12 oz (1.7 kg) but there are also baby Edams made to sell to tourists and the double Edam that is coloured with carotene and intended for export. The double-sized Edam used to be popular among the barge skippers on the inland waterways of Northern France. The French now make their own double-sized Edam-style cheese which they call Mimolette. Edam cheese sold in The Netherlands is rarely coated with paraffin wax as with export cheese, except during the tourist season. The red wax coating gives the cheese additional protection for shipping but helps their recognition in foreign shops. Occasionally you may see an Edam cheese abroad with a black wax coating. This cheese has been matured for at least 17 weeks. Most Edam is unfortunately sold far too young. Young Edam has a very mild, slightly sweet taste with a hint of nuts and the full taste only develops with age. When mature the cheese is both drier and more salty than a Gouda and also slightly sharper. Once fully matured an Edam cheese is ideal for grating. Genuine Edam cheese was once made in special wooden barrels that were also handy as head protection in times of trouble. It is from this that the nickname is derived of 'cheese-heads' or *kaaskoppen* that was given to people from the two provinces of North and South Holland.

Young Edam begs a light, fruity red wine, e.g. a Pinot Noir Burgundy or a Beaujolais, or a young red from the Loire (Chinon, Bourgueil). More mature Edam is better with a stronger wine such as a Rhône.

EDAM WITH CUMIN
Edam to which cumin seed has been added during making.

EDAM WITH HERBS
This variety is sometimes seen outside The Netherlands. The herb variety has a coating of green wax.

OLD FACTORS CHEESE
This type of cheese, known in The Netherlands as *oude commissiekaas* and in France as Mimolette, is better known in France than in The Netherlands. It is a double-size Edam with red-orange colouring from carotene. The cheese is now also made in Northern France. The origins of this cheese hark back to a feudal system in which the farmers had to supply all their cheeses to the landowner in exchange for a roof over their head and the squire's protection. The farmers asked if they might be permitted to make cheese for their own consumption and this was agreed provided the cheese was dyed red to identify it so that it could not be sold in The Netherlands. Dutch being Dutch they found a way to profit from this. A trade quickly flourished with the barge skippers who were shipping goods into Northern France and the south. The cheeses kept well and were popular additions to the galley of these barges. The skippers were able to make some extra money on the side from the trade and the farmers benefited too with the French becoming quite taken with the cheese. When young this cheese is not at all tasty because it needs time to develop. Once mature it is exceptionally tasty with a full flavour that has slightly salty undertones and a nutty finish. By the time the cheese becomes crumbly it is at its best. Drink a strong-tasting beer, a genever, of tasty glass of a full-bodied red wine with this cheese.

CRUMBLY FRIESIAN EDAM
These crumbly Edam cheeses were once common-place in the area along the river Zaan and in West Friesland. When the cheese is young one can taste fresh buttermilk in them and when more mature the taste is fuller and stronger but never too salty. There is a fruity undertone and this cheese is every bit as good as a crumbly old Parmesan. Small volume of this cheese is still made by the Friesian co-operative Frico which quickly sell on the strength of word of mouth recommendations to satisfied customers.

Edam

FRIESIAN CLOVE CHEESE/FRIESE NAGELKAAS

This is very much a cheese for those who like a sturdy cheese. The Friesians used to make this cheese from the skimmed milk left after butter and cream production and the dry, sharp-tasting cheese was flavoured with the juice from green herbs which in Friesian was known as *grien tsiss* pronounced not far from the English 'green cheese'. Later they add cumin and other spices to the cheese.

Today only the strongest of these cheeses is still made with the addition of cloves (and often cumin). The basic cheese is hard, dry, crumbly, and fairly sour. After maturing for four months the cloves impart a taste that is quite different and not to everyone's liking. The cheese is ideal after a day skating at temperatures of minus 15°C (5°F) with one or more glasses of Beerenburger, the local spiced bitter drink.

Those determined to drink wine with this very dominant-tasting cheese need to choose a truly robust one such as an old-fashioned Amarone from Valpolicella or a Barello, or strong and forceful Spanish wine.

Goat's-milk cheeses

The growth in goat's-milk cheeses in The Netherlands is considerable. Until recently most of these were made on small farms and tended to have a bit of an 'alternative' label attached to them. Although there are still many independent cheesemakers making them – largely with milk from organic farming –increasingly more of the big

Farm-made untreated goat's-milk cheese

producers are developing their own response to this demand. For blue mould goat's-milk cheese see blue mould cheeses and for red bacterial rind goat's-milk cheese see red bacterial rind cheese.

ARINA

Factory-made goat's-milk cheese of remarkably little character. Why should a factory seek to make a goat's-milk cheese that neither smells or tastes of goats' milk? Perhaps it is what the consumer wants?

Producers of goat's-milk cheese

BASTIAANSE

These cheesemakers from the province of Noord Brabant provide a wide range of different goat's-milk cheeses, mainly with organic and 'alternative agriculture' approval marks. Beside some of their very interesting goat's-milk cheeses with basil, garlic, stinging nettle, and goat's-milk 'Camembert' Bastiaanse also make a rather strange cheese for unusual tastes with potato peelings added.

COBERCO MEPPEL

This large dairy concern produces Belle Blanche cheese in Coberco's 'trade-mark' hexagonal form. Belle Blanche is factory made from pasteurised Dutch goat's-milk but the milk loses all its individuality through the process of pasteurisation and tastes little different to immature cow's milk cheese. This cheese has absolutely no interest for a lover of true goat's-milk cheese but is for those who wish to eat goat's-milk cheese with the

Belle Blanche

certainty that it will have none of the characteristic taste of goat's milk. Maturing time is four weeks to four months and the fat content is 48% of dry matter (30% in total).

Bettine Blanc

Chèvre de Bettine

Wonderful fresh goat's-milk cheese from Wolverlei

Bettinekaas

fresh goat's-milk cheese (not necessarily moist) drink a fresh white wine such as a Sauvignon Blanc from the Loire or similar from Alsace, the Savoie, northern Italy, or south-west France (Gascony). With white mould goat's-milk cheese it is better to choose a light red, ideally a Gamay.

Gouda (Goudse kaas)

Gouda is the best-known type of Dutch cheese both at home and abroad. Once this was true of Edam. The cheese gets its name from the picturesque town of Gouda where the cheese has been traded for centuries. The cheeses themselves actually originated in the provinces of Zuid

Gouda

EWIJK FAMILY
This family from Etten-Leur make superb goat's-milk cheeses such as Petite Bettine Blanc, that both smell and taste of goats' milk but are not strong. Bettine is a fine example of how such a cheese can be made acceptable for everyone.

SAANENHOF
Increasing numbers of small farms are producing goat's-milk cheese, particularly with organic and 'alternative agriculture' approval marks. Within that enormous choice this farm at Heeze in the province of Noord Brabant is one of the best. This cheese has become extremely well-known in the better-end of the catering trade and among the better special-ist cheese shops. Saanenhof provides a diverse range of cheeses made solely with untreated milk: white mould cheeses, blocks of goat's-milk cheese at various stages of maturing, cooking cheese, cheeses in herbal oil, herbal cheeses etc.

WOLVERLEI
A first-class goat's-milk farm cheesemaker in Ambt Delden with a varied assortment such as blocks of cheese. With factory-made goat's-milk cheese it is possible to choose any white or red wine because the cheese has too little character to matter. With

Holland (South Holland) and Utrecht but today are made almost throughout the entire country. Gouda cheese has three regional categories.

• Noord Holland Gouda, distinguished by the letters 'NH' on the little disc of cheese protein in the rind. This is made in the polders of North Holland to the north of Amsterdam and the Nordzee canal. This is the only type of Gouda that is afforded protected origin status by EC legislation. Many people object profusely to this since these are all factory-made cheeses while elsewhere the cheese is made with real regional individuality and care by hand. This was the result of successful political lobbying by the local milk co-operative Campina Melkunie.
• Holland-Brabantse Gouda, distinguished by the letters 'HB' on the rind and mainly produced in the provinces of Zuid Holland (south), Utrecht, and Noord Brabant.
• Friesian Gouda ('FF' on the disc) is made in the provinces of Friesland, Gronginen, Drenthe, Overijssel, and parts of Gelderland.

Normal Gouda is made as a large wheel of approx. 26 lb 6 oz (12 kg) with domed sides but for catering and cheese wholesalers there is also factory-made Gouda in large blocks that is intended for the cutting of regular sized slices. The quality and character of Gouda is determined by the origin and quality of the milk, the type of souring agent or rennet used, the amount of salt used, and other additives such as colourings and preservatives. The maturing process plays a very important role in the development of the taste in the cheese. Slow maturing in warehouses always leads to better results than the accelerated maturing of factory cheese.

With *Jonge* or young cheese drink a fresh red from e.g. Beaujolais, Rhône, or Provence or Northern Italy (e.g. Veneto, Trentino, or Alto-Adige). With *Belegen* or mature cheese a better quality red but not too sultry is recommended: a Bordeaux, Pécharmant, Côtes de Bergerac, or a fine Chianti Classico. The older cheese is best combined with a well-matured Bordeaux from the Medoc.

Gouda from untreated milk

Factory-made cheese and no pasteurisation? True, though do not expect the same flavour of a farm-made cheese from untreated milk. The milk for this type of cheese is not pasteurised or otherwise heated in its preparation but is rid of unwanted bacteria by other very high-technology processes. The milk is centrifuged and passed through micro or even ultra-micro filters under pressure which separates the curd from the whey. Because most bacteria thrive in a moist environment they are removed with the whey. This also means that the bacteria which cause the milk to go off are removed. The taste of cheese made by this process is certainly better than the more generally used pasteurisation.

KOLLUMER

This untreated milk cheese is made by natural traditional means from full-cream milk. The patient and careful maturing of Kollumer makes it a superb cheese that is full of flavour, creamy, and slightly salty. Fat content is 48% of the dry matter.

Kollumer

TEXEL/TEXELAAR

This cheese from Texel was the first non pasteurised but mechanically treated cheese to be made in The Netherlands. With these 'raw milk' Gouda cheeses you should choose a more full-bodied white from the Savoie, Jura, Alsace, or Switzerland or a full-bodied but not sultry red made from Syrah/Shiraz (Rhône, Australia, or South Africa). Other alternatives for the riper cheeses include a Californian Zinfandel or Pinotage.

Farm Gouda

Farm-produced Gouda is permitted to be made anywhere in The Netherlands but is hardly made, if at all, in Noord Holland. You will find good farm cheeses especially in Noord Brabant but also in Utrecht, Flevoland, Friesland, and Overijssel. Farm-made Gouda has a rich taste, is creamy and full of flavour when young with undertones of fresh hay and nuts. When more mature the taste is more intense, even quite strong. The curd of the cheese may contain some air bubbles and white crystals. Contrary to popular belief these are not common salt (sodium chloride) but calcium crystals.

STOLWIJK/STOLWIJKER

Genuine Stolwijk cheese bears no relation to modern factory-made versions of 26 lb 7 oz (12 kg). The real article is only made sporadically and is one of the best of all Dutch cheeses. A young Stolwijk cheese weighs 39 lb 9 oz–55 lb (18–25 kg) and it is displayed with great pride by every specialist cheese shop that can get their hands on one. Genuine Stolwijk is of course made from untreated milk and has a full, sweeter, and richer flavour than the factory-made imitation. Some cheeses contain quite large air bubbles and can smell of horse or chicken manure – but the taste is superb! On the farms themselves they call these cheeses *boerentik* in reference to the strange sound they make when tapped, or 'September' cheese, because of the month when they are sold.

JUMBO FARM CHEESE/BOERENJUMBO

A superb cheese weighing around 200 lb (90 kg) made by farmer De Groot of De Meije in a very careful hand-crafted manner from summertime-milk only, so available in limited volume. Matured for forty weeks.

Reduced salt Gouda

MAASLAND/MAASLANDER

This cheese by Westland cheese specialities has become renowned both at home and abroad. The instantly recognisable green and yellow logo on this cheese attracts attention to this cheese on sale. This cheese that weighs about 26 lb 6 oz (12 kg) is made like other Gouda (48% fat) but with less salt so that its taste is creamier and milder. Ideal on its own and perfect in salads or light dishes.

MATURE MAASLAND/MAASLANDER BELEGEN

In addition to the well-known green and yellow Maasland cheese a mature version presented in a red and yellow coat has been made for a number of years. The cheese is very similar to its younger companion but with a fuller and stronger taste while retaining the delicious creaminess.

OLD MAASLAND/MAASLANDER OUD

The latest addition to the Maasland family of cheeses but the oldest of them. This black and

Green and yellow and red and yellow Maasland

yellow coated cheese combines the strong mature cheese taste of old Gouda with the creaminess of the other Maasland cheeses. This cheese has found a gap in the market with a delicious mature cheese for those who appreciate such things without the crumbly nature and saltiness of a normal old Gouda.

This is due to the lower level of salt used in its preparation than Gouda of a similar age. By this means Westland are able to win over those people who find an Old Amsterdam too salty.

Gouda with cumin

Gouda cheese to which cumin has been added during preparation. This is less dry than the Leiden and Edam cumin cheeses.

May or grass Gouda

Some Dutch people confuse what they know as *meikaas* or *graskaas* with a fresh white 'May cheese' or *meikaas* made for Amsterdam's Jewish community, that is actually available year round with the help of freezers. That very young cheese is made under strict rabbinical *kosher* control and eaten while fresh. The Jewish 'May cheese' uses vegetable rennet derived from mushrooms, making it suitable for vegetarians. Gouda 'May' cheese or 'grass' cheese is the name given to young Gouda that is made in the spring when the cows are first turned out onto grass. Some light-heartedly call this the Beaujolais Nouveau among cheeses.

Drink a very mild white wine with this cheese if you are not eating it for breakfast.

Reduced fat Gouda

Reduced fat cheeses are fairly new on the scene for the Dutch. Most of these cheeses are similar to Gouda but have different names, presentation, and taste with fat content of 20+ and 30+.

CANTENAAR

An example of an intelligently and well made factory cheese. Cantenaar is made by Coberco in

Cantenaar

Gelderland according to old craft principles of cheesemaking. The cheese is actually made in a brand new factory with the very latest in equipment. The taste of this cheese is due not only to the 40% less fat and 25% less salt but to careful maturing over four months.

Cantenaar is delicious on its own but also makes a good cheese to cook with in view of its melting properties. It is a first class cheese that is well-suited to a healthy and sportive life-style and healthy diet.

MILNER
This is another reduced fat and reduced salt cheese made in a factory, by Campina. It is a 30+ cheese produced from semi-skimmed milk. In terms of taste Milner is comparable with a mature Gouda. Ideal on its own, in a sandwich, or in all manner of hot dishes.

Milner

MATURE MILNER
Cheese matured for a longer period (seven months), comparable with a extra mature Gouda.

MILNER EXTRA MATURE
An even more mature version of this cheese with less salt. The taste and texture is similar to an old Gouda.

MILNER WITH CUMIN
A *jong belegen* (young mature) Milner 30+ flavoured with cum seed. This cheese has less fat and salt than a Gouda with cumin and is much creamier than the equivalent Leiden cheese.

WESTLITE
A Gouda-type wheel-shaped cheese by Westland cheese specialities with only 30% fat in its dry matter.

This 30+ cheese of 26 lb 6 oz (12 kg) is matured for sixteen weeks (*belegen*) and hence has a full flavour, is creamy and unadulterated with a slightly sharp finish. Delicious on its own or for use in cheese dishes.

Full cream Gouda
This member of the Gouda family contains a much higher level of fat (60+). The taste is mild, creamy, and smoother.

Choose a light and fresh white or red wine to accompany this cheese such as Pinot Blanc or Pinot Gris from Alsace or a Gamay from Beaujolais or the Loire.

Gouda with a touch of Italian
A number of branded Dutch cheeses are sold that are slightly mature, contain less salt and that melt readily, making them ideal for culinary use. They are excellent grated for pasta but can also be used for cooking in slices or chunks and they also taste good on their own. Some of them are available at various levels of maturity. The brand names vary from country to country.

NAPOLI CONTADINO
In spite of its name this is farm cheese from Noord Holland which has garlic, olives, and sun-dried tomatoes added during its preparation. A delicious cheese for connoisseurs and a great discovery for the creative cook. There is also a goat's-milk cheese in olive oil.

OLD AMSTERDAM
This is a branded cheese from Westland cheese specialities that is the most popular old Gouda cheese with the Dutch. To emphasise its special characteristics and maturity the 22 lb (10 kg) cheese is presented in a very classy packaging together with the somewhat pompous self-designation 'Premier Grand Cru Classé' to reinforce its status as a luxury food. Nice bit of marketing for those to whom the label is everything but what about the cheese itself? Fortunately it is well matured, strong and full of flavour with a rich and unadulterated taste.

Delicious with a glass of good beer but also an excellent companion for a sturdy mature Bordeaux red or glass of vintage port.

Westlite

REIJPENAER

This cheese is certainly worth mentioning for it is of superb quality and slowly matured by natural means which is the factor that makes so much difference. The cheeses are stacked on miles of wooden racks in an old warehouse in Woerden that dates from 1906.

Factory-matured cheese is often matured more quickly because the temperature and humidity are strictly controlled with humidity held at about 85%. This does prevent the cheese from drying out. At the warehouse in Woerden where Reijpenaer is matured the only temperature control is ventilation in summer and very gentle heating in the winter. This does cause more drying out of the cheese which makes them denser than the factory-made varieties but they are also more intense in taste.

This is partly due to the exposure of the cheese to micro-organisms such as bacteria and mould that live among the wooden shelves, the beams, the shutters, and the floor. The flavour of this cheese has a greater range of different nuances than other cheeses of a similar type. Although the Reijpenaer is made from pasteurised milk it far better conveys the taste of the old-style classic Gouda.

A glass of port or a good red (Bordeaux or Bergerac) are entirely appropriate to accompany this cheese.

SPIJKER

This cheese has been developed comparatively recently and resembles a small Gouda of 48% of the dry matter. This offers a pleasing variant to the sharp Friesian clove cheese. It is made by Verbakel & Seggelink.

A sturdy red from the Rhône valley will taste good with this cheese.

Vegetarian Gouda

TRENTA

An unusual cheese from the Gouda family that it relatively small at 17 lb 9 oz (8 kg). At first glance it appears similar to a Gouda with fat of 48% and the usual wheel shape.

The major difference with this cheese is in the type of rennet used. Vegetable derived fats are used instead of animal-based rennet to produce Trenta which makes the cheese suitable for eating by

Trenta vegetarian cheese

vegetarians. It also contains less cholesterol with 78% of its fatty acids being unsaturated. This young and creamy cheese has a full and pure flavour and is also very healthy.

SMOKED CHEESE

This cheese, in the form of a long sausage, is known as 'smoked Gouda' outside The Netherlands although it has little relation to Gouda and the old-fashioned method of smoking above burning wood chips may often have been replaced by the addition of smoke flavouring to the cheese during its making.

A cheese for the enthusiast, ideally accompanied with a glass of beer or genever but if you insist on wine choose a spicy Portuguese one.

Smoked cheese

CHEESE WITH EYES (HOLLANDSE GATENKAAS)/MAASDAMMER/GOUTALER

These modern industrial creations have become very popular both at home and abroad. These Dutch cheeses with air bubbles or eyes in them are produced in the shape of large wheels with straight sides and a curved centre. The cheese is supple and springy with many large air bubbles created by the addition of specially selected bacteria. Both the air bubbles and the taste resemble Swiss cheese which is precisely what its creators intended – a cheaper version of a Swiss Emmental. Dutch 'hole cheese' (the literal translation of *Hollandse gatenkaas*) is also known as Maasdammer (cheese from Maasdam) and is sold under a variety of brand names including perhaps the most judicious: Goutaler. This is a blending of 'Gouda' and 'Emmentaler'.

LEERDAM/LEERDAMMER

The best-known and most important of Dutch cheeses with air bubbles in and probably the tastiest between the holes (a slogan used to advertise Maasdam) is Leerdam, known in The Netherlands as Leerdammer (from Leerdam). The cheese is in the form of a flattened wheel and bears the distinctive Leerdam mark on the rind. The soft and

supple cheese is springy with many large air bubbles. The taste is slightly sweet and creamy with nutty undertones that are reminiscent of Swiss cheese. Delicious on its own but also an excellent culinary cheese.

Drink the same with these Dutch cheeses with air bubbles in as you would with the large Swiss or French cheeses of this type: fresh white wine from the Savoie or Jura, or a Fendant du Valais. A light red from Alsace, the Jura, Beaujolais, or Switzerland will also make a good companion.

LIMBURG CAVES CHEESE (LIMBURG GROTTENKAAS)

A semi-hard cheese from Limburg that is mildly sharp through maturing in the caves in the ferruginous limestone. Also known in Dutch as *Heuvelland Grottenkaas* (hill country caves cheese). These 10 lb (4.5 kg) flat cheeses are a real delicacy as a result of the pure air, constant temperature, and high humidity of the caves. This is a first-class cheese with a glass of genever or to add to a cheeseboard but it is also very suitable for use in both hot and cold dishes. A Limburg

Limburg caves cheese

caves cheese would appear to be a perfect match for a glass of the local Limburg beer but a glass of Riesling is also a good combination, whether from Limburg or not.

Dutch cheese with herbs and spices

Cheese made in the Gouda manner can also have herbs and spices such as paprika, or other flavourings such as sun-dried tomatoes added during its preparation.

SUBENHARA

Cheese made by Coberco in a partially-crafted manner with a variety of flavours added: garden herbs, nettles, and garlic.

A beer or genever are the best companions with these cheeses but if you really must drink wine then choose a thirst-quenching fairly robust red or white, preferably from the south-west of France or the Midi.

Dutch flavoured cheeses sell well in export markets

ORIENTA/SENFORTE
Spicy cheeses by Coberco of Meppel that are extra creamy (50% of the dry matter is fat) with a slightly to quite spicy taste, but never sharp. This cheese needs to mature for at least four weeks and can happily continue to mature for a further three months in the shop. Consists in two varieties: the surprising Oriental Orienta with coriander and

Subenhara with garden herbs

Subenhara is also available in nettle or garlic versions

fenugreek and spicy Senforte with multi-coloured mustard seed. Both are hexagonal. These cheeses taste remarkably good with a glass of beer or a glass of smooth spirits. Orienta tolerates the

Coberca Senforte

Coberco Orienta

company of a fresh New Zealand Sauvignon while Senfort is better with a Burgundy or Beaujolais.

DELICATESS
A branded cheese by Campina from North Holland. Available as Delicatess Mustard with mustard seed and Delicatess de Saisons with seasonal ingredients such as asparagus and spring onions in springtime. Both cheeses have 50% fat of their dry matter. Choose a simple Pinot Noir for the mustard seed variety or simple Alsace Pinot Blanc for the seasonal one.

LANDANA
An oval cheese from the Leerdam cheese plant that cannot be compared with any other. It is creamy and slightly spicy with sweet undertones. Made without the use of preservatives by means of removal of both unwanted and desirable bacteria by centrifuging the milk. Fat content: 50% of the dry matter. Drink a red Rhône or wine from the Midi or an Alsace, Jura, of Swiss white.

LEIDEN CHEESE

Unlike Edam, farmhouse versions of Leiden cheese are made. The factory-produced cheeses only carry a state testing mark with 20+ or 40+ without the addition of "Boerenleidse" (Farmhouse Leiden). The 20+ cheese is intended for eating quickly when young but the 40+ cheese can be matured. This 40+ cheese then develops more flavour but the factory cheeses do not have the taste of a genuine farmhouse cheese. The Dutch call both types of cheese "Leidse" (of Leiden) but the cheese is usually sold as "Leyden" outside The Netherlands.

FARMHOUSE LEIDEN WITH KEYS

Skimmed milk is used to make farmhouse Leiden cheese with the crossed-key marking. During preparation part of the curd is kept white while the rest has caraway seed added. The top and bottom of the cheese moulds are layered with white cheese, without spices with the cheese with the caraway seed in the middle. This ensures a fine even rind.

The cheese is lightly pressed at first and then wrapped in a cloth and transferred to a cheese "barrel". After resting for about one day the cheese is pressed a second time when it developed its rounded sides. The cheese is then marked with the pair of crossed keys of the city of Leiden (Leidse-sleutels) and the indication of "Boerenleidse 30+ (Farmhouse Leiden 30+). The fat content of this cheese varies between 32 and 36% of its dry matter. The state testing mark has to indicate 20+ because 30+ is not legally recognised for Leiden cheese. The Farmhouse Leiden with crossed keys

Farmhouse Leiden with Keys, distinguished by its red colour and shape

is easily distinguished by its bright red colour. No wine is recommended for either type of Leiden cheese but instead a tasty beer or glass of genever. For those who insist on wine then pick a robust example e.g. a Rhône.

Red bacterial rind cheeses

FOUGEROND

Once a superb Dutch cheese known as Barselle

was made. This was a gorgeous red bacterial crust cheese with its own fragrant character. Because the culture of the red bacteria was not entirely under control this cheese disappeared from the Dutch shops. Its successor is Fougerond, a slightly less tasty and much drier version. This cheese was not a great success and has subsequently disappeared.

KERNHEM

An unusual example of a Dutch cheese that looks like a Port Salut but this cheese is more fully-flavoured.

The stronger taste is due to the culture of red bacteria that develops through the regular washing of the rind while the cheese is maturing. A whole Kernhem weighs approx. 6 lb 3 oz (2.8 kg).

Kernhem makes a tasty addition to a cheeseboard but is ideal to cook with. Matured for at least four weeks before sale to outlets and can be kept a maximum of a further three months in shops. Fat content is 60% of the dry matter.

Kernhem is often recommended with a glass of red port but I am not so fond of this combination, finding a light fruity red such as a chilled Loire or Beaujolais perhaps better partners.

Kernhem

Dutch sheep's-milk cheeses

When I came to The Netherlands in the 1970s, I discovered one of the tastiest of Dutch cheeses: a semi-hard sheep's-milk cheese from the island of Texel. Although there are masses of sheep in The Netherlands–especially in springtime–it is very difficult to find good sheep's-milk cheese. The Dutch are not terribly fond of hard sheep's-milk cheese with its clear tones of wool and lamb fat that starts somewhat salty and is quite sweet in the finish, often with a suggestion of caramel.

With a sheep's-milk cheese choose a quite acidic white from Gascony, the Pyrenees, or the Savoie or a tasty, expressive red from the French south-west, Midi, Provence, Navarra, Somontano, or Rioja in Spain, or Piedmont in Italy.

Belgium

The ancient Celtic inhabitants of Belgium made cheese. The Romans brought improved techniques and the monks of the many abbeys and monasteries during the time of Charlemagne spread the knowledge of cheesemaking among the people. All this seemed to be wasted activity in the Middle Ages. As part of the Low Countries (The Netherlands) Belgium tended to rely upon the cheeses made in the northern provinces and after the separation of the countries those in the southern provinces remained faithful for a long time to the types of cheese made in the provinces of Holland (in the Netherlands) which were either imported or copied for local production. Apart from in the monasteries and among a few shepherds cheese has never been a major Belgian priority. In the late nineteenth century a general agricultural malaise affected much of Europe, particularly in respect of the market for cereal crops. Traditional farmers were forced to moved to more profitable livestock when the price for grain dropped to unprofitable levels. This was more a matter of survival than a free choice. The *bleu-blanc-Belge* blue or white Belgian cows or Dutch Friesians increasingly became part of the landscape. There were far fewer goats and sheep. Initially the cows were primarily kept for their milk and cream production but after World War II production of cheese increased significantly. Belgian cheese is often made from skimmed milk left as a by-product of butter making. Semi-hard cheeses of a mild flavour are the most popular types but fresh cheese (cottage cheese etc.) are also made. In the final years of the twentieth century a significant movement got underway towards the making of hand-made farmhouse craft cheeses in Belgium. People sought out the old cheese recipes of the monks and introduced countless new cheeses that were inspired by the old traditional cheeses. The cheeses based on original Trappist abbey cheeses are particular popular, especially among lovers of Trappist beer. Cheese lovers though adore one cheese above all others: The Limburg cheese from the high plateau of Herve. Unfortunately the very best example of this cheese, Remoudou appears to be dying if not already dead.

TRAPPIST CHEESE
Soft to semi-hard Trappist (monastery) cheese, more or less mature. Belgium has numerous different cheeses of monastic origin.
If possible choose a beer from the same abbey or monastery.

ANTIGOONTJE
This cheese that is full of character is a creation of Luc Wouters, a highly-regarded Antwerp cheese retailer. During the period the cheese is maturing it is washed with Koninck beer (another speciality of Antwerp) which ensures a piquant taste.
You could of course drink a glass of Koninck with this cheese or a genever, or a sturdy and full-bodied Gewürztraminer from Alsace.

BEAUVOORDE
A semi-hard cheese from Passendaele distinguished by its hexagonal shape and natural grey-orange rind. This cow's-milk cheese is ivory-

Trappist cheese

Beauvorde

85

coloured inside with supple and springy cheese with irregular air bubbles. The cheese is fairly soft and has somewhat herbal undertones. Drink a glass of beer, genever, or wine with this cheese.

BOUQUET DES MOINES
A modern soft white mould cheese made from pasteurised cow's milk. A supremely well-made cheese that is both extremely creamy and very tasty. Fat content is 45%. Drink a full-bodied white wine that is none too dry such as Chardonnay or a fruity and full-bodied red like a Beaujolais.

Bouquet des moines

BRIGAND
A soft cheese with a red rind formed by the red bacteria *Brevibacterium limens*. The texture is smooth and soft but the taste has a slight bite to it.

Brigand has won many a heart

Brigand

Delicious with a glass of Belgian beer or a full-bodied but lightly spiced white or red wine.

BRUSSELS' CHEESE/FROMAGE DE BRUXELLES
A surprising and very traditional cheese from the Dutch/Belgian province of Brabant that is entirely made from skimmed milk. The fresh curd is cut into small pieces and then rested for twelve hours. During this time further whey drains from the curd and becomes quite sour. The still slightly moist curd is then further cut, salted, and formed into a clump which is left to drain further on a rack and then on reed mats in a warm and humid environment.
The young cheeses remain in the maturing rooms for two months and are dipped weekly in a bath of lukewarm water. After two months the cheese is immersed in brine, cleaned, and cut into small portions of no more than 7 oz. (200 grams). The cheese is then packed in cellophane in small trays. Brussels' cheese is sometimes also known as Hettekaas 40 + and has a distinctive taste that is fairly sour and remarkably salty.
Drink one of the more robust Belgian beers or a glass of genever with this cheese. The choice of wine is more difficult because of the sour and salty nature of this cheese. Try a green and salty wine such as a Gros Plant du Pays Nantais.

CHÂTEAU D'ARVILLE
Blue and white mould cheeses that are creamy and mildly flavoured. I regard them as the tastiest of the factory-made Belgian cheeses by the market leader Passendaele. Ideal for use in salads.
Delicious with a mild sweet white from the Loire or Germany.

CHEVAGNE
Passendaele cheese makers have studied how goat's-milk cheese is made by their northern neighbours and produce a plain goat's-milk cheese of an attractive shape that has neither the aroma or taste of goat's-milk cheese. Even the much vaunted "white mould culture" is mainly noted for its absence. The taste is fresh, slightly sour, and creamy.

The best choice of wines for this cheese are a house white or a simple fresh and fruity Gamay from Beaujolais.

Chevagne

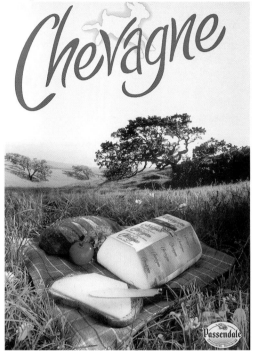

Château d'Arville

CHIMAY

A genuine Trappist cheese from the same abbey as the famous beer bearing this name. Superbly made cheese in four varieties of which the most delicious are the Chimay au lait cru made with untreated milk and Chimay à la bière (beer cheese) that are both matured for six weeks. The other two cheeses are Vieux Chimay, matured for six months and Chimay Grand Classique that is matured for three weeks. What better than a glass of Chimay Trappist beer to combine with these cheeses?

Chimay au lait cru made from untreated milk

The mature Chimay with beer

CORSENDONK

Another Belgian Trappist cheese of from pasteurised milk. A very mild semi-hard cheese for those who enjoy a snack with their beer provided it does not overpower the taste of the beer.

DAMME BRIE

A Brie type cheese made in the area around Damme, close to Bruges. This white mould cheese made biologically from cow's milk is delicious!

LOO/ECHTE LOO

A Trappist abbey cheese made with cow's milk recognisable by its black coating and ivory-coloured cheese. A soft texture cheese that is

Corsendonk

Trappist abbey Echte Loo

Herve cheese or Fromage de Herve is sold in long shapes like bricks of 7 oz (200 grams) or smaller blocks of 3½ oz (100 grams) and 1¾ oz (50 grams). The washed rind is moist, sticky, and light to dark orange depending on the age of the cheese. The cheese is soft, becoming creamier with age. The

Echte Loo or genuine Loo cheese

Herve, regarded by many as the finest aromatic cheese

Piquant, fragrant, and sharp Herve

creamy and slightly sharp. This "Echte Loo" cheese also comes from Passendaele. Drink a delicious glass of Trappist beer, preferably a Trippel with this cheese.

HERVE

A very popular cheese made along semi-craft cheese lines from the high plateau near Liege.

taste of a young Herve is creamy and almost sweet but the older fragrant examples are stronger in taste.

A glass of Duval or other Belgian beer taste good with this cheese or a young genever. If you wish to drink wine then choose a Pinot Gris or Gewürztraminer from Alsace rather than the fruit reds such as a Bordeaux that the Belgians tend to recommend.

LIMBURG/LIMBURGER

This cheese is the factory-made version of Herve made with pasteurised cow's milk. After pasteurisation the milk is allowed to cool and then enzymes or other rennet is added. After the souring process the curd is cut into small pieces and then heated.

The immature cheese is pressed into moulds and salted. The first maturing takes two weeks after which the cheese is allowed to mature at a cooler temperature and regularly washed with lukewarm brine. This process enhances the work of the enzymes close to the surface of the cheese that break down the lactic acid, giving the cheese its well-known aroma.

During maturing the cheese changes colour, aroma, texture, taste, moisture and fat content. A young Herve of about six weeks tastes superb with salads and various other dishes.

Limburger

MAREDSOUS

Well-known Trappist cheese from the abbey of the same name. The elongated cheese with a brown-orange rind lightly covered with white mould is semi-hard, supple, and springy to the touch. The washed rind imparts a piquant yet mild and subtle taste to this cheese.

Delicious with a glass of Maredsous beer or a young genever.

MERLIJN (MERLIN)

White mould goat's-milk cheese from organic farming. Soft, creamy, and slightly sweet.

ORVAL

A genuine Trappist cheese made by the abbey of the same name, using pasteurised milk. The washing of the rind gives Orval a sharp character and nutty flavour.

Drink an Orval Trappist beer with this cheese.

Orval

OLD BRUGES/OUD BRUGGE/VIEUX BRUGES

Fully-flavored Trappist-like beer cheese of cow's milk with a slightly sharp taste, matured for fifteen months. Bruges brown beer or a glass of full-bodied, somewhat spicy white or red wine.

Old Bruges/Oud Brugge/Vieux Bruges cheese

PAS DE BLEU

In spite of the humorous name (literally "not blue cheese") this is a top quality cheese made from organic cow's milk.

The addition of *Penicillium roqueforti* imparts

an entirely individual taste that becomes stronger with age.

Pas de bleu

PASSENDAELE
Well-known semi-hard factory-produced cheese from Flanders made in a round form with cow's milk. The brownish-yellow rind often has a little mould. Passendaele is fairly mild tasting, initially fresh with a buttery finish. The cheese is based on an old monk's recipe but modern marketers have seen fit to meddle extensively with that. Drink whatever you fancy with this very commercial cheese since the marketers have ensured it has little taste.

Passendaele in its usual rounded form

PASSENDAELE BEL AGE
Everything is semi or half about this cheese: semi-mature, semi-hard, and even half the work. A typi-cal factory-made cheese masquerading as a traditional craft-made product. But it does have more flavour than the ordinary Passendaele thanks to the half a year maturing. Drink a half pint of beer or small genever with this cheese.

Passendaele Bel Age

PATERKAAS/PATER CHEESE
Trappist-style cheese made by either craft or mass production methods. See abbey cheese.

Paterkaas/Pater cheese

PÈRE JOSEPH
A creation by Passendaele given the name of the patron saint of cheesemakers. This Trappist-style cheese is full of flavour, creamy, and has a sharp taste.
Delicious with a pint of beer, a genever, or a glass of red wine such as a Beaujolais.

Père Joseph

Père Joseph

the best-tasting cheeses in the world. Its original origin is on the high plateau of Herve but is also made on the other side of Limburg in the south of The Netherlands, although the Dutch version has all but vanished because the process of cheese-making for Remoudou is not profitable. Only a close group of five keep this cheese alive, of which three are craft cheesemakers.

The constantly ever tougher demands of the European Commission mean that the making of genuine red bacteria cheese from untreated milk by independent makers is becoming increasingly expensive and hence unprofitable. The surroundings must be so sterile under new regulations that it is virtually impossible to work with untreated milk.

What is so special about Remoudou? It is a seasonal version of Herve cheese of the very best quality, made only from milk from cows in the last two months of their lactation period. This makes the milk very rich and full of fat and this is further enhanced by not completing the first of the first two daily milkings so that the milk remaining from the morning, known as the *remoude*, enriches the milk taken from the cow during evening milking. Remoudou combines well with a beer or a Belgian *eau de vie de genievre* (genever). A robust Gewürztraminer from Alsace or Pinot Gris also combine well.

RUBENS

Modern factory-made cheese of Passendaele. This cheese named after the famous Flemish artist is more striking for its surprising oval form and the reddish-brown colour of its washed rind than for its taste. The semi-hard cheese is firm and almost entirely smooth with a creamy texture that is supple. The taste is rich and well-developed and yet Rubens fails to excite.

Delicious with a beer of whatever you have in house.

Rubens

POSTEL

Traditional rectangular red bacterial washed rind cheese made of cow's milk. Made in the abbey at Postel and only available in limited quantity. Exceptionally tasty!

PRINCE JEAN

This is a *triple-crème* factory-made cheese which as this suggests is very creamy with a well-developed rich flavour. There is a variety covered with pepper that has a soft downy covering of white mould.

REMOUDOU

The very best of Belgian cheeses, which–even though its smell may suggest otherwise–is one of

SINT JAN

Trappist-style cheese with lower salt and fat in the usual round loaf form. Fat content 18%.

Sint-Jan

WATOU

Another Trappist-style beer cheese made with cow's milk that is full of flavour and slightly sharp. Drink a Watou or other delicious beer with this cheese.

Watou

WIJNENDALE

Yet another Passendaele factory product made with pasteurised cow's milk. The taste resembles that of old craft-made cheeses but this is entirely due to modern technology. Wijnendale is mild in taste, creamy or even buttery, with a fresh nutty undertone.

This is a typical beer cheese but if you prefer wine the choose a Pinot Gris from Alsace, Luxembourg, or Germany.

Germany

German cheeses are so unknown outside the country's borders that it is as if the German's have no tradition of cheesemaking but nothing could be further from the truth. Apart from being a sweeping generalisation–some parts of Germany have a very well-developed cheesemaking tradition–this is a great pity for those living outside Germany.

The only German-made cheese known beyond the borders are imitation Camembert, canned Brie, and creamy factory-made versions of Italian Gorgonzola and Dolcelatte but Germany has much more to offer and to be discovered than soft cheeses with little taste. Germany has a number of quite strong cheeses from the area of Harz and the German Limburger and Romadur.

From barbarians to bon vivants

German cheese history dates back to the time of the first incursions of the Germanic tribes. At this time primitive forms of cheese were probably made as a sort of forerunner of today's quark and cottage cheese. These Germanic tribes from the north and other Barbarians spread across much of Europe reaching as far as Spain and Rome but were turned back with the establishment of the Frankish monarchy of Charlemagne. We saw in the section on Belgium that Charlemagne was a great lover of cheese and he encouraged the making of and trading in monastery cheeses throughout his realm including Germany such as Bremen and Hamburg. There was already a cheese tradition in existence in Eastern Friesland, Schleswig-Holstein, and Lower Saxony.

The renowned Fries-Holsteiner cheese originates from these areas. Other areas of present-day Germany also made cheese from early times but to a lesser extent that the north-west. One long important dairy region is the Allgäu on the border with Switzerland and Lake Constance.

In the Middle Ages mainly soft-types of cheese without use of rennet were produced, largely in the many monasteries where they were also eaten. These cheeses were similar to today's "sour milk cheeses" or *Sauermilchkäse*. The first cheeses using a souring agent to coagulate the milk originated in Prussia in the thirteenth and fourteenth centuries.

The Germans quickly took to this new cheese and the demand outstripped the supply so cheese was imported from various cheese towns in the provinces of Holland in the Low Countries. These salted Dutch cheeses caused a real sensation in northern parts of Germany but the southerners continued to prefer sweeter Allgäuer cheese that resembled a Swiss Emmental. The Limburger and Romadur cheeses that have been highly regarded for over two hundreds years also come from Allgäu. Other cheeses too have enjoyed a long period of popularity, such as Munster, Weinkäse, Tilsiter, and Trappist.

The German dairy industry today is among the world's leaders in the field with many of their cheeses being produced from pasteurised milk but fortunately there are still many wonderful cheeses such as the famous German Bergkäse from the Alps that are made with untreated milk.

German fat content indications

German cheese is often marked with an indication of its fat content. The fat content range of each of the grades described in German is indicated below.

Magerstufe	Low fat grade	less than 10% of the dry matter
Viertelfetstufe	Quarter fat grade	at least 10% of the dry matter
Halbfetstufe	Half fat grade	at least 20% of the dry matter
Dreiviertelfetstufe	Three-quarter fat grade	at least 30% of the dry matter
Fetstufe	Fat grade	at least 40% of the dry matter
Volfetstufe	Full fat grade	at least 45% of the dry matter
Rahmstufe	Cream grade	at least 50% of the dry matter
Doppelrahmstufe	Double cream grade	at least 60% but not more than 85% of the dry matter

German cheese that is exported generally adopts labelling that is accepted by EC or US regulations with descriptions such as Light or Low in Fat for the lower fat grades.

Allgäuer Bergkäse

The cheeses

ALLGÄUER BERGKÄSE
This is a hard cheese made from untreated milk that is darker in colour than Emmental. The cheese is more dense, the air bubbles are smaller, and its taste is also more pronounced, richer, and sharper than the Swiss Emmental. This is because the cheese is produced solely from milk from cows that graze high alpine pastures during the summer. Maturing time is three to nine months and fat content is 45%.

ALLGÄUER EMMENTAL
A hard cheese produced with a rennet agent that comes from the area close to Lake Constance (Bodensee) which is an excellent variation on the Swiss original. The Allgäuer Emmental has superb cheese with fine large air bubbles, is supple, slightly aromatic, slightly sweet, with nutty undertones. As this cheese matures its taste becomes sharper. This cheese is still made with untreated milk but is increasingly being produced with pasteurised milk.

Allgäuer Emmental

ALTENBURGER ZIEGENKÄSE
Small cylindrical cheese of about $8^{13}/_{16}$ oz (250 grams) from central Germany. This cheese is made from untreated cow's milk with a maximum of 15% goat's milk added. This hard cheese has a distinctive taste because of the addition of cumin. Fat content is 30%.
Delicious with a beer.

BRIE
White mould cheese in flat wheels of 2lbs 3 oz–6lb 10 oz (1–3 kg) that is mainly intended for sale in

portions in shops. German Brie is creamy and aromatic tending in taste from fresh acidity to distinctly sharp but otherwise of little character.

BUTTERKÄSE

The name of this cheese is rather confusing since it is neither made from especially creamy milk or by the addition of butter but the taste of this block cheese for cutting is buttery, making it a popular for breakfast.

The Germans also nickname it the "woman's cheese" or *Damenkäse*. Maturing time one month, fat content is 50%.

Butterkäse

CAMBAZOLA

A perfect example of successful marketing. A creamy, Brie-like cheese with some blue veining. Also ideal for those who like a mild cheese without too much character. See under its family name of White-Blue cheeses.

CAMEMBERT

White mould cheese in cylindrical form varying from 2⅛–14 oz (80–400 grams) and in fat content from 30–40% of dry matter. German Camembert is generally very mild in taste with little character.

CHESTER

A German variant of the mass-produced style of English Cheshire cheese. This German Chester is made by the Cheddar process in which the curd is first cut and then pressed (in this case into elongated forms). An interesting freshly acidic and slightly sharp cheese for cooking but also delicious for breakfast or lunch.

EDAMMER

German copy of a young mass-produced Edam cheese sometimes in the well-known cannonball shape but usually in catering blocks of 44 lb

(20 kg). The taste is as mild as that of a factory-produced Edam cheese. For eating on bread or in cheese dishes since it has too little taste for a place on a cheeseboard.

EDELPILZKÄSE

This "noble fungus cheese" or blue mould cheese is sold under a variety of brand names. There is a thin rind with a fine layer of fungus and the internal cheese is white to pale cream with well defined blue-green veins.

The texture of this cheese is creamy yet also crumbly. This cheese acquires a mild yet piquant taste through its maturing for at least five weeks. A good example of this "noble fungus cheese" is Bergader Blue.

Edelpilzkäse ("noble fungus cheese")

Geheimratkäse ("privy counsellor's cheese")

GEHEIMRATSKÄSE
This "privy counsellor's cheese" in cylindrical form resembles a cross between a Dutch Edam and an English Cheshire in appearance but tends in taste more towards a young mass-produced Edam.

GOUDA
A freshly acidic and mild to slightly sharp copy of the famous Dutch cheese.

HANDKÄSE/BAUERNHANDKÄSE/KORBKÄSE
A large family of cheeses made without rennet agents in a variety of sizes and shapes. The German

Handkäse

Harzerkäse

names refer to hand-made, farmhouse, and basket made cheeses and they include cylindrical and pointed form varieties. There is also variety in the flavour of these cheese from plain through kummel, and other spices, to types covered with white mould. The taste is lightly aromatic to quite strong.

HARZER/OLMÜTZER QUARGEL/MAINZER
Round golden-yellow cheeses made without rennet agent in the region of Harz and Mainz, ranging in size from half an ounce (15 grams) to $4^{13}/_{32}$ oz (125 grams). The cheese is firm but supple and slightly sharp but more pronounced with age. Available with or without cumin.

LIMBURGER
This is the German version of the Belgian cheese, that like German Romadur, originates in the Allgäu region. The cheeses resemble one another but the Limburger is stronger tasting and spicier than the Romadur (see entry). Unfortunately the German Limburger lacks the complexity of its Belgian forerunners and is dominated by a single taste of salt

Limburger

that is sharp but not exciting. The aroma is another matter entirely!

MÜNSTER KÄSE
This red bacterial rind cheese is produced on both sides of the German/ French border, in the Black Forest and also in Alsace and Vosges. Both 45% and 50% fat versions (percentage of the dry matter) are made with orange rind and smooth pale yellow cheese with few air bubbles. The cheese is slightly sharp in taste. Although three places in Germany are called Münster, none of them are the origin of this cheese because Munster is a bastardisation of *monastère* or monastery, dating from the time of Charlemagne. The monastery cheeses (many of

which were red bacteria rind cheeses at the time) were extremely popular in those days and Alsace was part of Germany for a very long time. German Münster is written in that country with an umlaut and the Alsatian variety without. The Munster cheese from Alsace became very popular throughout Germany and when Alsace became French the Germans started to make their own version. Although quite reasonable the German Münster does not begin to achieve the superb quality of a genuine Munster from Alsace.

ODENWÄLDER FRÜHSTÜCKSKÄSE
This "breakfast cheese" from the area of Odenwald is made from skimmed and pasteurised cow's milk in small rounds. The soft cheese has a mild taste that is ideal as the name suggests for breakfast. Maturing time is fifteen days and fat content is 45%.

ROMADUR
The Romadur name has a certain familiarity to it and indeed this cheese is a variety of red bacterial rind cheese based on Remoudou cheese of the Herve plateau in Belgium. The Belgian cheese was first imitated at least a century ago and this cheese is now a firm part of the German cheeseboard. Unlike Belgium, Romadur has always been popular. The cheese is produced in the same brick form as the Belgian original but is slightly smaller than a Belgian Limburger.
The orange washed rind hides a fine soft cheese with plenty of small to medium-sized and irregular air bubbles. Depending on the variety (Romadur is made in grades ranging from 20–60% fat content of the dry matter) and age, the taste can vary from mild to having a fair degree of bite.

QUARK/SPEISEQUARK
This young fresh cheese, known in Germany as Speisequark, is very soft with a pure fresh and slightly tart taste. It is hugely popular in Germany where it is eaten on its own or with herbs or jam and widely used in cooking. Quark consists of twelve per cent milk protein, four times as much as in natural milk. The fat content varies between the low fat (less than 10% of dry matter) through half-fat (20%+) and fat (40%+) varieties.

CREAM/DOUBLE-CREAM FRESH CHEESE
A very creamy fresh quark cheese similar to the Dutch Mon Chou and other fresh cream cheeses. These cheeses sometimes have flavouring of herbs or spices. Mainly intended for spreading on bread and use in cooking.

KÖRNIGER FRESH CHEESE
A fresh and acidic tasting German cottage cheese.

SCHICHTKÄSE/LAYERING CHEESE
This variety of quark is usually sold in blocks for use in cooking. Although creamy, this type of cheese retains its shape and it has a clean and freshly acidic taste. An ideal cheese to cook with.

STEINBUSHER
A cheese produced in the form of an elongated brick with a yellow-orange rind that is somewhat sticky. The inner cheese is lighter in colour and has several small air bubbles. The texture of this cheese is springy but the cheese can be sliced easily. Eaten when young (at least three weeks old) it is still quite mild and creamy but it becomes stronger with age.

STEPPENKÄSE
A low-fat hard cheese that is wider and flatter in shape than Tilsiter (see below) but shares some of

Steppenkäse

Steinbuscher

its character. The cheese is also supple and elastic but more uniform than Tilsiter with fewer air bubbles. The taste is mild and fresh, and slightly more pronounced than Tilsiter.

TILSITER
It is often thought that German Tilsiter is a copy of Swiss Tilsiter but this is not true. Tilsit was a town in East Prussia that is now part of Lithuania. This cheese is widely copied, especially in the Scandinavian countries. It was probably originally developed by Dutch immigrants who first made it in their traditional wheel shape and probably resulted from complete failure to make a Gouda-type cheese in Tilsit. Fortunately the failure was so good that this cheese soon became popular. Today this cheese is made in blocks for ease of slicing into portions. Maturing time is six months and fat content 30–50%.

TRAPPISTENKÄSE
The German variety of the famous monastic cheeses uses the old Port Salut of Entrammes as its model. A good cheese to slice for eating with bread for breakfast or with a glass of beer.

Trappistenkäse

VIERECK-HARTKÄSE
Swiss-like blocks of cheese with rind but with large air bubbles, this type of cheese is springy in texture with a mild and aromatic taste. Particularly delicious with breakfast or in cooking.

WEINKÄSE
This type of cheese was developed during the 1930s and closely resembles a Münster but its taste and aroma are milder than those of Romadur and Limburger cheeses.

WEISS-BLAU/WHITE-BLUE CHEESE
A collective name for white mould cheeses that are also injected with culture to form blue mould. Most of these cheeses resemble large mass-produced German Camembert on the outside but have distinct blue veins inside the cheese. Like German Camembert, this type of cheese is mild and creamy with a slightly piquant flavour from the blue mould.

White-blue cheese

Well-known brands include Cambazola, Bavarian Blue, and Blue Brie.

Weinkäse

WEISSLACKER

A pure white cheese that resembles a French Tomme or Greek Feta. It is fairly sharp to extremely strong in taste with considerable salt. As a snack cheese it combines best with a German beer from which its other name of "Bierkäse".

WISTERMARSCHKÄSE

This hard slicing cheese from northern Germany is

Wistermarschkäse

similar to Tilsiter. Its slightly spicy but fresh taste makes this an extremely popular breakfast cheese.

Which wine with German cheeses?

Because of the enormous variation in taste, fat content, and tartness among even the same types of German cheeses it is difficult to give specific advice about the types of wine to drink with an individual cheese. Most of these cheeses combine well with a glass of good beer or a genever, particularly in the case of the Trappist cheese, provided it has not been flavoured with kummel. The mild cheeses can be combined with an equally mild white wine while the fresher cheeses also demand a fresher-tasting white wine. Goat's-milk cheeses combine best with white wines from southern Germany or a light red. With hard and semi-hard cheeses either a good white or light red can be served. The white and blue-mould cheeses are so mild in flavour that they can be combined with a sweet Kabinett or Auslese German wine or a red wine that is not too full-bodied. The stronger cheeses demand sturdy wines in equal proportion. The best blue mould cheeses combine with a good Spätlese or a less expensive Beerenauslese. The really strong cheeses are better drunk with beer or spirits.

Switzerland

Small country, large cheeses

If there is a country in Europe that is automatically associated with mountains it is Switzerland. Life in much of the country is influenced or even dictated by the presence of the mountains. Despite this there is ample space in this idyllic country for considerable variety in both landscape and climate, which makes the country so exciting. Swiss gastronomy is also influenced by its multi-cultural nature: the country has four languages (French, Swiss-German, Italian, and Romanian). The north and south parts of the country have much in common with their neighbours in Germany and Austria, the west and south-west share character with neighbouring France, and the south-eastern corner is strongly Italian in influence.

The original Celtic inhabitants of Switzerland were the Helvetians who learned the art of cheesemaking in their–not always peaceful–contacts with neighbouring people. Swiss history is shot through with a love-hate relationship with the surrounding countries and between the different ethnic groups. The Swiss remain proud though of their country despite all the external and internal tensions. Making jokes about each other seems to be a national pastime but in the matter of working together for the future of their country the Swiss are rock solid. The country's federal structure is difficult for foreigners to grasp with the great variety and different interest groups and diversified local power yet when it comes to working together for the good of the country it happens. Although this co-operation affects many aspects of Swiss life it seems to be strongest among the country's dairy farmers and dairy industry. In the export markets Swiss cheese has just the one strong brand that everyone recognises: that of Switzerland itself rather than a trade name.

Cheese, pride of Switzerland

Principal alpine cheeses

Not surprisingly for a country with so many mountains, there are many alpine cheeses from Switzerland. Most Swiss cheeses originate in alpine regions but there are fewer different types of cheese than one might expect in view of the tremendous variety in the country between the twenty-six cantons and the often difficult transport links. People easily become cut off in the Alps and the large, slowly-maturing cheeses provide healthy nourishment during the long winter. Beside this it was safer and more efficient to transport a couple of the large cheeses in a cart from the high pasture where they were originally made to villages lower down.

In the less mountainous parts of Switzerland around Geneva and Neuchâtel more small and soft cheese could be made but the Swiss prefer the large alpine cheeses such as Emmental, Gruyère, Tilsit/Royalp, Sbrinz, and Appenzel. Fortunately one can also find some excellent white mould cheeses here and there such as Tomme and Tomme de Chèvre from the cantons of Fribourg and Vaud. Another popular cheese is Seré or Serac that is made from the final protein flakes that are dissolved in the whey.

One of the most unusual aspects of Swiss cheese is that it is hardly ever sold under a trade name but almost always by its regional name. All the cheeses that have a strictly defined area of origin are stamped with a distinguishing mark to set it apart from the many copies. This is particularly important because some of the countries that mass-produce cheese are striving to get a ban on the production of cheese with milk that is not pasteurised while Switzerland determines that quality cheese can only be made from milk that is not pasteurised.

This leads to a richer, fuller, more complex, and more exciting taste. The protected and strictly controlled cheeses of Switzerland are Appenzel, Emmental, Gruyère, Sbrinz, Spalen, Saanen,

Appenzel

Sapsago/Schabzieger, Tilsit, Tête de Moine/ Belle-lay, (Vacherin) Fribourgeois. The cheeses used for raclette are also protected such as Bagnes, Conches, Gomser, and Orsières although you are unlikely to encounter these cheeses outside Switzerland.

Finally there is the Vacherin du Mont d'Or that is found on both sides of the border in the Jura but the quality control here is regional rather than national.

The cheeses

APPENZEL

The old Appenzel or Appenzeller cheese was only produced in the canton of Appenzel but today is also made in the St. Gallen canton. This is a cheese with a century's-old tradition that is not only delicious on its own but has excellent culinary properties. Genuine Appenzel cheese is made from full-cream unpasteurised cow's milk but there is also a skimmed milk variety that is particularly popular in the export market. The cheese is made in the form of a flat wheel of 11–15lb 6 oz (5–7 kg).

The secret of the superb well-developed fruity full flavour of this cheese lies in the mixture with which the rind is washed to form its red bacterial culture on the outside of the cheese while the cheese is maturing.

The precise ingredients vary from one cheese-maker to another, each with their own secret recipe. The main ingredients are brine, white wine, wine dregs, spices, and pepper. The maturing time is at least one year but some are also matured for longer and known as Rässkäse. This cheese is much stronger than normal Appenzel and not to everyone's taste.

Very mature examples are especially strong, particularly in terms of their smell! Look for the wild bear mark when buying a genuine Appenzel cheese. Cheese without this mark has no guarantee of being genuine Appenzel.

Appenzel cheese can be accompanied by a wide choice of wines but its slightly spicy taste suggests a marriage with a spicy wine with a slightly peppery undertone. Choose a fine Syrah (Shiraz) from the Rhône valley, Australia, or South Africa.

ALPINE CHEESE

Swiss cheesemakers groups a number of cheeses such as Sbrinz, Saanen, and Spalen together under the generic title of Alpine cheese. The best-known of these is Sbrinz (see entry) but these cheeses are more or less identical in taste.

Saanen and Spalen are smaller in size though at 13 lb 3 oz–15 lb 6 oz (6–7 kg) and you will rarely if ever find them outside Switzerland unlike Sbrinz.

EMMENTAL

Emmental cheese gets its name from the valley of the River Emmen that runs through the canton of

Life in Appenzel (naive print)

Berne at the foot of the Alps. Emmental is one of the oldest types of cheese alongside Brie, Camembert, Cheddar, Gouda, and Edam, and is also one of the most widely copied of the world's cheeses. It is also known as the "king of cheeses." Originally Emmental was only made from mountain pastures but because demand outstripped supply it was decided to use milk also from lower-lying grazing land.

A genuine Swiss Emmental bears its seal of authenticity and takes the form of a large wheel of about 40 in (100 cm) diameter with domed sides, weighing 132–286 lb (60–130 kg). A true Emmental is certainly one of the largest cheeses of the world. The rind of mature cheeses is pale yellow, smooth, and clean.

When the cheese is cut the large regular air bubbles, as large as a walnut, are immediately apparent. These "eyes" are caused by large carbon dioxide bubbles forming during the maturing process. The maturing is done in relatively warm rooms at 22°C (71.6°F). Emmental cheese is matured for at least three months before it is sold to the trade but the process continues at the wholesaler or retailer.

Young Emmental is sold at four to six months old and mature cheese is sold at eight months to a year or even older. In contrast to other well-known Swiss cheeses, Emmental is a mild, sweet, and fruity cheese with distinct hints of hazelnut in its flavour. The best cheeses also both smell and taste of new-mown hay and possess a slightly tart finish. Emmental is a popular cheese to eat for its own sake but has many uses in the kitchen: grated or thinly sliced as a piquant addition to a salad, in a fondue, or for gratin dishes. The fat content is 45%.

Although many non-Swiss consumers of this cheese tend to reach for a red wine, a white wine that is not too green is a much better companion such as a glass of Fendant, A Swiss or French Jura white, Austrian Weissburgunder, or even an Alsace Pinot Blanc.

ETIVAZ

An alpine cheese from the west of Switzerland. The name relates to the summer grazing in the high alpine meadows. This protected-origin cheese is

Swiss cheese and Pinot Noir

only made between May 10 and October 10, must be matured for 135 days for the ordinary Etivaz and for thirty months for the Etivaz à rebibes, and tastes best in late summer, autumn, or winter. The cheeses are 12–25⅝ in (30–65 cm) in diameter and at least 3–4⁵/₁₆ in (8–11 cm) thick, weighing 22–83¾ lb. (10–38 kg). The fat content is 50%.

FRIBOURGEOIS

This cheese of the Gruyère type has a long history dating back at least to the fifteenth century. This is a more mature, fuller-flavoured, strong-tasting version of Gruyère.

Although this cheese is also sold when young at about three months it is best kept for one to two years.

If you should have an opportunity to taste a mature example then choose a fine Dôle or a red Pupillin from the Arbois as accompaniment to this superb cheese.

FROMAGE A RACLETTE

Anyone spending time in Switzerland will learn the meaning of *raclette* even if they do not speak French. The Swiss place a half cheese next to a natural source or heat or an electric element so that the surface cheese melts. This is scraped off by the chef, waiter, or host to serve with potatoes boiled in their skins, with gherkins, silver onions, and air-cured meat from Grisons (viande des Grisons) or the Valais.

This process is raclette. The French word means "a scraping." The pastime originated in Valais but has become popular throughout Switzerland and there are now handy table devices and all manner of factory-made cheeses are packaged as *fromage à raclette*. For the enthusiast nothing beats a true *raclette* cheese. Raclette cheeses are generally smaller versions of Gruyère weighing 13 lb 3 oz– 19 lb 13 oz (6–9 kg) and the best are made from untreated milk which gives them better aromatic properties. These alpine cheeses are semi-hard and they melt readily but this cheese is also eaten in slices.

Drink a fresh white wine with raclette, such as a Chasselas, Fendant, or Savoie white. If meat is also eaten with the cheese then a freshly served Gamay or Pinot Noir make good company.

GRUYÈRE

Like Emmental, Gruyère originates from the western of the central cantons of Fribourg, Vaud, Berne, Neuchâtel, Jura, Schwyz, and Lucerne. The name of this cheese is directly attributable to a village in Fribourg. Gruyère is another cheese with centuries-old tradition often passed down from generation to generation of cheesemakers. In appearance, Gruyère resembles a smaller and flatter Emmental.

The diameter of these wheels varies between $19^{11}/_{16}$–$23^{5}/_{8}$ in (50–60 cm) and the weight can be 66–99 lb. The biggest difference between these two cheeses is found inside where there are no large air bubbles as with an Emmental. Gruyère only has small air bubbles the size of a pea. This is because the maturing takes place in a cool, moist cellar in contrast with Emmental cheese.

Young Gruyère is matured for four to five months and mature cheese is kept five to fourteen months or longer. Emmental is characterised by its hazelnut taste while Gruyère has a more fully-developed flavour that is salty, and piquant with a finish reminiscent of walnuts. Because Gruyère is made from untreated full-cream milk the taste is also creamier than an Emmental.

Grated Gruyère is excellent in fondues or for gratin dishes. With younger Gruyère cheese you may choose the same wines as an Emmental but with more mature examples a more full-bodied wine is needed. Choose a fine white Burgundy, Jura, or Arbois, a fuller Austrian Chardonnay, or a rounded and full-bodied red Dôle, Burgundy, Jura, or Arbois.

ROYALP

Royalp is the name that was used for Swiss Tilsit cheese when it was exported (see Tilsit).

SBRINZ

This is the best known of the Swiss alpine cheeses and is also the cheese with the largest production volume of them (see Alpine cheese). Originally this cheese originated from the area around Brienz in the countryside of William Tell but the fame of this cheese quickly spread beyond the mountains and it was made in an increasing number of places. Swiss traders exchanged this cheese for Italian risotto rice, chestnuts, and chestnut meal for the classic chestnut polenta of Ticino and of course also for red wine, which is still produced in insufficient volume for local consumption. Sbrinz cheese and its compatriots are produced as large flat wheels of 77–88 lb (35–40 kg). This cheese, made from untreated milk, has a dark gold hard rind and the cheese itself is crumbly but hard as a result of extremely slow maturing during at least seventeen months and up to three years. In common with the hard Italian cheeses one can break pieces off, grate, or remove thin slices with a cheese "plane."

The cheese seems to melt on the tongue and the aroma and taste recall high alpine meadows filled with scented herbs and flowers. A rich nutty flavour develops in the mouth with warm caramel undertones. In general this cheese is grated as a topping for risottos, pasta, or polenta, or skimmed into curls for adding to salads but it is well-worth eating for its own sake.

Drink a tasty glass of white wine such as an Pinot Blanc from Alsace, Swiss white from Ticino or Grisons, or a fruity red such as a good Ticino Merlot.

Emmental, Sbrinz, and Tilsit

FONDUE AUX TOMATES

Just like Fondue Valaisanne but using tomato puree instead of Kirsch to mix the binding flour or meal, extended perhaps with some white wine mixed with the same binding agent. Do not serve this with bread but with pieces of firm potato.

Which cheese with which fondue?

People enjoy the whole process of fondue but often have a bloated feeling in their stomach the following day. Fondue is cheese and cheese is fatty. Hot fat flows readily but solidifies when it cools down. If you drink hot drinks while consuming fondue then this lump forming process is less of a problem for the digestive system. The drinking of chilled white wine (which is recommended on grounds of taste) equally cools the fat in the fondue so that it coagulates and is less readily digested.

The advice often given is to enjoy the fondue and not to eat or drink too quickly with it. First take some cheese and then later a sip of your drink, then some more cheese and so on. In this way there is less risk of lumps forming, which aids digestion. With a tomato fondue it is better to drink a rosé or fine red wine such as a Ticino.

Austria

The idyllic images of picturesque green alpine pastures of Austria are perhaps known to everyone.

Although the country has a strongly-developed tradition of cheesemaking, Austrian cheeses are almost non-existent outside the country. Perhaps this is because Austrians have copied too many foreign cheeses, especially from Switzerland and Germany.

Cheesemongers are always looking for something different and there are so many imitations–however successful–of Swiss and German cheeses. Another reason might be too little dynamic promotion of the country's produce. It seems to me that enough tourists visit Austria each year who would be interested in buying some Austrian cheese from time to time. But it is doubtful if the world is waiting for yet another imitation of Tilsit, Emmental, Gouda, Edam, Brie, Camembert, Trappist, Romadur, Butterkäse and so on.

Perhaps they are not but the first-class Austrian Alpine cheese, Mondseer, and Schlosskäse deserve better consideration.

ALPINE CHEESE/BERGKÄSE

Undoubtedly the best of Austrian cheeses. This traditional cheese made with untreated milk is made in both large and small versions in the well-known wheel shape of 13 lb 3 oz (6 kg) and 66 lb (30 kg). The rind is soft and conceals dense cheese with smaller air bubbles than the Allgäu alpine cheese. The taste is more fully developed also than Allgäu cheese, with greater hints of nuts and an almost sweet caramel undertone.

Although this cheese at not less than six months old is of great service in the kitchen it is also *the* cheese to eat with a glass of delicious Austrian wine.

Swiss brown cows on the border of Switzerland and Austria

EMMENTAL

Austrian Emmental is one of the country's most important cheeses, certainly in terms of its exports. The cheese is made from pasteurised milk, and is an extremely mild and rubbery imitation of the real thing from Switzerland and France. It is only suitable for use in cooking.

GAILTAIER ALMKÄSE

This hard alpine cheese, made with untreated milk cow's milk to which a maximum of ten per cent goat's milk is added, comes from the Galtai valley in Carinthia. The Almkäse can vary in weight between approx. 1 lb and 77 lb (500 grams and 35 kg). It is fully flavoured and delicious. Fat content is 45%.
The Gailtaier Almkäse demands a glass of not too dry Grauburgunder wine.

GAISHORNER EMMENTAL AUSLESE

This cheese does not share my comments about Austrian Emmental above. It is made from untreated cow's milk and matured for at least six months and possesses an excellent taste, somewhat piquant for an Emmental, and less sweet, being closer in taste to a Gruyère. Eat this cheese warm.
Delicious with a glass of Weissburgunder or Grauburgunder from the area around the Neusiedlersee.

GROYER

This an Austrian version of a Swiss Gruyère and once more this is a poor imitation of the real article. Use solely in cooking.

MONDSEER

The name appears to be a bastardisation of the French *monastère* or monastery and this cheese does have much in common with a German Münster although much less complex with less breadth of taste than a Munster from Alsace. Its taste is closer to a more mature Esrom. Not a strong-tasting cheese with little character but very pleasing with a drink.
Drink a Grauburguner (Pinot Gris) that is not too dry with this cheese or a well-matured red.

OSTERKRON

A very successful blue mould cheese with strong but not sharp aromas of mould. Delicious as a filling in strudel pastry. Drink a delicious sweet wine with this cheese such as a Ruster Ausbruch with a good balance between sweet and sour.

SANKT PATRON

A reasonable Trappist-type of cheese with a mild but pleasing taste. The cheese lacks sufficient character to be truly convincing.

SCHLOSSKÄSE

An Austrian version of Limburger that is not extreme but certainly strong and with a lot of character. The cheese is round and flat and has a rind covered with red bacterial mould but comes packed in aluminium foil. The cheese becomes stronger tasting with age.
Drink a Veltliner but not a really green one with this cheese.

TIROLER ALMKÄSE/ALPENKÄSE

These alpine cheeses from the Tyrol are made with untreated cow's milk and are matured for four to five months and taste delicious. Fat content is 45%. The weight 66–132 lb (30–60 kg).
Drink the tastiest wine you have available.

TIROLER BERGKÄSE/TYROL ALPINE CHEESE

This alpine cheese is likes a smaller version of the previous cheese and is also made from untreated cow's milk, although skimmed milk is used. The millstone-shaped cheeses weigh about 26 lb 6 oz (12 kg) and fat content is 45%.

TIROLER GRAUKÄSE

A rather dull looking cheese in cubes or brick-like forms of 2 lb 3 oz–8 lb 13 oz (1–4 kg). The ribbed grey exterior conceals a wonderful cheese made of pasteurised or untreated skimmed cow's milk. Choose the richer unpasteurised farmhouse versions of this cheese. Fat content is 40%.
You can drink either a Chardonnay or light fruity red with this cheese.

TRAUTENFELSER EDELSCHIMMEL

A very successful Austrian version of Roquefort, although less complex, less rich and fully-developed taste but still warmly recommended.

VORALBERGER ALPKÄSE

Another fine alpine cheese from the east of Austria. This Alpkäse is made from full-cream or skimmed cow's milk that has not been pasteurised. This is a sizeable hard cheese in the form of a millstone of about 77 lb (35 kg) that is matured for at least three months. The fat content is 45%.

VORALBERGER BERGKÄSE

Little brother of the previous cheese made from untreated skimmed cow's milk. The hard cheese is also matured for three months but is generally smaller in size with a thickness of 4–4$\frac{1}{2}$ in (10–12 cm), weighing between 17 lb 10 oz and 77 lb (8–35 kg) with fat content of 50%.

Eastern Europe

Although cheese has been made in Eastern Europe for a very long time the cheeses are little known outside the area. This is not surprising for cheese hardly comes into the picture for visitors to the countries of Eastern Europe. Many cheeses are used in cooking or as snacks. A few countries also eat cheese for breakfast. Many Eastern European cheeses are good to indifferent copies of cheeses from Western Europe such as Edam, Gouda, Cheddar, Emmental, Gruyère, Trappist, Harzkäse, Limburger, Tilsiter, Camembert, Brie, and Roquefort. There are also numerous sorts of different fresh cheeses made from both sheep's and cow's milk that are often inspired by Mediterranean cheeses. In this main chapter we deal with those countries furthest removed from the Mediterranean: Poland, the Czech Republic, Slovakia, and Hungary. The other south-east European countries are dealt with in the following chapter.

Poland

Poland had established extensive herds of cattle quite early and by the nineteenth century Poland was making successful copies of Gruyère, known as Grojer and of Trappist cheeses (see Trapistaw). The Polish dairy industry was developing successfully right up to World War II when half of all the Polish herds were destroyed. During the Communist period of Poland's history agriculture was given a lower priority than rebuilding the country's industrial base. Today things seem to be better with Poland's dairy farmers but despite this nondescript factory-made cheeses still dominate.

OSZCZYPEK
Oszczypek is one of the few remaining traditional Polish cheeses, originating from the Carpathian mountains across which it is made under the similar name of Oschtjepka on the other side of the border in Slovakia. Oszczypek is made from untreated sheep's and cow's milk by local farmers and small co-operatives. After the milk has been made to coagulate the curd is removed and kneaded. The immature cheese is then pressed into decorative forms usually made of wood which give the cheese an attractive appearance. Oszczypek cheese is hung for a time close to a chimney where it acquires both the aroma and taste of smoke. The cheese is matured in this way for two to four weeks. Both young and mature Oszczypek cheese is ideal for culinary use but be careful with adding salt because it is already quite salty. The fat content is 45%. Do not drink wine with this cheese but a glass of beer or a small genever combines well.

PODHALANSKI
Podhalanski cheese is still made by craft methods at small dairies. This cheese is made from untreated cow's and sheep's milk. The cheese comes in brick or loaf form weighing about 1 lb (500 grams).
The cheese is matured for about two months and is available in plain or smoked varieties. Polish cooks use it eagerly for gratin dishes.
Serve a glass of beer or a genever with this cheese.

Slovakia

On the other side of the Carpathian mountains the Slovaks also make the usual copies of other European cheeses that are mainly intended for the tourist trade and for export. There are few true Slovakian cheeses with most of the local cheeses also being made elsewhere in Eastern Europe. Kashkaval or Feta type cheeses are also made in Slovakia and the Slovaks consume a lot of fresh cheese (quark/cottage cheese) often mixed with herbs or onion.

BRYNDZA
This type of cheese is made through both Eastern and Central Europe. Bryndza is the basic type of sheep's-milk cheese but it can also be made from goat's milk or cow's milk or a mixture of all three. The cheese resembles Greek Feta or Turkish Beyaz Peynir but contains less salt. Maturing time is at least four weeks and fat content is 45%.
Raw vegetables or salad are usually served with this type of cheese or all manner of snacks. Depending on the garnish, choose a beer, a genever, or a fresh white wine.

OSCHTJEPKA
This is the Slovakian equivalent of the Polish Oszczypek. Both countries claim the cheese as their own but it is possible the cheese originates in the Ukraine or further east, being brought to this region by Slavic immigrants. The Polish version is often oval while the Slovakian cheese is round. The Slovaks knead the curd into a round form so the cheese does not have a regular shape produced from pressing in a mould.
The cheeses are then hung in their storehouses. This cheese of untreated sheep's and cow's milk matures in two to three months. Because the Slovakian Oschtjepka is not smoked it has a taste of its own that is less salty, slightly sweeter than Oszczypek, with a clear aroma and taste of sheep's milk. Fat content is 45%.
Drink a glass of good beer with this cheese.

Czech Republic

The Czechs too are partial to fresh cheese. Most types of cheese of Eastern and Central Europe can be found in the Czech Republic and there are also many indifferent to highly successful imitations of Western European cheeses.

ABERTAM

This cheese is the exception to the rule that Czech cheeses have little character. This traditional hard cheese made with sheep's milk has a distinctive character. The fairly small round cheese weighs about 1 lb (500 grams) is matured for at least two months and does not hide its origins. The cheese is characteristically sheep through and through with its sweet aroma, suggestions of onion, and caramel. Fat content is 45%.

A beer or genever go with this cheese but a red Bohemian wine will also do nicely.

Hungary

Much has altered in Hungary since the change in the country's political course in 1989 and although these changes were not immediately apparent more recent times have demonstrated that the Hungarian economy is being significantly restored. It is unfortunate that not all have yet benefited from this improvement and the extreme poor have suffered greatly while the middle and upper classes appear to lead increasingly more pleasant lives. Mass production of cheap copies of other European cheeses is not consigned entirely to the past though and Hungary predominantly makes reasonable to good versions of Camembert of different formats, poor to reasonable Trappist cheeses which the Hungarians call *Trappista sajt*, tasteless and rubbery Gouda and Emmental types. Increasingly though better quality craft-made sheep's milk and especially goat's-milk cheeses can be found being sold in the larger towns. With the growth in the Hungarian economy–of Budapest in particular–a middle class has arisen and with them the development of supermarkets.

This provides a large outlet potential and new possibilities for cheesemakers. With some help from the governments of the European Community they can look forward to a better future and I have a feeling that Hungary will become a good dairy producer within a few years.

BALATON

Traditional hard cheese made from cow's milk in the region around Lake Balaton. The bread-shaped cheeses have an average weight around 19 lb 13 oz–26 lb 6 oz (9–12 kg) and are quite firm in texture. The pale-coloured cheese has some air bubbles in it and slices easily. Hungarians eat this cheese for breakfast, with a drink, and in the kitchen for fried, grilled, and oven-baked dishes. Drink an Olasrizling, Chardonnay, Tihanyi kékfrankos, or Merlot wine with this cheese from the surroundings of Lake Balaton.

LAJTA

Traditional farmer's cheese made from untreated cow's milk. Lajta is a rectangular cheese of about 2 lb 3 oz (1 kg) in the Trappist style with red bacterial rind with a full and fairly strong taste. Maturing time is four to six weeks and fat content 50%.

This is a very interesting cheese to accompany with perhaps a fine late harvest Tramini, Sémillon, or even a Chardonnay from the firm of Orebaglas in the southern part of the Balaton area.

LIPTOI

Liptoi is a collective name for home-made sheep's-milk or cow's-milk cheese that has been made for generations from untreated milk, particularly in Hungary's northern mountains. Fresh Liptoi is soft and slightly granular and is either made plain or seasoned with herbs, onion, caraway seeds, and/or paprika powder (from mild to very hot). Fresh Liptoi is often eaten for lunch with fresh raw vegetables and salad. The cheese can also be hung up in cloths and allowed to drain over a number of weeks. In this case the cheese is flavoured with various additions such as onion, herbs, and spices, and often then used to fill peppers.

A fresh white wine of fairly moderate quality or large glass of beer provide the necessary liquid to quench the fiery paprika.

Trappista sajt

Typical spiral-form Hungarian smoked cheese

South-East Europe

The Balkans

In the south-east of Europe, the countries of Bulgaria, Romania, Macedonia, Serbia, Bosnia-Hercegovina, Croatia, and Slovenia all make more or less the same types of cheese and experience the same problems in their efforts to export them. Virtually everyone of these countries lacks adequate infrastructure and hence you are unlikely to encounter any of the many different types of cheese outside the country of origin although there are specialist importers who supply the Balkan restaurant trade in Western Europe.

A summary is given here of the cheeses from these Balkan countries listed above that are commonly found throughout the region. This is then followed by a separate section dealing with the cheeses of Greece, Turkey, and Cyprus.

BRINZ/BRINZ DE BURDUF

Brinzâ is the Romanian version of Hungary's Liptoi and it is made here from sheep's milk. Generally the Romanians eat this cheese within days of it being made while still fresh and spreadable, sometimes mixed with herbs or spices. Some of these cheeses are kept hanging for longer as in Hungary, making them more crumbly and drier like a Feta. This variant is known as Brinzâ de burduf because the cheese is hung up in a *burduf* or bag. These cheeses are mainly used for cooking with.

HALLOUMI

A well-known culinary cheese without a specific place of origin that is also made in Romania from cow's milk and other types of milk too. This is a small greyish-yellow to pale green cheese that is springy with a shiny coating on the outside. Certainly not a cheese to eat on its own but a superb culinary cheese for grilled and oven dishes. Halloumi is quite salty so avoid the use of too much salt in dishes in which it is incorporated. Some varieties are made with the addition of mint and these combine well with vegetable dishes such as baked courgettes or aubergines (zucchini or egg plant).

KASHKAVAL/KSKAVAL/CASCAVAL

This type of cheese is made throughout the Balkans and right through to the Polish border, sometimes being sold under the Greek name of Kaseri or Kasseri. Kashkaval is a fairly large cylindrical cheese that can weigh as much as 22 lb (10 kg).

The cheese is traditionally made from sheep's milk but today it is increasingly produced from cow's milk or a blend of the two. Kashkaval is very popu-lar in Bulgaria, Romania, and the countries of the former Yugoslavia. Although the cheese is also sold immature for use in cooking they are matured for six months to one year which gives them a fairly strong and salty taste that can be bitter. Only the traditionally-made sheep's-milk cheeses have the characteristic taste of caramelised onion. Some people do eat this cheese on its own but it is mainly a culinary cheese that is delicious in grilled and oven dishes or added to salads, pasta, and rice.

MANUR/MANDUR

Traditional sheep's-milk cheese from Serbia. Sold in a round form of 4 lb 6 oz–6 lb 10 oz (2–3 kg) under both names, this hard cheese is made from boiled milk.

It's taste is one of acidic freshness, sometimes combined with a caramel. The cheese is used for a wide range of culinary purposes from ingredient in salads to additional flavour for soup, rice, or vegetable dishes.

SIRAZ

This is a very popular cheese in Serbia that is made from untreated cow's milk and has much in common with a Feta (but made with cow's milk). The 6 in (15 cm) round discs of cheese are kept in brine.

The taste is of fresh acidity and salt. Siraz is eaten in chunks with a drink just like Feta or added to salads, vol-au-vents, or oven dishes.

Sirene and Greek Feta are very similar

SIRENE/BJALO SALAMURENO SIRENE

A traditional sheep's-milk or cow's-milk cheese from Bulgaria made from untreated milk. This is another cheese that closely resembles Greek Feta. It is sold in blocks that are preserved in brine. The taste is fresher than most of the other Feta-types and it is ideal to eat on its own but is mainly added to salads or oven dishes. The fat content is 45%.

TELEMEA

A soft sheep's-milk cheese from Romania. Telemea is either sold plain or with the flavouring of cumin seed after being matured in a bath of brine and whey for at least one month. This cheese is also mainly used for culinary purposes but can be eaten in its own right for breakfast or lunch.

Greece

Every year many tourists recall with some emotion the sun-drenched paradise that is Greece with its mountains, sea, fertile high plateaux, many harbours, and its monuments from the early Greek civilisation.

This quickly brings to mind bottles of retsina, ouzo, or delicious dry Greek wine that is coming into its own, and the wonderful Mezedes snacks with their tasty sheep's-milk and goat's-milk cheeses. You encounter the genuine original Greek sheep and goat's-milk cheese known as Feta in many things: *choriatiki* (rustic salad), the famous cheese patties (*tiriopita*), and many oven dishes together with courgettes and aubergines (zucchinis and egg plants). It is also used instead of meat, baked in slices.

Were you aware that the oldest known cookery book was written by a Greek? In the eighth century BC, Hesiodus wrote about the art of cooking. Plato too was a great lover of cookery books. In Homer's classic epics of the *Iliad* and the *Odyssey*, is it not perhaps a forerunner of Feta that Polyphemus the Cyclops made in his cave? And surely the warm mixture of grated goat's-milk cheese, white flour, and Pramnian wine described in the eleventh book of the epic poem is an ancient form of fondue?

Unfortunately the Greek's open nature and naïveté means they did not take steps to protect the age-old recipe for Feta cheese and it is now copied throughout the world. The best of these imitations are at least made from sheep's milk and or goat's milk but increasingly quite tasteless Feta is made from cow's milk. There are first-class sheep's and goat's-milk Feta made elsewhere in the Balkans and also in France and The Netherlands in recent years and the Greeks also manage to make exceptionally poor industrial Feta just like the Northern European countries.

Protection of genuine Greek Feta, made from sheep's milk or goat's milk is way beyond protection. The European Court found that it was impossible to define an area from which Feta originates and that in the meantime the cheese is so widely made elsewhere that no form of authenticity can

Telemea is made from sheep's milk and cow's milk

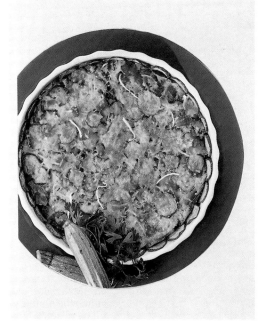

The Greek's have a characteristically sexist attitude towards the language of cheese. All cheeses made from full-cream milk are known as "first cheeses" or "masculine cheeses" while those made from heating the whey are known as "second cheeses" or "feminine cheeses."

The percentage fat given for Greek cheeses relate to the total fat percentage and not as a proportion of the dry matter. These figures would be much higher if they were calculated as a proportion of the dry matter.

Feta can be kept in its packaging in a refrigerator for several months

be linked to the name "Feta." The Greek name after all only describes a "slice" and this is far too vague for the protection of the European Court. This is a great pity since a tremendous chunk of history and also of quality will probably be lost forever.

Because so many cheaper–but incomparable cheeses in terms of their taste–are available most consumers will not understand the enormous price difference and choose the cheaper cheese. In this world of globalisation of taste as well as everything else it is certain that the worst versions of Feta, made from cow's milk will be purchased while the far better and more tasty sheep's-milk and cow's-milk Feta will be ignored. Fortunately there is a small minority of consumers who value the genuine article and continue to buy it.

Choose genuine Greek Feta

ANEVATO

A very soft fresh cheese made from goat's, cow's, or sheep's milk in the north-east of Greece around Grevana and Kozani. It is sold in containers of 17 lb 10 oz (8 kg) after maturing for two months. Fat content is 40%.

ANTHOTYROS

Anthotyro is a fresh sheep's-milk cheese (or made from a blend of sheep's and cow's milk) made like Myzithra from heating the whey from milk that has been separated. It is somewhat like an Italian Ricotta made with sheep's milk but has a fuller

111

and more nutty taste and creamy texture. The shape, weight, and size vary from area-to-area and even from house-to-house because this is classically a home-made cheese. The name *anthotyro* is given because of the aroma of meadow herbs and wild flowers of this cheese (*anthos* means "flower" and *tyro* is Greek for "cheese"). Anthotyros can be eaten fresh within a day or two but is also hung up to dry and mature as in the case of the Hungarian Liptoi cheese. The harder mature cheese is grated on pasta and rice dishes but also incorporated in a variety of dishes. The younger cheese is used to make desserts and also eaten for lunch with fresh figs. Fat content is 20–30%.

BATZOS

This semi-hard cheese is preserved in brine and made from pasteurised or untreated sheep's milk and/or goat's milk, or cow's milk. It resembles a young Edam without its rind but it has plenty of irregular air bubbles in its curd. Batzos originates from Thessalia or Western and Central Macedonia. It is matured for at least three months before being sold. Like Feta it is packed in brine and its own whey, in cans.

FETA

Widely imitated but never equalled, genuine Greek Feta made from sheep's and/or goat's milk is one of the world's oldest forms of cheese. The full flavour and distinctive aroma of Feta is due to the quality of the milk used. Sheep and goats graze freely on good pastures in areas such as Ipiros where air, water, and soil pollution are unknown. Craft made, often home-made Feta is produced from daily milk that is stored in sheep and goat leather bags which naturally curdle the milk through the presence of natural rennet. The curdled milk is then gently heated until flakes of milk protein form and the curd which floats to the top is skimmed off to dry, often in the sun. Factory-made Feta–some of the sheep's-milk versions are excellent–is made by the same manner but on a larger scale and with the help of modern technology. Unlike the craft-made Feta industrial versions though use pasteurised milk. Whether craft made or factory produced, sun dried in the open air, or in large industrial plants, once Feta has dried it is kept in a bath of brine and its own whey to both preserve it and allow it to mature. Traditionally, Feta was kept in wooden barrels, but today it is packed in cans or sturdy plastic containers, but always in a mixture of brine and whey. Because it is kept moist, Feta does not acquire a rind and it remains white.
Industrially made Feta from cow's milk does not have the same texture or aromatic properties of real Feta made from sheep's milk or goat's milk. All manner of tricks are resorted to in order to achieve the same white colour with these cheeses because cow's milk is naturally more yellow. The fat content of Feta varies according to the proportion of goat's, sheep's, or cow's milk used. Those

Also tasty on its own

wholly made of sheep's milk generally have higher levels of fat. This varies in practice between about 45 and 60%. The texture and taste of Feta varies according to the area in which the animals grazed, the quality of cheesemaking, the proportions of sheep's and/or goat's milk used, and the maturing time. It is typically fresh and slightly salty.
The Greeks drink Retsina or their favourite aniseed tipple, Ouzo with genuine sheep's-milk Feta, or those in which a little goat's milk is used. If you are only eating grilled almonds and Greek olives with chunks of Feta as an hors d'oeuvres then choose a better white wine but make sure it is a fresh one. Examples of good companions are Cephalonian Robola by Giannikosta Metaxa or a fresh Zitsa.

Top quality Feta from Greece

GREEK FETA "DODONI"

Naturally, the Best !

FORMAELLA ARACHOVAS PARNASSOU
An unusual goat's or sheep's-milk cheese usually weighing just under 1 lb (400 grams) made in the shape of a cork with a textured exterior. These cheeses from the area around Arachova in Volotia in central Greece are made from both pasteurised and untreated milk and are sold at varying stages of maturity from fresh (at least four days old) to mature (at least three months). Fat content is 33%. The Greeks eat this cheese on its own at table but also bake it as *saganaki*.
Drink a Greek white wine from the Savatiano such as a Semeli Attikos or a red made wholly from Agiogitiko at Nemea by Semeli.

GALOTYRI
Fresh, cottage-cheese type of full-cream pasteurised goat's or sheep's-milk cheese that is matured for two months. Fat content is 14%. This is Greece's oldest type of cheese with a protected origin status. Galotyri spreads easily and is often eaten for lunch or as a starter.

GRAVIERA AGRAFON
Version of Graviera cheese made in and around Agrapha in Thessalia. It is matured for at least three months and fat content is 32%.

GRAVIERA KRITIS
Version of Graviera cheese made on the island of Crete. This cheese is made from full-cream untreated goat's or sheep's milk from animals that have grazed in the mountains. The cheese is sold in cylinders of 13 lb 3 oz–55 lb (6–25 kg) that are matured for at least three months. Fat content is 40%. These mountain cheeses are much stronger than the winter cheeses and are only in short supply from late summer to autumn. The taste is very pleasant with a slightly sweet undertone of pureed onions.
Drink a spicy red Cretan wine with this cheese.

GRAVIERA NAXOU
Naxos is one of the best-known islands in the Cyclades to the south of the Greek mainland. A

Graviera Kritis

local variety of Graviera is made there from untreated cow's milk or a mixture of a maximum of 20% goat's and or sheep's milk with cow's milk. This cheese is also produced in cylindrical forms of 13 lb 3 oz–55 lb (6–25 kg) and matured for at least seventy days. Fat content is 40%. A superb cheese with a fully-flavoured nutty taste to eat in its own right or to use in cooking.
Try a Vin Santo from Santorini with this cheese.

KALATHAKI LYMNOU
This cheese originates from the island of Lymnos to the north-east of the mainland. This young springy cheese with lots of air bubbles and it is closest in style to a French or Italian Tomme. It is made from untreated sheep's milk or a mixture of milk from sheep and goats. The round cheeses still bear the marks of the basket in which they are matured for at least two months. After this they are packed in cans in a mixture of their own whey and brine. Fat content is 25%.
Surprisingly delicious with a dry Muscat wine from Lymnos.

KASSERI
A hard mountain cheese made on the mainland in the Greek provinces of Macedonia and Thessalia but also on the island of Lesbos. Just like Graviera, Kasseri (or Kaseri) is made in a flat cylinder without a rind.
Untreated full-cream milk from sheep or a mixture of milk from sheep and goats with at least 80% sheep's milk is used to make this cheese. It is mild and buttery with somewhat salty undertones. Initially the taste is quite salty but the sweetness of sheep's milk dominates the finish. Maturing time is at least three months and fat content 25%. Kaseri is eaten on its own but widely used as pizza topping.
Delicious with a glass of non sparkling Zitsa but also great with most red wines of the area such as a Rapsani or a Naoussa of Tsantali.

KATIKI DOMOKOU
A fresh cheese made from unpasteurised full-cream goat's milk or a mixture of milk from goats and sheep that is made on the high plateau of the Othrys mountain near Domokos in central Greece. Fat content is 30%.

KEFALOGRAVIERA
Kefalograviera is a cylindrical semi-hard cheese made from sheep's milk or a mixture milk from sheep and goats that is either pasteurised or untreated. This cheese mainly originates from the western part of the province of Macedonia and Ipiros in the north-eastern corner of the mainland. Kefalograviera does not really have a crust and the cheese is springy with large numbers of irregular air bubbles.
It is matured for at least three months and fat content is 31%. Kefalograviera is frequently used in cooking.

KEFALOTYRI

Kefalograviera is a cheese mid-way between Graviera and Kefalotyri which originates from Macedonia, Thessalia, the Peloponnese, Crete, Ipiros, or the Ionian and Cyclades islands where it is made from sheep or goat's milk or a mixture of them. This cheese is matured for at least three

Kefalograviera

months and is eaten in its own right, baked in slices as *saganaki*, or incorporated in cheese patties. Fat content is 28.8% (40% of the dry matter).

The taste is somewhat similar to that of Parmesan but more salty but less strong. The name of the cheese is derived from the Greek *kephalo* hat which it is said to resemble–according to one story–or is the same size as a *kephalo* hat according to another version.

KOPANISTI

This fresh but strong tasting cheese originates from the Cyclades where it is made full-cream unpasteurised cow, goat, or sheep's milk or a mixture of all three. The cheese is slightly granular but creamy after maturing for thirty days and has a fat content of 20%.

The cheese often has some blue veining which enhances the flavour with peppery hints.

Delicious with a glass of Ouzo or Retsina.

LADOTYRI MYTILINIS

An unusual shaped cheese in the form of a small barrel of 4 in (100 mm) diameter and 4³/₄ in (120 mm) deep weighing around 2 lb (1 kg). Ladotyri originates from the island of Mytilini near Lymnos in the north-east of Greece and this is a fairly hard mountain-type cheese with an individual taste resulting from being matured for at least three months in olive oil. This is where the name comes from: *lado* is Greek for "oil" and *tyros* means "cheese". The fat content is 32%.

Choose a wine that has full taste and sufficient acidity such as a red Lymnios or a sultry Muscat de Lymnos.

MANOURI

Manouri comes in the form of a somewhat clumsy cylinder that is flattened at the top, weighing 6 lb 10 oz–8 lb 13 oz (3–4 kg). It is made from full-cream untreated sheep's milk and or goat's milk in the centre and west of Macedonia and Thessalia in the north of Greece. Manouris is a *pasta filata* cheese.

That means the curd is kneaded like dough to shape it (as in the case of Provolone in the chapter on Italy). The cheese can be sold within four days of being made. Its taste is reminiscent of Ricotta but more pronounced and with distinct hints of butter and citrus fruit. Fat content is 40%. Delicious for breakfast or in a tasted sandwich.

METSOVONE

Metsovone is an elongated, sausage-like *pasta filata* cheese from the area around Metsovo (Ipirus). It resembles a small Italian Provolone and indeed the name exhibits a wink in that direction. The cheese is made using full-cream untreated milk from cows, or a mixture of milk from cows, sheep, and goats.

The sausage shape is 4–4³/₄ in (100–120 mm) in diameter and 7⁷/₈–12 in (20–30 cm) long, weighing about 5 lb 8 oz (2.5 kg). During the compulsory maturing of at least three months Metsovone is smoked, giving it additional flavour. Fat content is 26%. A superb cheese to eat for its own sake with a glass of Ouzo, Retsina or wine.

MYZITHRA/XINOMYZITHRA

Myzithra is another cheese made from heating the whey, like Anthotyro, but this one is made solely from sheep's milk (see Anthotyro). The more mature version of this cheese is known as Xinomyzithra.

The Cretan Xinomyzithra in particular enjoys great fame in Greece. Myzithra is the same type of cheese as Anthotyro and the names are interchangeable depending on where they are made. Both are made from the whey remaining after making sheep's-milk Feta.

PICHTOGALO CHANION

Fresh cheese from Canea on Crete that is made from untreated full-cream milk from goats, sheep, or a mixture of both. Fat content is 35%.

SAGANAKI

Saganaki itself is not actually a cheese but a dish made by coating a slice of cheese such as Kaseri in flour or breadcrumbs. The prepared cheese slice is then fried in olive oil or butter and then flavoured for serving with lemon juice and usually served with pitta bread.

A more spectacular version is served for tourists for which the cheese is first marinated in brandy and then flambéed, after being sprinkled with lemon juice. Saganaki is mainly eaten as a lunch dish or as a starter.

Saganaki

Turkey

The Turks and Greeks have a great deal more in common with each other than either will admit. Through the frequent invasions they have each acquired a great deal from each other. The differences between their cheeses are very small indeed. All the Greek and Turkish cheeses clearly have the same ancestors which originated in central parts of Asia. Nomadic people did not make cheeses for keeping over long periods. In addition to the daily yoghurt (*sivi tas*) large amounts of fresh sheep's milk and goat's milk fresh cheese were made in ancient Anatolia and Cappadocia. Although a great deal of cheese is made now by industrial processes, the traditional and ancient cheeses of the former nomadic tribes are still very popular. Turkish families consume a lot of Peynir cheese. In common with Greece and the Balkan countries around the Mediterranean much of this cheese is consumed in salads, in cooked dishes, as a snack, for lunch with bread and olives, or just when being sociable with a drink.

Peynir

The name Peynir appears to be etymologically associated with the name of the basic form of cheese in India and Pakistan known as Paneer. Both cheeses probably share the same ancestor somewhere in central Asia. Peynir is a generic name for many different sheep's-milk cheeses made with unpasteurised milk. Well-known examples are the fresh and hard Kasar Peynir, the light and creamy, almost yoghurt-like Los Peynir, made from heated whey, the *pasta filata* Dil Peynir, Tulum Peynir that is mixed with olive oil and matured in the stomach of a sheep or goat, or the ancient Koy Peynir, that is most similar to Indian Paneer. Two Peynir type cheeses are particularly popular.

SAN MICHALI
The island of Syros in the Cyclades of south-eastern Greece is the home of this hard cheese made from pasteurised skimmed cow's milk that is produced in cylinders of 13⅞ in (35 cm) diameter and a height of 4¾–5 ⁹⁄₁₆ in (120–140 mm), usually coated with black wax that contrasts boldly with the ivory-coloured cheese. Fat content is 27%.

SFELA
This cheese originates from Messinia and Lakonia in southern Greece where it is made from either pasteurised or untreated full-cream milk from sheep, goats, or from both. Sfela is matured for at least one month in brine and three months in attractive wooden tubs. Fat content is 30%.

TRIKALINO
This is a modern semi-hard cheese of the Kaseri type is made at Trikala from cow's milk to which 10% sheep and or goat's milk is added. Trikalino can be eaten for its own sake or in salads or as a pizza topping.

XINOMYZITHRA KRITIS
A fresh cheese made from untreated or pasteurised full-cream milk from sheep or goats, or from a mixture. This "sour" version of Myzithra (*xino* means "sour") is made on Crete. Fat content is 16%.

BEYAZ PEYNIR
Like all other Peynir cheeses, this one is made from untreated sheep's milk. Beyaz Peynir is with-

Trikalino

Beyaz Peynir

out doubt the most popular of these cheeses and Turkey's best-known cheese. This cheese closely resembles a Feta but this cheese is made without the use of an animal-derived rennet. Fat content is 45%.

MIHALIC PEYNIR

Mihalic Peynir is a local variety made in the area around Bursa that is sold in round slices unlike the elongated slices of Beyaz Peynir. Both cheeses are kept in brine. The texture of this cheese is less crumbly and more creamy than Bayaz.

Kaser

Kaser is a generic name for a great assortment of cheeses that are all made from untreated sheep's milk. The very young Taze Kaser is widely used in the kitchen for gratin dishes or melted in a sandwich. The older Eski Kaser resembles an Italian Pecorino or Greek Kaseri and the names here are similar too. This older type of Kaser is eaten in slices with some honey for breakfast.

Cyprus

Given the internal conflict between the Turkish and Greek inhabitants of Cyprus you will find both Turkish and Greek types of cheese on the island. I refer here to just two of them.

ANARI

A fresh sheep's-milk cheese with low fat content (20%) and a delicious mild taste with hints of nuts and caramel. Anari resembles a drier version of Greek Myzithra or Anthotyro or Italian Ricotta. This cheese is sold in large blocks of 22 lb (10 kg). The cheese can be sliced and then baked, added to salads, added to cooking, or eaten in chunks for lunch, with fruit or nuts.

HALLOUMI

Halloumi is a Cypriot speciality although this cheese is also made in the Lebanon and Romania. Present-day Halloumi is precisely the same as the cheese made when the Phoenicians were in power in the Mediterranean.

This small cheese 8⅞ oz (250 grams) with its shiny but irregular exterior is like a more rubbery version of Mozzarella but does not temp one into eating it because it has virtually no aroma, barely any colour, and almost no taste. This changes though when the cheese is grilled or placed on a barbecue, or fried.

The cheese does not lose its shape when heated and can therefore be used instead of meat, coated with flour or breadcrumbs. The outside of the cheese becomes crispy and brown while the inside is deliciously soft. Some cheeses (that connoisseurs regard as the best) are flavoured with mint. You should try Halloumi at least once in your life. After Gejtost/Gjetost, Halloumi is perhaps the most unusual cheese in the world. Although some eat the cheese on its own it really is just for cooking with.

Halloumi

South and South-West Europe

The Iberian Peninsula

Spain and Portugal are perhaps the most under-estimated countries in Europe in terms of cheese, together with the British Isles. Maybe this is because of the many poor or moderate cheeses that are served to tourists. No-one holds their breath for a Portuguese Queijo Flamengo (copy of Edam), nor are they charmed by the flabby, rubbery, industrially churned-out Manchego of Spain.

But those who take the trouble to discover these countries off the tourist beat will find that both countries have much to offer in terms of delightful cheeses. Of the two countries, Spain is under-standably the more varied with its greater size and geographic diversity. Compact Portugal has cheeses that all appear to resemble one another but a true cheese lover would happily be woken in the middle of the night for a well-matured Queijo de la Serra.

There is still plenty to discover in Spain and Portugal

Azeitão

Portugal

Portugal is a fairly small but elongated country. Cheese is made principally in the high plateaux in the mountains from north to south along the border with Spain. Good quality cheese is also made in the islands of the Azores.

The majority of these mountain cheeses are made with untreated sheep's milk but there are also goat's-milk cheeses from the Azores and also cow's-milk cheeses. In this book we deal only with the original Portuguese cheeses and ignore the many imitation Edam cheeses. In common with the making of all craft cheeses the activity is seasonal with virtually no cheese being made in summer and autumn.

QUEIJO AMARELO DA BEIRA BAIXA

The word *queijo* just means "cheese" in Portuguese and *amerelo* means "yellow", referring to the colour of the rind of this cheese made in the province of Beira Baixa in the east of central Portugal. This yellow cheese from Beira Baixa is a soft one of full-cream milk from sheep alone or sheep and goats. It measures $4^1/_2$–$6^5/_8$ in (120–160 mm) in diameter and $1^1/_8$–2 in (30–50 mm) thick, weighing 1 lb 5 oz–2 lb 3 oz (600 grams–1 kg). The cheese inside is pale yellow with several air bubbles. It is matured for at least forty-five days. You can serve any white or red wine of character with this cheese.

AZEITÃO

Azeitão is a village south of the Tagus river, about twenty-five miles south-east of Lisbon. A delight-ful round cheese is made here that is quite small (only $3^1/_2$–$8^7/_8$ oz/100–250 grams) with a diameter of 2–$4^5/_{16}$ in (50–110 mm) and $1^1/_8$–2 in (30–50 mm) thick. The rind is yellow-orange and

Portugal also has some special cheeses

117

covered with red bacteria. The cheese is soft and supple with a few small air bubbles. The cheese has a full flavour that is slightly sharp because of the use of untreated sheep's milk and the influence of the bacteria culture. Azeitão characteristically has an aroma and taste reminiscent of meadow herbs and flowers. Fat content is 40%. Choose a red wine such as an Alentejo.

QUEIJO DE CABRA SERRANO TRANSMONTANO
This cheese is solely made with untreated goat's milk. The rind of this flat cylindrical cheese is pale yellow and the cheese is quite hard as a result of maturing for at least two months. These cheeses are 4¾–7½ in in diameter and 1⅛–2⅜ in (30–60 mm) thick. The fat content varies during the seasons and the places where the goats graze in the mountains of north-eastern Portugal between 45–65%. The taste is lightly herbal and very pleasant.
Drink a tasty strong wine such as a Dão or Barrado branco, or a full-bodied and mature red such as an old-fashioned Garrafeira.

CABREIRO DE CASTELO BRANCO
A soft goat's-milk cheese from the same area as the Castelo Branco cheese below. This is a supple cheese that is mild-tasting when young but with a bite, hard, and salty after maturing for a few days. Widely consumed by the owners of specialist cheese shops. Serve a somewhat rustic white or young red with this cheese.

CASTELO BRANCO
Castelo Branco is a small cheese made from full-cream untreated sheep's milk in the town of this name in the province of Beira Baixa. The cheese has a distinctive aroma of its own, redolent of perspiration and sweaty feet, but the taste more than makes up for this with its balance of freshness, salt, and slight sweetness.
The cheeses are 4¾–6¼ in diameter and about 2–3⅛ in (50–80 mm) thick, weighing between 1 lb 12 oz and 2 lb 14 oz (800–1,300 grams). An infusion of cardoons are used to coagulate this cheese instead of any animal rennet, making this cheese suitable for vegetarians.
Try a robust Alentejo red from the area around Portalegre with this quite unusual cheese.

EVORA
Evora originates from Alento Alentejo, around ninety-four miles east of Lisbon. Because of its small size this cheese is sometimes known as Queijinhos Alentejo (literally little cheeses from Alentejo). They range in size from ⅞–5 9/16 in (20–140 mm) across, are not thicker than 1 9/16 in (40 mm), and weigh a little over 2 oz to 10⅝ oz (60–300 grams). There are several varieties of Evora ranging from a soft cheese matured for at least thirty days, a hard cheese matured for at least ninety days, and small cheeses that are stored in olive oil to keep them soft. Evora is made from skimmed but unpasteurised sheep's milk. The souring is done by an infusion of cardoon.
Evora combines well with red wines made from Periquita grapes. Choose an Alentejo Evora from the same area.

NISA
Queijo de Nisa, as this cheese is known in full, comes from the eastern part of central Portugal where it is made from the skimmed milk of Merina Branca sheep. These cheese–ranging in size from 4–6 5/8 in (100–160 mm) weigh 7–14 oz (200–400 grams) for the smaller cheeses and 1 lb 12 oz–2 lb 14 oz (800–1,300 grams) for the bigger ones–are matured for at least 90 days and are semi-hard. They are also produced using an infusion of cardoon. The taste is fresh and often slightly acidic and sharp.
Drink a delicious mature Dão or Bairrada red wine with Queijo de Nisa.

PICANTE DA BEIRA BAIXA
Another cheese from the eastern part of central Portugal: originating from Beira Baixa. This Picante cheese–in name and nature–is made with untreated full-cream sheep's milk or goat's milk, or from a mixture of both. The best cheeses are made in the mountains and are only available in late summer and early winter.
The cheeses look unremarkable as small cylinders of 4–6 in (100–150 mm) diameter and 1⅛–2 in (30–50 mm) thick that weigh 14 oz–2 lb 3oz (400–1,000 grams). The cheese is white to pale ivory in colour with a few air bubbles.
Depending on preference, drink Dão, Bairrada, or Douro with this strongly flavoured cheese.

PICO
Genuine Pico is made with untreated cow's milk on the Azores but home-made versions often contain a little goat's milk. The cheese is made as a flat disc of 6¼–6¾ in (160–170 mm) that is about ⅞–1⅛ in (20–30 mm) thick, weighing 1 lb 7 oz–1 lb 12 oz (650–800 grams). This cheese must be matured for at least fifteen days but the best cheeses are matured much longer and then benefit from a delicious full-on flavour with some bite and a wonderfully strong aroma.
Choose a mature white or red wine with this cheese.

RABAÇAL
There are two versions of this cheese, made from either sheep's milk or goat's milk but the milk is pasteurised in both cases. It originates in the north from the province of Beira Litoral. The cheese can be eaten fresh but is officially matured for at least twenty days. This another flat disc cheese of 4–4¾ in (100–120 mm) that is no thicker than 1 9/16 in (40 mm) with a weight of 10⅝ oz–1 lb (300–500 grams) although fresh cheeses sold without protected origin status can be as much as 2 lb 3 oz (1 kg).

Try a fine Vinho Verde (white) made wholly from Alvarinho grapes with this cheese.

REGUEIJAO
Regueijao is made with whey left over from making other cheeses to which 10% full cream milk is added. All the milk is then heated. The taste is good in spite of the low fat content.

SALOIO
Small cylindrical cheese of untreated sheep's milk. This fresh unsalted cheese is often used by the Portuguese as a starter.

SANTARÉM
Small cylindrical sheep's-milk cheese from Ribatejo that can be kept for a few weeks or a few months in olive oil, depending on taste. It weighs 5⅝ oz (150 grams).

The extensive landscape of Portugal

SAO JORGE
This cheese used to be protected under the name Queijo de ilha (cheese of the island). It comes from the island of Sao Jorge in the Azores. This is Portugal's greatest cheese, made wholly from untreated cow's milk. The cheese is hard yet crumbly and has irregular, fairly large air bubbles in it. The taste is quite sharp, certainly in the case

Sao Jorge

of older cheeses, with distinctive bitter and sweet notes that are its characteristic. The cheese is 10–14 in (250–350 mm) in diameter, 4– 6 in (100–150 mm) thick, and weighs 17 lb 10 oz–26 lb 6 oz (8–12 kg). Wonderful with a glass of Madeira that is not too sweet or a vintage port.

SERPA
This cheese gets its name from a town in central Portugal. It is a special cheese with a red rind formed by regular washing with olive oil with paprika powder in it. The cheeses are modest in size: 4–12 in (100–300 mm) diameter and 1⅛–3 in (30–80 mm) thick, weighing between 7 oz and 5 lb 8 oz (200 grams and 2.5 kg). This sheep's-milk cheese is made from untreated full-cream milk and it is matured for at least six months. The best of them though are aged up to two years and more, Serpa is a seasonal cheese that is only made between February and June. The cheese is soft and supple when immature but is semi-hard after lengthy maturing. The taste also develops during the life of the cheese from mild and deliciously full in flavour to very strong and sometimes even rather sharp. It is one of the least striking of Portuguese cheeses in appearance and it is coagulated with a cardoon infusion.
Choose a robust country-style red such as a Reserva from the Torres Vedra area.

SERRA DA ESTRELA
Queijo da serra da Estrela is made throughout the central and northern parts of Portugal. This wholly sheep's-milk cheese is made with skimmed but unpasteurised milk and it has a soft yellow rind and is creamy inside that becomes runny with age.

Fine cheeses are made on both sides of the border

This mountain cheese is certainly not large at 6–7⅞ in (15–20 cm) across and just 1⅝–2⅜ in (40–60 mm) thick, weighing 2 lb 3 oz–3 lb 12 oz (1–1.7 kg). The cheese is coagulated with a cardoon infusion.

Drink a tawny port or Colheita port with this cheese.

TERRINCHO

Queijo Terrincho comes from Tras-Os-Montes in the north of Portugal on the border with Spain. It is a fairly hard cheese made from untreated but skimmed sheep's milk obtained only from the Churra da Terra Quente breed. This small cheese is 5–7⅞ in (13–20 cm) across and 1⅛–2⅜ in (30–60 mm) thick and weighs 1 lb 12 oz–2 lb 10 oz (800 grams–1.2 kg).

A good Vinho Verde white or red will accompany this cheese but a better choice is a good Douro white or red.

TOMAR

Tomar is the name of a town to the north-east of Lisbon where a cheese also known as Queijinho da Tomar is made. The cheese is made from a mixture of milk and is fairly small at ¾–1¾ oz (20–50 grams).

Choose a red from Terras do Sado or the Torres Vedras area.

Spain

Spain truly is a cheese country although this is not at all apparent beyond its borders. Only their Manchego and occasionally Cabrales cheeses are ever found on sale outside of Spain and then it is rarely genuine Cabrales that is found but imitations that are not authentic. Why on earth do so few Spanish cheeses reach our shops when they are so delicious?

There are numerous reasons: firstly cheese production is often of an entirely local nature and the cheeses produced in an area are largely consumed by the local people, leaving little to export. Another factor is the huge cultural gulf between the small-scale producers of the finest craft-made cheeses in Europe and the cheese buyers elsewhere in Europe.

The cheesemakers are accustomed to getting their income immediately from the local population while cheese buyers do not normally pay for months after the cheese has been tested and more often than not already sold on. This gap could be bridged by introducing traders in Spain between the makers and European buyers which would increase prices, making Spanish cheese uncompetitive in the price-sensitive export market. Unfortunately for those living outside Spain this situation creates an impassable obstacle to our being able to enjoy Spanish cheeses of exceptional quality and extremely exciting tastes.

A tremendous variety

More than 100 different cheeses

Cheese is unlikely to spring to mind when you think of Spain and yet this country is a true paradise for cheese lovers. You will find a tremendous variety of cheese that is markedly different to cheese elsewhere. You will of course also encounter the factory-produced copies of internationally well-known cheeses in Spain but the main impression is one of originality.

Of the more than one hundred officially registered types of cheese with regional origins, twelve enjoy protection under European Commission regulations. These are distinguished by the blue-yellow of the European protected origin status logo known in Spain as *Denominación de Origen Protegida* that the Spanish generally reduce to "DO."

Virtually every type of cheese is made in Spain, from fresh ones through those matured for a short time to extremely well-matured cheese, plus white mould and blue mould cheeses, red bacteria cheeses, soft ones, semi-hard, and hard ones, smoked, or preserved in oil, mild and subtle in flavour to very strong and spicy. In other words, something for every taste. Spanish cheeses are made from milk from cows, sheep, and goats, and

Boffard, branded cheese made by the Osborne Group; not a DO but still delicious

also from mixtures of all three that the Spanish call *leche del ganado* or literally "milk of the herd." Apart from the cheeses of the big dairy concerns, most Spanish cheeses are made from unpasteurised milk that makes them additionally attractive for true cheese-lovers. The enormous variety in taste, shape, and type is largely the result of different climate and soil conditions.

Cow's milk cheeses largely originate from the mountainous areas in the north such as Galicia, Asturias, the Basque country, the Canary Islands, and the Balearics. Sheep's milk cheeses mainly come from the central high plateau or *Meseta* and its foothills in the north east. Sheep's-milk cheese is also made at the foot of the Pyrenees in Navarra, the Basque country, and Catalonia. One also encounters a pair of sheep's-milk cheeses in Andalusia: Calahorra and Grazalema.

Goat's-milk cheeses chiefly originate in the Basque country, Asturias, Leon, and Rioja in the north-west but also along the coastal strip of the Mediterranean of Catalonia and Andalusia, and on the Balearic and Canary Islands.

The cheeses

The best-known of Spain's great assortment of cheeses is listed below. All these cheeses must comply with strict rules governing their production area, type of milk used, and certain technical and sensory criteria (flavour and aroma) characteristics, regardless of whether they enjoy DO status or not.

ACEHUCHE
This wonderful cheese from Extremadura in the south-west is a flat cheese of about 2 lb 3 oz (1 kg) with a yellow-orange rind and rounded sides. Acehuche is a very creamy goat's-milk cheese (almost 55% fat of the dry matter) that is often hidden behind a fragrant red bacterial coating. The cheese is firm without air bubbles but fairly supple. The aroma is also to an extent found in the taste, making this a cheese for connoisseurs rather than beginners. The initial taste is fresh, slightly salty and buttery, with a very strong finish. This cheese is certainly worth trying.

Drink a delicious glass of dry sherry or a somewhat severe white made from Palomino grapes from Jerez.

AFUEGA'L PITU
The name means something along the lines of "the farm-hand choker," referring to the characteristic of the cheese to stick to the throat when fully mature, so you have been warned! Afuega'l Pitu, from Oviedo and Grado in Asturias, is made from full-cream cow's milk in a variety of forms (ball, knotted ball), different stages of maturity (fresh to old and mousetrap), and different levels of fat from "half fat" to full cream at around 41% of the dry matter. The rind of the normal cheese is soft and

thin, pale yellow, with the occasional white and or blue patches of mould. The curd is firm, without air bubbles, and is slightly crumbly. Depending on the level of fat and maturity the cheese can be either easily broken into pieces to eat or sliced (in the case of young cheeses that are still moist). The taste is rather sweet, milky, and very pleasant. Because of its strong character this cheese is difficult to select a companion drink for. Choose something thirst-quenching in red or white therefore.

ALIVA AHUMADO DO
Aliva Ahumado from Cantabria is also known as Quesos de los puertes de Aliva. As the name implies, this cheese is smoked (*ahumado* = smoked), which is done at the end of its period of maturing (not less than fifteen days) over a fire of juniper branches. This not only gives the cheese its attractive colour but also a distinctive aroma and taste. Alivo Ahumado is a fine example of a *leche del ganado* or mixed milk cheese using the output of cows, sheep, and goats. It is a medium-sized cylinder of approx. 1 lb to 4 lb. 6 oz (500 grams to 2 kg). The fat content varies between full-cream and extra creamy and is not less than 45% of the dry matter. Beneath the thin rough brown rind the cheese itself is dense, occasionally with horizontal weals in it. The curd is white to ivory in colour that makes a fine contrast

Spanish cheeses: Aliva ahumado in the foreground

with the rind. The taste is complex and quite sweet. The cheese has little salt but is creamy with a smoky aroma. It sticks slightly to the palate and melts on the tongue. The smoky fragrance of this cheese makes it difficult to combine with drinks but try a Txakoli or glass of farm cider.

ALBARRACÍN
This cheese from Teruel is a fairly general type of cheese with a plain cylindrical form and average weight of 2 lb 3 oz (1 kg). The appearance is not exciting but the taste of this goat's-milk cheese on the other hand is much more interesting and clearly originating with goats. There is also butter and salt. The finish with more mature examples

can be very strong. Fat content is 56% of the dry matter. Choose a full-bodied yet fresh white or a very fruity red that has not been cask aged.

ALHAMA DE GRANADA
See Zuheros.

ALICANTE
This cheese comes from the province of the same name in the south-east of the country. This fresh cheese is produced from goat's milk. Its curd is very white, dense without air bubbles, soft and supple. The taste is surprisingly pleasing and clearly originating from goats, being sweet yet fresh and slightly salty. The young age of this cheese tends to make it rubbery but the taste more than makes up for this. Fat content is 37% of the dry matter.
The same type of cheese is known as Formatge blanquet in Catalonia. Drink a dry Mediterranean white with Alicante.

ANSÓ-HECHO
Anso-Hecho derives its name from two high mountain valleys in the Pyrenees where this cheese is made, mid-way between Pamplona and Huesca. The cheeses are sold as Anso or Hecho, depending on which valley they come from and they are closely related to Roncal. These sheep's-milk cheeses are still produced by craft means and are fairly small cylinders of 3 lb 5 oz to 6 lb 10 oz or even 8 lb 13 oz (1.5–3 or 4 kg). The rind is smooth and pale yellow, the inner cheese is dense and firm with a few irregular small air bubbles. The taste is well-developed but not strong, tending towards creaminess, with a little salt and undertones of fresh hay. Fat content is 53–55% of the dry matter. Choose a full-bodied Navarra red.

ARACENA
This cheese originates from the picturesque surroundings of Aracena (Huelva). Immature Ararcena cheeses are available but rare with most being more mature (at least two months) and often more than a year, which is exceptional for a goat's-milk cheese.
This is not a large cheese, weighing around 2 lb 3 oz (1 kg). The rind of these cylindrical cheeses is dark, quite moist, and even slimy. The cheese inside is pale, making a fine contrast with the rind and it has a few small irregular air bubbles. The smell is quite strong and the taste likewise, with strong presence of salt but this is softened in the mouth by the creamy texture. The older *anejo* (more than one year old) cheeses are often kept in olive oil, which strengthens the flavour. Some cheeses are kept by this means without difficulty to a respectable age of two years. Fat content is 42–49% of the dry matter.
The fresher the cheese is the fresher needs to be its accompanying white wine and conversely the more mature it gets the better needs to be the quality of a red wine. In both cases choose wines that are not cask-aged.

ARMADA
A strange-looking cheese with an unattractive rustic appearance, once made in mortars used for grinding herbs and spices. For this reason it still sometimes bears its older name of Queso de mortera. The taste of this cheese, that is made from untreated cow's milk, is a real experience. It is firm, strong, sour, slightly bitter, can be sweet, and also salty, very fragrant, and creamy. In other words a cheese you should taste at least once in your life. Fat content is 69% of the dry matter.
The complexity of the taste of this cheese suggest an equally complex white or red such as those from Rioja but a good sherry that is not too dry is also an excellent combination.

ARZÚA
Arzúa cheese comes from Galicia in the northwest tip of Spain, above the border with Portugal. The taste of this cheese is similar to the other Galician classic, Tetilla. The appearance though is quite different, with Arzúa having the form of a fairly small but thick disc that varies in weight between $10^{19}/_{32}$ oz and 4 lb 6 oz (300 grams and 2 kg). In common with Tetilla, this cheese is made from cow's milk, with both pasteurised and untreated versions being available. The soft and smooth rind is pale yellow and can become split with age if the cheese is being kept too dry. The cheese itself is dense without air bubbles and very creamy, melting on the tongue. The taste is fresh, pure, slightly sweet and creamy, with a hint of bitterness. As the cheese ages the taste becomes stronger and more bitter. Depending on the season in which it was made the cheese can become more creamy or crumbly as it matures. Fat content is 40–55% of the dry matter.
This cheese combines perfectly with wines made wholly with Albariño grapes from Rias Baixas.

BABIA Y LACIANA
This cheese from Leon is made from full-cream unpasteurised goat's milk and its rind is rough with a light coating of mould. Its form is a thick wheel of about 2 lb 3 oz (1 kg). The cheese inside is dense with regular air bubbles and the taste is fresh and slightly salty with buttery undertones. Fat content is 52.7% of the dry matter.
Delicious with a glass of Rued or other fresh and dry white wine.

BENASQUE
Once made mainly with sheep's milk, this cheese has made a comeback now produced with very creamy and untreated cow's milk. The cheese originates from the Pyrenean town of the same name, to the north-east of Huesca. It comes in the form of a fairly small cylinder weighing 2 lb 3 oz–3 lb 5 oz (1–1.5 kg). After coagulation the curd is cut thoroughly and heated to 38°C (100.4°F) and the immature curd is heavily pressed for twenty-four hours and then place in brine. This cheese's characteristic flavour results from at least sixty days

maturing in a cool, slightly moist environment during which the rind is not allowed to become moist. Beneath the hard yellow rind–which is flecked with white–the cheese itself is quite dense but dotted with irregular air bubbles. The taste is well-developed and reminiscent of fresh hay. The fat content is 57% of the dry matter.
Choose a Navarra red wine.

BEYOS

A very rare cheese from the area around Amieva in Asturias that is generally made from milk from cows and goats with the occasional addition of sheep's milk. This cylindrical cheese has a very thin rind that is rough and often split, slightly sticky, and with white mould. The curd is a fine ivory colour and it is dense but can be friable. The taste is quite remarkably sweet initially and fresh and creamy in the mouth with an almost buttery finish. Fat content is 51% of the dry matter.
Choose an Albariño from Rias Baixas or a white Ribeiro.

BUELLES

A delicious but regrettably extremely rare small cheese from the area around the town of Buelles in Asturias that is mainly made from unpasteurised goat's milk but from time to time may also be made with pasteurised milk. The cheese weighs about 2 lb 3 oz (1 kg). Its rind is drab grey, often cracked, and sometimes lightly flecked with mould. The cheese inside has no air bubbles and it is fairly elastic and supple but slices easily. The whiteness of the inner cheese brightens the cheese up some-

what but the taste will be enjoyed by everyone. It is light and fresh initially, slightly sweet and not very salty. The cheese is creamy and melts on the tongue. Fat content is 49% of the dry matter.
Serve a fresh white or light fruity and fresh red with this cheese.

BUREBA

Bureba comes from north-western Spain, north of Burgos on the border with the Basque country. Through the use of decorative ceramic forms, this cheese resembles a cake of 2 lb 3 oz–4 lb 6 oz (1–2 kg). Bureba is also known as Queso de los altos and it is made from untreated full-cream sheep's milk. The fairly strong taste of this cheese results from months of maturing in cool moist storage which causes bacteria to form on the outside. The cheese is washed and dried before sale. The uneven surface of the rind is yellow-orange and the somewhat friable cheese inside is creamy yellow. The taste is robust and strong with a suggestion of nuts in its finish. Fat content is almost 47% of the dry matter.
For a taste explosion drink a totally sweet cream sherry with this cheese.

BURGOS

This is a somewhat generic cheese that was once made from sheep's milk but now uses pasteurised cow's milk with a little sheep's milk. The round plain cheese of 2 lb 3 oz–6 lb 13 oz (1–3 kg) is plainly marked by the container in which it was drained. The texture of this rindless fresh cheese is fairly sticky and smooth, while the taste is sweet,

Craft made cheeses: at the front a friable Cabrales

milky, and slightly salty. Burgos comes from the province of that name and it is a popular cheese with children who eat it for dessert with honey and or sugar. This cheese is mainly consumed for breakfast with some fruit. Its fat content is 52% of the dry matter.

CABRALES DO
The queen of Spanish cheeses but unfortunately you are unlikely to encounter genuine craft made Cabrales in your local shop. Many of the cheeses bearing this name are made in large plants or are Azul made by semi-industrialised processes that has no protected origin status. Ask to see the packaging in the shop: the real article must not only be described as Queso Cabrales Denominación de Origen it will usually also bear the AOP/DOP logo of the European denominated area of origin. Without this do not buy the cheese because it is certainly not Cabrales. True Cabrales is made in the east of the province of Asturias in the Picos de Europe chain of mountains and it is made from a mixture of milk from cows, sheep, and goats.

A good Cabrales is never sold before it has matured for at least three months while the best are kept in cellars for at least six months. Beneath the rough rind with its pronounced smell there is a fairly creamy cheese with lots of air bubbles shot through with lots of blue-green veins of mould. The flavour of Cabrales cannot be compared with any other cheese. It is strong, freshly tart, and slightly salty in taste. This is a cheese of world class that is completely under-estimated. Fat content is 45–55% of the dry matter.

Drink a full-bodied red or white with this cheese or for a veritable sensual adventure choose a glass of Pedro Ximinez sherry.

CÁCERES
This small sheep's-milk cheese from Extremadura looks like a mini Gouda cheese of about 2 lb 3 oz (1 kg). Its rind is smooth and yellow-brown, the cheese is dense with a few air bubbles, and an elastic texture. The taste is sweet and well-developed and the cheese contains little salt and is quite creamy. Fat content is slightly more than 44% of the dry matter.

Combines well with rosé wines from Ribera del Guadiana.

CÁDIZ
See Zuheros.

CALAHORRA
See Zuheros.

CAMERANO
Camerano is a clear example of an old-fashioned basket cheese, made from untreated goat's milk that is eaten fresh or within a few days of being made. The cheeses of less than 2 lb (less than 1 kg) are attractively presented for sale in a basket. This cheese from south of Logroño, which has no rind,

tastes of sweet milk but is also fresh on the palate. It melts on the tongue. Fat content is 58% of the dry matter.

Drink a fresh white wine or dry sherry with this cheese.

CANTABRIA DO
Cantabria is also known as Queso de Nata or Queso de Nata de Cantabria and it originates from the province of that name. This cheese has a history dating back several centuries but today it is made from pasteurised milk that comes from the ubiquitous black and white Friesians. Cantabrian cheese is oval or rectangular, weighing between 14 oz and 6 lb 3 oz (400 grams–2.8 kg). Its exterior is smooth and waxy and the cheese itself is supple, springy, smooth, and without air bubbles. The taste is very refined, mild, and creamy. Fat content is 50% of the dry matter.

Choose a white wine for preference with this cheese, such as a Txakoli, Bierzo, Rias Baixas, or Ribeiro.

CASIN
Particularly creamy untreated milk from cows is used to make this unusual flat cheese from Asturias, although milk from goats and sheep is also sometimes used. The taste is quite strong and well pronounced to an extent that not all value. Fat content is almost 49% of the dry matter.

This cheese is difficult to combine with wine and a glass of *aguardiente* is a better choice.

CASSOLETA
A *cassoleta* is a small earthenware dish in which the cheese of this name is made. Cassoleta originates from Castellón and Valencia and this cheese is also known as Formatge de Cassoleta or Saladito Valenciano, with the latter name making reference to the salty flavour of the cheese. At first distant glance this cheese resembles a young Tronchón –perhaps they have similar roots. Cassoleta is a fresh cheese made from mixed pasteurised milk from cows, sheep, and goats. After coagulation and the scooping of the cheese into their *cassoletas*,

Manchego sheep grazing

Small craft cheese store

they are then kept in a dilute brine bath for no longer than a week before being sold but they are not ready at this stage to be eaten. First they are dipped in a bath of milk and whey to flush away excessive salt. The fairly elastic cheese is initially sweet tasting but the salt quickly comes to the fore. This is more of a cheese to cook with or for combining with an aperitif and almonds and olives than as part of a cheeseboard. Fat content is slightly higher than 43% of the dry matter.

Delicious with a glass of fino sherry or a lighter Valencian white or red wine.

CASTELLANO

Castellano from Castilla y León closely resembles a Manchego and weighs 2 lb 3 oz–6 lb 10 oz (1–3 kg). Like a Manchego, this cheese is made from full-cream sheep's milk which is not pasteurised for the craft-made versions but is for other examples. This hard cheese must mature for at least three months but the best are older than this. The cheese is dense, without air bubbles but with a few irregularities. A Castellano is much moister in texture than a Manchego but otherwise shares the same fresh and salty flavour that is slightly sharp as the cheese becomes older. Creaminess is always present and the cheese melts on the tongue. Fat content is 52.9% of the dry matter.

Ideal with a fino sherry but a red from Castilla y León is also delicious.

CEBRERO/CEBREIRO

This classic cheese made from full-cream unpasteurised cow's milk from the Lugo region has an appearance akin to an old-fashioned baker's hat. This cheese is mainly produced in spring and summer and then matured a while in cool and moist storage. By either version of the name these are modest-sized cheeses of 2 lb 3 oz–4 lb 6 oz (1–2 kg) with a very thin rind and soft, creamy, yet friable white cheese. The taste is quite remarkably fresh and bitter and reminiscent of Bulgarian yoghurt, with little salt and extremely strong on cream. More mature cheese is broader in flavour and much stronger in common with a Tetilla. Fat content is 45% of the dry matter.

Choose a fresh white wine with plenty of character.

CONEJERO

This cheese from Lanzarote in the Canary Islands is made from full-cream goat's milk that is not pasteurised. It closely resembles the famous

Majorero. The cheese is cylindrical but squat with a fairly low weight. The external colour is yellow-orange resulting from constant massage of the cheese with butter and sweet paprika powder during maturing. The taste is freshly tart with little salt and bears the stamp of goat's milk. Fat content is 47.6% of the dry matter.

Serve a fresh dry white or glass of dry sherry with this cheese.

CUAJADA

This is a very fresh cheese made from sheep's or goat's milk that is kept in its own whey. There are several varieties including some that are suitable for vegetarians. A typical breakfast or culinary cheese.

FLOR DE GUÍA

Flor de Guía from Gran Canaria is made from the mixed milk of mainly cows and some sheep. It comes in the form of a flat wheel of more than 4 lb 6 oz (2 kg).

The use of a plant-based rennet agent is the unusual feature of this cheese which has a well-developed and sweet flavour with fresh and bitter undertones. This superb cheese is very creamy and melts on the tongue. Fat content is 50% of the dry matter.

This Flor calls for a like-named dry sherry.

GAMONEDO

This cheese from Asturias pronounced *gamenéo* will also be found described as Queso Gamonéu. Two factors are extremely important in its making: the moderate coastal climate of the area where it is made just inland from the coast and the presence of the Picos de Europa mountains. Gamonedo was once made from a combination of milk from cows, sheep, and goats but today is predominantly made from cow's milk so that the cheese is now available year round. The best examples are those made with mixed milk that has not been pasteurised. The cheesemaking process and the form of the cheese is similar to that of Cabrales.

Garrotxa (foreground) amid Spanish cheeses

This is a strong-tasting cheese that is full of character but very fresh, not salty, and with a creamy finish in which a suggestion of hazelnuts emerges. Fat content is 45% of the dry matter.

A glass of sherry will taste delicious with this cheese provided it is not too sweet.

GARROTXA

The name is pronounced *garrotscha*. This cheese from Catalonia is also known as Formatge pell Florida or cheese with the mould on its skin. Like French, Spanish and Catalan describe a cheese with mould as "floral." Garrotxa is not widely made any more with increasing numbers of cheeses being produced from pasteurised goat's milk rather than untreated milk. Even made this way Garrotxa is still a tasty cheese with a drab grey exterior but ivory cheese inside, weighing about 2 lb 3 oz (1 kg). The flavour bears memories of the cheese's time in a cold moist environment while it matured for several weeks. In addition to the fragrance of thyme, rosemary, mimosa, damp hay, walnuts, and hazelnuts, Garrotxa also offers a buttery and creamy texture. Fat content is almost 57% of the dry matter.

The idiosyncratic flavours of this cheese demands an equally idiosyncratic Oloroso secco sherry with plenty of oxidisation flavours.

GATA-HURDES

This relatively small cheese of 2–3 lb 5 oz (1–1.5 kg) from the north-western boundary of the Cáceres province (Extremadura) has much in common with Ibores and Acehuche cheeses. This goat's-milk cheese with a washed rind is kept in olive oil before consumption. The soft and creamy cheese contrasts pleasingly with the quite strong taste of this red bacterial cheese. Fat content is about 55% of the dry matter.

Drink a Vino de la tierra from Extremadura, preferably red.

GAZTAZARRA

The name means "old cheese" in the Basque language and it refers to the means of making the cheese. Some fresh curd and mature sheep's-milk cheese that has not developed properly are cut into pieces the size of chick peas and placed together in an earthenware container to ferment. To kick start the fermentation process a bit of the old cheese is added to the new. To prevent the cheese from drying out during fermentation liquid is added in the form of water, sheep's milk, or a local liquor known as Pacharán that is made from aniseed, herbs, and small wild plums (*Prunus espinosas*).

The taste is very strong and those that were sprinkled with the liquor bear clear traces of it. This cheese is quite an unusual but pleasing surprise. Fat content is 52% of the dry matter (see the Catalan version at "Tupi").

Drink a glass of Pacharán with this cheese and certainly no wine.

Tierno/Oreado (young and fresh)

Viejo (very mature (old) cheese)

Curado (mature)

cheese was once made from all three main types of milk but these days is mainly made with cow's milk that is not pasteurised. The young cheese (matured for at least three weeks) is fresh tasting, slightly salty, and creamy. With greater age this cheese can be quite strong. Fat content is about 55% of the dry matter.

Serve a fresh white wine from north-west Spain or a fresh fruity red such as a Ribeiro.

GOMERA
This cheese from Gomera in the Canary Islands is a variant of Herreño that is supplied as squat cylinders of 2–4 lb 6 oz. (1–2 kg). The top and bottom of the cheese are coarsely ribbed but the sides are smooth. The better craft-made versions of this cheese–that is matured for at least five months and often more than one year–are made from full-cream milk from sheep and goats that is not pasteurised, but the mass production versions use pasteurised milk. Unlike Herreño the curd is further handled for this cheese to form a denser, smooth cheese without air bubbles. The flavour is distinct and often strong. Because these cheeses are often smoked they develop a quite unusual taste. Craft-made versions can vary in flavour, depending on the type of wood and herbs used for smoking. Fat content is 50–55% of the dry matter. This cheese is difficult to combine with wine but try a glass of dry sherry with it.

GRAZALEMA
See Zuheros.

HERREÑO
Herreño comes form Hierro in the Canary Islands and is also known as Queso de Hierro. It is a thick wheel of a cheese of 4 lb 6 oz–13 lb 3 oz (2–6 kg) with a thin but coarse rind and rounded sides. This cheese was once mainly made with milk from sheep and goats but today it is increasingly more commonly made with cow's milk. Herreño generally has a mixture of all three types of milk with goat's milk playing the principal role but young

GENESTOSO/XENESTOSO
A very rare smaller cheese (less than 2 lb/1 kg) from the south-west of Asuturias. The locals know this cheese by the name of Xenestoso but the "X" is pronounced as a soft "G." The cheese resembles a large diabolo with a decorative zigzag. The

Semicurado (semi-mature)

cheeses are also made solely from cow's milk for use in the kitchen that are somewhat like a soft French Tomme. With the mass-produced versions of this cheese, pasteurised cow's milk is used but untreated milk continues to be utilised for the craft made cheeses. The cheese itself is quite elastic and riddled with small to medium-sized air bubbles. Herreño is generally a fresh cheese without a strong flavour that is slightly salty and creamy. Fat content is approx. 51% of the dry matter.

IBERICO

Mainly factory-produced cheese made with mixed milk from cows, sheep, and goats that comes from throughout the country and is often pasteurised. It is a fine cheese for use in cooking that is mild and not too salty but with less character than a really good Manchego. Fortunately there are some well-made crafted cheeses that quickly make one forget the inferior kind.

If you eat this cheese for its own sake then any Spanish red wine that is not too full-bodied is the best choice and this comes from throughout the country, like this cheese. With the tastier craft-made Iberico you can enjoy yourself with a glass of cream sherry.

IBORES DO

Ibores cheese comes from Extremadura, to the east of Cáceres, around Trujillo. The cheese is a flat cylinder of around 2 lb (1 kg) but both smaller and larger ones can be found. The rind in the usual variety of this cheese is pale yellow and dry but a moist variety also exists that is washed with olive oil and treated with olive oil and powdered paprika. Full-cream unpasteurised goat's milk is used to make this cheese which results in a high fat content of 56% of the dry matter. This cheese is pure in taste and freshly tart, slightly salty, buttery, and moist. With its fresh yet creamy taste this cheese demands

Hand-made Idiazábal

Unsmoked Idiazábal

Smoked Idiazábal ahumado

a fresh wine with elegant acidity. Drink a glass of good fino sherry with it.

IDIAZÁBAL DO

The famous semi-hard cheese from the Basque country and the valleys of Navarra is solely made from full-cream sheep's milk that is not pasteurised but is heated to 35–45°C (95–113°F) after which the cheese is firmly pressed. The cheese is 4–12 in (100–300 mm) in diameter, 3–4¾ in (80–120 mm) thick and weighs about 2 lb–4 lb 6 oz (1–2 kg).

The carefully hand-made cheeses are hand-salted during the process but the mass-produced ones are dipped in brine baths. Both types are made with unpasteurised milk and both are matured for at least two months. The craft cheeses vary in taste depending on the quality of milk and the place in which they were matured which adds to their interest. The mass-produced ones comply with the same requirements but are more consistent in quality and avoid surprises. The rind of an Idiazábal is quite smooth and also dry, although slightly greasy. The cheese inside is dense and has just a few small air bubbles. The aroma is characteristic of good dry sheep's-milk cheeses and is reminiscent of lanolin. The taste has a slight bite and is freshly tart at first but creamy on the tongue. Once all the cheeses made in the mountains were smoked because the absence of a chimney in the shepherd's hut meant that the cheese absorbed the smoke from the cooking fire. These old-fashioned hand-made cheeses still exist but there are also cheeses that are intentionally smoked after maturing over a fire of birch, beech, pine, or cherry wood. The colour of the rind of an *ahumado* cheese is browner than the normal Idiazábal. The flavour too is more pronounced with a greater bite. The taste varies widely, depending on the type of wood used and also the duration of the smoking. Fat content is 49% of the dry matter.

Idiazábal is wonderful to eat just for its own sake, perhaps with quince jelly or black cherry jam but it can also be used in dishes. The cheese is perfect to add to salads as slivers or chunks and can also be grated on top of pasta or rice dishes. An equally strong wine is needed for this strong cheese, such as a Navarra or Rioja but a full-bodied old-fashioned cask-aged Rioja white will be better suited for the smoked variety.

LEÓN

León is also known as Queso de Sajambre. It is a fairly small cheese of less than 2 lb (1 kg) that is made from full-cream unpasteurised cow's milk. The cheese resembles a Beyos but a León cheese is generally matured for less time than a Beyos and is therefore fresher in taste. The Léon also has a bitter undertone and it is not as creamy as a Beyos, resulting from the use of cow's milk instead of a mixture of three different types of milk as in the case of Beyos. Fat content is 52% of the dry matter. It does not matter if you drink white or red wine with this cheese provided it is fresh and strong on fruit.

LIÉBANA DO

These are small cheeses or *quesucos* from the area around Liébana in Cantabria. They are discs of 3–4³⁄₄ in (80–120 mm) in diameter and 1¹⁄₈–4 in (30–100 mm) thick with a weight of 3¹⁄₂ oz–1 lb 1 oz (100–500 grams). Liébana cheeses are made

Mahon

from full-cream pasteurised milk from cows, sheep, and goats. Fat content is 46% of the dry matter. Choose a white wine with this cheese such as a Bierzo or Rias Baixas.

MAHON DO

Mahon is a traditional cheese from the island of Minorca in the Balearics for which either pasteurised or untreated cow's milk is used, full-cream or skimmed, depending on the variety of this cheese being made. It is also permitted to add up to 5% sheep's milk to this cheese. The square shape of this cheese is quite distinctive with its rounded sides and relative thickness 2–3⁹⁄₁₆ in (50–90 mm) that look rather like a cushion. This shape is created by the use of a cloth or *fogasser* to wrap the curd in, which is knotted at the middle. The weight of Mahon cheeses vary between 2 lb 3 oz and 11 lb (1–5 kg) and the are sold at various stages of maturity: fresh, young, semi-mature (at least two months old), mature, and even more than one-year old cheese. With cheeses of more than one month the rind is regularly rubbed with a mixture of olive oil and paprika which turns the rind red-orange which contrasts with the yellow of the cheese itself. The texture of this cheese is soft and supple with few air bubbles. Depending on the length of maturing, this cheese is mild, fresh, milky, and slightly salty to strong with a bite. Fat content is 38% of the dry matter.

Mahon is especially tasty as an aperitif with some olives and olive oil and although a fine white or red wine is not out of place with this cheese its ideal companion is a glass of Palo Cortado sherry.

MAJORERO DO

Majorero or Queso de Fuerteventura of the Canary Islands is a fairly large and very interesting cheese of 6 lb 10 oz–15 lb 7 oz (3–7 kg) in the form of a flat wheel with rounded sides. It is made from full-cream goat's milk that is not pasteurised. The beige to brown rind bears the traces of the decorative container in which the curd was pressed. The inner cheese is dense, elastic, with some irregular air bubbles. During the maturing process the rind is rubbed with olive oil with both mild and hot paprika and *golfio* a local and ancient form of cereal crop that is like a cross between maize and wheat. This gives the cheese a quite distinctive taste that is quite special: fresh, slightly salty, and can be fairly piquant and peppery with spices, hints of the paprika, honey, almonds, and a slightly roasted taste to the finish. Fat content is 50% of the dry matter.

Drink a glass of a robust but dry white wine with this complex-tasting cheese.

MÁLAGA

See Zuheros.

MALLORQUÍN

This cheese from Mallorca or Majorca in the Balearics is still craft made. It takes the form of an

The well-known ribs of hard sheep's-milk cheeses come from the mould

Factory-made sheep's-milk Manchego DO

Extra mature or viejo Manchego (factory-made)

Craft-made Manchego is identified by its label

Craft-made Manchego

irregular rectangle with rounded sides and weighs 4 lb 6 oz–6 lb 10 oz (2–3 kg). During the maturing time the rind is rubbed with buttermilk or lard. The craft-made versions are produced from sheep's milk that is not pasteurised but the mass-produced version is made with pasteurised cow's milk. The dairy companies use plastic forms that give the cheese a more standardised and neat appearance. The fragrance and flavour of these industrial cheeses are both milder and less interesting than the craft-made examples. As you can imagine, the rubbing of the rind of these sheep's-milk cheeses with butter or lard gives it a smell all of its own but not at all unpleasant. The taste is a big surprise, very fresh and slightly salty. The cheese feels granular on the tongue but the finish is really creamy. Fat content is 52% of the dry matter. Choose a full-bodied white or red that has been cask-aged.

MANCHEGO DO

The craft made Manchego from La Mancha is made with full-cream unpasteurised sheep's milk that has been taken solely from the Manchego breed. The mass-produced version though use pasteurised milk. For both types of this cheese it is important that the milk used is high in fat (more than 6%). After coagulation at temperatures between 28 and 32°C (82.4–89.6°F) a fairly dense curd is quickly achieved which is then cut while being heated to 40°C (104°F). The curd is then scooped into moulds and pressed. The cheese is salted by hand or dipped in brine before being matured for at least two months in a cool and not too moist place. Manchego is a cylindrical cheese of 3^7/$_{16}$–8^3/$_4$ in (9–22 cm) diameter and 2^3/$_4$–4^3/$_4$ in (70–120 mm) thick, weighing 5–11 lb (2.3–5 kg). Its rind is light to dark brown and attractively ribbed. The taste and texture vary depending how mature the cheese is. Manchego is sold as *tierno* (literally young and soft), *semicurado* (semi-mature), *curado* (mature, at least thirteen weeks), or viejo (old, or extra mature, after three months). Take good notice of the labels and make sure they indicate either DO or DOP. Check also that the cheese is made solely of sheep's milk. Some of the mass-produced versions of this cheese are made from a mixture of three different types of milk and these have less taste than a genuine 100% sheep's-milk Manchego DO or DOP. Fat content is at least 50% of the dry matter.

Drink a robust red from La Mancha or Valdepeñas.

MATÓ

The charm of this fresh cheese from Catalonia starts with the decorative pattern on the outside left by the mould. Mató is made in a variety of shapes and sizes that are mainly less than 4 lb 6 oz (2 kg) but always fresh – from a few hours to several days. The texture is jelly-like and sticky but the flavour is fine, fresh, slightly sweet, milky, and creamy. Depending on the type of milk used Mató's colour and taste can vary. A high percentage of cow's milk makes the colour creamier and the taste milder. The more goat's milk there is in the cheese the whiter the cheese is and the stronger is its taste. The fat content is also higher with more goat's milk. Both types of milk used for this cheese are pasteurised and the fat content varies between 45-55% of the dry matter.

If the cheese is served as a dessert then drink a sherry such as a pale cream that is not too sweet.

MONTSEC

This cheese from the small village of Clúa in the Sierra de Montsac in Lerida is a fairly recent addition (1978). The cheese is made from full-cream goat's-milk that is not pasteurised. The cheese has the form of a flat cylinder of about 3 lb 5 oz (1.5 kg) or of a circular rod. The exterior is speckled dark

Fine collection of well-matured craft-made Manchego cheeses

grey and brown, quite sticky, and moist. This is because the cheese was first coated with ash and then left for at least sixty days in damp cellars to mature. Inside the cheese is smooth without air bubbles and quite pale. The smell is quite strong and not unlike a mouldy cheese but if this does not put you off you are in for a huge and pleasant surprise in the taste. The flavour is milky, very fresh, and creamy initially. The fat content is 61% of the dry matter.

Serve a fresh white or fruity but robust red from Catalonia such as a Costers del Segre.

MURCIA

Most cheese sold under this name is fresh pasteurised goat's-milk cheese that comes from the Murcia region. This is cylindrical with a weight of 1–3 lb 5 oz (500 grams–1.5 kg). This cheese is predominantly intended for use in cooking. It has no rind and is pure white, soft, dense, and slightly elastic with lots of air bubbles. Fat content is 55%. Choose a fresh young Spanish white with this wine.

MURCIA AL VINO

A fairly recent addition from the province of Murcia that resembles a more mature version of the standard cheese from this region, with a weight of around 2 lb (1 kg). The rind is reddish-brown from being washed with red wine while it was maturing. This Murcia al vino is also made from pasteurised goat's milk. It is somewhat sweet and fairly fresh, very creamy, and melts on the tongue. Distant memories of the red wine can just be detected too. Fat content is 56% of the dry matter. Drink a young Spanish red with this cheese, preferably made with Tempranillo grapes.

NUCÍA

This cheese from Alicante resembles a fine Turk's head cake. Pasteurised milk from cows, goats, and sheep is used to make this cheese. This fresh cheese of 2–4 lb 6 oz (1–2 kg) has no rind, is sweet, milky, slightly salty, and it melts on the tongue. Fat content is at least 30% of the dry matter. Serve a full-bodied Mediterranean white with it.

OROPESA

Oropesa from Toledo is made from full-cream sheep's milk that is not pasteurised in the form of a cylinder that is smooth on top and bottom but marked with esparto grass on the side. Beneath its smooth yellow rind Oropesa is a very dense cheese like Manchego. The cheese has a very pronounced flavour that is slightly salty and fatty. Fat content is 46% of the dry matter.

Choose a full-bodied but fresh white or robust tannin-rich red wine from Mentrida or Madrid.

PALMERO

This cheese from Las Palmas in the Canary islands is a fairly large cheese in the form of a flat wheel of 11–15 lb 7 oz (5–7 kg). Occasionally smaller versions of this cheese are also made of about 2 lb

(1 kg). Full cream goat's milk that is not pasteurised is used to make this cheese, sometimes with the addition of some sheep's milk. After maturing for one week the cheese is then stored until it is sold and immediately before this it is smoked over a fire of deal and almond shells. This gives the cheese a light smoky aroma that just emerges above the fresh milky taste. Fat content is 50%.

Choose a delicious glass of dry wine or a fino sherry with this cheese.

PASIEGO

A very craft-made cheese of untreated cow's milk from Cantabria. The shape and size of these cheeses is not recorded but they generally resemble a thick pizza or tart. The weight is on the low side, around 1 lb (500 grams). The maturer examples of this soft cheese are a few weeks old and have a more developed taste than the fresher ones. The cheese is very creamy and the taste is very pleasing, creamy, and slightly sweet. Fat content is 48% of the dry matter.

With this cheese you could drink either a full-bodied white such as a Chardonnay or an Albariño, or a well-rounded red from Bierzo, Ribeiro, or Toro.

PEDROCHES

This cheese from Córdoba, made with unpasteurised full-cream sheep's-milk, is a flat cylinder of 1–3 lb 5 oz (900 grams–1.5 kg). Coagulation of the cheese is brought about by a rennet agent derived from cardoons. After at least two months maturing the cheese is pale yellow inside with a well-pronounced fresh acidic taste that has a slight bite, is creamy and slightly bitter. Fat content is 48–48% of the dry matter.

Delicious with a glass of dry white wine such as Palomino from Jerez or a glass of fino sherry.

PEÑAMELLERA

Small cheeses made from a blend of milk from cows, sheep, and goats from the small town of Alles south of Oviedo. Beneath the thin rind of these cheeses weighing around 1 lb or less (500 grams or less) the cheese is dense and yellow with few air bubbles. The taste is well-developed but not in any sense strong, with cream being the most prominent factor. The cheese is matured for at least two weeks and the fat content is 53% of the dry matter.

Drink a full-bodied white or red wine from the north of Spain but avoid cask-matured wines.

PERAL

Peral from Asturias is a less well-known semicrafted blue-veined cheese made with pasteurised cow's milk. The cylindrical cheeses weigh 2 lb 3 oz–6lb 10 oz (1–3 kg) and they are usually sold wrapped in silver foil.

The rindless cheese is quite pale with an open texture and it is fairly crumbly with only a few blue veins. The cheese is quite soft for a blue cheese tending towards creamy and buttery rather than strong, making it suitable for newcomers to blue cheeses.

Because the blue veining does not dominate this cheese can be combined with almost any drink.

PICÓN DO

This cheese is a blue cheese not unlike Cabrales. Picón comes from a number of administrative districts of Liebana south-west of Santander such as Bejes and Treviso. Another name from this cheese is Picón de Europa. If this cheese is made in the Valdeón valley in León if carries the DO or DOP markings for that locality. These cheeses are cylindrical in form and are still wrapped in the traditional manner with sycamore leaves. Milk from cows, sheep, and goats that is not pasteurised is used to make this cheese.

The almost rindless cheese has a fairly moist and sticky exterior and it is slightly fragrant. This is a cheese that tastes better than it smells. It is simultaneously tart and creamy with a very fresh undertone. Fat content is at least 45% of the dry matter. Choose a full-bodied sweet sherry such as an Oloroso dulce for this cheese.

PIDO

Pido from Liébana in Cantabria is very similar to Liébana and it is traditionally made from unpasteurised cow's milk although pasteurised versions are becoming more commonplace. Some makers also incorporate some sheep's milk with the cow's milk. This cheese is sold from fresh through to mature but never at any real age. It is exceedingly fresh and pure tasting, slightly sweet and milky, very creamy, and slightly moist. Fat content is 45–55% of the dry matter.

Serve a fresh white with it from north-western Spain or Portugal.

PORRÚA

Fresh young Porrúa from Llanes in Asturias is a small cheese rarely weighing much more than 1 lb (maximum 500 grams). It is made from milk from cows and or sheep that is usually not pasteurised. It is very similar to a Liébana or Pido. This is a fresh cheese that is very moist, milky, slightly sweet, barely salted, and quite creamy. Fat content is 52% of the dry matter.

A delicious cheese for breakfast or to eat with fruit.

QUESAÍLLA

Quesaílla from Badajoz in Extremadura is a small hard cheese of 1 lb or less (less than 500 grams) that is made from unpasteurised goat's milk. It resembles an Ibores in its cylindrical shape with rounded edges but the rind is moister and more sticky with a much stronger aroma. The cheese has a nickname of *pestoso* or "stinking" which refers to this strong smell.

The cheese itself is quite dense in texture without air bubbles. Quesaílla tastes mature with a slight bite with little salt and much less fresh-tasting than

you might expect from a goat's-milk cheese. Fat content is 50–59% of the dry matter.

Drink a rosé or red wine from Ribera del Guadana with this cheese.

Roncal

QUESUCO DO

There are various cheeses in Cantabria that are known by this name, which refers to the smallness of this cheese. These *quesucos* of not more than 1 lb 10 oz (750 grams) are made from mixed milk from cow's and goats that is not pasteurised for the increasingly rare craft-made versions but treated for the now more common cheeses made by mass-production methods. These round cheeses are sold when young or slightly mature. When young they have a soft and sticky rind. The cheese is fresh and sweet, milky, creamy, and buttery, with slightly bitter undertones. Fat content is 46% of the dry matter.

Delicious with white wine from Bierzo or Galicia (Rias Baixas).

RONCAL DO

Roncal from Navarra is a fairly small cylindrical mountain cheese of 4 lb 6 oz–6 lb 10z (2–3 kg) that is about 3–4¾ in (80–120 mm). The rind of this sheep's-milk cheese made without pasteurisation is quite dark and covered with downy blue-grey mould. The cheese is fairly dense but somewhat granular with small irregular air bubbles and it is white to ivory in colour. The taste is quite strong with a slight bite and full of character that is reminiscent of mountain pastures. Fat content is 53% of the dry matter.

Roncal combines well with a full-bodied red from Navarra but you can also drink a white from the same area.

SAN SIMÓN

San Simón from Lugo in Galicia has an unusual pear-shaped or conical form that the Spanish jokingly refer to as *bufones* or fool's cap. This traditional cheese is made from unpasteurised cow's milk with the morning and evening milking being mixed together. After coagulation the curd is pressed into shape by hand and then left to rest in a cool and well-ventilated place. After one or two days the newly-formed cheese is dipped in a bath of hot whey and after ten to fifteen days they are smoked over a fire of green birch prior to sale. The cheese is dense in texture yet open with small air bubbles and is also quite supple and elastic. The taste is fresh with a slight bite to it. The combination of the mild smoky taste and a creamy undertone provide this cheese with a distinctive and pleasurable flavour of its own. Fat content is 45% of the dry matter. Choose a white wine such as a Rias Baixas from Galicia wholly pressed from Alvariño grapes or Vinho Verde of Albarinho grapes. Do not waste a good quality wine with the more heavily smoked examples of this cheese.

SELVA

Selva cheese from Gerona in Catalonia is made from pasteurised cow's milk that is high in fat (more than 4%). Its form is cylindrical with weights between 2 lb and 4 lb 6 oz (1–2 kg). Both the soft smooth rind and the cheese are light in colour and the cheese itself is fairly dense but with air bubbles

Serena in the foreground of these Spanish cheeses

and cracks. The texture is quite elastic and supple while the taste is quite strongly sweet, fresh, and milky, with a creamy and buttery finish. Fat content is 47% of the dry matter.
Select a dry white or fresh-tasting fruity red wine.

SERENA DO

This cheese from Badajos in Extremadura is small and round in flat cylindrical form but with rounded sides. Full-cream milk from Merino sheep that is not pasteurised forms the basis for this superb creamy cheese that is similar to the very best Portuguese cheeses. The Merino sheep's milk yield is quite low but the quality of its milk is excellent, with a concentrated and complex taste. The young cheeses are salted the day after coagulation and placed in a basket on planks of oak or poplar to

mature, where they are regularly turned and washed. Mature Serena cheese is modest in size at 7–9 3/4 in (18–24 cm) diameter, 1 9/16–3 in (40–80 mm) thick, and weighing 1 lb 10 oz–4 lb 6 oz (750 grams to 2 kg). The cheese itself is dense but with a few air bubbles and it is also supple and elastic. The taste is very creamy, slightly bitter, and a touch piquant, with a buttery finish. Fat content is 50–53%. Such strength of flavour demands a full-bodied wine such as a Colheita port, or to keep it Spanish a Pedro Ximénez sherry.

SERRAT

The name of this cheese from Catalonia, Formatge Serrat comes from the Catalan equivalent of *cerrado* in Spanish, which refers to the "closed" or dense texture of this cheese. Serrat is clearly a mountain-type cheese that is made from full-cream and unpasteurised sheep's milk supplied by local breeds. After coagulation the curd is salted by hand

One of the many forms of "serviette" cheese

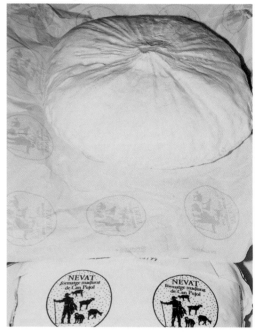

and then matured for at least two months in a cool place that is not too humid. During this time careful attention is paid to ensuring the rind remains dry. Beneath the hard waxy rind that smells of lanolin the cheese itself is equally firm without air bubbles but quite brittle. The flavour is well-developed, sweet and intense, and unmistakably of sheep's milk. Fat content is 50% of the dry matter. Choose a robust white or red wine such as a Costers del Segre.

SERVILLETA

Servilleta from Alicante is also known as Formatge de Tovalló which refers to the manner in which the curd is pressed in a linen cloth or large "serviette" the four corners of which are tied together in the middle. This gives the cheese its characteristic shape. It is made with pasteurised milk from goats and or sheep and sold when fresh or slightly mature. The rind is smooth and marked by the folding and knotting of the cloth in which it was wrapped. The colour is white to cream and the dense cheese is less elastic and has fewer air bubbles than might be anticipated. The cheese is sweet, milky, with little salt, and has no really pronounced taste. Fat content is 48% of the dry matter.

Choose a fruity white or red wine such as those from Alicante or Valencia.

SIBERIA

This cheese from Badajoz in Extremadura is also known as Queso de Castilblanco. The means of making of this cheese is quite unusual, combining the traditional methods of making goat's-milk cheeses of Extremadura with those used by the shepherds on the large Meseta plateau. Coagulation is done slowly over two to three hours at a relatively low temperature of between 25 and 30°C (77–86°F). The curd created is quite dense and firm. This is then cut to remove excessive whey and then further processes are manual as in the case of Queso de la Serena. The cheese is not allowed to mature though and is kept plain and fresh, if necessary by keeping it in olive oil. The cheese is sold as a relatively compact flat wheel of 2–3 lb 5 oz (1–2 kg). The taste is mild with fresh undertones and final hints of walnut. Fat content is 49% of the dry matter.

Especially tasty for use in the kitchen or in *tapas* with a glass of dry sherry or dry white wine.

SIERRA MORENA

A cylindrical mountain cheese from south-western Spain, near Seville. The cheese is sold in local markets both fresh or matured. Sierra Morena is made from full-cream untreated goat's milk that is sold at a week old, although some are matured for a few weeks or months. This cheese weighs 1 lb 12 oz–3 lb 4 oz (800 grams–1.5 kg). The rind of the

Tetilla, the "nipple" cheese

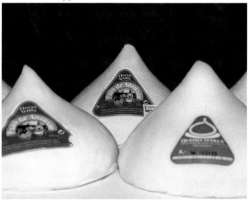

young cheeses is the same as the cheese and this is quite supple but firm with a few irregular air bubbles. The taste is very milky, slightly salty, and clearly reminiscent of goat's milk. Fat content is 45–50% of the dry matter.

Delightful with a glass of ultra dry Palomino from Jerez but also with a fino or Manzanilla sherry.

TENERIFE

This cheese from Tenerife in the Canary Islands is sold as a fresh or young cheese of 4 lb 6 oz–6 lb 10 oz (2–3 kg). It is made with goat's milk that is not pasteurised, sometimes supplemented with cow's or sheep's milk. In form and taste it is similar to the white springtime "May" cheese produced in The Netherlands. It is fresh and slightly tart, slightly salty, and milky. Fat content is 45–50% of the dry matter. Mainly of interest in use in dishes.

TETILLA DO

Tetilla has traditionally been made in small Galician villages for centuries. Currently this cheese relies less on hand-crafted methods than previously but the shape and taste remain as does the respect for tradition. Modern technology guarantees excellent quality and hygiene. Tetilla gets its name from its similarity to a woman's nipple or *tetilla* in Spanish. This cheese has a taste of its own similar to the best Portuguese cheeses. Although Galicia makes other cheeses, this is the most original of them to come out of this part of Spain. Tetilla is made with milk from Friesians, Pardo Alpino, and native Rubia Gallega cows that may or may not be pasteurised. The cheese is conical (or nipple shaped) with a diameter of $3^3/_8$–6 in (9–15 cm) at the bottom and weighs between 1 lb and 3 lb 5 oz (500 grams–1.5 kg). The elastic straw-coloured smooth rind is edible. The colour is natural, without colouring and hence fairly light. The cheese is soft, creamy, and uniform with occasional ivory markings. Its taste is fresh, of milk, creamy, with fresh acidity. Fat content is 40–55% of the dry matter. Tetilla demands a dry and fresh white wine that is aromatic. The perfect combination is a Galician Rias Baixas, preferably made wholly from Albariño grapes.

TIÉTAR

This cheese from Arenas de San Pedro in the mid-western part of Spain is a fairly classical straight-sided cylinder, weighing a little over 2 lb (1 kg). Tiétar cheese falls mid-way between Ibores and Garrotxa cheeses and is also made from untreated goat's milk. It is sold at varying stages of maturity from fresh to semi-mature. The pale rind is quite thin and the cheese itself fresh and creamy. Some Tiétar cheeses have a light covering of mould on the rind and these taste more mature. The taste is reminiscent of evaporated milk with hints of meadow herbs and flowers and then hazelnut in the finish. Fat content is 58% of the dry matter.

A dry sherry combines supremely well with the hazelnut finish.

TORTA DEL CASAR ⚙

Tortar del Casar (Casar de Cáceres, Extremadura) looks much like a Serena which is also sometimes made as a *tortas* (flat disc). This cheese is made from full-cream sheep's milk that is not pasteurised and using a natural plant-derived rennet agent. The difference with Serena lies in the quality of milk used. Lower fat milk of lower acidity that is richer in protein is used for this cheese and coagulation takes place at a lower temperature and takes longer than with most cheeses. This results in a soft but compact curd. Another difference with Serena is the greater use of salt for Tortar del Casar. Its rind is smooth, thin, and waxy. The cheese itself is quite compact with occasional air bubbles but it is also elastic and creamy. The taste is superb, well-developed and strong with slight bitterness and tart undertones. The finish is creamy with the character of goat's milk well to the fore. Fat content is 47% of the dry matter.

Spoon this cheese out like a French or Swiss Vacherin and drink a full-bodied white or glass of a good dry sherry with it.

TRONCHON DO

This cheese from Tarragona, Castellón and Teruel is cylindrical with straight sides but there is a dimple in middle of the domed top. It weighs 2 lb 3 oz–4 lb 6 oz (1–2 kg) and is made from either untreated or pasteurised milk from sheep and or goats. After coagulation the cheese must be matured for at least one month. The rind is dense, shiny, and slightly greasy.

The cheese is also dense but its texture is slightly elastic. The taste bears clear hallmarks of sheep's milk with hints of meadow flowers and herbs and there is a freshly tart finish. Fat content is 56% of the dry matter.

You can choose either white or red provided they are fresh and fruity such as the wines from Tarragona or Terra Alta.

TUPI DO

Tupi is a Catalan name for the small earthenware jars in which these cheeses ferment. Excess curd from the other local cheese, Serrat, made here at the foot of the Pyrenees, is used as the basis for Tupi. The immature curd is allowed to mature as small pieces and are then placed in the *tupi* (or in glass jars, plastic containers, or earthenware pots). The curd then ferments.

Each maker has his or her own secret recipe for the ingredients that they add to the fermenting mass, ranging through aniseed liquor to olive oil, whey, milk, salt, other alcoholic liquors, etc. Tupi is mainly eaten on bread or used as a dip. Fat content is 70%.

No wine can cope with the might of this cheese. Depending on the ingredients used to make Tupi choose a Catalan brandy or aniseed liquor.

ULLOA

See Arzúa, the official name of this cheese.

URBIÉS

Urbiés from Asturias is a strong, fermented cheese in the manner of Tupi. It is made from full-cream cow's milk that is not pasteurised. This is kept at an ambient temperature of around 20°C (68°F) for two to three days during which it curdles in the old-fashioned manner of cheesemaking. After coagulation the curd is cut into small pieces and hung up in a linen cloth for a week. Once the curd is drier it is salted, and transferred to wooden or earthenware containers. After a time mould forms on the surface of the cheese. This is regularly washed and the cheese is turned to ensure the mould is uniform throughout the cheese. The process lasts at least five months. The result is a very creamy cheese with a sharp, almost biting taste full of character and flavour with a finish like rancid butter. Certainly not a cheese for beginners but well worth trying at least once. Fat content is around 44% of the dry matter.

This is not really a cheese to combine with wine.

VALDEÓN DO

Local name for the blue-veined Picón or Picos de Europa cheeses made in the north-west of León.

VALDETEJA

Valdateja is a village in the north of León in northwest Spain. The cheese from here is a small one of about 2 lb (1 kg) in the form of a cylinder that has crumpled in on itself. It is made from full-cream goat's milk that is not pasteurised and it has lots of character due to a period of at least one month's maturing in a cool but moist place, which causes it to be covered with a well-developed culture of mould. The taste is quite pronounced, slightly piquant, and clearly influenced by the method of maturing. Fat content is 50% of the dry matter.

Drink an old-fashioned cask-aged white Rioja with it.

VALLE DE ARÁN

This cheese from the Arán valley near Lérida in Catalonia, close to the border with France, is made with full-cream cow's milk that is not pasteurised and is also high in fat. The immature curd is pressed into its form by hand and is then salted. After one day the cheese is removed from the mould and left close to a chimney to encourage the formation of a rind.

The cheese matures in this way for a month, absorbing aromas of smoke and in order to enhance its flavour the cheese is regularly washed with sour wine, brandy, and rum. This makes the rind coarser, moister, and extremely aromatic. The cheese inside is open in texture but quite hard. The taste is slightly tart and bears clear evidence of the smoke and washing of its rind. Fat content is 45% of the dry matter.

It is difficult to combine this cheese with drinks but a glass of Catalan brandy is the best match. If you insist on drinking wine then pick a cheap one that is cask aged.

VERA

Vera comes from Cáceres in Extremadura. It is an absolutely white cheese of 1–2 lb (500 grams–1 kg) in a cylindrical form with curved sides. This is another goat's-milk cheese that resembles Ibores, and it is made with unpasteurised milk. This cheese though is eaten fresh or very young. The cheese has virtually no rind and its texture is soft and friable while the taste is fresh, slightly salty, and fatty. Fat content is 53.5% of the dry matter. Serve a fresh dry white wine from Extremadura or a glass of fino sherry with it.

VIDIAGO

This cheese from Llanes in Asturias is made with cow's milk and resembles a bleached unfired brick with white patches on its slightly roughened rind. The weight varies around the 2 lb (1 kg) and the taste is similar to Nata de Cantabria. The cheese is fairly dense without any air bubbles but it is also supple and elastic. Vidagio is a mild and creamy tasting cheese with milky flavours including a finish of buttermilk. Fat content is 44% of the dry matter. Chose a delicious white wine from north-western Spain or Portugal.

VILLALÓN

This strange cheese made of cow's and or sheep's milk comes from Castilla y León. It is eaten fresh or slightly matured and its form is an irregular cube with rounded sides. Beneath the thin but rough rind the cheese is fairly dense while being both elastic and slightly friable. The cheese is riddled with air bubbles. The more mature cheeses can be quite crumbly. The taste is sweet, milky, moist, slightly salty, and fatty with young examples. The matured ones are kept in moist cellars and this is apparent in their taste. Fat content is 53% of the dry matter.
Try a delicious Rueda with this Villalón.

ZAMORANO DO

Zamorano originates from the place of this name in Castilla y León. It is a tall cylindrical cheese of up to 9$^{7}/_{16}$ in (24 cm) diameter and height and weighs 6 lb 10 oz–8 lb 13 oz (3–4 kg). The decorative marking of the rind (once wrapped in esparto grass but now often in plastic) is easily seen because of its darkness. The cheese is made with full-cream sheep's milk some of which is unfortunately pasteurised. The method of making is the same as with Castellano and Manchego cheeses. Zamorano is matured for at least six months in a cold and humid place which causes moulds to grow on the rind. Beneath this grey-brown greasy rind the cheese inside is firm in texture without air bubbles although casein crystals may be seen that look like grains of salt. The taste is clearly reminiscent of sheep's milk, cellar-storage, and old nuts. Fat content is 45–51% of the dry matter. Zamorano is a superb cheese to eat in its own right with a glass of full-bodied red wine such as those of Castilla y León, Bierzo, or Toro. Choose cask-aged Crianza versions of these wines. The combination of several chunks of Zamorano with a cream sherry is a heart-warming mid-winter treat.

ZUHEROS

Zuheros is a collective name for a number of Andalusian cheeses from the south of Spain. These cheeses are cylindrical in form but vary from flat wheels to medium height. They all bear the distinctive markings of being wrapped in esparto grass.

CALAHORRA (GRANADA)

Made from untreated fresh full-cream sheep's milk to which a little goat's milk is added. The rind is soft and the cheese is open textured with lots of air bubbles and is quite elastic. The taste is typical of the milk used, well-developed, slightly piquant, clearly originating from sheep's milk, and has a creamy finish. Fat content is 42–50% of the dry matter.

ALHAMA DE GRANADA

Made with untreated full-cream milk that is turned into cheese immediately after milking. Once the curd is pressed into shape and salted the cheese is then matured for forty-five to seventy days before being sold. The rind is hard and dark yellow, the cheese inside is dense and firm with a few air bubbles. Its colour varies between off white and pale yellow. The taste is quite sharp, fatty, and quite salty. Fat content is 42–47% of the dry matter.

MÁLAGA

Fresh or young cheese made from full-cream goat's milk that is still unpasteurised for the craft-made versions but pasteurised for the more mechanised forms. The fresh cheese is white while the young ones are more yellow. The cheese is fairly firm, even with the fresh cheese, with some air bubbles. The taste brings the best aspects of goat's milk to the fore: sweetness, creaminess, and little sign of salt. Fat content is 5–54% of the dry matter.

GRAZALEMA

Young or matured full-cream cheese of sheep or goat's milk. The cheese is quite pale, almost bleached yellow and fairly dense with a few air bubbles. The taste is very pleasant, being creamy, even buttery with the young cheeses (minimum age thirty days) and stronger with the more mature ones (at least sixty days). Fat content is 49–55% of the dry matter.

CÁDIZ

A mountain cheese made with full-cream goat's milk that is not pasteurised. White on the outside, its smooth cheese has a few air bubbles and has a classic goat's-milk taste: sweet, milky, slightly salted, moist, and creamy. Fat content is 39–43% of the dry matter. Drink a dry fino or Manzanilla sherry, Huelva, or Montilla-Moriles with these cheeses.

Italy

Surprisingly, Italy is less well-known for cheese than neighbouring France, when in reality many French cheeses owe their origins to the Romans. Only a few cheeses such as Cantal existed before the arrival of the Roman legions. Most Anglo-Saxons derive their word for cheese from the Latin *caseum* of the Romans. How has Italy managed then to become such a relatively unknown producer of cheese when it makes more than four hundred different types?

Long history but a quite new country

The geography of the Italian peninsula in the Mediterranean ensures great variety in its agriculture. The country is almost 1,000 miles (1,500 km) from north to south, has 5,000 miles (8,000 km) of coastline, and yet is only around 150 miles (250 km) wide for much of the country. The country seems to fall into two parts: the more expansive north, roughly north of a line between Genoa and Venice and the elongated but narrower south. There are also two large islands that also have characters of their own: hence you have a country ripe for considerable diversity.

It does not end there though for the north is greatly influenced by the presence of the Alps while the low-lying fertile parts are constantly threatened by urbanisation and industrialisation, leading to fragmentation of the land. The south and the two large islands are also divided by high mountain chains, leaving minimal land for agriculture.

In addition to this geographical fragmentation there are historical and climatic reasons why Italian cheese is little known outside the country's borders. Clearly the north of the country at the foot of the Alps and less influenced by surrounding sea has a more moderate climate than provinces 600 miles (almost 1,000 km) to the south.

Finally, Italy enjoyed a reasonable level of political and military union until the fall of the Roman Empire in the fifth century. It was not achieved without effort and not everyone felt as "Roman" as the Caesar, but the country was united. After the invasions of Barbarians this unity was shattered and the once mighty Italy became divided into myriad large and small states. Series of wars led to French, then Spanish, and finally Austrian domination of the northern states. A united Italy only became a reality once more in the nineteenth century.

Political and military unity though did not immediately bring about economic unity. Italian infrastructure was so poor that most agricultural produce could only be sold locally because of its rapid deterioration in transit.

Great lovers of cheese

Italians have been great lovers of cheese for as long as anyone can recall. Italian gastronomy and its many great dishes are better known though outside the country than its cheeses. This is because many of the Italian cheeses are consumed locally and have no outside economic significance, having perhaps been eaten in the same valley for centuries. Only a few Italian cheeses have international recognition: Parmigiano (Parmesan), Grana Padano, Pecorino, Gorgonzola, Taleggio, Fontina, Provolone, and of course those indispensable cooking cheeses of Ricotta, Mascarpone, and Mozzarella—just ten cheeses from more than four hundred Italian cheeses! You are rarely likely to encounter Montasio, Asiago, Fromai de Mut, Bra, Castelmagno, Fiore Sardo, Murazzano, Quartirolo, or Ragusano outside Italy. In Italy itself the selection of cheeses in specialist shops tends only to reflect cheeses from that region. Italians are regionalists rather than nationalists, which can perhaps be explained by history and circumstances.

Goats, sheep, cows, and buffalo

One of the most remarkable aspects of Italian animal husbandry is the presence of water buffalo in the south and on the southern islands. Wide-scale felling of trees has led to serious soil erosion on the slopes of the volcanic mountains of central and southern Italy and it is here that goats and sheep can best cope with the harsh conditions, high summer temperatures, and extensive drought. This makes them the most important suppliers of milk for the southern parts of the country and also on the islands of Sicily and Sardinia. The cow, which forms an image of northern Italy, is unable to cope with the inhospitable conditions further south although its distant relative the water buffalo can. Not only are these animals better able to withstand the heat, they are greatly valued as draught animals that are much stronger than oxen. More than 90% of Italy's milk is produced by cows or buffalo.

Well before Christ

Long before the time of Christ, Roman poets and authors enthused about local cheeses made mainly from milk from goats and sheep. Baked, Ricotta-like cheeses were being made then that were sweetened with honey and the ancestors of the *pasta filata* cheeses like Provolone and Mozzarella were being used in baked dough dishes that bear great resemblance to today's lasagne before Marco Polo left for China.

In the Roman era cheeses were made according to well-established methods. Milk from the morning milking was used for example in the making of fresh cheeses and the evening milk for harder cheeses. The morning milk was mainly curdled in the evening with the use of the flower forms or the sap of cardoons (a kind of thistle). After the cheese was pressed it was salted and then sometimes smoked or dried. During the time of the empire many different types of cheeses existed from stretched ones that are the ancestors of Mozzarella and Provolone, kneaded cheeses (Caciocavallo), smoked cheeses in all manner of decorative form, cream cheese, herbal cheese, and hard cheeses (Pecorino). This all virtually disappeared with the fall of the Roman Empire in the fifth century. Fortunately recipes were kept in ancient manuscripts by monks so that traditional cheesemaking could return once the Barbarians had disappeared from the country.

Often imitated, rarely equalled

The best-known of the Italian cheeses, including those from antiquity, are made throughout Europe and the New World to meet the demand for them at a lower price. Pecorino, Mozzarella, Ricotta, Mascarpone, Provolone, and Gorgonzola are among the most imitated of cheeses.

These cheeses are to be found in every country where Italians emigrated such as the USA, Argentina, Uruguay, Australia, and New Zealand. Some of these cheeses achieve a very respectable standard but cannot equal the quality of the handmade originals from the motherland.

North and South: worlds apart

Apart from the tremendous differences of climate and geology between the north and south of Italy there are also great economic and social gulfs between the two parts of the country that make them worlds apart. The wealthy north is able to buy more luxury cheeses with a limited storage life while the poorer south has greater need of cheeses that will keep. The gastronomy of the north is also more refined than the more rustic nature of the southern cuisine which in the extreme south is very spicy. Greater numbers of strong and spicy cheeses will be encountered in the south and on the large islands than in the north where there are more creamy soft cheeses. The northern cheeses are mainly produced with cow's milk while those of the south are chiefly with the milk of sheep, goats, and buffalo.

Protected origin names

Each of the four hundred types of Italian cheese have their own regional characteristics, some of which are more specifically defined geographically than others. At present there are thirty Italian cheeses that are recognised by the European Commission with protected origin status, known in Italy as DOC or *Denominazione di Origine Controllata*. This recognition and protection carries with it strict minimum quality standards, limitations on the origin of the milk, the method of cheesemaking, and other technical matters that are all checked regularly. These are minimum standards of course because the quality of the cheeses can vary within an area and between craft-made and mass-produced examples, and whether they are made from pasteurised or untreated milk. There can also be a difference from village to village and one cheesemaker to another, before the seasonal influences are taken into account. Purchase of a DOC cheese is always a guarantee of reasonable quality.

The cheeses

The cheeses listed below are a representative selection of the better-known Italian cheeses. Those that have been omitted are not by inference poorer (or better) quality but they are less well-known and more difficult to obtain. Italian cheeses come in all manner of types, tastes, and forms: fresh cheese, soft, semi-hard, and hard cheeses, kneaded, smoked, cylindrical, wheel-form, knotted balls, rectangular, round, pear-shaped (or conical), oval, plaited, and with weights from a few ounces or grams to tens of pounds or kilograms.

ASÌNO

Although the name and its advertising make reference to asses this fresh cheese from Friuli is made with cow's milk. Although Asìno in Italian is "ass" in reality the name refers to Mt. As from which it comes. Centuries of tradition ensure a mild and delicate freshly tart taste and creamy texture.

The fresh acidic taste of this cheese demands a fresh and fruity wine such as a Furlan or Sauvignon from Friuli or Collio.

ASIAGO DOC

This wheel-form cheese of $3^9/_{16}$–$4^3/_4$ in (90–120 mm) in thickness and almost 20–$26^1/_2$ lb (9–12 kg) is made on the Asiago plateau in the provinces of Vincenza, Trento, Padua, and Treviso. The same type of cheese has been made for over a thousand years. There are actually two different types with quite different tastes. Asiago Pressato is the least mature of them and more recent arrival. This comparatively modern form is very popular because it meets the current taste demands of consumers.

It is made with milk from Holstein and Bruna Alpina cows from just a single milking to ensure milk that has fuller cream and fat than that used for the "normal" Asiago cheese. The Pressato is slightly thicker at about 6 in (15 cm) than the other version and it is lighter in colour inside, has a thinner rind, more elastic consistency, and milder taste. The name Pressato just means "pressed". It is only matured for twenty to forty days, which is shorter than the other version. Fat content is 48%. With the younger cheese all manner of wines can be drunk ranging from a fruity Valpolicella classico to Refosco del peduncolo rosso. The locals give preference to a red or rosé wine. The best combination though is a fresh white such as Grave del Fruili.

The Asiago d'Allevo or matured Asiego is a cheese with more than a thousand years of tradition. This cheese is also made of untreated cow's milk. After salting the cheeses are matured for at least three months and up to nine months (for a vecchio or "old"), for twelve months or even up to two years for a Stravecchio or extra mature version. As the cheese becomes older it becomes harder and more granular. The taste also strengthens. The exterior of this cheese is difference from the Pressato with a thicker and harder rind and far more air bubbles in the cheese itself.

A red wine combines best with a mature Asiago. The more mature the cheese is the more full-bodied the wine should be. Choose perhaps a fine Cabernet Sauvignon, or Merlot from Trento or Piave.

BEL PAESE

A branded cheese from the Galbani company. The name is derived from an expression of Dante about Italy of "bel paese" or "beautiful country". The cheese is made in Lombardy from pasteurised cow's milk.

These are small round cheeses with a thin smooth rind. The cheese is ivory to yellow, and is creamy and soft in texture. The smell and taste are reminiscent of fresh milk with a hint of butter, fresh grass, and green herbs. Maturing time is six to eight weeks.

Fat content is 45–52%. Because this cheese melts readily it is much used in cooking. There is also a cheese spread version of Bel Paese known as Crema Bel Paese that is popular with children.

Drink a red or white without too dominant a taste such as a Favorita, Pinot Bianco, Chardonnay, or Solcetto, Barbera, or Freisa.

Bel Paese and Crema Bel Paese

BITTO DOC

Flat, wheel-form cheese of 12–20 in diameter (30–50 cm) that is made in the Valtellina valley near Bergamo in northern Italy using untreated cow's milk with the addition of up to 10% goat's milk. This still fairly unknown cheese is a classic small scale mountain cheese that is only made between June 1 and September 31 that must be matured for at least seventy days. Two types of this cheese are sold, one matured on average for six months and the other kept for at least one year.

Most of these older cheeses are eaten between one and three years old but you might encounter one up to ten years old. The rind becomes darker and thicker with age. The inside of the cheese is riddled with air bubbles and it is creamy and easy to slice at medium age. As it gets older the cheese also becomes stronger tasting and much harder. Whether young, medium mature, or old, Bitto's taste is characterised by the many herbs and wild flowers of the alpine pastures and in its young and medium mature state the cheese is widely used in the culinary specialities of Valtellina because it melts easily and has a wonderful flavour. More mature cheeses are served at table. Fat content is 45%.

Drink a wine of equal character with this cheese such as a fine Valtellina Superiore Sassella or Inferno. The Italians prefer red wine with this cheese.

BOCCONCINI

See Mozzarella and Mozzarella di Bufala.

BRA DOC

This cheese gets its name from the town of Bra in which it is sold but has never been made. This cheese comes from the mountain valleys and is matured in cellars in small towns between Cuneo, Asti, and Turin. These days Bra can only be made in the province of Cuneo, by craft methods in the mountain valleys and on a semi-industrial scale in the larger valleys around Cuneo. It is permitted to use full-cream cow's milk that is pasteurised or not and also to add a small amount of sheep and or goat's milk. Like Asiago there are two forms of this cheese: the traditional hard cheese or *duro* and the modern softer version or *tenero* (literally tender).

The rind is smooth, uniform, and pale grey while the soft cheese inside is ivory-coloured, slightly aromatic, and has a delicate flavour. The duro version as the name implies is hard (at least semi-hard) and both types come in a flat cylindrical form of 12–16 in (30–40 cm) diameter and 2 3/4–3 9/16 in (70–90 mm) thick. The weight is 13 lb 3 oz–17 lb 10 oz (6–8 kg). The brown rind is hard and thicker than the tenero cheeses. The cheese inside is also darker, tending towards yellow ochre or even brown. The taste and smell are stronger than with tenero cheeses, with greater bite and intensity. The best cheeses are made in the mountain pastures during the season and these bear the addition of *di alpeggio* in the name. Fat is about 32%.

With the tenero you can drink various young fruity wines of any colour. A young Piedmont Barbera or Dolcetto combines well. With the duro version red wine is the better choice such as a Barbera, Dolcetto, or Nebbiolo.

CACIOCAVALLO SILANO DOC

Caciocavallo is one of the oldest types of Italian cheese with direct links to cheeses from Central Europe, the Middle East, and even Asia. All its various manifestations have connections with horses: *caciocavallo, kashkaval, qasquawal,*

Bra tenero and duro

kackavalj etc. Experts do agree though about the origins of the name: Mongolia, but it is not entirely certain why this ancient cheese is linked by its name to horses. One expert says the original cheese was made from mare's milk while others say it relates to milk being carried on Mongolian horses in large saddle bags made from a stomach which curdled through the constant motion, heat of the sun, and reaction with acids in the leather, resulting in a primitive form of cheese. During the many invasions by the Mongols these cheeses spread to Europe. These cheeses came to Italy via the Balkans but also through the many voyages of Genovese traders to the Middle East. Caciocavallo is made in a great swathe of southern Italy, in Molise, Basilicata, Apulia, and Calabria. Its taste can be mild or quite strong, depending on the quality of the milk and the rennet agent chosen. The best cheeses start life in the mountain pastures and the best of these come from Podolica cows. The best Caciocavallo cheese is matured for at least two years during which time it becomes covered with dust and mould. Beneath this is a smooth and lustrous rind and intense yellow and very aromatic cheese with a soft and creamy texture. Fat content is 38%.

For one of the simple factory-made cheeses choose a fruity white, rosé, or red wine from the areas mentioned.

CANESTRATO PUGLIESE DOC

This hard sheep's-milk cheese comes from Apulia (Foggia, Bari) in the south of Italy. Full-cream unpasteurised milk is used from Merino or Gentile sheep that may only be fed prescribed fodder of mainly grass and hay. The ewes are milked twice each day and the milk is then heated to not more than 45°C (113°F). The curd is then transferred to rush baskets which create the attractive patterns on the cheeses. The salted cheeses are matured in baskets for at least two months, and some for up to a year. The mature cheeses weigh 15 lb 6 oz–30 lb 13 oz (7–14 kg) and have the form of a thick wheel of 10–13 in (25–34 cm) diameter that is 4–9/16 in (100–140 mm) thick. The rind is thick and ribbed while the cheese itself is dense and crumbly with a taste that varies from village to village but is always extremely creamy, with aromas of lanolin and caramel toffee. Fat content is 38%. Drink an ordinary southern Italian rosé or red with young cheese and a Salice Salentino Riserva with the more mature ones.

CAPRINI

A collective name for small cheeses of the Robiola type made wholly from goat's milk, mainly from Piedmont.

CASCIOTTA D'URBINO DOC

Those encountering this cheese from the Marches of Pesaro for the first time associate it with Belgium or The Netherlands rather than Italy. This is due to the rounded cylinder form of these cheeses of 8 in (20 cm) diameter and 4 in (100 mm) thick. They weigh 2 lb 10 oz (1.2 kg). Beneath the thin yellow rind however you will discover a surprising cheese made with full-cream unpasteurised sheep's milk with up to 30% of cow's milk added. The cheese itself is dense yet soft and breaks easily. The taste is fresh, sweet, and delicate, with aromas of the grass of mountain pastures and their wild flowers. The finish is nutty. Maturing time is fifteen to thirty days and fat content is 40%.

Choose a local red wine that is not too heavy, preferably fruity and rounded, with sufficient body to balance the full flavour of the cheese.

CASTELMAGNO DOC

This cheese is virtually unknown outside Italy but it has been an Italian classic for more than eight centuries. It is made with full-cream milk that is not pasteurised in the Grana valley of Cuneo province in north-west Italy. The main source of milk is from cows but this can be supplemented with milk from mountain-pasture grazing sheep and goats. Despite its long history and tradition, Castelmagno was virtually neglected but has staged a comeback. For this cheese too there are strict rules concerning the fodder for the milking stock of fresh grass of mountain pasture and hay only which is to be found back in the milk and its cheese. Cheesemaking is still done by hand on a

Milan, Padua, and Vercelli. Just milk from a single milking is used to make this cheese and in order to ensure the blue veins of *Penicillium gorgonzolai* the cheese is impregnated with culture during the fifty days maturing period by means of long needles of brass or stainless steel. The injection is always half-way into the cheese which is then turned after two days for the other side to be treated.

Both types of cheese are matured in relatively warm surroundings at 20–22°C (68–71.6°F) at very high humidity of 95%. After maturing the cheese is wrapped in silver foil to prevent loss of weight through evaporation and to keep the rind intact. Gorgonzola cheese is a cylinder of 10–12 in (25–30 cm) diameter and 6¼–8 in (16–20 cm) deep, weighing 13 lb 3oz–26 lb 6 oz (6–12 kg). Beneath the foil the rind is hard, rough, and reddish orange with clear traces of the cheese being penetrated with probes. The cheese itself is

Picante: with a bite and firmer texture

Dolce: creamy and mild

soft and creamy (48% fat), white to pale ivory with uniform green veins of mould. The cheese is soft and creamy, delicate and subtle in flavour in the modern version and somewhat stronger in the traditional combined milkings version which also has a denser and less creamy texture.

Gorgonzola is a very popular cheese both inside Italy and out. It is a great pity that the more tasty version is so rarely exported.

With the young modern cheese the most mollifying of wines is the best choice, such as a Caluso. With the more traditional version that has a greater taste people generally choose a red wine such as a Piedmontese Ghemme, Bramaterra, Barolo, or Barbaresco.

GORMAS
See Torte di Gorgonzola.

GRANA PADANO DOC
This is another cheese with a history stretching back more than a thousand years. The Cistercian monks of Chiaravalle were the first to introduce

cows to the Po valley which had been the domain of sheep and goats until then. Grana Padano gets its name from the Padano (or Po) valley and also from its "granular" texture. Today this cheese is made in parts of Piedmont, Lombardy, and Emilia-Romagna using good quality organic and unpasteurised cow's milk. Its size of almost 14–18 in (35–45 cm) diameter and 8–10 in (20–25 cm) high catches the eye first with this heavy cheese of 52 lb 13 oz–88 lb (24–40 kg).

The eye is then taken by the control stamps and the heat stamped chequering with *Grana Padano* imprinted into the cheese. Those made in Trentino are permitted to identify this on the rind. Beneath the smooth yellow-orange rind the cheese is friable.

The taste of this dry granular and hard cheese is of partially skimmed unpasteurised cow's milk that is well-developed and with a slight bite after maturing for about a year. Those intended for use in dishes are generally about one year old but those intended for grating are generally at least two years old. The comparatively low fat (30% of the dry matter) and high protein and mineral salts makes Gran Padano a healthy cheese that is recommended for older people, those convalescing, and growing children.

With an aperitif the preference is usually for a dry white, possibly sparkling such as a Spumante made from Riesling or an ordinary Riesling e.g. an Oltrepò Pavese. With the older cheese at the end of a meal red wine is a better choice, e.g. a Barbera or a Bonarda from Oltrepò Pavese.

MAGOR
See Torta di Gorgonzola.

MASCARPONE
Mascarpone is a cheese product made from the cream of milk from cows and buffalo. This is made throughout Italy by heating cream to 75–90°C (167–194°F) which is then curdled by the addition of vinegar, citric acid, or white wine. The fresh "cheese" is mainly sold in plastic containers and is

Grana Padano

very popular for spreading on bread for breakfast and is widely used in preparing desserts. It is often used as a replacement for cream (75% fat) and is an essential ingredient of the Italian treat of tiramisu.

MONTASIO DOC
Montasio is the pride of Fruili where much of it is made (it is also made in parts of the provinces of Veneto, Padua, Belluno, and Treviso in north-eastern Italy). Montasio is by origin a typical mountain cheese but was improved in the thirteenth century and made popular by the Benedictine monks of Moggio. Currently the area

Mascarpone

in which Montasio is permitted to be made has become so extended that it is less typically a mountain cheese. The cheese is still made in the traditional manner though. Both full-cream and skimmed milk that is not pasteurised is used from Pezzata Rosa (red spotted), Bruna Alpina, or Friesian cows. The form of the cheese is a classic flat wheel of 12–16 in (30–40 cm) diameter and a thickness of 2³/₈–4 in (60–10 mm) that weighs 11–14 lb 6 oz (5–7 kg). Fresh Montasio is soft and delicate with a mild milky taste while the mature cheese is stronger, firmer, and drier. Fat content is 30% of the dry matter.

As an aperitif and generally with the younger cheese a white wine such as a Furlan or Pinot Bianco is a good choice but fruity wines also combine well such as a Merlot or Pinot Nero from Collio, Isonzo, or Grave del Fruili.

MONTE VERONESE DOC
Monte Veronese originates from the province of Lessinia in north-eastern Italy in an area where many people live whose ancestors were German immigrants in the thirteenth century. Two types of this cheese are made: one with full-cream of 44% fat and a reduced fat (35%) version made with skimmed milk.

Milk that has not been pasteurised is used for both types in the making of hand-made cheese but modern versions often use pasteurised milk. The fresh cheeses are in reality young immature cheeses that must be matured for at least two months while the mature ones are kept for six months to two years. Both types of cheese are

Montasio

made in the form of a flat wheel of about 12 in (30 cm) diameter and a thickness of 4 in (100 mm). They weigh 15 lb 6 oz–17 lb 10 oz(7–8 kg).

You might choose an Alto-Adige or Veneto white with the younger cheese but a full-bodied red is preferable with the mature cheese, such as a Valpolicella Classico Superiore.

Mozzarella

Mozzarella originated in southern Italy, between Rome and Salerno. The best Mozzarella is made with the milk of free-ranging herds of buffalo and is permitted the designation of Mozzarella di Bufala DOC. Most of the Mozzarella sold throughout the world is mass-produced and in terms of world volume largely from countries other than Italy, such as Denmark.

Many countries with Italian immigrants also make this type of cheese. Mass-produced Mozzarella is always made with cow's milk and has virtually no taste and an unattractive texture akin to rubber. This is not a cheese for adding to salads but is wonderful melted on top of pizzas or incorporated in oven-cooked dishes. Much of the mass-produced Mozzarella originates as milk from the notorious "improved" Holstein breed that are walking dairies on legs with enormous yields of low quality milk.

Ordinary Mozzarella is sold in small packs that contain a small amount of whey to prevent the cheese from drying out. The shape can vary from large rectangular blocks (not originally an Italian manner but popular with caterers) to miniature balls or *bocconcini* ("single bite cheeses"). The commonly found Mozzarella starts life like the real thing as a soft fresh cheese with which the curd is kneaded into shape, which the Italians call *pasta filata*.

The *bocconcini* are mainly added to salads as an hors d'oeuvres, perhaps with olives. The larger cheese is really only used as a cooking ingredient. Because this cheese has little taste there is little point in eating it for its own sake. With *bocconcini* eaten as a light snack with aperitifs you can serve whatever you like since the cheese makes no imprint on the taste buds.

MOZZARELLA AFFUMICATA

Balls of Mozzarella or Mozzarella di Bufula are sometimes hung above a fire of local wood that gives them a dark colour and a smoky flavour and aroma.

This smoked Mozzarella is known as Mozzarella Affumicata. A smaller form known as Scamorza is smoked above a wood fire in northern Italy in Piedmont.

MOZZARELLA DI BUFALA CAMPANA DOC

Experts are uncertain whether buffalo were brought to Italy by the Barbarians in the sixth century or whether they are indigenous although DNA profiles suggest that perhaps these beasts were native to the country because similar DNA has been found among breeds of cow that are known to have existed in Italy for a long time. In any event, the history of Mozzarella has been linked to buffalo for centuries and these animals still play an important role in central and southern parts of Italy in addition to their milk production and not just in those once marshy areas that have been drained.

The buffalo's strength and ability to cope with the heat made it a first-class draught animal. Once herds of buffalo roamed free that were rounded up each day for milking. Today buffalo are being bred for their milk. Now buffalo can be found also in northern Italy and even in France, The Netherlands, and some other European countries in order to be able to make the tastier forms of Mozzarella. The cheese made from buffalo that are kept and fed like cows does not have such a distinctive taste and aroma (akin to a musk ox) of the free-ranging animals but it is of significantly better quality than the mass-produced cow's milk version.

Mozzarella DOC is only permitted to be made from full-cream buffalo milk–pasteurised or not–from Campana as indicated in the full DOC designation but also from slightly outside this area. The milk may originate from one of seven provinces: the whole of Caserto and Salerno, parts of Naples, Benvento, Frosinone, Latina, and Rome (the last two of which are part of Lazio).

The Mozzarella name is derived from *mozzare*, meaning "kneaded by hand." The curd is heated slightly to make it more pliable so that it can be drawn into long "threads" which is an art in itself in common with the *al mozzando* process of kneading the curd into shape. This type of cheese that is first stretched and then kneaded is known as *pasta filata*.

The cheese is dipped in brine after the kneading process. The final form of a Mozzarella di Bufala is of a somewhat flattened ball of 3–4 in (75–100 mm) diameter and 2–2³/₈ in (50–60 mm) thick.

Mozzarella di Bufala Campana

They weigh 3½–10⅝ oz (100–300 grams). Fat content is 52%.

Mozzarella di Bufala is soft and slightly springy in texture but not rubbery and when sliced the inner cheese weeps or as the Italians put it "sheds tears." It is a fresh and mild cheese with suggestions of musk ox and wild plants, especially in the unpasteurised versions.

This Mozzarella is at its best when freshest. All Mozzarella, including the best, is not normally eaten on its own but added to salads or incorporated in dishes. For those wanting to serve Mozzarella with aperitifs it is best to select a fresh and firm white such as Asprinio di Averso, Taburno Falanghina, or Falerno del Massico bianco from the south of Italy.

MURAZZANO DOC

This cheese from the eponymous province is not well known. The cheese is also made in parts of Cuneo in the north of Piedmont. It is made with full-cream and unpasteurised sheep's milk that can be supplemented to as much as 60% with cow's milk. Murazzano is a soft fresh cheese that is not larger across than 4⅛ in (105 mm) and quite thin. The weight varies between 9 lb 8 oz and 13 oz (270 and 375 grams).

There is no great secret in the method of cheese-making but the quality of the ingredients makes Murazzano a superb and much sought after cheese. After the milk has been received it is heated to 37°C (98.6°F) and then soured. Once coagulated the curd is allowed to rest for several hours before being scooped into moulds. After draining for twenty-four hours it is then salted by hand and left to mature for four to five days. Some cheeses are matured slightly longer, which makes them firmer and stronger tasting but the majority of cheese enthusiasts prefer Murazzano as fresh as possible.

The creamy cheese has a few air bubbles and varies in colour between ivory and straw gold, depending on its age, and it can have a slightly granular texture. Fat content is 50%. The aroma and taste betray the use of fresh sheep's milk. A local

Murazzano

speciality is also made using this cheese, known as Bruz di Murazzano. This is a strong cheese based on young cheese, sheep's milk, and some grappa liquor.

The Italians mainly drink a young red Piedmont Dolcetto wine with this cheese but the local white made with Favorita grapes is also recommended.

PARMIGIANO REGGIANO DOC/PARMESAN

True Parmesan cheese is Parmigiano Reggiano, made in the province of Parma and also in those of Bologna and Mantua. Because part of the production area overlaps with that of Grana Padano these cheeses are sometimes confused with each other.

Both the generic and official names indicate the Parma origins, while the official name of the true Parmesan indicates its origins in the Reggio Emilia. In common with Grana Padano, Parmesan is made with semi-skimmed but unpasteurised cow's milk from two separate milkings. The shape and size of Parmesan is also similar with a diameter of 13⅞–17¾ in (35–45 cm), thickness of 7–9⅛ in (18–25 cm) and a weight of 44–88 lb (20–40 kg). Parmesan is a classic *grana* type cheese with its hardness, nutritional value, fat content of 30% and lengthy maturing period of two years. What then makes this *grana* so different from the others? The source of the milk from cows grazing fresh spring pastures with grass, clover, wild flowers, and herbs is part of it but also the small-scale manual production that is still a craft. True Parmigiano Reggiano can be recognised by the brand in the rind.

Outside Italy this cheese is predominantly grated as a topping for pasta, polenta, and risotto. The

Parmigiano Reggiano (Parmesan)

different stages of maturity are *giovane* or young at fourteen months, *vecchio* or old at eighteen to twenty-four months, *stravecchio* is older at two to three years and *stravecchione* is an extra mature cheese of three to four years old.

With shavings of Parmesan served with aperitifs, good choices are a dry white such as Malvasia secco or a fine Spumante. Served with dessert, Parmesan demands a red wine: the older the cheese the stronger bodied the wine should be.

Pecorino

Pecorino is a collective name for all sheep's-milk cheeses. The differences in these cheeses is created by the origin of the milk, the method of cheese-making, and the period of maturing. The best known pecorino cheeses are the Romano and Tuscano

PECORINO ROMANO DOC

Pecorino Romano has a long history, having existed at the time of the classical ancient Roman civilisation. The praises of this cheese have been sung by many famous Roman authors. In reality this cheese is only partially Roman because it is made in the provinces of Lazio and Roma and also for as long as anyone can recall has also been made in Sardinia. The mass-production of this cheese became centred on Rome in the nineteenth century but most of this cheese now comes from Sardinia.

Fresh full-cream sheep's milk is heated to above 57°C (134.6°F) for fifteen seconds to eradicate any pathogens. Because this also kills off all the lactic acid bacteria they have to be re-introduced in the form of a culture. After coagulation the curd is cut into small pieces and heated to 45–48°C (113–118.4°F). The curd is then transferred to a mould and is pressed. The cheese is then still salted by hand in the craft manner. Maturing takes place over at least five months for young cheese (which does not bear the DOC designation), eight months for mature cheese, and a year for extra mature ones.

This cheese is a tall cylinder of 8–12 in (20–30 cm) that is 5½–8⅝ in high, weighing 48 lb 6 oz– 72 lb 10 oz (22–3 kg). The outside of the cheese can be covered with a colourless or black protective layer. The attractive seal of Pecorino Romano can be seen beneath this in the form of a stylised sheep's head imprinted into the rind together with the name of the cheese and identification numbers of the producer, and month and year in which it was made.

The colour of the cheese itself is white to pale straw yellow with a few air bubbles. The aroma and taste are strong and full of character and this is more intense with older cheese. Pecorino Romana is a "healthy eating" cheese with low fat of 30% and forms part of the famous low fat Mediterranean diet.

The strength of this sheep's-milk cheese demands a red wine from Lazio such as a Cesanese di Affile or del Piglio but Sardinia reds like a Canonau or Carignan del Sulcis are also a good choice.

PECORINO SARDO DOC

The Sardinian Pecorino has recently been elevated to DOC status. The milk for this cheese is not pasteurised and comes from Sardinian sheep and this cheese is still made wholly by hand on the farms. Pecorino Sardo is a more modestly sized cylinder than the Romano, with slightly curved sides. It is 6–7 in (15–18 cm) across and 2⅜–4 in (60–100 mm) thick, weighing 2 lb 3 oz–5 lb (1–2.3 kg). The rind is white to pale yellow and quite thin.

The cheese itself is white, through ivory to pale yellow, firm, and almost without any air bubbles. The aroma and taste are reminiscent of the wild bushes and herbs of this island in the Mediterranean. Pecorino Sardo is made as a "fresh" cheese that is only matured for twenty to sixty days after being salted and a mature variety that develops more slowly during eight to twelve months. The mature variety is much stronger in fragrance and flavour than the fresher cheese. Fat content is 35%.

Drink white wine with the younger type of cheese such as a Vermentino but for the mature variety you are better off with a full-bodied red like a Cannonau or Velletri.

PECORINO SICILIANO DOC

Sicilian Pecorino is extremely varied and has a plethora of names depending on the area from which the cheese comes. Often this cheese is named after the basket in which it acquired its form: Canistratu from *canestro*, or rush basket. Other common names are Maiorchino, Marzulinu, and Musciu, referring to the mildness of the cheese, Primusali (or "first salt", referring to the youth of this variety), and finally also Caciu from the Latin *caseus* for home-made cheese, and Tuma or Tumazzu with its link to Toma and Tomme.

Pecorino Siciliano is *the* cheese of Sicily with a history stretching back before records were kept. Milk from local sheep that is not pasteurised is used in its making with the cheese being made in the same manner as Pecorino Romano. The differences in these cheeses flow from the different quality of milk used, different grazing and habitat, and different breeds of sheep. The size of these Sicilian cheeses is 13⅞ in (35 cm) diameter with a thickness of 4–7 in (100–180 mm). Fat content is higher at 40%.

The aroma and taste of the Sicilian cheese are both stronger than the Romano and Toscano varieties. There is also a spicy version with peppercorns known as Pipatu.

A white wine is called for with the young cheese such as an Etna or Alcamo but the mature cheese requires a full-bodied and powerful red like a Cerasuolo di Vittoria or an Etna Rosso.

PECORINO TOSCANO DOC

The Tuscan variety of Pecorino is also known as Cacio and was the most popular cheese of Italy until the mid nineteenth century. This was as a cheese for the table, for consumption by the peasants, and in cooked dishes.

Either pasteurised or untreated full-cream milk is used from Sarda, Comisana, Massese, Sopravissana, and Appenninica breeds of sheep. In Tuscany the milk from two separate milkings is used but otherwise cheesemaking is as for other pecorino.

Much of the production is still a hand-crafted affair. This Tuscan cheese is shaped like a thick wheel of 6–8⅝ in (15–22 cm) diameter and 2¾–4⁵/₁₆ in (70–110 mm) thick that weighs between 1 lb and 7 lb 11 oz (1–3.5 kg). There are two main varieties, the "fresh" variety that is matured for at least twenty days and a mature one that is kept for at least four months. The fresh variety is 45% fat while the mature cheese is 40%.

In common with the other pecorino cheeses white wine is the best choice for the younger cheese, such as a Vernaccia or Orvieto while the mature one requires a full-bodied red such as a Chianti or Carmignano.

PROVOLONE VALPADANA DOC

Provolone is perhaps the most spectacular cheese in the world in terms of its size, at least as far as the *giganti* or giant-sized variety is concerned. These are made in the form of a 5 ft (150 cm) long sausage that weighs 220 lb (100 kg). These large Provolone cheeses and the equally massive Mortadella sausages are always big attractions at exhibitions for the delicatessen trade. Apart from its various physical forms (pear-shaped, sausage, cylinder, ball, and cube) Provolone is no different in terms of its production from other *pasta filata* cheeses such as Mozzarella and Scamorza.

Originally Provolone was made with buffalo milk that was not pasteurised but today full-cream pasteurised cow's milk is used. Provolone originates from northern Italy in the provinces of

Cremona, Brescia, Vicenza, Roviga, Padua, Piacenza, and parts of Bergamo, Lodi, Mantua, and Trente. The soft variety is matured for at least three months while the stronger tasting type is matured for much longer.

Fat content is 45%. Provolone is an excellent cheese to use in cooking, grated over all manner of dishes. The more mature *picante* variety is used for this purpose while the milder *dolce* is eaten in its own right, perhaps with a milder white such as a Chardonnay or Pinot Bianco from Fruili or Grave del Fruili. The *picante* needs a robust

Provolone Valdapana

red wine if it is eaten at the end of a tasty meal. You might choose a Ghemme or Refosco from Fruili.

Provolone in its famous sausage form

Pecorino Toscano

QUARTIROLO LOMBARDO DOC

The name of this cheese, which relatively recently attained DOC status, is derived from a custom in the hills of Lombardy of northern Italy. At the end of summer, just before the cows return to their farms in the valleys, they are allowed to eat grass from the pasture that has been mown four times. This fourth mowing is known as *quartirola*. The milk of this new grass following the fourth mow makes wonderful soft cheese known as *quartirolo* but alas today *quartiroli* is made throughout the year when milk is available.

Only a few cheesemakers still know the secret of making these traditional cheeses by hand for the most delightful flavour through the aromatic properties of the milk from cows fed on the new grass that is filled with wild flowers after the fourth mow.

The use of unpasteurised milk is diminishing and more and more homogenised and pasteurised milk is now being used. The area in which this cheese is made has also been extended to meet the demand for it. Today Quartirolo is made in the provinces of Brescia, Bergamo, Como, Cremona, Milan, Pavia, and Varese, all in the north of Italy. A selected culture is added to the milk after pasteurisation and after coagulation the curd is moulded and then salted. While the cheese is maturing for at least two months, its rind is regularly washed.

Quartirolo is similar to Taleggio but is milder and with a more consistent flavour. The cheeses are rectangular blocks of 8–9 in (20–23 cm) across and $1^9/_{16}$–2 in (40–50 mm) in thickness. They weigh 2 lb 3 oz–7 lb 11 oz (1–3.5 kg).

The decoratively marked rind of the young cheese is white but this becomes reddish-orange with more mature ones. The cheese is firm but springy with young cheese and creamy with older ones. Fat content if 30%.

Drink a fruity white or red with the young cheese e.g. Lugana, Garda Orientale Bianco, or Botticino but the mature cheese requires a more full-bodied red wine such as a Valcalepio.

Quartirolo Lombardo

RAGUSANO DOC

Sicily has many different local cheeses that are varieties of Ricotta, Provola Pecorino, goat's-milk cheeses (*formaggi caprini*) and two DOC cheeses: Pecorino Siciliano and Ragusano. This latter cheese is not well known outside Italy with the exception of the USA, which is a pity in several respects.

Ragusano, originating from the south-eastern tip of the island (Iblea), is the soul of the island, its people, and its cuisine. The shape of the cheese is reminiscent of the many rectangular houses apparently piled one on top of the other in the typical Sicilian village.

Ragusano is made with full-cream cow's milk that is not pasteurised so that it can be made with great care by hand using the natural cultures in the milk. This is turned by wizardry into a delicious cheese. The secret of the fragrance and flavour is largely due to the quality of milk from the native breed of Sicilian cows, the Modica. Fat content is 44% and maturing takes four to six months. For lovers of strong flavours there are also cheeses that are matured for a year or more that are extremely strong.

A glass of good Marsala Vergine is a supreme experience with the young cheese and for the more mature cheese you might try a robust red from Etna or Faro.

RASCHERA DOC

Raschera is a cheese from the area around Cuneo in Piedmont. Raschera Tipico is made in the valleys throughout the Cuneo region and Raschera d'Alpeggio is made in the mountains. Both vari-

Ragusano

eties of cheese may be either rectangular or round in shape, measuring of the order of $13^7/_8$–$15^3/_4$ in (35–40 cm) across with a thickness of $2^3/_4$–$3^9/_{16}$ in (70–90 mm). The weight is 15 lb 6 oz–22 lb (7–10 kg). This cheese is made with full-cream cow's milk that is not pasteurised although it is permitted to add some milk from sheep and or goats. After coagulation the curd is pressed without being heated to form a semi-hard cheese and salting is still done manually. The maturing process used to be much longer but today's demand is for cheeses of one to two months old. Beneath the drab grey or brown rind this mild cheese is firm, ivory to pale yellow and is riddled with lots of irregular air bubbles. The large rectangular cheeses are generally stronger tasting than the smaller round ones which have a more refined flavour. Fat content is 32%.

The younger cheese, and especially the round ones, combine well with a white wine or fruity red such as a Favorita, Pinot Bianco, Dolcetto, or young Barbera that is not cask aged. The more mature cheese and the stronger rectangular ones need a more full-bodied red such as a well matured Barbera.

RICOTTA

Ricotta means "cooked again", which indicates the method of cheesemaking employed for this popular soft cheese. The whey left over from making other cheese is heated so that the remaining milk proteins form a soft curd that is then treated in the

Raschera

same way as making fresh cheese. Ricotta can be made with the whey from the milk of cows, sheep, or goats or with a mixture of them. There are many varieties of Ricotta cheese available in Italy but they can be summed up in two main types: Ricotta Dolce (sweet ricotta) that is soft and milky, with a consistency just slightly firmer than quark and Ricotta Salata (salted ricotta) that is made at a much higher temperature, is considerably firmer, and keeps longer. Outside Italy and the USA the sweet ricotta is better known. In Italy the salted variety is incorporated in all manner of dishes such

Ricotta, Provolone, Mozzarella di Bufala, and Mascarpone

as filled pasta (ravioli, lasagne, cannelloni). Ricotta is also delicious on bread for breakfast or in a salad for lunch.

ROBIOLA

Robiola is a soft cheese from Piedmont that was once made with goat's milk but nowadays uses cow's milk. This is a small round cheese of just 12 oz (350 grams) that is usually matured in two weeks. The rind is uneven and thin with soft cheese beneath.

Fat content is 50%. An examples of a good Robiola is Robiola di Mondovi of Ocelli of Valcasotto. During a visit to Piedmont it is possible to hunt down a number of different versions of this cheese: Robiola del Bek (goat's milk), Robiola Caramagna, Robiola Bossolasco, and Robiola

Robiola

Cocconata, that are all cow's milk cheeses, and Robiola delle Langhe that is made with milk from cows and sheep.

It is traditional to serve a fruity red wine with this cheese e.g. a Piedmont Dolcetto but a fresh and fruity white such as a Prosecco is also a good combination.

ROBIOLA DI ROCCAVERANO DOC

Roccaverno lies on the border of the three provinces of Cuneo, Acqui (Alexandria), and Asti. The Robiola cheese unites these three provinces of Piedmont through this cheese that is common to them. The delight of this cheese was once provided by the goats of Roccaverno but now up to 85% of the milk used comes from cows with full cream milk being used from goat, sheep, and cows. The small farm producers still use milk that is not pasteurised but the diary concerns pasteurise their milk, which also removes some of the characteristic flavour.

The soft curd is moulded after coagulation and this cheese can be eaten within a matter of days. This cheese is produced either in the form of a flattened ball or of a small cylinder of 4–6¼ in (100–160 mm) diameter and 1³/₁₆–2 in (30–50 mm) with weights in the region of 7–14 oz (200–400 grams). The outside of the cheese is very white, without any rind. The cheese is also white inside, without any air bubbles, and it has a slightly granular texture. Robiola is fresh, slightly tart, mild and delicate in flavour, and very pleasing. Fat content is 45–55%.

Serve a fresh white wine from Piedmont with this young fresh cheese, such as a Favorita, Arneis, or Langhe Bianco. The mature cheese combines well with a fresh fruity red like a Grignolino d'Asti or a young Nebbiolo.

STRACCHINO

This is a collective name for fresh soft cheese that was once made from cows on their way to the

Robiola di Roccaverano

spring pastures in the mountains or on their way back to the farm in autumn. The name comes from *stracca* with connotations of "tiredness" but also of "mild" or "weak." Today this milk from "tired" cows (with their higher butterfat content) is no longer used to make this cheese but the name remains. Well-known Stracchino cheeses include Gorgonzola and Crescenza. Fat content is 45–55%.

TALEGGIO DOC

Taleggio is a typical northern Italian cheese which is linked with the Val Taleggio in the province of Bergamo. In addition to the Teleggio valley, this cheese is also produced in the provinces of Brescia, Como, Cremona, Milan, Pavia, Novare, and Treviso.

Taleggio is one of many typical northern Italian soft cheeses that have been popular here for as long as memories can recall. Although a small amount of craft-produced cheese is still made from

Taleggio

untreated milk, the majority of this cheese is now made from pasteurised full-cream cow's milk. This has been done to reduced the number of reject cheeses and to maintain constant quality. Unfortunately this also removes much of the character from the hand-made traditional Teleggio, which is a seasonal product, unlike the modern version that is made throughout the year. Although the milk is now homogenised and pasteurised for most of this cheese, the cheese-making process remains the same. Animal rennet is added to the milk to coagulate it and the milk is heated.

The milk coagulates within fifteen minutes. The dense curd is cut into small pieces the size of a hazelnut and is then scooped into moulds. After draining for a time the cheeses are turned at regular intervals. The fresh cheese remains for eighteen hours in a fairly warm and humid (90%) environment. During this time the cheese develops its characteristic texture and taste. The cheese is salted by hand or dipped in brine and maturing these days is mainly in well ventilated cool rooms. Slightly less than one third of the production is

Taleggio: at its best after maturing in caves

milk in Cuneo province. The cheese is sold by the Piedmont firm of Ocelli that is based in Valcasotto. These flat wheels of 11–15 lb 6 oz (5–7 kg) have a grey-brown rind with some evidence of mould. Maturing time is four to twelve months. Testun has an extremely individual taste that is filled with flavour, creamy, and quite intense, and reminiscent of damp cellars in which it was stored.
Drink a red wine from Piedmont such as a mature Barbaresco or Gattinara with this cheese.

TOMA PIEMONTESE DOC
The name clearly indicates the origins of Toma from Piedmont in north-west Italy. This cheese is made in the provinces of Novara, Vercelli, Torino, and Cuneo. Similar types of cheese can also be

Testun

still matured in the traditional manner in local caves. The rind is brushed every seven days to prevent mould forming. This gives the cheese its characteristic red colour. Total maturing takes forty days but the first cheeses often leave the dairy plants after twenty-five days. A brand is burnt into the ribbed and moist rind of Taleggio. The cheese is a rectangular block of 8–9⅝ in across and 2–2¾ in (50–70 mm) thick, weighing 3 lb 12 oz–4 lb 13 oz (1.7–2.2 kg).
The cheese itself inside is white to ivory, densely formed but springy with only a few air bubbles. The more mature the cheese is the more creamy its texture becomes and the taste also develops but is never overpoweringly strong, in common with many cheeses that have their rinds washed. The aroma and flavour are reminiscent of damp cellars, possibly also of fungi or even truffle. The traditional cheese made with unpasteurised milk and matured in caves often possess a suggestion of freshly-mown mountain grass with lots of wild flowers and herbs. This is an excellent cheese to incorporate in dishes. The fat content is 48%.
With the young cheese you could serve a glass of dry Spumante or other white wine. The older, more carefully matured cheese calls for a full-bodied white or red. Traditionally the locals drink Pinot Nero from Oltrepò Pavese but any good red wine will do.

TESTUN
Like its name in the Piedmont dialect suggest, this is a precocious cheese made with sheep and cow's

found along the border of France and Italy. All these cheeses are generally semi-hard and made by gently warming the curd. Known as Toma, Tomme, or Tome, they take various forms from flat wheels to squat cylinders. This Piedmont Toma is the only one of these cheeses with designated origin status and it is made with full-cream and/or skimmed cow's milk. The fresh cheese is matured for at least fifteen days and the harder varieties for many months. Piedmont Toma's wheel is 6–13⅞ in

Toma Piemontese

153

(15–35 cm) diameter and 1⁹/₁₆–4³/₄ in (40–120 mm) thick. It weighs between 4 lb and 17 lb 10 oz (1.8–8 kg). Fat content can be 40% but as high as 48%. The cheese itself is pale in colour with few air bubbles and its aroma and flavour become more intense with age, ranging from sweet and refined with young Toma to very full flavour and a strong smell with age. Many fresh white or fruity red wines are ideal with a young Toma but for the mature cheese a more mature wine such as a fine Gattinara is a better

TORTA DI GORGONZOLA

World famous modern creation that is known by a variety of names such as "Magor" (*ma*-scarpone and *gor*-gonzola) and "Gormas" (*gor*-gonzola and zzma-scarpone). This is a "cheesecake" made from alternate layers of soft gorgonzola and mascarpone cheese. It is an absolutely delicious dessert combined with pears or peaches.

Torta di Gorgonzola

TUMA D'LA PAJA

This delightful Italian cheese is all the rage in the USA where Americans are mad about it and it also

Layers of gorgonzola and mascarpone to form a "tart"

Italy still has a few traditional soft cheeses that are matured on straw

won the distinction of best cheese at the International Fancy Food Fair in New York. This is indeed a very unusual cheese that is made by a very small dairy co-operative concern based at Farigliano in Cuneo within Piedmont. Although this is not a truly craft-made cheese it is still superb. The cheese is a modern version of a traditional cheese that was formerly dried and matured by the shepherds and goatherds of Piedmont on beds of straw. The Piedmont word for straw is *paja* and the name "Tuma" has clear links with "Tomme" or "Toma."

Today's cheese is made with milk from cows (*mucca*) and sheep (*pecora*) rather than milk from goats or sheep. After natural rennet is added to coagulate the milk it forms a natural soft white crust that is slightly ribbed and covered in white mould, which is a sign of quality. The aroma is quite subtle but fresh with hints of musty cellars while the taste is quite extensive and richly creamy with clear suggestions of walnuts. This cheese demands a delicious fresh white wine, preferably from northern Italy, such as a Collio or Alto-Adige.

VALLE D'AOSTA FROMADZO DOC

In the extreme north-west of Italy in the Valle D'Aosta this cheese that was recently promoted to

Tuma d'la paja

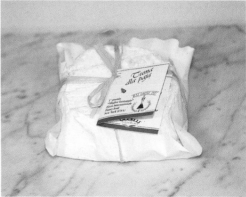

DOC status is made with unpasteurised cow's milk, although a little goat's milk is sometimes added. The milk used comes from at least two separate daily milkings and depending on the type of cheese to be made the milk may be semi-skimmed or skimmed. Fromadzo is an alliance of French *fromage* and Italian *formaggio* and this cheese is in reality a lighter version of Fontina that is made from full-cream milk. This Fromadzo is cylindrical but with slightly rounded top and bottom and fairly straight sides. The rind is straw-coloured to pale grey, depending on the age of the cheese. Some examples have occasional light red patches. The taste is somewhat similar to that of Fontina. Maturing time is sixty days but can be up to eight to ten months. The flavour intensifies with age.

Choose a Piedmont white or fruity red wine for the younger cheese but a full-bodied and mature red for older cheese.

VALTELLINA CASERA DOC

This mountain cheese from the Sondrio region of northern Italy is made with full-cream cow's milk that is not pasteurised. The milk used comes from Bruna Alpina cows that graze the mountain pastures. This semi-hard and medium fat cheese is produced in the form of wheels of 13⅞–17¾ in (35–45 cm) that are 3⅛–4 in (80–100 mm) thick and weight 15 lb 6 oz–26 lb 6 oz (7–12 kg). Fat content is 34% and the taste is milky and clearly reminiscent of mountain pasture. This is an excellent cheese for use in the kitchen and a superb cheese to serve at table.

Other cheeses

Italy has more than four hundred different types of cheese which it is not possible to review fully here. If you are visiting Italy I can recommend heartily that you seek out and try the following additional cheeses: Casolet della Val Camonica (Trentino, Lombardy), Silter della Val Camonica (Brescia), Bagòss di Bagolino (Brescia), Bettelmatt della Valdossola (Novara), Branzi dell'alta val Brembana (Bergamo), Bruss delle Langhe (Piedmont), Burrata delle murge (Basilicata), Cacioricotta Lucano (Puglia, Campania, Basilicata), Casieddu di Moliterno (Podenza), Casale de Elva/Elva (Piedmont), Formaggio di Fossa (Sogliano al Rubicone, Talamello), Formaio embriago (Trevisa), Graukäse della Valle Aurina (Sud-Tyrol), Paglierina di Rifreddo (Piedmont), Pecorino di Filiano (Podenza), Piacintinu di Enna (Sicily), Provula di Floresta (Sicily), Salato morbido (Friuli), and Scamorza (Molise).

France

France is the largest producer of cheese in terms of quality and diversity of cheese. Each region has its own specialities and cheese is simply an integral part of French life. Currently there are some five hundred different cheeses in France although with slightly different branded versions this increases to 750. Many French cheeses are exported.

At the present time the French dairy industry like those elsewhere is doing everything possible to make matters worse for the craft-made cheeses. Together with the Danish, British, German, Dutch, and Belgian diary industries they are trying to get the making of cheese with milk that is not pasteurised banned. The French dairy industry is busily engaged in undermining centuries of tradition in cheesemaking.

This is a disturbing case in which the bureaucrats of the European Commission – who are not always well informed – play an essential part through adopting measures often in panic and ignorance and also self-serving. It is no surprise at all that these measures threaten the end of the craft cheesemakers in favour of the large dairy concerns. Fortunately for true cheese lovers the battle is not yet over. Some cheeses have already more or less loss the struggle, such as Camembert and Epoisses but resistance is growing everywhere and consumers are becoming more quality conscious. French cheese ought to remain as it always has been: capricious, precocious and lively, and exciting to the last mouthful.

From cave dwellers to the Romans

Long before the influence of the Greeks and Romans, people living in present day France made simple cheese from the milk of sheep and goats which were soured naturally. This young moist cheese was allowed to drain in earthenware containers and was generally eaten while still fresh. Such cheese is now known in France as

Quality and tradition in French cheese

faisselle from the basket in which the cheese is drained and sold. The nomadic herders found from time to time that mould formed on their cheese and since food was scarce they also ate the mouldy cheese but found the cheese none the worse for it...

The process of making and keeping cheese was improved by the Greeks and a Feta-like cheese existed in southern France in the sixth century BC. The Greek's influence extended far into the interior of France. The Greeks travelled along the Rhône into what is now Burgundy from Antiopolis (Antibes), Massilia (Marseille), Nikaia (Nice), Agathé Tyché (Agde), and other trading posts along the Mediterranean coast. Wherever they went they influenced the local wine and cheese-making. In Roman times certain cheeses were extremely popular, such as the hard cheese of the Auvergne, and it appears that a blue sheep's-milk cheese from the southern chalk plateaux around present day Roquefort was also popular in Rome at the time of Julius Caesar.

The Romans and the monks

During the long period that the Gauls were subdued by the Romans they improved their cheeses and developed new ones. It is possible too with the arrival of the Romans that the Gauls switched from natural souring of the milk for their cheese to the use of vegetable or animal rennet or *coagulum*.

The famous monastic cheese of Port Salut

After the fall of the Roman empire the area that is France experienced a dark age that lasted until the Middle Ages. During this time it was monks who were mainly responsible for the maintenance and improvement of the old recipes and the monastery

The Romans enjoyed cheese

cheeses that later became known as Munster stem from this period.

During the holy wars many holy men sought safe shelter with the peasants in the countryside and recipes were exchanged, leading to the continuation of old traditional cheeses. The same happened once more during the French Revolution so that cheeses like Camembert were kept for posterity.

The present day

It is apparent from two comments made during World War II that cheese plays an important role in France and that it is important for all those who are lovers of French cuisine. Churchill remarked about the German occupation of France: "A country that gave the world some three hundred cheeses must not be defeated," and the Free French leader General de Gaulle referring to Hitler's subjection of his country added: "One cannot expect him to be able to govern a country that makes 365 different cheeses." Both these statements refer to the extraordinary diversity in cheese, many of which are solely of regional significance, but which collectively amount to a tremendous cultural heritage.

Unfortunately France has once again been subjected to all manner of attacks on its cultural existence since the late twentieth century. The arrival of supermarkets and hypermarkets even in the most remote parts of France has led to a uniformity and lowering of standards in what is sold and has led to many specialist suppliers disappearing.

Because the running of a specialist cheese shop is a highly skilled affair and skills cost money, many supermarkets kept their staff costs down by buying in from the big dairy concerns. Because these dairy concerns can offer product with a set sell by date, made from pasteurised or heat treated milk that is homogenised, the supermarkets also chose for a substantial levelling down in terms of flavour. This is understandable on the part of these large shops which depend on the speed of their throughput

but genuine lovers of cheese can only look on in dismay at these developments. In the final decades of the twentieth century the consumers were starting to become fed up with this loss of quality and individuality and specialist cheese shops started to experience a growth in their trade.

European community regulations have also done great harm to French cheese. New laws were created on the basis of research that was influenced by (and sometimes financed by) the big dairy concerns whose motives are clear.

I believe the consumer should be free to choose between traditional cheese and modern cheese made according to European community regulations.

The "danger" of untreated milk

The future is uncertain for the producers of traditional French cheese. Is the end of such cheeses in sight? Under pressure from the public and influenced by the major European food industry the bureaucrats of the European Community seem set to follow the American lead to a wholly hygienic world. The entire realm of French gastronomy is threatened if we do not resist this urge for uniformity. Countless organisations, cheese experts, food writers, leading lights from the restaurant world, and consumers are fighting the "hysterical attacks" on unpasteurised milk. It is not just France's gastronomic heritage that is at risk but also the jobs of more than 40,000 people.

By the drastic reduction of the permitted level of bacteria permitted in the area in which cheese is produced (the famous zero *Listeria monocytogene* rule) cheesemakers have been forced to take drastic measures such as micro-filtration, heat treatment, and pasteurisation) that not only eliminate pathogens but also eradicate other living organisms that impart much of the character in traditional cheese.

This is especially true of cheese made with milk that is not pasteurised, accounting for two thirds of the French cheeses with designated origin

A centuries old tradition of cheesemaking

Will making cheese by hand be forbidden?

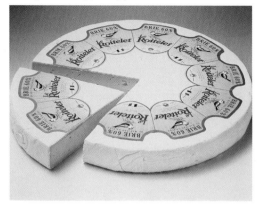

status. Without their living cultures of organisms these cheeses made with untreated milk will entirely lose their character. In reality unpasteurised milk is only potentially harmful to a small proportion of the population (those already ill or recovering from illness and pregnant women).

The French cheese families

The French categorise their cheese into a number of large families. The most important of these are described below.

FROMAGES FRAIS/FROMAGES BLANCS
These fresh or white cheeses are eaten young, often with salt and pepper but also with green vegetables. Fromage frais is also sold with sugar and fruit added.

PÂTES MOLLES CROÛTE FLEURIE
These soft cheeses with moulds growing on their rind are made with both cow's and goat's milk.

Fromage frais with herbs: Le Roulé

The cultures of white mould spread from the rind to the inner cheese and often create a downy layer on the outside of the cheese. Examples of this type

of cheese include Camembert, Brie, Coulommiers, and Bougon (goat's-milk cheese).

PÂTES MOLLES CROÛTE LAVÉE
These are soft cheeses which have a rind that is "washed". The washing referred to is a regular cleaning of the rind with a cloth or brush which has been moistened with brine and some other "secret" ingredients such as wine, hard liquor, and herbs or spices.
These "washed rind" cheeses always develop a distinctive aroma resulting from the breaking down of proteins in the rind. The flavour of this type of cheese is also considerably influenced by the choice of washing mixture. Examples of this type of cheese include Munster, Livarot, Maroilles, and Epoisses.

Soft cheese with washed rind

PÂTES PERSILLÉES/FROMAGES BLEUS

These cheeses have natural or cultured blue-green moulds and with the larger examples the mould is spread through the cheese by injecting it with probes. Examples include Roquefort, Bleu d'Auvergne, and Fourme d'Ambert.

Blue cheese

FROMAGE DE CHÈVRE

Most goat's-milk cheeses are made by hand on the farm. The best-known of them are those made with untreated milk from the Loire, Languedoc-Roussillon, Provence, and the Rhône valley. These cheeses are sold at varying stages of maturity from fresh and moist through creamy, to extremely hard. Examples include Crottin de Chavignol, St-Maure, Pouligny-St-Pierre, and Selles-sur-Cher.

Goat's-milk cheese

PÂTES PRESSÉES NON CUITES

These cheeses are made with curd that is not additionally heated before pressing such as Cantal, Salers, Reblochon, and St-Nectaire.

PÂTES PRESSÉES CUITES

Cheese made from heated curd (above 50°C/122°F), which is then pressed, such as Comté, Beaufort, and Abondance.

Heated and pressed curd

FROMAGES FONDUS

This category includes all the melted cheeses which in French have the name preceded by *Crème de.*

These cheese are created by mincing pressed cheese (whether made by heating or not) and then adding cream, butter, or milk powder. The mixture is heated with citric acid salt or phosphoric acid salt to improve the melting process and then moulding into the desired form, perhaps with the addition of nuts or sultanas.

All manner of other ingredients are added to these melted cheeses such as ham and garden herbs. This type of cheese is not dealt with further in this book.

Pressed but unheated curd

Keeping French cheese

There is no special difficulty attached to keeping semi-hard and hard cheese but taking good care of white mould cheeses, soft cheeses, and those with a washed rind demands greater attention. The best way to keep these cheeses is in a well ventilated cheese cellar, preferably on a bed of straw, at a temperature between 10–15°C (50–59°F) at a high level of humidity. Unfortunately few of us have such conditions available to us and furthermore few consumers dare to leave cheese to develop.

A good alternative is the refrigerator. Place the cheese in the salad tray because this is usually the least cold part of the fridge. Alternatively place the cheese in a special covered dish with ventilation. Keep the cheese in its original packaging and if using the salad tray do not place anything other than cheese in the tray.

Cheese kept in a refrigerator will not continue to develop so make sure you buy cheese from a specialist cheese shop that is at the stage of maturity you wish. Depending on the temperature of your refrigerator the cheese needs to be taken out of chilled storage fifteen minutes to an hour before serving. Do not take too much cheese out of the fridge at a time. Moist cheese made from unpasteurised milk that is out of the fridge for more than an hour needs to be consumed immediately or cooked as part of a dish. If the cheese is to be kept for cooking store it apart from the other cheese. With a little care you will be able to enjoy superb traditional French cheese throughout your life.

Appellation d'Origine Contrôlée (AC)

The notion of indicating the origin of a product in its name is an old one. The Greeks and Romans did it and others have followed their example. Most people know of Appellation Contrôlée or AC for wines that are made according to strict rules within a defined geographical area. The same approach is used for cheese. Certain cheeses are historically linked with a particular locality. They may be copied elsewhere but the result is never the same.

Cheeses which bear the AC mark of designated origin provide a certain guarantee that is perhaps of greater value than that of wine. These cheeses come from a defined area and have been made in accordance with strictly defined and legally enforceable rules. Unfortunately the AC designation does not provide any guarantee in respect of the transport or storage in the country to which the cheese is exported. For this reason it is best to buy such cheese from a specialist cheese shop.

The cheeses

Given the tremendous assortment of different French cheese this book has restricted the selec-

tion to the AC cheeses, the best-known non AC traditional cheeses, and a few modern branded cheeses.

Monastery cheeses (Abbaye de ...)

There are a number of craft-made monastery cheeses produced in France. These are rarely found outside the area in which they are made but are well worth seeking out and always individual in character.

ABBAYE DU MONT DES CATS
A speciality of the French part of Flanders made with unpasteurised cow's milk. The curd of this hard cheese is pressed but not heated and is then matured in baskets for one to two months. A mild-flavoured cheese that is delicious on bread for breakfast.

Drink a French of Belgian beer from Flanders with the mature cheese but for those preferring wine I suggest a red from the Loire, Burgundy, or even a Bordeaux.

ABBAYE DE BELLOC
Made on the slopes of the Pyrenees exclusively

Abbaye du Mont des Cats

from unpasteurised sheep's milk with rennet and salt. A superb cheese that is matured for at least six months.

Drink a local wine such as Pacherenc du Vic-Bilh, Jurançon, Tursan, or Irouléguy with this cheese.

ABONDANCE AOC
Abondance originates solely from the mountain pastures and farms of the Abondance valley and the Aravis mountain chain of Haute-Savoie at the foot of Mont Blanc. This cheese dates back to the fifth century when monks encouraged the Barbarian Burgundians to make cheese with the milk from their red spotted cows that they had brought with them. Cheese from the Abondance abbey was regularly served at the papal court in the fourteenth century. In the meantime the red spotted Burgundian cow that is known locally as

Abondance has been joined by two other breeds: Tarine and Montbéliarde.

Abondance is a soft cheese made with untreated cow's milk that is slightly heated and the curd pressed. It comes in the form of a wagon wheel of 15–17 in (38–43 cm) diameter that is 2³/₄–3¹/₈ in (70–80 mm) thick and weighs 15 lb 6 oz–26 lb 6 oz (7–12 kg). The rind is brownish-yellow to orange with a clear impression of the cloth in which the cheese was made. Genuine Abondance can be distinguished by the blue casein patches on the exterior of the cheese. The cheese itself is ivory to yellow, soft, supple, and slightly creamy with the occasional air bubble. The aroma is mild and pleasing and the flavour is fresh and pure with a suggestion of hazelnut in the finish. The minimum maturing time is ninety days and the cheese is available throughout the year. Connoisseurs however prefer the cheese made during summer which is then eaten at the end of the year. This summer cheese has a more subtle aroma and richer flavour as a result of the wild flowers and lush grass eaten by the cows. Fat content is 48%. Abondance is a multi-faceted cheese which is delicious in all manner of uses.

Because of the mild and subtle taste a light and equally subtle white wine is most suitable, such as

Abondance

a Swiss Savoie. Good alternatives include a Pinot Blanc from Alsace, or a mellow Mâcon Blanc, or white Beaujolais. For those preferring a red wine the best choice is a Swiss Savoie or a mellow wine from the Diois region.

AFFIDÉLICE AU CHABLIS

This cheese is also just known as Chablis. This is a local variant of Epoisses that is washed during maturing with Chablis instead of Marc de Bourgogne. The taste is milder than that of Epoisses or Munster and is quite delicious and creamy, melting in the mouth.

Burgundian fare with Affidélice au Chablis in the centre

Drink a glass of Chablis with this cheese but not an expensive one.

AISY CENDRÉ

This is more the name of a method of adding flavour to cheese than a cheese in itself. Young cheese such as Epoisses is placed in a basket of ash

Aisy Cendré

so that the creamy cheese acquires a distinctive taste, often without salt. It is difficult to combine this cheese with any wine.

Ami du Chambertin

AMI DU CHAMBERTIN
A craft-made variety of the many red bacteria cheeses that come from Burgundy. In common with Epoisses, this cheese is washed with water and Marc de Bourgogne during its period of at least four weeks maturing. Fat content is 50%.
A red Burgundy is a perfect accompaniment with examples that are not fully mature but a glass of Marc de Bourgogne is better once the cheese has developed its very strong aroma.

Superb cheese including Anneau du Vic-Bilh

Bouchons (corks) of Vic-Bilh

ANNEAU DU VIC-BILH
A ring-form goat's-milk cheese from south-western France that is soft, creamy, slightly salty, and a touch bitter. At its best when young, after ten to fifteen days.
Serve a dry Pacherenc di Vic-Bilh with this cheese. Don't imagine the hole in the middle is wasted cheese. The small cork-shaped cheese is sold by the appropriate name of Bouchon.

ARDI GASNA
A farm-made sheep's-milk cheese from the French Pyrenees made with unpasteurised milk from ewes of the black-headed Basque Manex breed. The sheep are fed solely on natural fodder of fresh mountain grass, clover, maize, and hay. The ewes spend the summer on the Iraty mountain at

Typical black-headed Basque Manex ewes.

4,265 ft (1,300 metres), where they are free to graze over large areas of very aromatic grass.
The craft-made Ardi Grasna (sheep's-milk cheese in Basque) is wheel-shaped and weighs 5 lb 8 oz–6 lb 10 oz (2.5–3 kg). This cheese is made without

Ardi Gasna, Basque sheep's-milk cheese

Ahuntz Gasna: Basque for goat's-milk cheese

Arômes au vin blanc

heating or pressing the curd. Ardi Grasna has a slender natural rind that develops through turning the cheese regularly, The cheese itself is dense and slightly elastic, mainly without air bubbles, but occasionally with indentations. The creamy colour is uniform. Through at least four months maturing in a cool damp place the cheese develops a mild nutty flavour. The young cheese (four months) tastes slightly of sheep's milk and the aroma is mild and slightly reminiscent of lactic acid. Later (after six months) the cheese acquires greater flavour and more character. The Basques prefer this cheese more mature at about one year old. They eat the then crumbly cheese in thin slices with cherry jam from Itxassou and drink a strong red Basque wine from Irouléguy with it.

There is also a goat's milk cheese, Ahuntz Gasna, from this same area of the Pyrenees.

ARÔME
Seasonal and local cheeses from the area around Lyon. The local cheeses such as Rigote, Pelardon, St-Marcellin etc. are placed in a basket in a barrel

of marc or moist wine sediment. The cheese absorbs the taste of the grape pips and skins and becomes stronger flavoured. These cheeses are known as Arômes aux gènes de marc. Similar treatment is given to St-Marcellin made with goat's milk but this is immersed in wine. These cheeses are very popular in restaurants around Lyon where they are known as Arômes au vin blanc.

With Arômes aux gènes de marc a glass of marc from the Rhône or Burgundy tastes delicious. Arômes au vin blanc combines well with a full-bodied white wine from the Mâconnais or Châlonnais.

BANON
Cheese bearing the Banon name is widely found

Arômes aux gènes de marc

Banon Fermier, made only with untreated goat's milk

both inside France and elsewhere but unfortunately many of these are mass-produced cheeses that bear little resemblance to craft-made Banon. The only similarity is the wrapping of chestnut leaves and straw. For those who search, especially in Provence, the traditional craft-made cheese can still be found. This is wholly made from unpasteurised goat's milk. Genuine Banon is bought while fresh and without flavouring of herbs and spices. Real Banon is not sharp in taste but mild, creaming, and heavenly.

Choose a fine white wine from Provence, a Cassis, Palette, or a good Côtes de Provence from the area around the Montagne-Ste-Victoire, e.g. a Mas de Cadenet.

BEAUFORT AOC

This cheese is named after the territory of Beaufort in Savoie but is also made in Tarentaise and Maurienne in Savoie and a small enclave in Haute-Savoie. Beaufort is a member of the Gruyère family and many connoisseurs regard it as the best of these cheeses. It is a typical mountain cheese that derives its aroma and flavour to the great diversity and richness of flowers in the alpine pastures of the Savoie.

The cows that provide the milk are Tarine and Abondance breeds that spend two thirds of the year in pasture at 2,600–8,200 ft (800 to 2,500 meters). The cheese is still solely made in the high summer quarters and the farms lower down by traditional means. Milk straight from the cows that is still warm is used and after coagulation and cutting the curd is heated in a large vessel until it forms a soft and unctuous mass. The curd is captured in a large cloth and then placed in wooden forms. Once it has been pressed, the young cheese is salted and matured for five to six months in well ventilated cool cellars.

These cheeses are shaped like a wagon wheel of 13³/₄–29¹/₂ in (35–75 cm) diameter of 4⁵/₁₆–6⁵/₁₆ in (11–16 cm) thickness, weighing 44–154 lb (20–70 kg). There is a blue casein patch on the rind on which the word Beaufort is imprinted with a code

Beaufort

for the cheesemaker. The rind is dry, pure, and firm. The cheese inside is dense, almost without air bubbles, but with occasional splits. The aroma is fresh and fruity and quite untainted while the flavour is very pleasant with a hint of hazelnut in its finish.

Fat content is 48%. Beaufort is at its tastiest in the autumn, winter, or spring and it makes a superb cheese for the end of a meal on a cheeseboard, but is also delicious eaten as a chunk on its own. It is widely used in cooking for gratin dishes, grated for pasta or risotto, or incorporated in flaky or choux pastry. It is also used of course in local fondue recipes.

Choose either a red or white wine with this cheese provided it is fresh and fruity and not too ponderous. Select a local wine such as those from Savoie, Diois, Switzerland, of the Valle d'Aosta.

Bleu de …/Fromage bleu

France has many different types and tastes of blue cheese of which several are dealt with here.

Bleu d'Auvergne

Several highly recommended blue cheeses that are omitted here include Bleu de Laqueuille (the Auvergne) and Petit Bayard (Dauphiné).

BLEU D'AUVERGNE AC

As the name indicates, this is a blue cheese from the Auvergne in central France. The territory of this cheese is spread across seven different *departements* including Cantal and Puy-de-Dôme. Bleu d'Auvergne was created in 1845

Naturally pure

through chance. A local cheesemaker called Antoine Roussel who had been apprenticed to a Normandy apothecary discovered that the texture of his cheese was too irregular, which made it difficult to sell. The white cow's milk cheese quickly started to turn mouldy but the frugal Roussel did not throw the mouldy cheese away but ate it himself. When he discovered in 1854 that his stale rye bread also turned mouldy he injected the mould into his cheese with a needle. The result was outstanding. Since that time the method has been consistently improved. This *fromage façon Roquefort* quickly became successful in the Auvergne and later throughout France. Over the years the manual craft production has gradually been replaced by more industrial processes and since 1955 there has not been any craft-made Bleu d'Auvergne.

To make Bleu d'Auvergne pasteurised milk (or more rarely unpasteurised milk) has a culture of *Penicillium roqueforti* added to it and it is then warmed. After coagulation the immature white curd is cut, carefully agitated, separated from the whey, and then placed in forms. After draining for two days the cheeses are salted in pairs by hand so that only one side of the cheese is salted. The

Bleu d'Auvergne

cheese is then injected with probes to encourage the veins to form throughout the cheese. This is assisted by ensuring the cheese is well ventilated. For a considerable time the culture was achieved by allowing rye bread to turn mouldy before baking the bread to dry it out and then grinding it to breadcrumbs. Since 1975 though pure cultures of the mould have been used. The cheese is matured at a temperature in the range 7–9°C (44.6–48.2°F) at humidity of 100%. Small cheeses (up to 2 lb/ 1 kg) mature in three weeks and those of more than this in four weeks in cool cellars. Larger wheels of Bleu d'Auvergne of 8 in (20 cm) diameter are 3^{1}/$_{8}$– 4 in (80–100 mm) thick and weigh 4 lb 6 oz– 6 lb 10 oz (2–3 kg). The smaller ones are 4^{1}/$_{8}$ in (10.5 cm) diameter and weigh 12 oz, 1 lb, or 2lb (350, 500 grams or 1 kg). The cheese is protected by silver foil for transport and to prevent it drying out. The rind is thick, rough, and covered with white grey-blue, and orange moulds. The cheese itself is dense with many dark green to blue veins and indentations of mould. The texture is both firm and creamy while the aroma is quite strong. The taste is also strong and well developed and very characteristic of the cheese. Fat content is 50%. Bleu d'Auvergne is an excellent cheese to conclude a meal but also enjoyable with a drink. It is ideal on toast (made creamy with a little butter), in choux pastry, quiches, as pizza topping, in cheese soufflés, added to pasta, in salads (with walnuts), on pancakes, in short a multi-faceted cheese.

On toast with an aperitif or as a snack with a drink it combines well with a mollifying full-bodied wine. Choose a Rivesaltes Ambré, delicious oloroso sherry, or a white meio seco port. After a meal drink a robust and rustic red such as a traditional St-Pourçain, Côtes d'Auvergne, Boudes, Marcillac, Madiran, Gaillac, Cahors, Rhône, or even a Burgundy. For those preferring sweet white

Bleu d'Auvergne

wines then choose a Moelleux or Liquoreux one from Bergerac, Ste-Croix-du-Mont, Loupiac, Cadillac, Cérons, or Jurançon. Delicious sweet fortified wines with this cheese include Maury, Banyuls, or Rivesaltes/Grenache Tuilé.

Boursault

Any mellow fruity red or white wine combines well with this cheese.

BOURSIN

A branded mass-produced cheese made from cow's milk that is enriched with cream and flavoured with garlic and herbs and spices.

Boursin

BREBIOU

A fine modern sheep's-milk cheese that is surprisingly tasty, creamy, appetising and attractive! Fat content is 50% of dry matter, 42% in total. Drink a white wine from south-west France e.g. from Languedoc-Roussillon.

BREBIS

The collective name *brebis* or "ewe" covers a range from craft-made shepherd's cheese to semi-mass produced ones and from creamy farm-made sheep's-milk cheese to large and extremely hard mountain cheeses. They can be encountered in every mountain region. Some of them are made at just one farm or in a particular village. If possible choose from the craft-made cheeses.

BREBIS DES PYRÉNÉES

A collective name for various sheep's-milk cheeses from the Pyrenees. The well-known sheep's-milk cheeses such as Ossau-Iraty and Ardi Gasna are described separately but virtually every valley, village, and shepherd has its or his or her own Brebis des Pyrénées. The best of them are the craft-made cheeses like Laruns, Ossau-Laruns, and Ossau Fermier.

Cayolar, the summer quarters of the Basque shepherds in Iraty

Brie

Brie is a region to the south-east of Paris where many different types of white mould cheeses are made. Common or garden Brie is not a protected

Brebiou

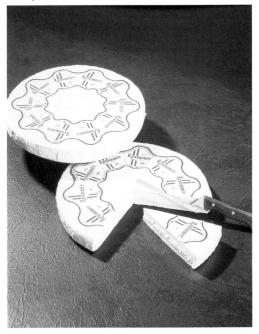

name and may be made anywhere but there is also craft-made Brie such as Coulommiers and the AC Brie de Meaux and Brie de Melun.

Farm-made Brie de Meaux, with real character!

BRIE FERMIER

Farm-made Brie cheese is still made throughout Brie. These are smaller (12⅝ "/32 cm) versions of Brie de Meaux that are mainly sold at local markets. The rind has white mould and a few patches of red. The taste is exceptionally fully developed and mature. Drink a robust red wine or a white Alsace wine such as Pinot Gris or Gewürztraminer with this cheese.

BRIE ARTISANAL DE COULOMMIERS

The *Brie artisanal* cheeses such as those of Coulommiers (probably the original form of all

Brie) are generally smaller at 8–12 in (20–30 cm) diameter than Brie de Meaux. They are often milder too than Brie de Melun, de Meaux, and *Brie fermier*.

A fine Burgundy is recommended with sufficient finesse and rounded character to flatter the cheese, such as a Givry or a Rhône Hermitage or from Bordeaux a St-Emilion, Pomerol, or St-Julien. For those preferring white then choose the same wine from Alsace one would drink with Camembert or a Chardonnay or Blancs de blancs from Champagne.

BRIE DE MEAUX AC

Although the town of Meaux can be regarded as the epicentre of the area in which this cheese may be produced, the Brie de Meaux territory is quite extensive, encompassing the entire *departement* of Seine-et-Marne and parts of the *departements* of Aube, Loiret, Marne, Haute-Marne, Meuse, and Yonne. The historical origins of Brie are not entirely clear but it is certain that the cheese has existed for four or five centuries. Many gastronomes describe Brie de Meaux as the queen of cheeses. Brie de Meaux became the people's cheese after the French Revolution but the elite continued to enjoy it in secrecy. The cheese acquire an international reputation in the late nineteenth century.

Brie de Meaux and Brie de Melun are both produced on farms in the same traditional manner. After the slow coagulation of the cow's milk the curd is carefully scooped out into the moulds with a slotted spoon. While the cheeses are draining they are carefully turned several times and salted by hand. Both these types of Brie mature for at least four weeks (generally six to eight).

Brie de Meaux is a flat disc of 13¾–14⁹⁄₁₆ in (35–37 cm) about 1 in (25 mm) thick, weighing 5 lb 12 oz (2.6 kg), making it larger than Brie de Melun. Brie de Meaux is never covered with packaging but is presented in a box on a bed of straw. The rind is extremely thin and is often covered with a downy film of white mould with the occasional reddish-orange patch. The cheese itself is the colour of straw, is soft, creamy but compact, unctuous and yet never runny. The aroma is both well developed

Brie de Meaux

and delicate while the taste is slightly sweet with a tinge of hazelnut. The cheese is at its best in summer, autumn, and winter but do not allow it to become too warm while carrying it home in summer. Fat content is 45%. Brie de Meaux is delicious in its own right, at the end of a meal, or with a late evening drink but it is also excellent in salads, on toast, or for gratin dishes.

Drink a good Chardonnay from the Auxerrois or Chablis but best of all is a Blanc de blancs from Champagne. Those favouring red wine are recommended to try a Pinot Noir or Merlot but neither too young or too strong in tannin.

BRIE DE MELUN AC

Just as with Meaux, Melun is the centre of the production area for this version of Brie, although the cheese is made in precisely the same territory as Brie de Meaux. Brie de Melun was formerly solely made on the farms but today it comes from small craft-style cheese producers. The cheesemaking is similar to that of Brie de Meaux but at a slower pace, especially in the beginning and final phase. The coagulation of the milk occurs at a lower temperature (maximum 30°C/86°F) so that the milk sours naturally first through the lactic acid. The cheese is matured for at least four weeks but in practice much longer. Brie de Melun is flat and rounded with a diameter of 10⅝ in (27 cm) and thickness of 1³/₁₆ in (30 mm), weighing about 3 lb 5 oz (1.5 kg). The cheese has a definite rind that is rough and covered with white mould and patches and stripes of reddish-orange. The cheese itself is more yellow than Brie de Meaux, very elastic, but denser and firmer than Brie de Meaux. The aroma is more fully developed and somewhat more rustic with suggestions of hay, cellars, stables, and fungi. The taste is also more fully developed and fruitier. Fat content is 45%. This cheese is at its best in summer, autumn, and winter. Brie de Melun has a precocious, fairly rustic character with a less broad culinary range of uses than Brie de Meaux or ordinary Brie. It is superb though in choux pastry and it at its best at the end of a meal with some farmhouse bread. Drink a red wine such

Brie de Melun

as a Pinot Noir from Côteaux Champenois or an Irancy or red Burgundy from Auxerrois or Alsace. A Rhône wine is also a possibility.

BRILLAT-SAVARIN

Brillat-Savarin was one of the greatest French gastronomes of any age so it is not surprising that this extremely creamy cheese appeals to most gourmets. This is no slimmer's cheese at more than 75% fat content, which the French refer to a *triple-crème*. In order to make this cheese so creamy, additional cream is added during the cheesemaking process. This is a relatively modern cheese from Normandy which is a very popular addition to the gourmet cheeseboard. The cheese is round with a diameter of at least 4 in (100 mm). It is matured for one to three weeks and is very soft and creamy with a mild aroma and creamy taste that is almost buttery.

This cheese combines well with a fresh white wine

Brillat-Savarin

possessing sufficient acidity and full-bodied taste such as those from Alsace or a German Riesling or Sauvignon Blanc from the Loire. Another delicious partnership is formed with a glass of chilled Normandy brut cider. For those preferring a red it is best to select a more mellow Bordeaux or Burgundy.

BRIN D'AFFINOIS

A soft cheese with a varied rind that is washed and covered with white mould. The cheese itself is soft, creamy, and fresh. A branded cheese from one of France's most successful dairy companies. Maturing time is two weeks and fat content is 50%. Delicious with a glass of red Burgundy or Beaujolais.

BRIQUE .../BRIQUETTE ...

These names refer to the brick or block like shape of these cheeses. There are many local varieties of these soft, creamy cheeses that are produced on a craft scale or by semi-industrial processes. The most recommended of them is Briquette du Forez. The best choice for these cheeses is a Côtes de Forez or wines from the Roannais or Lyonnais.

Brocciu, Broccio, or Brousse

BROCCIU CORSE/BROCCIU AOC

Corsican Brocciu is made from whey in the manner of Ricotta. The remaining whey is used to make this hard cheese from sheep's milk that is not pasteurised. The whey is heated to 35°C (95°F), salted, and supplemented with full-cream milk to a maximum of 10–15% of the total volume. The mixture is then stirred and heated to 90°C (194°F) which causes the albumin protein in the whey to coagulate. These flakes of milk protein are collected and drained. Brocciu is a craft-made farm product that can be eaten throughout the year. In France it is known as "Broccio."

There is no minimum maturing period for this cheese and it is mainly eaten fresh within forty-eight hours of being made but it can be matured and it is sometimes rolled in pepper or dried herbs and spices. The moist fresh cheese is traditionally

Brin d'Affinois

sold in reed baskets while the firmer but still moist cheese is formed into a curved and irregular cylinder, a small straight cylinder, or a flattened ball. The weights vary from approx. 1 lb (500 grams) to 2 lb (1 kg). Fat content is 40–50%. Young, fresh Brocciu is widely used as filling for cannelloni, crepes, or pastries. The mature cheese is delicious for lunch with some farmhouse loaf, tomatoes, and olives. Drink a simple but not too dry white wine with fresh Brocciu and with the more mature cheese select a robust Corsican wine or a red from Provence, the Rhône, or Languedoc-Roussillon.

CAMEMBERT DE NORMANDIE AC

The origin of Camembert is unknown but there are all manner of stories of cheeses relating to the village of Camembert, the oldest of which date from 1554. A certain Marie Harel is named as the creator

Lid of a Camembert box

of this cheese and her statue adorns the picturesque Normandy village although Marie Harel was not yet born in 1554. The man behind the famous wooden box that dates from 1890, an engineer called Ridel, is certainly known. He developed the wooden boxes so that the cheese could be transported further afield, which increased its fame.

The cheese was originally only made on farms but through its tremendous popularity small-scale production plants were established to reproduce the cheese even far from Normandy. It was not until 1983 that the genuine Normandy Camembert gained protection through AC status but this only applies to the original and genuine article made from unpasteurised milk (*au lait cru*) that is spooned into its form (*moulé à la louche*). Commonplace Camembert copies can be made anywhere in France but also in Germany, Denmark, the United Kingdom, Canada, the USA, and Australia. For many people Camembert is simply a commonplace supermarket cheese but those who have sampled genuine Camembert de Normandie (the only Camembert AC) made with milk that is not pasteurised from cows grazing in Normandy will never regard this cheese as commonplace. Unfortunately it is increasingly diffi-

cult to find genuine farm-made Camembert and you will never find one outside Normandy itself. Most AC Camembert is made by craft or semi-craft means by farmer's co-operatives or dairy concerns but by the traditional means. Genuine Camembert de Normandie AC is only be made in the Normandy *departements* of Calvados, Eure, Manche, Orne, and Seine-Maritime. Mass-produced Camembert without AC designation can be made anywhere. Mass-produced article is often preferred by "the masses" who like their cheese creamy and mild tasting. Most are sweet while the genuine is salty.

Real Camembert de Normandie AC is made with semi-skimmed unpasteurised milk heated to 37°C (98.6°F) transferred to large containers of 100 litres (approx. 26 gallons) rennet is added. Once coagulated the curd is scooped out with a special slotted spoon into perforated forms. Once the form is filled the air is removed by striking the mould on a hard surface and after the cheese has drained for four or five hours the cheese is turned. The following day the mould is removed. Previously the formation of the mould was left to nature but now the cheese is sprayed with solutions containing three different types of *Penicillium candidum camembertii* mould. Following this the cheese is salted at a

Heat treated Camembert: tasty but not AC status

temperature of 18–20°C (64.4–68°F). On the third day the cheeses are moved to a large storage space where they are kept at a constant temperature of 13°C (55.4°F) and humidity of 85% for twelve days. The cheese has by this time acquired a downy covering of white mould. Camembert is further matured for another twenty-one days of which at least sixteen must be at the place they were produced. The cheeses are turned every forty-eight hours to encourage the growth of the downy coating. The best examples are matured for another week on a board before being sold. Camembert develops its full flavour between thirty and thirty-five days after the curd is first formed, at which point the heart of the cheese still contains a small layer of immature cheese and the outside of the cheese exhibits some pale red patches. The cheese itself is ivory-coloured and slightly elastic. Runny Camembert contains too much water. The aroma is of a good cheese cellar, slightly earthy, but never of ammonia. The taste is mild, fruity (hazelnut), somewhat rustic and earthy, sometimes a bit peppery, with a hint of salt. Mass-produced Camembert's fat content is less than 40% but traditional cheese is 45%. Good Camembert forms a regular circle of 4$\frac{1}{8}$–4$\frac{1}{2}$ in (105–115 mm) about 1$\frac{3}{16}$ in (30 mm) thick. The weight of these cheeses that are packed in the well-known wooden boxes is approx. 8$\frac{7}{8}$ oz (250 grams). The dimensions and weights are prescribed in law. Large double-thickness and especially creamy Camembert for slicing is therefore never the genuine article with AC status.

Serve the real Camembert made with unpasteurised milk at room temperature (18°C/64.4°F). Choose a good red wine from the Rhône or Beaujolais for a Camembert that is not over mature

The best-known Camembert from Isigny

or a mellow Merlot from the Libournais, a young Pinot Noir from Burgundy, or a red Touraine. Some firm dry whites combine surprisingly well with a creamy Camembert. With the more mature Camemberts the choice of wine is more difficult but a glass of brut cider or calvados is always suitable.

CAMEMBERT AU CIDRE

The full official name is *Camembert affiné au cidre*. The recipe for this cheese is remarkably simple but the end result is determined by the quality of ingredients used. A whole immature farm-made (and unpasteurised) Camembert, rind and all, is dipped in good quality apple cider for fifteen days. The cheese absorbs the apple flavour and aroma but the cheese remains very creamy. The apple cider fragrance is not strident but does excite the nose.

Drink a dry farmhouse cider with this cheese.

CAMEMBERT AU CALVADOS

In reality only the *coeur de Camembert* or hart of the cheese is used for this delicacy. The rind and outer part of the cheese is removed before the

heart is immersed in the classic Normandy apple brandy known as calvados. Following this the cheese is covered with breadcrumbs. The aroma of this cheese is quite pronounced and the outside of this cheese has a fairly strong flavour. It is also salty and somewhat granular. The inner part of this treated cheese is soft and creamy.

Do not try wine with this cheese but drink either a strong farm cider or a good calvados liqueur.

CANCOILLOTTE

This too is a cheese speciality rather than a cheese in itself. The delicacy is made in Franche-Comté, between the Jura and Alsace. The basis of this speciality is *metton*, the curd from cow's milk, that is first carefully coagulated with the help of lactic acid. The curd is then heated to 60°C (140°F), pressed, and agitated and then left to ferment. The *metton* is then melted, salted, and layered with butter, garlic, and white wine to create a sort of fondue. The cooled mass is then placed in jars or cans. The creamy but no longer liquid mass has a very distinctive flavour. Cancoillotte is spread on bread and also eaten with hot potatoes baked in the jackets and local sausage delicacies from the Jura.

CANTAL AC

This famous cheese from the Auvergne comes from the department of Cantal and parts of Aveyron, Corrèze, Haute-Loire, and Puy-de-Dôme. Cantal has been made for two thousand years and once was made by farmers who survived the winter in remote parts with large stocks of cheese in summer to last them all winter. These cheeses were so popular with the Romans that they took supplies with them on their voyages to Britannia. The French insist that Cantal is the precursor of Cheddar. Until 1910 this cheese was solely made by farmers but is now increasingly produced by dairy concerns. The best Cantal is made with milk from the native Salers cows that have a fine coat and striking horns. The taste is largely due to the tender grass and many mountain flowers and herbs such as gentian, arnica, liquorice, saxifrage, anemone etc.

It takes 10 litres (21 pints) of milk to produce one kilogram (2 lb 3 oz) of Cantal cheese. The milk is heated to 32° (89.6°F) and rennet is added. The immature curd is cut and agitated thoroughly and separated from the whey. In order to achieve a fine texture for the cheese and to remove as much whey as possible the immature cheese is cut several more times and pressed. The immature cheese (*tomme*) is placed in a large storage area for about eight hours at a temperature of 12–15°C (53.6–59°F) to allow

Cancoillotte

Cantal–one of France's oldest cheeses

the lactic acid to do its work. The immature cheese is then cut once more, dipped in brine and returned to the same storage space. Eventually the chunks of curd are pressed in moulds to form cheeses that are 19¹¹/₁₆ in (50 cm) tall with a diameter of almost 15 in (38 cm). The cheese is pressed for forty-eight hours during which time the pressure is gradually increased. After pressing, the cheese is placed in cellars to mature at a temperature of 10–12°C (50–53.6°F) and humidity of 90% for from thirty days up to a year. While the cheese is maturing its rind is constantly brushed and turned twice each week. The cheeses are sold at three stages, as young, mature, or extra mature (old) cheese. The eventual weight varies between 77 and 99 lb (35–45 kg). Both mass-produced pasteurised and unpasteurised varieties of Cantal exist. The factory-made version is generally made in a smaller size as Petit Cantal of 33–44 lb (15–20 kg) and Cantalet of 17 lb 10 oz–26 lb 6 oz (8–12 kg). Fat content is 45%. Young Cantal is mainly fed to children or incorporated in dishes. Both of the more mature types are also used in cooking but are also ideal to serve at table.

Select a fresh and fruity red wine such as Côtes du Forez, Côtes Roannaises, Côtes d'Auvergne, Chantargue, Boudes, Châteaugay, Madargue, St-Pourçain, or another Gamay or Pinot Noir.

CANTAL JEUNE/DOUX
This young cheese has a light rind that is thin and greyish-white. The cheese is ivory in colour and has a mild and milky taste. Must be at least thirty days old.

CANTAL ENTRE-DEUX/DORÉ
This cheese is literally "between young and old." The rind is thicker and pale golden. The taste is initially fresh and mild but is stronger in its finish. You will detect hints of wild herbs from the pasture, including the bitterness of gentian. Between two and six months old.

CANTAL VIEUX/CANTAL DE CARACTÈRE
This extra mature or old cheese has been matured somewhat longer. It has a very thick rind that is

Caprice des Dieux

attractively marked by reddish-orange mould patches and the cheese itself is also darker. The taste is stronger, more rustic, and breathes the power of the land from which it has come, with salty and nutty undertones. A cheese for the connoisseur that is at least six months old.

CAPRICE DES DIEUX
A modern branded cheese developed in the 1950s that is best known for its creaminess and unusual

Delicious Carré de l'Est washed down with eau-de-vie

shape. Beneath the thin rind that is covered with white mould the cheese is very soft, creamy, and unctuous. This cheese is adored by those who prefer a cheese without any bite. They are made in varying sizes but the most common size is 9 oz (250 grams) measuring about 4¹/₂ by 2³/₈ by 1⁵/₈ in (115 x 60 x 41 mm). Virtually any mild and fruity wine can be drunk with this cheese.

CARRÉ DE L'EST
A rectangular hybrid of a Munster and Coulommiers that is made on medium to mass scale. It can be tasty.

CHABICHOU DU POITOU AC
Chabichou is the local name for a goat's-milk cheese, possibly derived from Arabic from the time when the Moors had reach Poitiers where they

A mature Chabichou du Poitou

were resisted in 732 by Charles Martel. *Chabi* is probably a bastardisation of the Arabic *chebli* for "goat." Poitou is the region around the town of Poitiers. The grass that the goats graze is grown on chalk and this is reflected in the freshness of the cheese. Only cheese made according to strict rules governing the origins and quality of the full-cream goat's milk is permitted as AC Chabichou du Poitou. The most delicious is that made from untreated full-cream goat's milk in the traditional manner by spooning the curd into the mould, known as Chabichou du Poitou *au lait cru, moulé à la louche*. Chabichou du Poitou is conical in shape with a diameter of 2–2³/₈ in (50–60 mm), about 2³/₈ in (60 mm) high, and weighs about 5⁵/₈ oz (150 grams) after ten days maturing. The rough rind of the young cheese is covered with grey-blue mould while older cheese, and especially those made with milk that is not pasteurised, can show pale orange to red patches. The cheese is hard but can be crumbly when mature. The aroma is reminiscent of goat's milk while the taste is mild, creamy, fresh, and slightly salty. Fat content is 50%

Fresh Chabichou du Poitou

with unpasteurised versions and 45% with others. The non pasteurised cheese is at its best in late summer and autumn. Chabichou is an ideal cheese to serve at table. When young it is great with French bread but when mature is better at the end of a fine

Chabis is sold under many names

meal. Choose a fresh white wine as accompaniment, preferably a Sauvignon Blanc from Haut-Poitou or a similar wine from Touraine.

CHABIS
This is a collective name for various goat's-milk cheeses from the Loire valley that are always worth

Chamois d'Or

considering. Drink a dry white Loire wine with them, preferably a Sauvignon Blanc.

CHAMOIS D'OR
A modern branded cheese of pasteurised cow's milk. The soft rind is covered with white mould. The cheese is dense, smooth, creamy, and mild and ideal cheese for beginners. Fat is 60%. Choose a not too dry white Loire wine.

CHAOURCE AC
Connoisseurs consider Chaource to be one of France's tastiest cheeses. This cheese comes from Champagne and the Auxerrois, the area around Chablis, Tonnerre, and Auxerre. Chaource is made with full-cream milk from cows that graze lush green pastures.
After coagulation the curd is allowed to drain in its form and the immature cheese is then salted. The young cheeses dry on mats of rye straw where they

Chaource

mature for at least two weeks. This cheese is sold in two sizes: the smaller weighs approx. 7 oz (200 grams) measuring 3 1/8 by 2 3/8 in (80 x 60 mm), while the larger ones are approx. 1 lb (450 grams) and 4 5/16 by 2 3/8 in (110 mm x 60 mm). Both have at least 50% fat content.

Chaource has a thin white rind spotted with red as it matures with fine white soft cheese inside. The cheese should never become runny (a sign of too

Enjoy delicious Chaource

much water remaining in the curd). The aroma should not be overpowering and certainly not tend towards ammonia. Good Chaource smells of fresh cream and field mushrooms (*Psalliota campestris*). The taste is luxuriant, creamy, mild but fresh, with a hint of hazelnut. The most tasty of these cheeses are made with milk that is not pasteurised (*au lait cru*).

Drink a Champagne or a young Chablis with this cheese or a fruity white or red Burgundy such as an Irancy.

CHAROLAIS

A small cylindrical cheese from Burgundy that is made with a mixture of unpasteurised milk from cows and goats. Delicious, mild, and from fresh to rock hard. Choose a red Beaujolais or Burgundy.

Chaumes, the modestly smelly cheese

CHAUMES

A renowned modern branded cheese from the south-west of France. It is a soft cheese of cow's milk with a washed rind. The taste varies from mild and creamy to slightly sharp, depending on the

Fresh goat's-milk cheese

Fresh goat's-milk cheese

A roll of mature goat's-milk cheese

maturity of the cheese, but is never really strong. Choose a good mellow dry to sweet white wine from the south-west of France such as a Jurançon, Haut-Montravel, or Rosette. For those who prefer red wine try a Bergerac, Marmandais, Frontonnais, or Tursan.

Bûche literally means "stump"

Banon-like goat's-milk cheese

Chevrotin des Aravis

CHÈVRE/FROMAGE DE CHÈVRE

There are many different goat's-milk cheeses, some well-known, others not, available throughout France or perhaps locally from just one farm. They are made with both pasteurised and untreated goat's milk and some include cow's milk. These cheeses come in all forms from a dished (Apérobic), a small barrel, a cork, a plaited cone, pyramid, disc, heart, bell, "horse-droppings", rectangular, semi-circular, oval, in a roll, or even in the form of a Camembert (Bougon). They are sold plain or with mould, coated in ash, or pepper...too many varieties to mention. Chevrotin des Aravits deserves a mention for this superb cheese with washed rind from Savoie. Fantastic semi-hard mountain cheeses are made of goat's milk in the Pyrenees, such as Bethmale.

COMTÉ AC

Famous Comté cheese originates in eastern France in the Jura – the departments of Doubs, Jura, and Nord-Ain. The name is derived from the province of Franche-Comté to the south of Alsace.

Comté cheese has a long history and was made in the Jura long ago by the Celts and the Sequani, later inhabitants of Champagne and the Seine valley. In the thirteenth century these large cow's milk cheeses were known as *Vachelin* from the French word *vache* for cow. Comté is made with milk from the Montbéliarde and Abondance breeds of cow that is not pasteurised. These cows graze high pastures and produce quality milk which is always made into cheese with twenty-four hours. Storage of the milk is prohibited. Once coagulated, the curd is cut, agitated and heated in a copper vessel to 54°C (129.2°F) for at least forty-five minutes. The curd is placed in moulds and pressed for at least

Superb Comté cheese with a green band

twenty hours. Following this the cheeses are removed from their forms and are then salted by hand, and regularly brushed and turned. Maturing lasts for at least four months and averages a year. Note the side of the cheese where the quality is indicated. Average quality cheese has a brown band while the best ones bear a green band and a cow bell. The cheese is a large wheel with straight or slightly curved sides of 15¾–27¾ in (40–70 cm) diameter with a thickness of 3⁹⁄₁₆–5 in (90–130 mm). The weight is 66–121 lb (30–55 kg). The rind is yellow to brown, slightly granular, and dry. Because no additives are allowed, colour varies

Four-month-old Comté

according to season and location. Winter cheese, when more hay is eaten, is straw yellow while the summer cheese (more grass and flowers) is a richer yellow. Although dense it is fairly supple and elastic. The aroma and flavour vary with age and

Seven-month-old Comté

Ten-month-old Comté

season. Young cheese tastes of fresh milk and is milder than the sharper mature cheese. Winter cheese has a more burnt aroma including hazelnut and hay while the summer cheese smell of grass and alpine and meadow flowers. Fat content is 45%.

Young Comté is tasty on bread, in toasted sandwiches, grated on pasta, used for gratin dishes, in salads, for fondue and so on. The more mature cheese is perfect to conclude a meal but is also ideal for gratin topping for poultry or even fish and shellfish. Any good wine will do this cheese but for the *terroir* choose a delicious Crémant de Jura. After a meal with drink a *vin jaune* from the Jura, or a red or rosé from Pupillin, or choice of white or red Arbois, or Côtes de Jura.

CORSE

Corsica has many different types of cheese but these are generally only available on the island. Ranging from fresh or mature, moist or rock hard, and mild to very sharp. Most cheese is made from sheep and/or goat's milk. Fermier de Brebis, Niolo, Tomme Corse, and Venaco are highly recommended.

COULOMMIERS

From the same family as Brie and Camembert and regarded as the common ancestor. Avoid confusion with Brie de Coulommiers. This cheese is rarely sold outside of France. Coulommiers resembles a small but Brie and it originates from the area around the town of Coulommiers in Brie. The cheese has a diameter of 5–6 in (125–150 mm) and usually 1⁹⁄₁₆ in (40 mm) thick. Pasteurised versions of this cheese are available year round while the farm-made variety is only available in later summer. The rind is white with red spotting. The cheese itself is less creamy than Brie and the local people find it at its most tasty before the cheese becomes

Coulommiers

runny. The flavour is well-developed, somewhat sweet, freshly acidic, with a hint of almond. This cheese is tasty on fresh bread. Serve a fruity red from Burgundy or the Loire with this cheese.

CROTTIN DE CHAVIGNOL/CHAVIGNOL AC

Crottin is derived from Latin *crusta* or crust that in modern French is known as croûte. The Romans called the crust which forms as mud dries *crusta luti* from *lutum* (mud). Simple earthenware objects were made out of mud, including the *crottet* a container for draining cheese that has coarse channels to allow the whey to drain. This local type of goat's-milk cheese acquired its name from the earthenware in which the curd was drained.

Chavignol is a village in the Sancerrois, the area surrounding the town of Sancerre on the Loire. The cheese though is permitted to be made in a larger area that includes almost the entire department of Cher and parts of Loiret and Nièvre. Crottin is made with very fresh full-cream goat's milk. After a slow coagulation lasting twenty-four to forty-eight hours the curd is suspended in a cloth to drain. The curd is subsequently scooped into forms and further whey drains off. The immature cheese is then removed from the form and salted and matured for at least ten days. The small cheeses are ball-like with a diameter of 1⁹/₁₆–2 in (40–50 mm) and about 1³/₁₆–1⁹/₁₆ in (30–40 mm) thick. They weigh about 2 oz (60 grams). As these small cheeses mature they lose moisture and become harder and smaller.

The exterior can be coated in white and or blue mould that does not harm the cheese but does add to the taste. The cheese itself is quite fine, pure, and smooth, and is airy when young but crumbly and hard with older ones. The aroma of the young cheese is reminiscent of cream and fresh goat's milk while the older cheese invokes memories of fallen leaves in a wood in autumn and mushrooms. The strength of both the fragrance and flavour of this cheese varies according to the season. Spring cheese is the mildest and autumn cheese the strongest. The texture varies between very creamy and melting on the tongue with young cheese to crumbly and rock hard with old cheese. The best time is March to November. Fat content is not less than 45%.

Crottin de Chavignol is often eaten as a quick snack for local farm workers and those working in the vineyards and wineries. Outside the area the cheese is mainly eaten as part of a cheeseboard at the end of a meal. The combination of this goat's-milk cheese with red wine is often not very pleasing. Only the really mature old cheese can be combined with a red wine if you really insist and then it is best to choose a Pinot Noir from Sancerre or a Côteaux du Giennois. The younger cheeses really demand a fresh white wine such as a Sancerre Chavignol or Sancerre, Quincy, Reuilly, Menetou-Salon, Pouilly-Fumé, or Côteaux du Giennois.

CURÉ NANTAIS

A cheese made from Pasteurised cow's milk from Pays de Nantes. It is a local and strong-tasting variety of the old traditional St-Paulin. Choose a local white wine such as Gros Plant du Pays Nantais or a Muscadet.

Curé Nantais

DAUPHIN

A cheese for those who love strong sensations. This cheese gets its name from its shape of a dolphin. It is said that the name was granted by Louis XV when he was the *dauphin* or crown prince because he found it delicious. This is a cheese product

Dauphin cheese for slicing without its traditional dolphin shape

Crottin de Chavignol

rather than a cheese that is made from remnants of white Maroilles that are ground and mixed with pepper, cloves, parsley, and tarragon. The mixture is matured for three to four months, during which time the rind is regularly washed to give the cheese its eventual strong aroma and taste. Delicious with a robust brown ale or stout.

DREUX

A variant of Coulommiers from Touraine that is wrapped in chestnut leaves.

EDEL DE CLÉRON

A local variety of the Vacherin cheese of Franche-Comté. A soft cow's-milk cheese that is packed in a wrapping of spruce like Vacherin and Tourrée de l'Aubier. It has a distinctive aroma and taste. See also Tourrée de l'Aubier and Mont-d'Or.

EMMENTAL FRANÇAIS/EMMENTAL GRAND CRU

French variety of the famous Swiss cheese that is made in the same manner as the Swiss cheese and is very tasty and fruity. It stems from the Vosges, Jura, and parts of Franche-Comté, Burgundy, Savoie, and Rhône. The cows only eat fresh grass and hay and the milk is turned into cheese without pasteurisation. This makes a very good unpasteurised hard cheese from heated and pressed curd. French Emmental is also made in large

wheels that weigh approx. 154 lb (70 kg). Maturing time is at least ten weeks and fat content is 45%. Usually sold in portions or as grated cheese.

EMMENTAL DE SAVOIE

Another French variety of the famous Swiss cheese but from the Savoie. Made with unpasteurised or heat treated cow's milk. The large cheeses are wheel-shaped but tend to be more rounded at the side and smaller than other French Emmental cheeses with a diameter of 28¾–31¼ in (72–80 cm) weighing 132 lb (60 kg). They are matured for at least seventy days and fat content is 45%. Mainly sold packed in portions or ready-grated.

EPOISSES AC

Epoisses is made within the boundaries of a small and strictly defined area of the Côte d'Or, Yonne, and Haute-Marne. The name is derived from the village where the cheese was first made. It was developed in the sixteenth century by Cistercian monks of the Abbey of Citeaux who revealed the secret to local farmers. Similar cheese was discovered elsewhere in the nineteenth century.

Epoisses was once a quiet village in Burgundy. One farmer and three industrial concerns made the cheese but then suddenly there was panic following the death of two consumers who had eaten "Epoisses" that was infected with Listeria. The hysteria that followed was mainly whipped up by the poorly informed media. The victims had eaten cheese from a producer who was no longer licensed to make the cheese. The cheese in question had been made with pasteurised milk, and the infection was caused by poor hygiene in the place where the cheese was made. As a result of the pressure from the media and public opinion some producers felt obliged to switch to the use of pasteurised milk, thereby losing much of the individuality of this cheese. The best-known of the Epoisses products, Berthaut, recently decided to heat treat its milk for fifteen seconds at 57–68°C (134.6–154.4°F). Cheese made with such heat-treated milk can no longer bear the words *au lait cru* but is still permitted to be accorded AC status.

Emmental Français Grand Cru

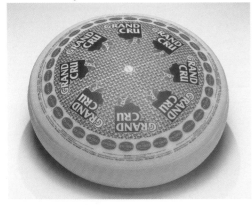

Epoisses: a pity no longer from untreated milk

Consumers continue to have lost faith in Epoisses and other red bacteria cheeses despite these measures.

Epoisses is a soft cheese with a washed rind that is made with full-cream cow's milk. The coagulation process is carried out very slowly over sixteen to twenty-four hours. After this the curd is drained in its mould for two days and after forty-eight hours the cheese is removed from the form and salted by hand before being matured in cool damp surroundings. The cheeses mature for at least four weeks and are washed twice each week, first with brine and then with a mixture of water and Marc de Bourgogne. The reddish-orange colour is created by natural colouring during washing. Epoisses is a cylindrical cheese of 3³/₄–4¹/₂ in (95–115 mm) diameter for the small ones that are 1³/₈–1³/₄ in (35–45) mm thick and weigh 8³/₄–12 oz (250–350 grams). The bigger ones are 6¹/₂–7¹/₂ in (165–190 mm) in diameter, are 1³/₁₆–1³/₄ in (30–45 mm) thick, and weigh 1 lb 8 oz–2 lb 3 oz (700 grams to 1kg). The cheese is creamy, soft, and supple. Young Epoisses still has a hard centre that is brittle and fragile but more mature cheese is often very creamy. The fragrance is dependent on the extent of the maturity. Young ones smell fruity and pleasant while older ones are strong, pungent, and penetrating. The taste is always creamy and melting but the older cheese has a more complex and sharper taste than the younger cheese. Fat content is 50%. This cheese is delicious in salads, quiches, and for snacks but is best of all as a dessert, especially in the case of really mature cheese.

Choose a Burgundy – white for the young cheese, red for the older – but Pinot Gris from Alsace or a good Marc de Bourgogne is better with older cheese.

ETORKI

This is a good example of what marketing can do for a cheese. This modern branded pasteurised sheep's-milk cheese is a soft variety of the genuine mountain cheeses such as Ossau-Iraty, Laruns etc. It does possess the fiery character of the Basque country but no longer speaks the language of the

Etorki

terroir. Despite this, this is a superb cheese for those who prefer their sheep's-milk cheese less obviously tasting of sheep's milk.

Serve a white or red wine from south-west France with it such as an Irouléguy from the Basque country, or a Jurançon or Tursan.

EXPLORATEUR

A delicious cow's-milk cheese that is further enriched with cream. A extremely creamy taste and a hint of mould.

Explorateur

FAISSELLE

A *faisselle* is actually an open pot in which the young cheese is drained. These cheeses are generally made with milk from goats or cows and are spooned from the pot to be eaten with salt and pepper and a little whipped cream.

Faisselle

FOURME D'AMBERT/FOURME DE MONTBRISON AC

The word *fourme* is derived from Latin and relates to the form in which these cheeses are made. These cheeses of the Auvergne actually predate the arrival of the Romans and their language. Archaeological finds near Pierre-sur-Haute suggest the Gallic druids made cheese in this way. It is in any event

Laguiole is an outstanding cheese to use in cooking. The very young cheese (tomme) is used for the best-known cheese dish of France: Aligot. The more mature cheese can be grated and is delicious with pasta or as a gratin topping with white meat and also with trout, or as a filling for e.g. pancakes. The locals drink regional red or white wines with Laguiole from such less well-known wine areas as Marcillac, Millau, Estaing, or Entraygues et Fel. You could also try a Côtes d'Auvergne Gamay or Beaujolais, a Costières de Nimes, a Frontonnais, or a Mamandais.

LANGRES AC

Langres has acquired a reputation for a fragrant-smelling Burgundian cheese but this is not wholly justified. This cheese only becomes strong after a long period of maturing and the cheese is not solely made in Burgundy but also in parts of the Vosges and in Champagne. Unlike Epoisses, this is not an ancient cheese and it probably first made an appearance in the eighteenth century but was first recorded in official documents from the mid nineteenth century. It was clearly a farm-made cheese with which the still warm milk was placed in earthenware forms where it soured naturally. The young, fresh cheese was then dried on sycamore leaves and then matured on a bed of straw. Slowly but surely this cheese became successful. People travelled from neighbouring villages and even further afield to buy the young cheese and even to mature the cheese further. In the nineteenth century the fame of this cheese reached Lyon, then Paris, then Switzerland before eventually achieving worldwide renown. Langres is a cow's-milk cheese with which the curd is neither washed or stirred but immediately placed in moulds. After draining under its own weight for twenty-four hours the cheese is removed from its mould, salted by hand, and placed on a rack to dry. There are two sizes of Langres: a large cylinder of 6¼–8 in (16–20 cm) diameter and 2–2¾ in (50–70 mm) thick that weighs at least 1 lb 12 oz (80 grams) or a smaller one of 3–3½ in (75–90 mm) diameter, 1½–2⅜ in (40–60 mm)of at least 5¼ oz (150 grams). The maturing time for the two sizes of cheese differ: the small one for at least fifteen days while the larger cheese is matured for at least twenty-one days. The cheese is regularly washed with brine while it matures. At the end of this time a distinct hollow forms in the top of the cheese and traditionally this is filled with Marc de Bourgogne to aid the ripening of the cheese. This *fontein* as the French call it is visible in the young cheese but much clearer in older ones.

The locals drink a glass of a good red Burgundy with Langres such as a Mercurey or Nuits-St-Georges but a Pinot Gris from Alsace is a much better choice.

LIVAROT AOC

This cheese gets its name from the small town of Livarot in the heart of Normandy's Pays d'Auge. The history of this cheese remains shrouded in mist. Quite probably it is a local variety of the many *fromages de monastère* or monastery cheeses. Livarot can be traced back to 1693 and it gained popularity in the eighteenth and nineteenth centuries. At the end of the nineteenth century around two hundred cheesemakers produced some 4,500,000 cheeses each year and Livarot was the most popular cheese of Normandy where it often served as a substitute for meat among poorer people. Until the middle of the previous century the cheeses were made on the farms and then stored elsewhere to mature in special cool but damp places. Originally Livarot was a low fat cheese containing a mere 10–15% fat with skimmed milk being used as a by-product of butter making. In the previous century the level of fat was first raised to 25% then to 30% and currently it is 40%.

Today Livarot AC can only be made in the south of the Pays d'Auge where the meadows are green and lush because of the mild climate that enables cows to graze longer in the meadows. Livarot is a cow's-milk cheese with soft cheese surrounded by a washed rind. The cylindrical cheeses are made in four standard sizes: *Livarot, Trois-quart, Petit,* and quart.

Livarot is 4½ in (12 cm) in diameter and weighs at least 8 oz (230 grams) of dry matter; *trois-quart* is 4³⁄₁₆ in (106 mm) and *weighs* at least 4¾ oz (135 grams), *petit* is 3½ in (90 mm), weighing at least 4¼ oz (120 grams), and *quart* is 2¾ in (70 mm) and weighs not less than 2 oz (60 grams) of dry matter. Occasionally you may also encounter a large or *Grand* but this is not standard and weighs up to a little over 1lb (500 grams). Livarot continues to be made in the traditional way with rennet being added at a temperature of 37°C (98.6°F). The curd is cut into grains and allowed to rest before being cut again and agitated after which it is allowed to drain in its mould.

After regular turning the young cheese is removed from its mould and salted with coarse sea salt or immersed in a brine bath. After draining for twenty-four hours the cheese is taken for a period

The Colonel-in-chief of cheese

Livarot

of three weeks to one month to cool damp cellars. During this time the cheese is turned and washed with brine at least three times. The final wash is made with annato natural dyestuff known in French as *roucou* added to the salt water. The rind of Livarot is smooth and often lustrous and coloured reddish-brown to dark brown. The texture of the cheese is smooth, dense, fine-grained, and slightly elastic. The cheese develops a stronger aroma with age. The taste is well-developed, rich, and powerful. Fat content is at least 40%.

Livarot is sometimes used as a culinary cheese but is better suited to eating with bread.

A sturdy red wine can be tried with a normally matured Livarot, e.g. Burgundy, Rhône, or Languedoc-Roussillon, but a good Pinot Gris from Alsace is not out of place either. For those seeking something special try a glass of the local farm cider from Normandy.

With the very mature cheese forget cider and switch to a glass of the delicious Calvados apple liqueur from Pays d'Auge.

MAROILLES AOC

Maroilles is also known as Marolles. This cheese comes from the Thierache region of northern France close to the Belgian border and acquired its name from the village of Maroilles. This ancient village in turn gets its name from the fine land-scape which it describes in the old Celtic language of the Gauls: *Maro Lalo* or "clearing in a wood," which French knows as *bocage*: rich, green mead-ows surrounded by woods. This cheese is yet another example of the industry of local monks some thousand years ago who made their own version of the *fromage de monastère*. It is quite possibly though that the recipe for this cheese predates even this time. Its fame spread almost as rapidly as its distinctive aroma, making Maroilles a renowned cheese at the French court. Maroilles is a soft cheese made from cow's milk with a rind that is washed during its maturing. The cheese is

Maroilles

rectangular and the standard size is 5⅛ in by 5⅛ in (130 mm by 130 mm) and 2⅜ in (60 mm) thick with a weight of 1 lb 8 oz (720 grams). There are also smaller versions known locally as *Sorbais*

Livarot

Maroilles

of 1 lb 3 oz (540 grams), *Mignon* 12¾ oz (360 grams), and *Quart* 6⅜ oz (180 grams). After the milk has coagulated the fresh white curd is moulded in forms and salted. After draining for a time the cheese is removed from its mould and transferred to a well ventilated area where it remains for ten days during which time it acquires a natural culture of mould on the outside. During the maturing period of three to five weeks the cheeses are turned regularly, brushed, and washed to produce a fine natural red rind and the formidable aroma. Properly matured Maroilles should still have brittle cheese at its the heart surrounded by very creamy cheese. The aroma is quite distinctive and typical of red bacteria cheese. The taste is strong and earthy and not at all for the uninitiated. Fat content is at least 45%.

There is often a demand for robust country fare in the wet and cold northern part of France. The fragrant Maroilles is incorporated in the renowned local dishes of *Flamiche* – a kind of quiche – and *Goyère* – a type of tart, for which the cheese is notorious. It is also used in potato gratin dishes and other oven dishes. Fortunately most people in the area also serve this cheese at table as well at the end of the meal.

There are those who like a glass of a robust red wine with this cheese but most such confrontations will be won by the cheese. A safer combination is a well-rounded and full-bodied white that is none too dry such as a Côteaux du Layon. The locals though choose a more thirst-quenching companion for this very rustic cheese in the form of a *blond* beer, a glass of brown ale, or farm cider.

MIMOLETTE

Dutch barge skippers who voyaged to the south of France took double Edam cheese with them that was coated with an orange colour. The colour indicated this was cheese for local consumption by the farmers and locals and not for sale but of course this really did not work... The French became so fond of this cheese that the French court banned its import and ordered that it should be copied and made in France. Since those times the Mimolette has been the counterpart of the double Edam cheese but French production could not fulfil all the demand and hence the Dutch export "Mimolette" cheese to France. French Mimolette is a hard cow's-milk cheese made by lightly heating the curd and then pressing it in the form of a 7 lb 11 oz (3.5 kg) ball. The fat content is at least 45%. The rind is pale yellow and the cheese itself is smooth and dense and can even be crumbly when older. The striking orange colour is created with natural *roucou* colouring which comes from annato. The maturing period depends on the quality of the cheese. The French are particularly fond of year old Mimolette *extra vielle* that is matured for at least twelve months.

Although a delicious glass of white or red wine combines quite well with Mimolette the local tradition in northern France is to drink a glass of cold beer with this cheese.

MONTBRIAC/ROCHEBARON

This cheese became very popular when the Montignac diet was all the rage. It is a fine and successful modern branded cheese with a slightly rustic appearance – the work of the marketing people – which gives the impression the cheese has a thousand years of tradition behind it. Beneath the drab exterior of the rind there is a soft and creamy cheese brought to life by the blue veins running through it which impart a very slightly piquant bite to the finish of the cheese's taste. Fat content is 55% of the dry matter but only 33% of the overall content.

Drink a simple fruity country wine from the Auvergne, Rouergue (e.g. a Marcillac), south-west of France, or Languedoc-Rousillon.

MONT D'OR/VACHERIN DU HAUT-DOUBS AC

This cheese is also often known as Vacherin du Mont d'Or, although this is actually the name of a Swiss cheese from the other side of the border with France. The French version gets its name from the same high pasture land in the French Jura. The Mont d'Or of both Swiss and French cheeses refers to a peak above the slopes of the Jura that the cows graze on both sides of the border. The history of these Vacherin cheeses dates back to the twelfth century when monks led the clearance of large areas of woodland to create pasture for livestock farming.

Vacherin is very much a seasonal cheese that may only be made between August 15 and March 31 so that you will only come across these French cheeses in the autumn and winter months. The cheese is made with milk from the local Montbéliarde and red-spotted or Abondance breeds of cow that is not pasteurised. After coagulation the curd is placed in moulds and then

Mimolette

Mont d'Or, a moist and creamy cheese

removed from these forms after draining for a time but the mould is replaced with an outer ring of spruce wood and the cheeses are also matured on spruce planks. This gives the cheese quite distinctive resinous aromas. During the three weeks of maturing, the cheese is regularly turned and the rind is washed with brine. Finally, the Vacherin is placed in the round wooden box for which it is known. There are various sizes of these cheeses – all of them round – from 8–12 in (20–30 cm) that are 1³/₁₆–2 in (30–50 mm) thick. The weight varies from approx. 1 lb to 2 lb or more (500 grams–1 kg) for the smaller ones and 4 lb–6 lb 10 oz (1.8–3 kg) for the larger ones. The top of the cheeses has soft

"pleats" or creases and the colour is pale pink covered with a thin layer of white. The cheese has a gentle aroma that is subtle and balsamic, invoking thoughts of lactic acid and spruce wood. The cheese is often so moist and creamy (fat content 45%) that it has to be served with a spoon but this is a wonderful experience for the true lover of cheese.

There are different opinions about the best accompaniment for this cheese. Some prefer a red wine from the Jura or Arbois but the white wines from these same places and those of Switzerland and the Savoie are also recommended.

MONTJOUX

A first-class cheese of unpasteurised cow's milk from eastern France (Franche-Comté, Doubs). The rind is washed but only displays white mould. The taste is well-developed and creamy. Fat content is 50%.

Wonderful with a glass of white, rosé, or red wine from the Jura, Arbois, Burgundy, or Alsace

MORBIER AOC

Morbier is France's newest AC cheese (granted in December 2000) and it gets its name from the village in the Jura near Morez. The cheese's history though dates back at least to the nineteenth century when left-over curd from making Comté cheese was kept for the following day. To keep insects off the curd it was covered with a layer of branches from the local conifers. The next day new curd was added to the left-overs and both were pressed together into a cheese which was then left in cold moist cellars to mature for two to three months and they were subsequently brushed with a brine solution to develop their natural grey to light brown rind. This tradition has been continued.

Modern Morbier is no longer regarded as a by-product but as a worthy cheese in its own right. It is made with unpasteurised milk. Morbier made with pasteurised milk is not permitted AC status. For this reason the cheesemaking must not be delayed. Once the milk has been skimmed it is

Mont d'Or

Morbier de Montagne, au lait cru

Morbier, a dessert on its own

coagulated slowly for twenty-four to thirty-six hours and the curd is heated slightly to 34°C (93.2°F) in two parts, separated from each other by a layer of black ash. These are then brought together and pressed to form flat wheels of 13⁷/₈–15³/₄ in (35–40 cm) diameter and 3¹/₈–3¹/₂ in (80–90 mm) thick, weighing 6 lb 10 oz–17 lb 10 oz (3–8 kg). Beneath the thick but often split rind you will find a soft and creamy cheese divided into two sections by a layer of ash. This is no longer merely taken from the fire beneath the vessel in which the curd is heated but brought in specially. The cheese is fresh and fruity with both milky and plant derived flavours present. Fat content is 45%. Available from March to October.

Morbier is a tasty cheese to eat with bread or for the end of a meal. Drink a fresh white or fruity red from the Jura, Arbois, Savoie, or Bugey with it.

MOULIS

Morbier is a superb craft-made cheese from the Ariège at the foot of the Pyrenees. The coarse-looking cheese is an irregular wheel of varied format. The milk from the morning milking in the surrounding mountains and valleys is collected for this cheese each day. After the milk is filtered

Le Moulis

rennet of animal origin is added at a temperature of 33°C (91.4°F). Coagulation of the milk takes about forty-five minutes after which the curd is cut into small pieces with a tool resembling an upside down lyre but with blades instead of strings. After being vigorously stirred to get rid of excess whey the curd is rested for a time to improve its texture. Once the whey has been drained off the curd is placed in forms and lightly pressed and regularly turned. After the cheese is salted by hand it is left on spruce planks to mature for one to two months in a cool damp place and is also regularly dipped in a brine solution and brushed during this time to acquire its distinctive taste that is simultaneously both strong and mild. Young cheeses are riddled with irregular air bubbles but still quite moist and creamy in texture. Older cheese is harder and more dense with a stronger aroma and flavour.

With the young cheese drink a fresh dry Jurançon or a rosé or white Irouléguy, Tursan, or Bearn-Bellocq. With the more mature cheese choose a full-bodied red from south-west France e.g. Irouléguy, Madiran, Frontonnais, Marmandais, Gaillac, or Cahors.

Le Moulis's milk comes from cows like these

Munster

THE FIRST EUROPEAN CHEESE

Munster is undoubtedly the most authentic European cheese, dating from times long before people dreamed of a united Europe. The story starts in the seventh century when a number of Italian monks established a monastery in the Fecht valley. This *Monasterium Confluentis* later became *monastère* and still later *munster*. The

Munster, the first European cheese

cheese that the monks made was originally for their own consumption but it quickly became the subject of barter. New recruits joined the monastery's ranks from Ireland and present-day Germany, perhaps attracted by the fame and maybe also the aroma of the cheese so that a small village became established surrounding the monastery. More and more woodland was felled to create pasture and they began to eye up the other side of the mountain. Behind the mountains of Alsace are the gently undulating hills of Lorraine. Relations were sufficiently good between the people of Alsace and Lorraine through trade in the thirteenth century that they jointly built a new town on the border to improve mutual trade at *Sancti Gerardi mare* or Gérardmer. Because the cheesemakers–known in German as *melker* and in Alsace as *malker*, later becoming *macaire* in French–regularly criss-crossed the mountains, the Munster cheese became commonplace to the people of both Alsace and Lorraine. Meanwhile countless new monasteries copied this Munster cheese and were now producing it. However the relations between Alsace and Lorraine deteriorated appallingly and the border was closed to the exchange of cheese.

THE THIRTY YEARS WAR

Alsace was beset by disasters at the start of the seventeenth century. Because of the continuing wars between Catholics and Protestants, the allied Protestant armies put Catholic Alsace to the torch. The mountains of Alsace were declared an area devoid of inhabitants for thirty-six years. It was only when French troops occupied Alsace in 1675 that life returned to the valleys of Alsace and Munster cheese once more started to be made. The original cows used by the cheesemakers had more

or less disappeared and there was also a tidal wave of immigrants, including Danes, Bavarians, Tyroleans, and Swiss. The Scandinavians brought their own fine black spotted cows with them which they quickly renamed Vosgienne from the Vosges mountains. The cows of the Vosgienne breed are superb milk cows that produce low yields of excellent quality.

PROTESTANTS AND CATHOLICS

Despite the peace which had meanwhile been reached between Catholics and Protestants the two communities really continued to live in their own manner. The effusive Catholics used full-cream milk from both daily milkings to make their cheese, Munster-Géromé. The more frugal Protestants living in the "Munster" valley removed the cream from the evening milking and added it to the following morning's full-cream milk. Hence the "Catholic" cheese was both creamier and more complex while the "Protestant" cheese was more down-to-earth and less pronounced in its flavour. The two types of cheese exist to this day and are both permitted within the AC of Munster and Munster-Géromé.

Present-day cheeses though are no longer precisely the same. The extensive introduction of industrial processes has led to new types of Munster cheese being developed. Today there are a number of varieties of Munster:

- Munster au lait pasteurisé made with pasteurised milk (usually fairly mild to tasteless)

Superb cheese without equal

189

- Munster au lait thermisé made with heat-treated milk (generally has a reasonable flavour)
- Munster au lait cru made by semi-industrial processes but with milk that is not pasteurised (with a good flavour but not always possessing much character)
- Munster fermier au lait cru made on the farm with unpasteurised milk for the best and most tasty version (very well-developed flavour and with character that changes with the season).

MAKING MUNSTER FERMIER GEROME

The process starts with the milking of the cows. It takes 21 pints (10 litres) of milk to make just over 1 lb (500 grams) of cheese. The fresh milk is placed in a copper boiler and warmed to 35°C (95°F). Following rapid lactic acid souring that takes about thirty minutes, animal rennet is added to the curdled milk. The curd is cut into coarse cubes and then into smaller pieces before it is ladled into spruce wood moulds with a copper scoop. The bottom of the mould allows the curd to quickly drain and after three days in the moulds at a temperature around 20°C (68°F) the fresh white cheese is removed from its form and is salted by hand.

The immature cheeses are then moved to a cool damp place where they mature for three to five weeks at a temperature of around 13°C (55.4°F). During this time the cheeses are washed every two days with brine to keep the rind free from mould. This also causes the rind eventually to form its natural reddish-orange colour. These farm cheeses made with unpasteurised milk are at their best in summer and autumn.

Farm-made Munster

MANY CHEESE BUT ONE AC

The AC rules require Munster or Munster-Géromé to come from the slopes of the Vosges in one of seven *departements* of Alsace-Lorraine. These cheeses must contain soft cheese with a washed rind with a fat content of not less than 45%. The standard size is a flat disc of 5¹/₈–7¹/₂ in (13–19 cm) diameter and 1–3¹/₈ in (24–80 mm) thick, weighing 1 lb–3 lb 5 oz (450 grams–1.5 kg).

The smaller Petit-Munster and Petit-Munster-Géromé are also covered by the AC with their modest dimensions of 2³/₄–4⁵/₈ in (70–120 mm) diameter, ⁷/₈–2³/₈ in (20–60 mm) thickness and lighter 4¹/₄ oz (120 grams). The rind of the various Munster cheeses varies from smooth to slightly uneven and often bears traces of a rack. It appears slightly moist and shiny and varying in colour from yellow-orange to red-orange. The cheese inside is paler, smooth, dense, supple, and creamy. The aroma is quite distinctive and gets stronger with age. The taste of the type of cheese varies from mild to quite strong according to type but should never be sharp or burn the tongue. Cheeses that smell of ammonia are best ignored.

True connoisseurs of Munster and Munster-Géromé eat their cheese at room temperature with potatoes cooked in their jackets. Munster is also incorporated in all manner of local specialities but is mainly served at the end of a meal, with or without a bowl of cumin seed.

Although some insist on red wine with Munster (a thirst-quenching fruity Pinot Noir) a full-bodied white that is not over acidic is preferable such as a Pinot Gris or Gewurztraminer from Alsace. Those who like to eat cumin seed with the cheese are advised to forget the wine and drink a glass of the local beer from Alsace instead.

Petit-munster

MUROL/MUROLET

Like Anneau de Vic-Bilh (see there also) this is a ring-form cheese with a hole in the middle. The cheese is actually related to the St-Nectaire but made with pasteurised cow's milk. To differentiate between the two cheeses and to speed up the cheese's maturing, the middle of the cheese is removed. This centre part is sold separately coated in paraffin wax as snack cheese under the name of Murolet.

Drink a light Gamay with either Murol or Murolet

Murol and Murolet

e.g. from the Auvergne, Forez, Roannais, Lyonnais, or Beaujolais.

NEUFCHÂTEL AOC

Neuchâtel is a soft cheese from Normandy with a rind coated in white mould. The cheese has been made by local farmers for more than eleven hundred years and this cheese was extremely popular at the time of the Hundred Years War between France and England. Treacherous Norman maidens offered the marauding English soldiers their heart in the form of a soft heart-shaped cheese.

Whether they did this from love or for survival the story does not say. Today Neuchâtel is available in six different shapes: the large heart (*gros coeur*) of 1 lb 5 oz (600 grams), small heart (*petit coeur*) of

Neufchâtel

7 oz (200 grams), small cork-shaped cylinder (*bonde*) of 3½ oz (100 grams), large cork-shaped cylinder (*double-bonde*) of 7 oz (200 grams), square (*carré*) of 3½ oz (100 grams), and a block (*briquette*) of 3½ oz (100 grams). Neuchâtel is made with either pasteurised or untreated milk from Normandy.

The unpasteurised cheeses are presented on a bed of straw but the others from dairies are packed in paper. A small quantity of rennet is added to full-cream milk to prepare it for cheesemaking and the milk is curdled slowly for twenty-four hours. The curd is then lightly pressed before it is placed in its mould.

A downy white covering of mould forms on the outer skin of the cheese after several days and the cheeses are sold after at least ten days maturing but the more tasty ones are left for a further three or four weeks. The texture is always soft and creamy, the aroma is reminiscent of a cheese or wine cellar and the taste is delicate but with the character of a rich cow's-milk cheese. Fat content is 45%. Neuchâtel has little culinary use but it is a welcome addition to the cheeseboard or eaten on its own at the end of a meal or with bread for lunch.

The locals enjoy Neuchâtel with a glass of farm cider for a superb combination but for those who prefer wine you may chose white, rosé, or red, provided it is fruity and fresh.

NUITS D'OR

A delicious modern branded cheese from the area around the small town of Nuits-St-Georges of Burgundy's Côtes d'Or. This cheese is made with pasteurised cow's milk and is made by half cooking the curd but not pressing it. The rind of the cheese is then washed. The taste is fruity and creamy with hints of nut. Fat content is 50%.
Delicious with a glass of red Burgundy.

Nuits d'Or

OLIVET CENDRE/OLIVET AU FOIN

A modern craft-made cheese from the Loire region. The basic cheese somewhat resembles a

Olivet cendré

coulommiers. The cheese is attractively packed in a layer of ash (*cendré*) or with a few pieces of straw (*au foin*). Worthy cheese of pasteurised cow's milk that is unlikely to disappoint.

Drink a dry Loire wine with this cheese, preferably made with Sauvignon (blanc) grapes.

OSSAU-IRATY AC

Ossau-Iraty is certainly not the only hard sheep's-milk cheese from the Pyrenees and also not the only one of France but it certainly is the best known. The name is a fusion of the names of the Bearnais Ossau valley at the foot of the Pic du Midi d'Ossau and the magnificent conifer forests of Iraty in the Basque country. During the hot part of the

year more than two thousands flocks of sheep numbering some 300,000 ewes freely roam this land, which is also home to the famous Pottok ponies. The territory of the Ossau valley and Iraty are the domain of Basco-Bearnaise sheep for several months. Cheeses are made during these balmy hot days for the sheep that will be sold the following autumn, winter, and spring. These cheeses are still made in the summer quarters of the shepherds known as *cujalas* by the Bearnais or *cayolars* in the Basque language.

The still warm milk is used or if collected from further afield it is heated to 30°C (86°C). After the addition of animal rennet a sturdy curd is formed which is cut to small pieces by hand and further lightly heated. After vigorous stirring of the curd to separate the whey and make the curd more pliable it is then scooped into moulds with drainage holes in. The curd is left to drain naturally for a while before it is pressed, after which it is salted and allowed to drain further. Once the cheese has assumed the required form it is moved to cool damp cellars where it then matures for at least three months. Ossau-Iraty cheese is an attractive cylindrical form of 10 1/4 in (26 cm) diameter and 4 5/8–5 1/2 in diameter (12–14 cm) high that weighs 8 lb 13 oz–11 lb (4–5 kg). The old-fashioned hand-made farm cheeses though can weigh up to 15 lb 6 oz (7 kg) while the small Petit Ossau-Iraty weighs a mere 4 lb 6 oz–6 lb 10 oz (2–3 kg). The natural rind is brushed dry and is whitish-grey to yellow-orange in colour. The cheese is smooth without air bubbles and its texture is firm and dense, varying from

The landscape of Iraty

creamy with young cheese to very hard with more mature ones. Fat content is at least 50%. The aroma and flavour of this cheese is a perfect translation of the *terroir* of the Béarnaise/Basque countryside with its pasture, aromatic wild herbs, flowers, summer thicket, blueberries, liquorice, gentian, and ...Ossau-Iraty is very much a table cheese but it can also be grated into farmhouse-style soups when old and makes an excellent snack on slices

Ossau-Iraty-cheese

of bread. The younger cheese is a perfect combination with a dry or sweet white wine and also with the local rosé. For local authenticity chose a Jurançon, Pacherenc du Vic-Bilh white or Béarn-Bellocq or Irouléguy for a rosé. The stronger older cheese demands a more robust red wine and here too the regional choices include Irouléguy, Tursan, or Madiran. If these are not available then their cousins from the south-west of France or Aquitaines will suffice: Marmande, Fronton, Côtes du Duras, Côtes de Bergerac, Cahors, Gaillac, Marcillac, or a wine from Languedoc-Roussillon.

PAVÉ

Pavé (the French name for the cobblestones used to pave their roads) is also a collective name for certain square and rectangular cheeses.

Delicious: well-matured Pavé d'Our

PAVÉ D'AFFINOIS

A successful product from the Guilloteau dairy company which is one of Europe's best large-scale dairy concerns. Pavé d'Affinois is a creamy soft fresh cheese with white mould in a form so simple it is slick. In addition to the ordinary Pavé d'Affinois (fat content 45%) there is also a lower-fat variety, Pavé d'Affinois Léger (fat content 25%) and an organic variety was introduced at the end of 2000.

Pavé d'Affinois

Low-fat Pavé d'Affinois Léger

This Pavé tastes best combined with a light fruity white or red such as a Chardonnay or Pinot Noir.

PÉLARDON AOC
Pélardon was granted its AC status in August 2000, making it the second newest AC cheese in France after Morbier. The cheese is actually one of the country's oldest. A small goat's-milk cheese from the Cévennes mountains south of the Massif Central was renowned in ancient Rome. Since those times Pélardon has managed to capture the hearts and a place at the tables of both the local population and cheese lovers in France and elsewhere. In addition to grass, the diet of the goats that provide milk for this cheese includes wild flowers and herbs, hay, and chestnuts.

The full-cream unpasteurised goat's milk is coagulated each day during the season, spooned into moulds, and then salted after draining. This work is normally done by the farmers and goatherds themselves but occasionally milk is sold to a small-scale dairy concern. The most delicate part of the process of cheesemaking is yet to come. The young cheese is matured under controlled temperature and humidity to give the cheese its characteristic flavour and character. Pélardon cheeses are small in the form of a flat disc of just $2^{1}/_{8}$–$2^{3}/_{4}$ in (60–70 mm) diameter and $2^{1}/_{4}$–$1^{1}/_{16}$ in (22–27 mm) thick, weighing at least 2 oz (60 grams), but usually $3^{1}/_{2}$–$3^{7}/_{8}$ oz (100–110 grams). The natural thin rind is covered with various white, grey, blue, or pale orange moulds depending on the place the cheese was matured and its age. The cheese itself varies in texture and colour as the cheese matures. Pélardon can be eaten young, semi-mature, mature, or old. There is an especially creamy Pélardon Crémeux with aromas of hazelnut. Fat content is at least 45 and often 50%.

A simple but wonderful way to enjoy Pélardon is in a warm salad. Coat the cheese with a thin covering of breadcrumbs and fry in good olive oil and place on a bed of crunchy, fresh lettuce.

Drink a fresh white wine such as a Clairette de Bellegarde, Clairette du Languedoc, or Picpoul de

Pélardon and Pérail

Pinet with the young cheese. Drink a more rounded white such as a Chardonnay from Pays d'Oc, Viognier from the Ardèche, or a Condrieu with the creamy cheese. With the mature cheese choose a delicious red that is low in tannin from the Languedoc, or a Costieres de Nîmes.

PÉRAIL
Smooth in texture but strongly flavoured, this small cheese of just $4^{1}/_{4}$ oz (120 grams) comes from Aveyron, to the south of the Auvergne.

Pour a full-bodied white wine into your glass for this cheese and by preference a Jurançon or Pacherenc du Vic-Bilh.

PERSILLÉ
A farm-made goat's-milk cheese from the Rhône-Alpes region varing from soft to semi-hard. This unheated cheese that is not pressed gets its name from the blue veins that the French call *persillé*.

PETIT BRETON
A modern cheese of pasteurised cow's milk that comes from Ille-et-Vilaine in Brittany. It is a semi-hard cheese of lightly-pressed curd with a washed rind and somewhat resembles St-Paulin.

Drink what you will with this cheese: beer, white wine, or even spirits.

Petit Breton

PICODON DE L'ARDECHE/PICODON DE LA DROME AC
These cheeses are more or less made in the same manner in two different areas of the mountainous *departements* of Drôme and Ardêche in the south-east. Picodon cheeses were eaten fresh with olive oil and bread two thousand years ago by local goatherds. Because the goats gave no milk in winter some of the cheese was kept back for this season. Picodon is a soft full-cream goat's-milk cheese. After the milk is slowly coagulated the curd is scooped out and placed in small forms to drain. Once it has drained, the cheese is salted manually and left to dry on a rack for at least twelve days. The cheeses made by the method

known as Picodon *affiné méthode Dieulefit* are stronger than the others because they are matured longer and their rind is regularly washed with water.

Picodon cheeses are more of a ball than a cylinder with a diameter of 2–3 1/8 in (50–80 mm) and 3/8–1 3/16 in (10–30 mm) thickness. They weigh 1 3/4–3 1/2 (50–100 grams). The exterior of the cheese and its internal texture vary between the types and also with age and these cheeses are sold at various stages of maturity from young and fresh to hard and crumbly. The outside of the cheese can be pale yellow but also have signs of white, greyish, blue, or red moulds. When cut the cheese is always smooth, but creaminess and moistness are dependant on age. The aroma is of fresh goat's milk and this is fresher with young cheese but more pronounced with mature cheese. Fat content is at least 45%. These goat's-milk cheeses can be incorporated in salads or eaten hot or cold with bread. Picodon is sometimes kept in white wine, perhaps with a shot of marc or eau-de-vie but the large glass jars with them in olive oil with Provençal herbs is more traditional. Cheese kept this way is out-of-this-world when grilled.

With young Picodon drink a fresh and fruity white, rosé, or red wine. For the mature cheese select a fuller-bodied rosé or red that has not been cask-aged such as those from villages in the south.

PIÉ D'ANGLOYS

A modern branded cheese with a very rustic-looking appearance. Beneath the fine rind there is a soft and unctuous extra creamy cheese. Choose a ripe cheese and take it out of the refrigerator some time before eating it.

With its 62% fat and creaminess Pié d'Angloys demands a creamy and mollifying wine such as a Vouvray, Montlouis, or Côteaux de l'Aubance. If you prefer more down-to-earth tastes you could choose a tasty white or red Côtes du Rhône instead.

Pié d'Angloys

PITHIVIERS AU FOIN

A local variety of white mould cheese from the Loire that is packed in a little hay from which it derives its distinctive flavour.

Picodon

PONT-L'EVEQUE AC

It was probably the local monks who first made Pont-l'Evêque in the thirteenth century. This superb cheese quickly became known as *l'angelot* or "the cherub" which became modified to *Augelot* because this cheese originates in the Pays d'Auge. The present-day name dates from the seventeenth century when the best of this cheese came from the small town of Pont-l'Evêque between Lisieux and Deauville. Today Pont-l'Evêque is made in five departments of Normandy and neighbouring Mayenne.

Petit Pont-l'Évêque

Pont-l'Évêque

Pont-l'Evêque is a soft cheese made with cow's milk that has its rind washed. The form is always rectangular but the size varies. The larger Grand Pont-l'Evêque is a square with sides of 7¹/₂–8¹/₄ in (19–21 cm) and weighs at least 1 lb 7 oz–1 lb 14 oz (650–850 grams) of dry matter. The normal Pont-l'Evêque has sides of 4¹/₈–4¹/₂ in (105–115 mm) and weighs at least 5 oz (140 grams) of dry matter. There are also Demi Pont-l'Evêque (also 4¹/₈–4¹/₂ in/105–115 mm long but 2–2¹/₄ in 52–57 mm wide and at least 2¹/₂ oz (70 grams) of dry matter) and Petit Pont-l'Evêque that is square with sides of (85–95 mm) and at least 3 oz (86 grams) of dry matter. The normal Pont-l'Evêque has a total weight of 12³/₄ oz–1 lb (350–450 grams) and its fat content is at least 45%.

Pont-l'Evêque is made with fresh full-cream milk, both pasteurised or not, to which animal rennet is added. Following coagulation the curd is cut, stirred, and placed in forms. After draining during which the cheese is regularly turned it is removed from the form and then further matured on wooden racks in a cool place where it is also turned regularly. After five days the cheese is either manually salted or immersed in brine and after seven days the exterior is washed or brushed with brine. A white mould forms which later becomes reddish-orange through the action of the natural carotene colouring in the milk. The maturing continues, depending on the size of the cheese, for thirteen days to six weeks. The cheeses are at their best from June to mid-March – and those made with unpasteurised milk are the tastiest. Buy Pont-l'Evêque with a smooth golden-yellow to orange rind that sticks to the wrapping but easily comes free. Avoid sticky and moist cheese that remains stuck to the box. The aroma can be strong and earthy but should never be pungent or of ammonia. The flavour should be creamy and strong without burning the tongue or throat.

Wine lovers have a tendency to choose a robust but fruity red from Champagne, Burgundy, or the Loire but true gastronomes choose a robust farm cider from the Pays d'Auge in Normandy instead.

Pont-l'Évêque

PORT SALUT

The cheese from the monastery of Entrammes was once *the* model for cheesemakers throughout the world. The monastery of Port-du-Salut produced a good semi-hard cheese made by pressing the curd without heating it and then washing the rind. This craft-made cheese with a well-developed and rich taste disappeared though at the end of the 1950s when the monks were no longer able to cope with demand because of financial problems. The name

Port Salut

and the recipe were sold and since that time Port Salut has been mass-produced. The cheese is soft and creamy and has a passing resemblance to the superb cheese of yesteryear. It is matured for one month and fat content is 50%. Port Salut is far tastier as an ingredient in the kitchen e.g. for gratins than to eat in its own right.

Drink a beer or light-bodied red wine from the Loire with it.

POULIGNY-SAINT-PIERRE AOC

Pouligny-St-Pierre is a soft goat's-milk cheese made in the form of a pyramid without its point. It comes from just twenty-two *communes* in the department of Indre, south of the Loire, in the Berry region. The cheese is 5 in (125 mm) square at the base and 1 in (25 mm) square at the top and is also 5 in (125 mm) tall. The weight is 8³/₄ oz (250 grams but there is also a smaller version of 5¹/₄ oz (150 grams).

Full-cream milk is used from Saanen or Poitevine goats that graze sparse scrub that is plentiful in aromatic plants and bushes. The milk, which is not pasteurised, is turned into cheese immediately following milking. After animal rennet has been added the coagulation takes at least eighteen hours

Pouligny-Saint-Pierre

before a smooth and homogenous firm curd is formed. The curd is scooped into forms with a ladle and left to drain in them for at least twenty-four hours. After this the cheese is removed from the form and salted. After three days the cheese is moved to a cool damp place where it remains for at least a further seven days to mature. The fine rind is covered with a soft natural moulds of white, grey, and blue. The cheese is firm but slightly friable and yet supple and creamy. The aroma is reminiscent of fresh goat's milk and is fresh and slightly sour. The taste is well-developed, fresh, fruity, and characteristic of its *terroir*, with a hint of hazelnut in the finish. Fat content is at least 45%.

The French use the cheese widely in their cuisine. Young cheese is often added with walnut oil to salads or served slightly warmed on toast. The ripe cheese with mould is a table cheese that everyone can enjoy.

There are no doubts about the wine to accompany this cheese: it must be white, fresh, and fruity, and preferably from the area, e.g. a Reuilly, Quincy, Menetou-Salon, Sancerre, or Pouilly-Fumé.

RACLETTE
See Fromage à raclette.

REBLOCHON (DE SAVOIE) AC

Local taxes were often very high in the Middle Ages but farmers were not beyond intelligent ways to mitigate this. On the day that the tax inspector visited they squeezed the cow's teats less hard so that less milk was produced. Once the inspector had noted the low yield (this data was used to determine the tax for the farm) the farmer milked

Reblochon

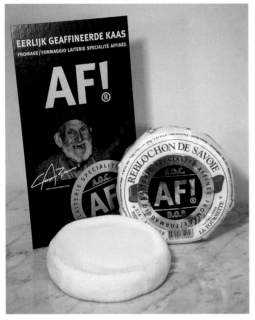

the cows again to produce more milk. This "squeezing again" was known in the local dialect as *reblocher* and the cheese made from this milk became known as *reblochon*. The cheeses from this second milking were high in fat and more creamy than other cheese. Reblochon though

became outlawed in the seventeenth century.This cheese made with full-cream milk that is not pasteurised may now only be made in two hundred *communes* in the departments of Savoie and Haut-Savoie, specifically in the Aravis mountains and the Abondance valley. The unpasteurised milk from Abondance, Montbéliarde, and Tarine cows must be used within twenty-fours hours. After souring with animal rennet the curd is placed in forms and left to drain before salting and is then matured for at least two but usually three or four weeks.

Reblochon is cylindrical with a diameter of $3^9/_{16}$–$5^1/_2$ in (90–140 mm), thickness of $1^3/_{16}$–$1^3/_8$ in (30–35 mm) and weight of 1 lb–1 lb 3 oz (450–550 grams). The rind is quite thin, yellow to yellow-orange, and generally is covered with a fine white coating. The cheese is firm but supple and springy, yet creamy with some air bubbles. The aroma has two aspects: on the one hand it is reminiscent of alpine pastures and flowers but on the other it recalls damp cellars. The taste is creamy, velvet smooth, with a distinct presence of hazelnut, The farm cheeses made of untreated milk are much deeper in flavour with a more complex taste than those made on a larger scale or in factories. The farm cheese can be recognised by a round green casein patch on the rind while the others have a red patch. Fat content is at least 45%.

Reblochon is widely used in the local cuisine. Pela and Tartiflette are variants of the same dish with baked onions, potatoes, garlic, fresh herbs, and melted Reblochon that are popular with winter sports enthusiasts. Reblochon is also ideal for

Rigotte

198

pancakes, with poultry, fried fare, and in quiches. Beside these uses, Reblochon is also an ideal conclusion to a meal.

Traditionally a fresh white or fruity red from Savoie is drunk with Reblochon but wines from Switzerland, Diois, the Jura, Rhône, or Beaujolais taste fine too.

Rigotte

A collective name for craft-made cheeses and those made on a larger scale from the Rhône valley. They were probably once made with heated whey, from which this name is derived. Today these cheeses are not made from whey. Fat content is 40–50%.

RIGOTTE DE CONDRIEU

A very specific form of Rigotte made with unpasteurised goat's milk from the Rhône-Alpes region. A superbly delicious cheese of just 1¼ oz (35 grams) that is soft, creamy, and sweet, with aromas of acacia honey.

Drink a Condrieu or possibly a Viognier Vin de Pays d'Ardêche with it.

ROCAMADOUR AC (PREVIOUSLY CABECOU DE ROCAMADOUR)

Rocamadour is a small goat's-milk cheese made on the high chalk plateau of Causses in the Quercy region of the department of Lot (Cahors and Rocamadour) and certain *communes* in the surrounding departments of Dordorgne, Corrèze,

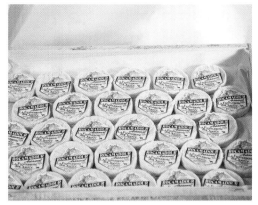

Rocamadour Artisanal

Aveyron, and Tarn et Garonne. The former name of *cabecou* means "goat's-milk cheese" in the Provençal language of Occitan, quite possibly derived from Arabic *chebli* for "goat." It is entirely possible that this cheese is very old but it was first written about in the fifteenth century. The name Rocamadour comes from the picturesque hill town in the north of the department of Lot. This very historic town that is unfortunately extremely popular with tourists is built on three levels and is partially hewn from the chalk rock itself.

Rocamadour is made entirely with goat's milk and is a fairly small cheese of just 2³⁄₈ in (60 mm) diameter and ⁵⁄₈ in (16 mm) thick that weighs about 1¼ oz (35 grams). It uses unpasteurised goat's

Rocamadour Fermier

milk that is dealt with shortly after milking. A very small amount of rennet coagulates the milk in at least twelve hours after which the curd is collected and drained for twelve hours. Once most of the whey has drained the curd is broken, lightly kneaded by hand, and scooped into the forms. The young cheese matures in cold damp cellars for at least six more days. The cheese has no rind, more a thin skin with the mature cheese. It is soft, supple, and creamy (fat content is 45%). The aroma is strongly evocative of fresh goat's milk. The cheese melts in the mouth, has a creamy or velvety texture, and a sweet finish with hint of hazelnut. There are three types made with unpasteurised milk. Rocamadour AC is made by craft or industrial means within a defined area, Rocamadour AC Artisanal is craft-made from very small-scale dairy companies and the milk of herders; Rocamadour AC Fermier is craft-made by farmers with their own milk.

Rocamadour can be eaten as a very young and very creamy cheese but it becomes less moist with age. Locally the cheese is added to dishes, includes in salads, quiches, tarts, and such specialities as fried Rocamadour with a coating of ground walnuts. Most cheese connoisseurs though prefer to eat it at the conclusion of a meal.

Drink a robust red wine from the area with the mature cheese, e.g. Cahors, Côtes de Bergerac, Montravel Rouge, or Gaillac. With the creamier young cheese white wine is better such as a Gaillac, dry Bergerac, Montravel Blanc, etc.

ROCHEBARON/MONTBRIAC
See Monbriac.

ROLLOT
Related to Maroilles, originating from Picardy in northern France. Once all Rollot cheese was made on farms of unpasteurised milk but today most are made in large plants with pasteurised and homogenised cow's milk so that they have lost their fiery character and taste. If you are given the opportunity to sample a farm-made Rollot of unpasteurised milk then grab the chance with both hands and enjoy it. The mass-produced version is not bad cheese but it does not compare with the authentic article. Rollot is a round disc of 2³/₄–3¹/₈ in (70–80 mm) diameter that is 1³/₁₆–1¹/₂ in (30–40 mm) thick, weighing 7–10⁵/₈ oz (200–300 grams). The yellow-orange rind hides a soft ivory-yellow cheese that is initially creamy on the palate but then sharp in its finish, with saltiness and bitterness, resulting from at least four weeks maturing and regular washing of the rind. Fat content is 45%.

If you drink a robust red wine with this cheese the battle between the cheese and the tannin will always be won by the cheese. With young cheese a dry white such as a Jurançon, Pacherenc du Vic-Bilh, Tursan, Côteaux Champenois, Sancerre, or Pouilly-Fumé tastes fine. With the salty and bitter older cheese a more anonymous thirst quencher possessing fresh acidity, sufficient body, and a bittersweet finish is better: in other words a beer from Picardy such as Les 3-monts or Col Vert, or possibly a Jeanlain. Genever from northern France is also good.

ROQUEFORT AOC
The origins of this famous blue sheep's milk cheese is protected. The milk comes solely from the surroundings of Roquefort-sur-Soulzon in Aveyron and five bordering departments. The cheese is matured in huge underground cellars in the village. Roquefort has a long and glorious history. The cheese was first officially protected by the French king in 1666 and also recognised by the French Revolution.

Roquefort is a round cheese of about 8 in (20 cm) diameter and 4 in (100 mm) high that weighs 5 lb 8 oz–6 lb 10 oz (2.5–3 kg) made only with full-cream pasteurised sheep's milk from the immediate area of Aveyron. Animal rennet is added to warm milk, sometimes also with a culture of *Penicillium roqueforti* but can also be added when the curd is scooped into its forms, or when the curd is cut. Young cheeses are turned five times each day so that excess whey is drained off. Once salted the cheese is transferred to cellars for at least three months deep underground in the Combalou high plateau of the Massif Central. The ventilation is excellent and ensures the development of the blue mould which imparts such a unique taste to this cheese. The aroma is reminiscent of mould and of sheep's milk and the flavour is quite subtle, complex, and yet robust. The cheese is packed in foil bearing the Roquefort name with the AC insignia and a small logo of a red ewe, which is Roquefort's emblem. The cheese itself should be firm and not too crumbly. Fat content is at least 52%. Roquefort does not readily withstand changes in temperature so keep it in a cool place and put it at room temperature an hour before serving. Never return Roquefort that has been at room temperature to storage with other Roquefort that has been kept cool. Use up any Roquefort that has become too warm in vol-

Roquefort

au-vents, soufflés, quiches, and such like. Drink a full-bodied and rounded sweet white with Roquefort such as a classic Sauternes, but a fine Barsac, Loupiac, Ste-Croix-du-Mont, Monbazillac, Saussignac, Jurançon, or Pacherenc du Vic-Bilh Moelleux/Liquoreux is also good. For those seeking a taste adventure try a fortified red wine such as a Maury or Banyuls. Alternatively you could drink a fine Ambré from Domaines Cazes or a Rasteau.

Many regard this as the best Roquefort

ROUCOULONS
A modern branded cheese from Haut-Saône (in eastern France) made with pasteurised cow's milk that has a washed rind coated with white mould. Ideal for not demanding too much of their cheese with a creamy taste. Fat content is 55%. Drink a Chardonnay or Pinot Noir with this cheese.

Roucoulons

ROUY
Rouy is a soft branded cheese with red washed rind from Brittany, made with pasteurised cow's milk to which lactic acid is first added and then animal rennet. A square cheese of 6⅞ in (175 mm) that is

Rouy

1½ in (40 mm) thick, weighing approx. 2lb (1 kg). Fat content is at least 50%. The taste is creamy, supple, unctuous, and of harsh in appearance suggests. Drink a tasty beer or spirits or simple red Loire wine.

ST-AGUR
A branded blue cheese made with cow's milk from the Auvergne that is a creamier and milder version of Bleu d'Auvergne.

ST-ALBRAY
There is little of note to say about this branded cheese from the Pyrenees apart from its somewhat rustic-looking crown shape. St-Albray has an aroma and taste of heated milk with hints of nuts and dried fruit. It appears harsh but is quite mild and amenable in taste. A fine cheese for those who do not like too prominent a flavour in their cheese. Drink a dry white wine with this cheese, preferably a Jurançon or Tursan. For those who prefer red choose one from the sunny south of France.

St-Albray

ST-ANDRÉ

A modern cheese made with pasteurised cow's milk from Villefranche-de-Rouergue in central France. This large white mould cheese of 4 lb 6 oz (2 kg) is mainly sold in shops as cheese slices. There is an extremely mild and creamy cheese beneath the thin outer crust that is ideal for those who prefer a cheese without a distinctive taste. Fat content is an amazing 70%.

Drink a fruity red wine with St-André, such as a mellow Frontonnais or Marmandais that has not been cask-aged, or a mollifying choice such as a Haut-Montravel or Rosette if you like a sensual experience.

St-André

ST-AUBIN

A modern branded cheese made with pasteurised cow's milk that comes from Anjou. It looks fantastic and has a very acceptable taste.

Delicious with a light fruity red wine such as those of the Loire.

St-Aubin

STE-MAURE DE TOURAINE AC

This goat's-milk cheese of the Touraine was a by-word in the eighth and ninth centuries. A lot of goat's-milk cheese is produced in Touraine and elsewhere under this name. Only of cheeses from Indre-et-Loire and a few enclaves of neighbouring Indre and Vienne that meet strict requirements are permitted to bear the AC of Ste-Maure de Touraine. Little animal rennet is added to fresh full-cream goat's milk so that coagulation occurs

Not all Ste-Maure is permitted AC status

slowly over about twenty-four hours, mainly through the working of lactic acid. The curd is placed in long cylindrical forms but after drying is removed and holes are bored with long reeds to aid ventilation. The young cheese is salted and covered with ash. The cheese matures for at least ten days but this can last six weeks. These cheeses are rolls 5$\frac{1}{2}$–6$\frac{1}{2}$ in (14–16 cm) long and 1$\frac{3}{16}$–1$\frac{1}{2}$ in (30–40 mm) thick at the thinner end and 1$\frac{1}{2}$–2 in (40–50 mm) at the wider end. They weigh at least 8$\frac{1}{8}$ oz (250 grams) and contain at least 3$\frac{1}{2}$ oz (100 grams) of dry matter. The outside is covered with a thin layer of mould and ash. The inside is white but ivory-coloured with older cheese. Texture depends on how maturity ranging from moist and creamy with young ones to firm and dry with older ones. The taste is fresh, salty, slightly creamy, and has a slight hint of walnut or hazelnut but lots of goat's milk. Fat content is at least 45%. The cheese is at its tastiest between

Unpasteurised Ste-Maure

March and November. In its home territory they use this cheese widely in cooking but it is mainly served at the end of a meal.

Serve a fresh-tasting white from the Touraine with the young cheese and a lighter fresh and fruity red such as those of Touraine, Bourgueil, Chinon, or Anjou with the older cheese. During the season the cheese is delicious with fresh strawberries, a little pepper, and a good Cabernet d'Anjou rosé from Domaine de Bablut.

ST-FELICIEN

A small cheese of 5¼ oz (150 grams) from the region of Rhônes-Alpes made with unpasteurised cow's milk that is always delicious, always creamy, and never disappoints.

Drink a white or light red Lubéron, Diois, or Tricastin with St-Félicien.

ST-MARCELLIN

An ultra lightweight cheese of 2⅞ oz (80 grams) from the Isère valley in Rhônes-Alpes. A very creamy cheese with a full and very creamy taste for those who like a creamy taste but also those who enjoy the taste of real cheese.

Drink the great white wine Condrieu Recolte Tardive with it such as those of Yves Cuilleron.

ST-MORGON

A modern branded cheese from Normandy made with pasteurised cow's milk. It is first made as a white mould cheese and is then matured in cool damp cellars where the outer crust is regularly

St-Marcellin

Buy St-Marcellin when really mature

St-Félicien and St-Marcellin

St-Morgon

washed so that it acquires extra bite. Otherwise it is a quite ordinary mild and slightly creamy cheese. Try a Cru du Beaujolais such as a Morgon with it but a full-bodied white or red wine from the Loire, Burgundy, or Alsace make tasty companions.

ST-NECTAIRE

St-Nectaire comes from fertile land of volcanic origin which is criss-crossed by streams and rivers at an average altitude of 3,280 ft (1,000 m). The cheese is only allowed to be made in seventy-two *communes* (52 in Puy-de-Dôme, 20 in Cantal) and the milk must also stem from this same area. The classical taste of this cheese is in part derived from the grass and myriad wild flowers and herbs of the pastures. St-Nectaire has a long and glorious history and was regularly served to Louis XIV in the seventeenth century.

St-Nectaire from Salers cows

ST-NECTAIRE FERMIER

Unpasteurised St-Nectaire is made twice per day on the farms of the region after morning and evening milking. The milk is coagulated, the curd finely cut with large knives and separated from the whey before being placed in forms. After pressing the rind of the cheese is marked with a green seal and is then salted. After a final pressing lasting twenty-four hours the cheese is stored for three to six weeks to mature.

This cheese is flat, round and semi-hard. The rind is coated with mould of varying colours from drab grey-white to yellow or even orange. The cheese contains 52% dry matter and 45% fat. In addition to St-Nectaire of $8^{1}/_{4}$ x 2 in (21 cm x 50 mm) and 3 lb 12 oz (1.7 kg) there is also the Petit St-Nectaire of $5^{1}/_{8}$ x $1^{3}/_{8}$–$1^{1}/_{2}$ in (13 cm x 35–40 mm) that weighs 1 lb 5 oz (600 grams).

Farm-made St-Nectaire

ST-NECTAIRE LAITIER

This version of St-Nectaire is made by dairy companies using homogenised milk that is heated. The cheese is distinguished by the square green seal on the rind. The cheese is matured for three to four weeks.

St-Nectaire is a prized addition to the cheeseboard whether *Fermier* or *Laitier* but it is also a useful

Superb cheese from the Auvergne

cheese for cooking e.g. flans, gratins, etc. It is at its best in summer and autumn.

Drink a Pomerol or Burgundy with it although a good white from the Auvergne is equally suitable e.g. Madrague, Chanturgues, Châteaugay, or Bourdes, or perhaps a St-Pourçain, Côtes du Forez, or a Beaujolais.

ST-PAULIN

This was once a monastery cheese like Port Salut. Today it is a semi-hard cheese of unpressed curd made by hand or in large dairies with pasteurised cow's milk. It is mild, creamy, and slightly sweet. Very much a cheese for the uninitiated.

Select a light Gamay red from Touraine or fruity Pinot Noir or Merlot.

St-Paulin

Salers AC

The history of Salers is also the history of Cantal and the town of this name in the department of Cantal.

The requirements for AC Salers were drastically changed in the year 2000 in order to maintain a quality product. Other areas were able legally to mass-produce cheese they could call Salers but which did not share the taste of the real thing. Since March 2000 Salers is only permitted to be produced on the volcanic plateau at the centre of Cantal and Puy-de-Dôme with milk from this same area that is made into cheese on the same farm as the milk is produced. The former production area has been cut by more than one third and Salers can no longer be made by dairy companies. Furthermore the use of stainless steel tanks has been forbidden in favour of the traditional wooden vats or *gerles*, which ensures small scale production. The farmers are forced to work extremely hygienically because of their use of wood and the wood also ensures the development of natural lactic acid bacteria which determine the quality of the cheese. The characteristics of Salers cheese are mainly due to the volcanic soil which is rich in phosphoric

acid, calcium, and magnesium. The grass is greener here than elsewhere and wild berries, gentian, liquorice, clover, and many other aromatic plants grow here too. The very best cheese is made with milk from the native Salers cows. This is a sturdy breed with a low milk yield that produces milk of the highest quality. Only cheeses made with their milk can bear the name *Tradition Salers*.

Salers resembles an old-fashioned Cantal cheese but is far more delicious. Both types of cheese are pressed twice and matured for a long time under similar circumstances. The big difference is that Salers is only produced on the farms. The unpasteurised milk is never heated and the cheese is only made when there is lush grass (between April 15 to November 15 from 2000 onwards). Each cheese has its own individual character, with taste and aroma largely determined by what the cows have eaten. Maturing time is at least three months but usually ten to eighteen months. Salers is made into a large cylinder of varying sizes ranging from 15–18$^7/_8$ in (38–48 cm) in diameter, 11$^7/_8$–15$^3/_4$ in (30–40 cm) high, and weighing 77–121 lb (35–55 kg). In addition to the marking *Tradition Salers* the cheese can be recognised by the large decorative lettering, the heads of several cows, and a red aluminium plate with the maker's code. Salers is a hard cheese made by pressing unheated curd. The rind is thick and dry and frequently covered with red to reddish-orange cellar mould. The cheese itself is firm but supple and creamy and melts slightly on the tongue. There is a delicate fruity fragrance reminiscent of wild flowers in high pasture. The taste is rich, fully-developed, and strong with suggestions of summer flowers, herbs,

Salers

and a slightly bitter finish in which gentian can be readily recognised. Fat content is at least 45%.
Eat Salers on its own or at most with some fresh red fruit or a fresh-tasting apple. Choose a fruity red wine that is not too heavy as company such as a Châteaugay, Boudes, Côtes du Forez, Beaujolais, or Gamay from the Loire. Alternatively choose a good full-bodied white such as those of the Rhône e.g. a Condrieu by Yves Cuilleron.

SELLES-SUR-CHER AC

This cheese comes from a strictly-defined area surrounding the small town of Selles-sur-Cher on the banks of the Cher river, a southern tributary of the Loire. The local wild flowers impart their distinctive fragrance to the milk. Once this cheese was really made by the farmers for their own consumption and it was only in the nineteenth century that wider-scale trade took place from Selles-sur-Cher.
The cheese is made with full-cream unpasteurised milk from Alpine and Saanen goats and contains at least 45% fat. The cheeses are flat discs of approx. 3¾ in (95 mm) diameter and 1–1³⁄₁₆ in (25–30 mm) thickness that weigh approx. 5¼ oz (150 grams). The mild flavour is partly due to the moderate climate that ensures plenty of lush green grass for the goats. After the milk has been coagulated by addition of natural rennet the curd is shaped by hand. The young cheese is lightly sprayed with a mixture of brine and charcoal ash. Maturing time is ten days to three weeks. Selles-sur-Cher is very much a soft cheese with a firm and fine texture. The taste is quite refined and

Selles-sur-Cher

freshly milky with a hint of hazelnut and there can be a sweet finish. Fat content is at least 45%. Eat this cheese on toast as a starter or at the end of a meal. Do not remove the layer of ash on the rind under any circumstances for this adds greatly to the flavour.
Drink a fresh white or young red wine with this cheese, preferably from the same area, e.g. Touraine blanc or red Chinon, Bourgueil, or Touraine Gamay etc.

SOUMAINTRAIN

A local variety of Epoisses that is made from either fresh or pasteurised cow's milk. It is a soft cheese with a washed rind. See also Epoisses.

Selles-sur-Cher

TOMME

Collective name for countless different cheeses from the mountains of France. These are mainly made with unpasteurised milk from cows or goats that are sold both young and mature. Some of them are small and soft while others are huge and hard. There are also varieties with a washed rind such as the superb Tomme de Chèvre du Pays Nantais.

TOMME DE SAVOIE

A centuries old semi-hard cow's-milk cheese of curd that is pressed but not heated from the departments of Savoie and Haute-Savoie and a few *communes* in the department of Ain. These cheeses are 7–8¼ in (18–21 cm) in diameter and weigh 2 lb 10 oz–4 lb 6 oz (1.2–2 kg) and they are sold both whole and as portions. The cheese is made with either unpasteurised or heat-treated/pasteurised milk. Animal rennet is added at a temperature of 30–35°C (86–95°F) and following coagulation the curd is cut into small pieces, stirred, and then placed in moulds layer-by-layer over a space of five to eight hours. Once the mould is entirely filled the curd is lightly squeezed and then pressed. After pressing the cheese is turned and provided with a casein plate with the

Tomme de chèvre du pays Nantais

Tomme de Savoie

producer's code. After this the cheese is salted by hand or immersed in brine. Maturing time is at least six weeks. The rind is grey and covered with red and yellow-orange moulds. The cheese itself is supple and soft with irregular air bubbles. The taste is reminiscent of mountain pastures with a finish that includes hints of hazelnut. Fat content is 20–40%.

TOURRÉE DE L'AUBIER

A modern variety of Vacherin from Lorraine. The cheese is girded with a ring of spruce wood (*épicéa*) which gives the cheese a resinous aroma. Tourrée de l'Aubier is made with pasteurised cow's milk and is matured for three weeks. It has a

Bethmale, Vache des Pyrénées

washed rind. Fat content is 60% of the dry matter. The penetrating aroma of resin makes it difficult to combine this cheese with wine. Drink a simple rustic wine that has not been cask aged, such as a Burgundy, Beaujolais, or wine from Alsace but maybe a wine from the Jura or Arbois is better still.

VACHE DES PYRÉNÉES

A collective name for various mountain cheeses made with unpasteurised cow's milk that are generally semi-hard. Heartily recommended cheeses of this type include Barousse/Esbareich and Bethmale. See also Moulis.

VALENÇAY AC

This cheese was granted AC status quite recently. It comes from the area around the small town of Valençay in Berry and may only be made in the department of Indre and several *communes* of the departments of Cher, Indre-et-Loire, and Loir-et-Cher. The precise origin of this cheese is not known but we do know that its knotted pyramid form was the idea of Talleyrand who inhabited the castle of Valençay and was a famous politician of the French Revolution and under Napoleon and subsequent French monarchs. In the nineteenth century the cheeses from Valençay were very popular in the markets of Paris. Napoleon saw the pyramid form of Valençay during a visit to

Talleyrand's castle after his disastrous Egyptian campaign. He drew his sword and hacked off the top of the cheese because its pyramid shape reminded him of his failure in Egypt.

The cheese is still made in the same manner as long ago. After animal rennet has been added to the fresh and unpasteurised goat's milk (from Alpine and Saanen goats) the process of coagulation takes twenty-four to thirty-six hours. The soft curd is spooned directly into forms in which the curd drains. After passage of time the cheese is removed from the form and is salted by hand and coated with ash. The cheeses are matured in a minimum of eleven days from the time the rennet was added. The base of the pyramid is 2⁹/₁₆ x 2⁹/₁₆ in (65 x 65 mm) and the cheese weighs at least 7³/₄ oz (220 grams). The cheese is soft and has a grey to grey-blue exterior with patches of white or blue mould. The cheese is firm and smooth with a fine white colour. The aroma is fresh with notes redolent of an autumn walk in a wood. The taste is fresh and milky with elegant nuances of fresh walnuts and dried fruit. Fat content is at least 45%. Valençay has a wide range of uses: with bread, for lunch, with an aperitif, or at the end of a meal. Drink a fresh white, rosé, or red wine from the locality such as Valençay of course or a Châteaumeillant, Reuilly, Quincy, Menetou-Salon, or Sancerre.

VIEUX-LILLE

This Maroilles-like cheese is made in Thiérache in northern France. It is not a cheese for the uninitiated and needs to be eaten locally in view of its very strong aroma. Not surprisingly the local name is *le vieux puant* (the old stinker). The pungent smell is caused by a drab grey layer of bacteria that appears on the outside of the cheese while it is maturing. The cheese is matured in brine for at least three months. The cheese is square and weighs 7 oz–1 lb 12 oz (200–800 grams). Those who dare to confront the smell discover soft but firm cheese with a strong, earthy, but wonderful taste. Fat content is 45%.

Do not drink wine with this cheese. Much better is a glass of a good local beer from northern France of a Belgian genever.

Vieux-Lille, the "old stinker"

WINZERKÄSE

A speciality soft cheese from Alsace that is washed with Alsatian wine.

Winzerkäse

Middle East and Africa

The cultures of many countries around the Mediterranean Sea were significantly influenced by the urge to migrate of the nomadic people of central Europe and also by the Babylonians, Assyrians, Phoenicians, Phocaeans, Phrygians, Etruscans, Greeks, Egyptians, Romans, and of course the Ottomans (Turks). All these peoples have left their mark via the Middle East on countries from Austria and Hungary through the Balkans to North Africa where the original inhabitants (the Berbers and Kabyles) were driven out by the Phoenicians (who founded Carthage), the Romans, and later the Ottomans.

It is little wonder therefore that there is so much in common in the culinary cultures of the countries of the southern and eastern Mediterranean. Hence many similar types of cheese are to be found in a number of countries, perhaps slightly differently named. Here we limit ourselves to the more commonly found cheeses, their geographic origins, and any variations in name. The major cities of this part of the world are increasingly eating locally-produced variants of well-known Western European cheeses and in this Israel leads the way.

AKKAWI

Akkawi is the name given in the Lebanon to a flat, round hard cheese of cow's milk. Such cheese is

Lebanese Akkawi

regarded as a special delicacy that is far more special than the everyday sheep's-milk cheese. Other varieties though are made with sheep's milk. Akkawi is also made outside the Lebanon in Syria (Akavi), and Algeria (Akaawi). The main difference in these cheeses is the extent of their maturing but most are sold when young. Young cheese is soft, and mild and fresh in taste becoming stronger and drier with age. All these cheeses can be eaten on their own, as part of lunch, or be incorporated in all manner of dishes. The size of them varies between 14 oz (400 grams) to more than 22 lb (10 kg). The smaller cheeses can be allowed to mature for a further month or so but the larger ones for a shorter time. Fat content is 20–25% (slightly more than 50% of the dry matter).

BALADI

Baladi is a typical Lebanese cheese with a long history and this is incorporated in the name "native" cheese. Baladi is a soft cheese that is white with a creamy to crumbly texture. Traditional Baladi is still made with unpasteurised sheep's milk but cow's milk is increasingly being used. Baladi is mainly eaten on bread for breakfast or as a snack between meals.

BRYNZA

Good quality Brynza is also made in Israel. Originally these small cheeses were made with sheep's milk but today a small proportion of milk from cows and or goats is permitted.

HALLOUM

Halloum is the Lebanese name for Halloumi. It closely resembles the Cypriot cheese and is also made with sheep's milk, both with and without the addition of mint (see Cyprus).

JIBNEH

Jibneh is a simple cheese that is extremely popular in the Middle East and also in Egypt and Morocco. In Morocco the cheese is known as Jbane and is made with unpasteurised goat's milk. In Saudi Arabia it is known as Jupneh or Jubna and is made with goat's or sheep's milk. In Israel it is called Jibna. All these cheeses are made in the same manner. The curd is wrapped in a cloth and placed between two boards for pressing (stones are placed on the uppermost board to bear down on the curd). Full-cream milk is used in each case. Young Jibneh is a superb cheese for breakfast, lunch, or combined with a raw vegetables and bread.

KASHKAWAN

The Syrian name for Kashkaval. This cheese is made as Kashkaval in Israel.

LABNEH

This cheese is best-known from the Lebanon but is also made elsewhere. In Syria it is Lebnye or Laniya which is made by heating sour milk with rice or barley until it coagulates. The young cheese is then mixed with thyme or other herbs and made into balls.

The cheese is eaten fresh or sun dried. This same cheese is known in Israel as Lebbene. The dried form is known in Syria as Lebbene be-zet and Duberki in Israel. If the cheese has dried rock hard in the sun the Israelis call it Kislik. The young watery version of this cheese is known as Laban in Jordan and the thicker older form as Labaneh. Although all these countries allow a small proportion of this cheese to mature the great majority of it is eaten while fresh.

In reality this young Labneh is not actually a cheese but a form of yoghurt akin to the Sauermilchkäse of the Germans. It is delicious as a cheese dip, as a cheese spread, or to eat with fresh fruit. The texture is creamy and soft, the taste is fairly neutral and fresh. Fat content is 12% (48% of the dry matter).

Lebanese goat's milk Labneh in oil

LOUR

Fresh cheese, generally made with sheep's milk, from Iraq that is eaten within a few days of being made.

MEIRA

The way that Meira–a typical Iraqi cheese–is made is very similar to Jibneh (see also). The difference is in the cutting of the young cheese into strips after the curd has been pressed. These strips are then kept in sheepskin for up to twelve months. Young Meira is readily sliced and supple but the old cheese is very hard and has to be grated.

NABOULSI

This cheese is found in the Lebanon, Syria, and Jordan. It is a fresh cheese that just like Feta is

Akkawi, labneh en nabulsi

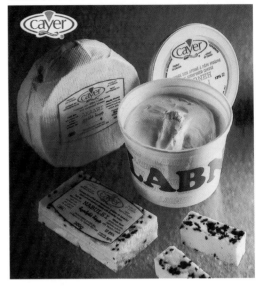

sold in slices in brine. The taste is exotic through the addition of cumin to the curd. It is used in salads but is also placed on skewers and grilled. The taste and texture of this cheese is somewhere between Feta and Halloumi or Halloum. In common with Halloumi, Naboulsi is rather salty and quite rubbery. Fat content is 25% (50% of the dry matter).

SERET PENIR

This cheese from Iran would appear to be the missing link between Indian Panir and Turkish Peyir. The nomads of Iraq make Seret Panir with whatever milk is available from camel's milk to milk from asses, goats, or sheep. The milk is allowed to sour through the heat of the sun in earthenware containers.

After several days the curd is scooped out and placed in cloths. Excess whey is removed by pressing and the young cheese is then smoked above a fire. Once the curd is hard enough it is fashioned into balls that are dried in the sun. After a time the cheeses are immersed in brine and coated with a layer of wax. Seret Penir can be kept for a long time. There are other ancient cheeses made by nomads in Iran, such as Lighvan, which is a Feta-like cheese of milk from sheep and or goats and Kaschgaii, which is a hard cheese for which the milk is heated.

ZWATIT GEWINA

Zwatit Gewina is a fresh cheese of pasteurised sheep's milk from Israel. The young curd is lightly pressed in round baskets which leave their impression. The texture of this white cheese is similar to that of Feta and the taste is rather salty. Modern mass-produced versions are now made with a mixture of milk from cows, goats, and sheep. Fat content is 30–40%.

North Africa

Reference has already been made to cheesemaking in North Africa in the sections on Greece, Turkey, and the Middle East. A new development not referred to in those previous details is the production of cheese with pasteurised camel's milk by an English woman living in Mauritania. The first results of this cheese and its sales look very promising. The appropriate name of Caravane has been chosen for this Mauritanian cheese of Nancy Abeiderrahmane.

Cheese is also made in darkest Africa, albeit in limited volume. It is strange that Africans have kept cattle since ancient times but have little knowledge of dairy production, perhaps through the constant drought. Milk and cheese are high in animal protein which is missing in the diet of poorer parts of Africa.

The nomadic life style of many of the people of Central Africa makes it difficult for them to develop organised dairy production. Countless projects have been carried out since the 1980s to set up small dairy plants in Central Africa but unfortunately not all the results have been hopeful. People are keen but so far levels of quality have been wanting, in part because of low yields resulting from insufficient fodder for cattle.

Mediterranean goat's-milk cheese balls

Increasing amounts of cheese are being made in Africa in a manner that is strange for those from Europe and North America. The basic milk for cheesemaking is often reconstituted from dried milk powder. This milk is pasteurised and turned into "fresh" cheeses that resemble Feta and Labneh. One advantage of this is that people get enhanced animal protein in their diet in a safer

Fresh North African cheese

Vegetarian cheese from the Middle East

The fiery Mediterranean aperitif: Mezze

way in terms of health. It is doubtful if such cheese has much taste.

South Africa

There is one country in Africa that is entirely different when it comes to an established dairy industry. This is not surprising because of the large numbers living in this country that originated from Britain, The Netherlands, Germany, and France. Cattle herds existed before the arrival of European colonists but the many native tribes were not aware that their cows could be milked as well as eaten.

The present cattle are mainly cross-breeds of the native African cows of the Nama and other people with Friesians brought by the Dutch, and Ayrshire and Jersey cows brought by the British.

Many copies of European cheeses

The different immigrants brought their own customs and cheesemaking practices to South Africa so that it is possible to find first-class Cheddar, Gouda, Edam, Camembert, and Brie type cheeses. Towards the end of the twentieth century increasing amounts of cheeses such as

Delicious with a few olives

Feta, and Italian and even Danish cheeses were also copied. The results of these vary from poor to excellent. Unfortunately most of the cheese is made with pasteurised milk so that they are never able to attain or deserve the epithet of "outstanding." One cheese that is recommended is Fairview Estate of Suider Paarl, makers of specialist cheeses from Jersey cows and Saanen goats. This estate also produces some very good wines.

South Africa copies many European cheeses

South African goat's-milk Camembert

Asia

The history of cheese probably began in Asia several thousand years ago when nomadic tribes hung milk in saddle bags made from the stomachs of young animals during their long treks. Through the heat, shaking, and contact with the leather the milk soured and coagulated. There is very little difference in Asia today between present-day cheese and this ancient form, except where western influence is more clearly apparent.

Afghanistan, Pakistan, Nepal, Mongolia, and Tibet

Many Asian countries still make the same types of cheese as thousands of years ago. In these countries cheese is not a luxury but a by-product. The clarified butter or ghee made from milk is a sumptuous experience not to be missed. Ghee is widely used in almost anything, including curry and even tea.

In Afghanistan, Pakistan, and Nepal they make special basket cheeses with the buttermilk remaining from making ghee, known as *krut, karut,* or *qurut.* This is similar to the cheese made in Europe from whey. After the buttermilk has been heated, which causes the albumin to solidify, the curd is placed in baskets to drain. After a while salt is added to the curd which is then thoroughly kneaded. The cheeses dry in the sun until extremely hard so that they are easy to transport and to keep. Before use some of the cheese is broken off and allowed to absorb moisture. Sometimes these cheeses are formed into rectangular blocks between bricks or stones. This type of cheese is known as Chura in Tibet.

In Pakistan and Afghanistan fresh cheese is also made by souring the milk in the stomach of a newly-born lamb or calf, in common with many countries of the Middle East. These cheeses are known as *panire* in central Asia, and as *panir* elsewhere in Asia. In both Afghanistan and Pakistan cheese is made with milk from sheep and buffalo.

A single Panir and pieces of this cheese

masses from the 1970s and visited its famous vineyards. And while the majority of Japanese prefer a cheese spread such as *La Vache qui rit* they feel obliged to take even the smelliest of cheese home with them. Since then there are now far more French cheeses but also those from Australia and New Zealand to be found in Japan.

A lot of imports

Currently slightly more than one third of dairy production is of cheese. The largest volume dairy product is ice cream.

In Japan too the emphasis is on the health benefits of dairy products. Hence milk is praised as a means to prevent what advertising agencies describe as the world's biggest health problem: osteoporosis. Where previously the Japanese authorities gave scant regard to this problem they now warn of a chronic lack of calcium. "Milk is good, milk is essential," is the slogan. Cheese is becoming increasingly more important with this attitude. Drinking milk is seen as a medical necessity and eating cheese as virtuous and healthy.

The Japanese like to use the Internet to buy cheese, ordering by e-mail and paying on receipt. The cheese is carefully packed and delivered chilled. Foreign cheese is still quite new for the Japanese and tends to be eaten in the better off families. The Japanese do not seem to concern themselves that these "luxury" foreign cheeses are often merely branded mass produced products we can find in our supermarkets.

French or Italian? No Australian!

Oceania

There are two extremely productive dairy nations on the far side of the world: New Zealand and Australia. In addition to meeting the growing demands of their domestic markets both these countries also export, especially to Asia but New Zealand and Australian cheese is also readily to be found in Europe and North America.

This is not surprising since most of these cheeses are copies of European cheeses. Despite this it is well worth trying some of these cheeses for they can easily stand up to comparison with the originals.

New Zealand

The Maoris and Morioris knew nothing of cheese before the first British colonists reach New Zealand. It was the British who introduced cows to the islands, in particular Jerseys, Guernseys, and black and white Friesians.

The first blue cheeses were made for their own consumption in the nineteenth century but the breakthrough for the New Zealand dairy industry happened during World War II when the starving British became acquainted with New Zealand Cheddar. In the second half of the twentieth century the New Zealand dairy industry successfully developed new markets in Russia, Japan, Asia, and the Middle East. New Zealand is a very green country that lends itself to milk production. The new inhabitants of these islands eventually also gained the help of Dutch colonists who brought their experience and knowledge with them.

In addition to the large volumes of English-type cheese there soon followed copies of Edam, Gouda, Leiden, and Maasdam and other Dutch cheeses. Because Australia was such an important market for them the New Zealand cheesemakers also developed copies of French, Italian, and Greek cheeses.

At the start of the twenty-first century the New Zealand dairy industry is in very good health and on the verge of an astonishing breakthrough that can only be compared to that made by New Zealand wines. Only one thing holds them back before world-wide success is theirs: they need to scrap the ban on use of unpasteurised milk that limits their quality.

Australian pyramids of goat's-milk cheeses by Richard Thomas

The cheeses

There are outstanding New Zealand Cheddars (Barry's Bay), Gouda (Mercer, Mahoe Aged, Meyer Vintage), Gouda Herb Cheese, Brie, Colby, blue cheeses, brick cheeses, goat's-milk cheeses, and various English-style farmhouse cheeses but you cannot expect much in terms of originality. It is a strange experience though to enjoy a home-made "Brie" or "Ste-Maure", Cheddar, or Gouda that was made on the other side of the world. Perhaps the most interesting cheese is a very good quality Feta-type cheese marinated in herb oil with the exotic name of "Hipi iti" or "lamb" in Maori but the fiery strong blue cheese made with cow's milk called Kikorangi that is very creamy is also well worth trying.

Australia

The original inhabitants of Australia also knew nothing of cheese and again it was European cows, goats, and sheep that introduced the art of cheese-making. After their arrival in the late eighteenth century cheesemaking for a long time was merely a household activity from which some extra money could be earned.

Eventually dairy co-operatives arose which up to World War II all made Cheddar-type cheese. After the war and particularly in the 1960s many Greeks, Italians, Yugoslavs, Czechs, Dutch, and German immigrants arrived in Australia which led to a cultural and gastronomic revolution. The demand grew from these immigrants for cheeses from their home country so from the 1950s efforts were made to produce Camembert, Brie, Gouda, Edam, and Pecorino type cheeses.

The major changes happened though in the 1980s when the Australian economy boomed and people could afford all manner of delicious cheeses from Europe. These were so popular that a new generation of cheesemakers began to experiment with

Maturing of Australian goat's-milk cheeses

imitations of various European cheeses. In the 1990s there was explosive growth in speciality cheeses but of course all this is relative. The vast majority of the cheese production is still of Cheddar-type cheese. This is not just because of the domestic consumption but also through the important exports to Asia. Unfortunately the Australian dairy organisations have not understood the potential of the enormous unsullied areas of grassland which cows can graze the whole year. Cheese is mainly regarded as nutritious and healthy with too little consideration given to how delicious it can be. It is unbelievable that the making of cheese from unpasteurised milk in such a healthy and unsullied environment as this is banned, just as in New Zealand and South Africa. It will need several more generations before this can be changed.

The cheeses

Unlike Europe, Australia has few true regional cheeses. Cheddar, Gouda, Pecorino, and Feta etc. can in principle be made anywhere. The style of the cheesemaker, the trusted brand, and a known taste are far more important for the Australian consumer than geographical origins although these are indirectly very important. Australia is a huge country and not every cheese is available everywhere.

Only the mass-produced cheeses can be found anywhere while the specialist cheese from small producers is unlikely to find its way to consumers on the other side of this vast land.

Australians classify their cheese by types which we will also adopt. According to the Daisy Corporation the making of cheese is child's play or so they suggest in a brochure in which they tell consumers "how easy" it is for them to make their own cheese.

1. Milk the cow and pasteurise the milk to remove all harmful bacteria.
2. Add lactic acid to convert lactose into further lactic acid (the quantity depends on the type of cheese).
3. Add rennet (normally animal derived).
4. Cut the curd into pieces to separate the whey (the method and size of pieces depend on the type of cheese).
5. Heat the mixture of curd and whey so that the curd shrinks and sheds further whey.
6. Separate the curd from the whey.
7. Do what is required to create the type of cheese you want. Scoop the curd into a mould and press it.
8. Add salt if required.
9. Wrap the cheese in foil or wax, depending on the type.
10. Allow the cheese to mature in storage.

If only it was so easy to make cheese...

Australian cheddar

Just as elsewhere in the Commonwealth a great deal of Cheddar-type cheese is made in Australia. Australian Cheddar is at least equal to mass-produced English Cheddar but not comparable with top quality farmhouse Cheddar. This Cheddar is mainly sold in pre-packs in many varieties including those with added flavours. The following are the main types.

AUSTRALIAN MILD CHEDDAR
Pale yellow, firm and dense texture with mild and refined taste; matured for three months.

AUSTRALIAN SEMI-MATURED CHEDDAR
Yellow, firm and dense texture, rich-tasting, matured for three to six months.

AUSTRALIAN MATURED (TASTY) CHEDDAR
Yellow, firm and dense texture but crumbles slightly, strong-tasting; matured for six to twelve months.

AUSTRALIAN VINTAGE (EXTRA TASTY) CHEDDAR
Golden yellow, hard but crumbles slightly, strong-tasting; matured for twelve to fifteen months.

AUSTRALIAN COLBY
Pale yellow, firm, mild-tasting, matured for three months.

AUSTRALIAN CHESHIRE
Very pale yellow, firm but slightly flaky, pleasing fresh acidity, matured for four to twelve months.

AUSTRALIAN GLOUCESTER
Very pale orange, firm but crumbles, strong-tasting, matured for four to twelve months.

AUSTRALIAN LEICESTER
Yellow, firm but crumbles, strong-tasting, matured for four to twelve months.

AUSTRALIAN RED LEICESTER
Orange-red (with colouring), firm but crumbles, strong-tasting, matured for four to twelve months.

Finally there is Cheddar for cheese-on-toast and many flavoured varieties.

AUSTRALIAN PROCESSED CHEDDAR
Grated and melted, pale yellow, soft but dense and mild-tasting.

AUSTRALIAN FLAVOURED CHEDDAR
Flavoured with port, alcohol, bacon, pepper, herbs and spices, chives, onion, garlic etc.

Australian stretched curd
Stretched curd is the Australian equivalent of Italian *pasta filata*. These are cheeses with which the curd is kneaded and then stretched such as Mozzarella and Provolone. Australia has the following varieties: Australian Mozzarella, Australian Bocconcini, and Australian Scamorze.

AUSTRALIAN PROVOLONE
Available in smoked and unsmoked varieties.

AUSTRALIAN PROVOLETTE
A small version of Provolone but is smoked.

AUSTRALIAN HALOUMY
A local variant and spelling of Halloumi, the popular Mediterranean cheese.
For more information about these cheeses, which are successful copies of mass-produced versions of the original, see entries about Italy and the Middle East.

Australian stretched curd

Australian eye cheeses

The eye referred to here are the holes left by carbon dioxide bubbles while the cheese is maturing. This is generally referred to elsewhere in this book as "air bubbles." The Australians put the

Australian Cheddar

Australian eye cheese

well-known "holey" cheeses of Swiss origin but also others like Gouda and Edam in this category.

AUSTRALIAN EDAM
Always coated in the recognisable red wax; yellow, firm, with small eyes, mild, matured for two to six months.

AUSTRALIAN FONTINA
Very pale yellow, semi-hard and creamy, slight nutty aroma, matured for three to six months.

AUSTRALIAN GOUDA
Golden yellow, often in the same form as an Edam, firm and creamy, with eyes the size of a pea; mild and matured for three to six months.

AUSTRALIAN SWISS TYPES
These are Emmental and Gruyère-type cheeses with large eyes. The taste is dimly reminiscent of Swiss or (far worse) French mass-produced cheeses with a hint of nuts. It can hardly be otherwise with only three to six months maturing.
An excellent example of a good Australian cheese is the Tasmanian Heidi Gruyère. This both looks and tastes like a Beaufort with a mellow and fruit sweetness with a nutty finish.

AUSTRALIAN HAVARTI
Pale yellow with small eyes, firm, buttery, and mild; matured for two to six months.

Australian white mould, surface ripened cheese

This category includes all the white mould soft cheeses.

AUSTRALIAN BRIE
Soft and creamy with aromas of mushrooms, mould, and nuts; matured for four to seven weeks.

AUSTRALIAN CAMEMBERT
Often sold when not fully ripened with a core that is still brittle. Otherwise creamy, with aromas of mushrooms and nuts. The Australians often add peppercorns in order to pep up the flavour. Maturing time is four to seven weeks.

AUSTRALIAN DOUBLE AND TRIPLE CREAM
Creamy and even creamier...matured for four to seven weeks. This category includes excellent mature goat's-milk cheeses with different rinds such as those of Gabrielle Kervella (Kervella Affine) and Richard Thomas (Cairo and Crottin), two important new Australian cheesemakers.

Cairo pyramid and Crottin of Richard Thomas

AUSTRALIAN BLUE-VEINED CHEESE
Australian blue-veined cheeses are often well worth trying. They are inspired by French, German, Italian, and English cheeses and hence available in a wide variety of types and tastes from creamy and mild to crumbly and strong. Average maturing time is four months.

Australian white mould

Look for craft-made blue cheeses such as those of Richard Thomas whose source of inspiration is northern Italian cheeses.

Australian blue-veined cheese

Australian hard grating cheese

In typical Australian manner hard cheeses are not particularly regarded as cheese to be eaten at table but more readily for grating over pasta, as topping for gratin dishes, and in sauces. Yet many of these cheeses are well worth eating in their own right perhaps with a glass of Australian Shiraz.

AUSTRALIAN PARMESAN
A fine, strong-tasting cheese that is matured for fifteen to eighteen months.

The latest creation of Richard Thomas is maturing here

AUSTRALIAN PECORINO
Strong, salty, with a bite, not always made with sheep's milk. Young cheese is matured for one to three months; mature for four to twelve.

AUSTRALIAN PEPATO
As if this cheese was not strong enough already it also has a lot of peppercorns added to it. Matured for four to twelve months.

AUSTRALIAN RIGATINO
The mildest of these hard cheeses, matured for four to eight months.

AUSTRALIAN ROMANO
Very strong matured four to twelve months.

Australian hard grating cheese

Australian fresh unripened cheese

The Australian category for fresh cheeses. The term "unripened" is somewhat misleading since some of these "fresh" cheeses such as Feta are actually matured for six months. These cheeses are popular for culinary use.

Australian fresh, unripened cheese

AUSTRALIAN CREAMED COTTAGECHEESE
Although the name suggests otherwise, this type of cheese often forms part of slimming diets on toast or in salads. The experience of these moist soft cheeses is best described as a cross between the creaminess of quark and the granular texture of English cottage cheese.

AUSTRALIAN COTTAGECHEESE
Much firmer than European cottage cheese, being more akin to ricotta in texture.

AUSTRALIAN CREAM CHEESE
Absolutely the creamiest cheese that can be flavoured with herbs or fruit.

AUSTRALIAN NEUFCHATEL
Do not expect the fully-flavoured and creamy cheese of Normandy. The Australian version is closer in style to a French "petit Suisse," the very creamy cheese loved by children big and small, with or without chocolate or strawberry.

AUSTRALIAN RICOTTA
Looks much like the Italian original and is also made from whey but is perhaps sweeter in taste.

AUSTRALIAN QUARK/QUARG
This cheese looks nothing like the smooth and creamy quark of Europe being much more akin to European cottage cheese. It is granular and freshly acidic.

AUSTRALIAN MASCARPONE
Just as creamy as the Italian cheese if not even creamier.

AUSTRALIAN STRACCHINO
A somewhat firmer version of Italian Stracchino.

AUSTRALIAN FETA
Made with cow's milk and kept in whey for six weeks to six months, varying from soft and smooth to coarse and crumbly; slightly salty.
Other outstanding cheeses in this category include the superb fresh goat's-milk cheeses of Gabrielle Kervella (Kervella Chèvre Frais).

Australian washed rind cheeses

Do not expect the fragrance of such cheeses from Belgium, France, and Germany but certainly these washed rind cheeses are stronger smelling and tasting. Similar to Swiss mountain cheeses.

Australian washed rind cheese

AUSTRALIAN TILSIT
Deliciously full flavoured with a bit of bite. Maturing time is two to four months.

AUSTRALIAN RACLETTE
On the strong side but with a sweeter taste. Maturing time is three to six months.
The craft-made cheeses with a washed rind by makers such as Richard Thomas with his Pastorello are much more interesting.

A creation of Richard Thomas: Pastorello, a goat's-milk cheese with washed rind

America

The only countries in the vast continent of America with intensive dairy herds are Argentina, Brazil, Canada, Chile, Mexico, the USA, and Uruguay. There are no native breeds of cows, sheep, or goats and also no native cheeses. Every cheese in both North and South America is based on a European example and adapted to local circumstances and requirements.

Canada

The first cows to set hoof on Canadian soil were brought by Samuel de Champlain in the early seventeenth century to an area then known as Nouvelle-France. The numbers of colonists grew rapidly after 1610 and hence the herd grew too. Black spotted Breton and Norman cows with a later injection of Jerseys quickly formed the basic blood for the present-day Canadian cow, the Black Jersey. Cheese was made as early as the seventeenth century by French and British immigrants who used the methods known in their own countries.
Later immigrants from Switzerland, Germany, Scandinavia, and the Netherlands brought their cheesemaking knowledge and experience to Canada. The number of dairy companies grew rapidly in the nineteenth century. In the early twentieth century and also during World War II Canadian Cheddar was the rage of Britain but exports later dropped significantly. In the meantime the Canadians had found new markets in the USA and Asia.

Canadian Cheddar

The cheeses

Cheddar still dominates in the English-speaking part of Canada. In Quebec province the Trappist-like Oka and cheeses resembling mountain area raclette cheeses are the most popular. More than a hundred different types of cheese are produced in Canada, the majority of which are more or less successful imitations of European cheeses. The most popular cheeses include Canadian versions of Bocconcini, brick, Brie, Camembert, Cheddar, Colby, cottage cheese, Emmental, farmer, Feta, Friulano (also known in Canada as Montasio), cream cheese, Gouda, Gruyère, Havarti, Marbré/marble (an amusing mixture of light Canadian Cheddar, brick, and orange Canadian Cheddar or Colby), Monterey Jack, Mozzarella, Parmesan, Provolone, quark, raclette, Ricotta, St-Paulin, Canadian Swiss, and Vacherin. Because these cheeses are copies we will pay them no further attention, even though some are quite tasty. The following cheeses though deserve attention.

CANTONNIER
Semi-hard cheese of the old original monastic Port Salut type. Well made, aromatic, full of character, creamy and unctuous, with hints of nuts and fresh apples; and surprising delicious.

OKA
A semi-hard monastery-type cheese that is creamy and unctuous with delicate aromas of walnuts and apples and a somewhat salty undertone.

The USA

The present US dairy herd is a colourful mixture of old European breeds from Scandinavia, France, The Netherlands, Britain, and Switzerland. Although the making of cheese flourished on a small scale during the pioneer days the first glimmering of a true dairy industry only got under way in the nineteenth century. The first co-operatives that were established suffered during the American Civil War. After an extremely boring period in which American cheese appeared to consist solely of variations on the Cheddar theme a cheesemaking revolution seems to be happening in the USA. The demand for good foreign cheeses and for domestic craft-made cheese is increasing. Ever greater numbers of Americans appear to be turning their backs on junk food and becoming interested in culinary traditions and the making of food with care by small scale craft methods. This greater interest in craft-made cheese on the part of

Americans has also benefited European producers selling to American tourists. It is the cheeses that are on sale in the USA that mainly attract the tourists and once back home these tourists turn to a growing group of "artisan cheesemakers" who produce hand-made cheeses, sometimes even using milk that has not been pasteurised. Hand-made cheese is enjoying a real renaissance in California in particular.

Mainly cow's milk cheese

The best-known cheesemaking areas of the USA were originally the states of New York, Wisconsin,

Hubbardston Blue Cow

Hubbardston Blue Cow

California, Vermont, Massachussets, Ohio, and Oregon. American cheese production is chiefly based on cow's milk and is dominated still by Cheddar and Brick but a company such as Westfield Farm has successfully launched a fine soft cow's-milk cheese that tastes particularly good because of the addition of a blue mould to the outside of the cheese.

AMERICAN CHEDDAR
American Cheddar-type cheese can be a major disappointment. It is often rubbery and tasteless and simply intended for adding to toast, for toasted sandwiches, or use in cooking. Many of these cheeses do not even use the Cheddar process

American cheese returning to the pioneer days

Classic Vermont Cheddar by Cabot

in their cheesemaking and yet they remain extremely popular with Americans. There is really good Cheddar-type cheese though in America, even some made with milk of Jersey cows. Examples are Grafton Village and Shelburne of

Vermont and Oregon's Tillamook which is also of excellent quality.

BRICK

Originally coming from Wisconsin this in reality was a failed attempt at a spreading cheese that was previously made by forming the curd between

Mild brick of Widmar Cellars

bricks. Generally a tasteless breakfast cheese and only a very few of these cheeses can provide any degree of pleasure.

COLBY

Another classic of the crude melting pot: this cheese is often a mass-produced effort with little taste and an artificial-looking colour.

COLD PACK

This creation of the American dairy industry can be found in every supermarket. It consists of a pureed mixture of Cheddar-type cheeses that has been fused together by melting and flavouring with wine, beer, nuts, etc. This is a very popular mass product that barely deserves to be called cheese.

Tillamook's white Extra Sharp Vintage Cheddar

COUGAR GOLD

Canned Cheddar-type cheese from Oregon that is actually quite tasty.

CREAM CHEESE

A fresh and somewhat sour-tasting fresh cheese that is mainly eaten on bagels, the round Jewish American rolls with a hole in the middle.

CROWLEY

Is regarded as like Cheddar by many but is closer to Colby of Vermont. A very interesting and tasty cheese than can be matured well–at least three months and up to twelve. The mature (matured for six months) and longer matured Extra Sharp examples are among the best of American cheeses.

DRY JACK

Few cheeses in America have the symbolic significance of the various Californian Dry Jack cheeses. In a state that is so clearly influenced by Hispanic culture and history, you might not expect an Italian-style cheese to be so popular. Yet the Italians have had a major influence upon California. Just think of all the Italian names among the Californian wines.

Dry Jack is mainly intended as grating cheese. It is a dry cheese with a maturing period that can stretch to several years.

The taste is rich and strong and yet smoothly creamy with definite hints of nuts and a sweet finish. The cheese is delicious grated as pizza or soup topping but try it at least once on a cracker or with bread and some fruit.

The success of Dry Jack stems from World War II when the Italian Americans were denied Parmigiano or Pecorino. The Californian Jacks were widely available at the time and quickly caught the taste buds of the Italian community as a worthy replacement for their beloved Grana or Pecorino.

Dry Jack

MONTEREY JACK

Monterey is a bastardisation of the Spanish for "king's hill" and also the name of a well-known town in California. Both Spanish and Mexican influences are clearly apparent here. Monterey Jack, also sometimes somewhat erroneously called Fresh Jack, is a less mature version of Dry Jack that is also known as Regular Jack. It is an essential ingredient for those who adore Mexican food. Currently Monterey Jack is produced in eighteen towns in California but not in Monterey itself.

Monterey Jack is superb and multi-faceted in its use in cooking. It is mild and melts easily. But what is the origin of "Jack"? David Jacks was a Californian landowner who had his name branded on cheeses made by his tenants of Monterey. The "s" quickly disappeared from the name and Monterey Jack was born and became a huge success across America.

Monterey Jack and Dry Jack are now firmly part of the Californian history and culture. They are the descendants of the local cheese *queso del pais* of Spanish colonial times.

Monterey Jack

MOZZARELLA

Is American Mozzarella worth considering? No, not really. In reality a number of different types of cheese are lumped together under this name. Hand-made smoked and unsmoked Mozzarella is sold in plenty of specialist shops while the industrial blocks of Mozzarella seem to have just one use: for pizza.

There is good news though from the Mozzarella Company in Dallas, Texas. Through the leadership of Paula Lambert very good Mozzarella is being

Smoked Mozzarella

Capri Hubbardston Blue Goat

Capri Hubbardston Blue Goat

made from the milk of cows and or goats. The goat's-milk cheeses from this company are also of excellent quality.

TELEME
Franklin Peluso of Los Banos in California makes truly marvellous cheeses with cow's milk. This cheese cannot really be compared with any other, being somewhat of a cross between a French double crème, a Scandinavian Havarti, a Greek Feta, and the local *queso del pais* (Jack). It is soft, creamy, and unctuous.

GOAT'S-MILK CHEESE
Goat's-milk cheese became popular in the 1970s when Laura Chenel of California launched an assortment of them.

Laura Chenel had to fight the large dairy concerns as both a woman and small entrepreneur but her astonishing personality saw to it that her cheeses survived. Today she is seen by the present generation of makers of goat's-milk cheeses as the founder of modern American goat's-milk cheese. Two other women are worthy of a mention too: Judy Schad (Capriole Inc. of Indiana) with her outstanding Mont Saint Francis and Capriole Banon and Mary Keehn (Cypress Grove, Californian).

Capri Hubbardston Blue of Westfield Farm (Massachusetts) is a supremely tasty cheese on French lines (*Penicillium roqueforti* is applied to the outside of the cheese) but with a taste all of its own.

SHEEP'S-MILK CHEESE
The makers of sheep's-milk cheeses have suffered greatly but their hard struggle over twenty years or so now appears to be paying off. Two names are pre-eminent among makers of American sheep's-milk cheese: Sally Jackson (Washington State) and Jane North (Northland Sheep Dairy, New York State).

Central America

The term Central America here refers principally to Mexico and the Spanish language languages of the Caribbean.

The cheese culture in this part of the world has its origins with the Spanish colonists. The monks who came with them to convert the native people also made cheeses from the milk of cows, sheep, and goats. After the end of intensive trade between Europe and Central America most of these cheeses disappeared with the only remnant of Spanish colonial times being *queso fresco* or fresh cheese which is based on the Spanish Burgos. Other cheeses are mainly used in cooking for enchiladas, tortillas, and tacos. One good property of the

Mexican cooking cheeses is that they do not run when melted.

COTIJA
A strong Spanish version of Parmesan that is very popular in Mexico. The locals sprinkle the grated cheese literally on anything and everything that they eat..

PANELA
Very popular Mexican fresh cheese that is mainly used in cooking.

QUESO ASADERO
Semi-hard cow's-milk cheese of the *pasta filata* type that is reminiscent of Provolone. The name refers to the good melting properties of the cheese under a grill or in a hot oven. This unctuous cheese is mainly found in Mexico. The first of them were made in the state of Oaxaca and therefore bear this name.

QUESO AÑEJO
Literally "year old" cheese and hence well matured. When fresh this cheese resembles Feta but once mature and dry it is much more like the texture and taste of a reasonable Parmesan. Once this cheese was only made with goat's milk but nowadays only a very small amount of goat's milk is used to make it.

QUESO BLANCO
This "white" cheese made of cow's milk seems like a cross between cottage cheese and Mozzarella. The cheese is quite salty and freshly acidic with a hint of lemon. Its texture is like that of Halloumi. It is also flavoured with fresh fruit such as pineapple and mango.

QUESO FRESCO
This fresh cheese is based on Spanish Burgos (see there also). It is soft, moist, and freshly acidic, melts easily, and tastes delicious in salads and with fresh fruit.

QUESO JALAPEÑO
Soft cheese with flavouring of jalapeño peppers.

QUESO MEDIO LUNA/ QUESO DE PAPA
Colby-like orange cheese that is very popular with Puerto Ricans.

QUESO QUESADILLA
A soft, mild, white family cheese that is also eaten as dessert.

South America

There is little to say about South America in terms of cheese. Cheese was introduced here too by the Spanish and Portuguese. Wherever the Spanish settled the *queso fresco* described for Central America is made.

A cheese industry only got under way when immigrants arrived from other European countries. In Chile Basque immigrants make Pyrenees-like cheese with sheep's milk. In Argentina people of Italian origin produce copies of their favourite cheeses and give them their own names, such as Reggianito (Argentine Parmigiano Reggiano), and Sardo (an Argentine version of Sardinian Pecorino Romano). In Brazil a dairy industry has never really become fully established. Much cheese is imported and only a few are made locally on a small scale. Cheeses such as Minas Frescal and Minas Prensado (*pasta filato*) are related to ancient cheeses made by monks in the neighbourhood of Minas Gerais to the north of Rio de Janeiro.

Recipes with cheese

Mustard cheese rolls with fresh cream cheese and beer

(quick cheese snack or lunch dish)

FOR FOUR

50 g (1³/₄ oz) fresh cream cheese
1¹/₂ tbsp of beer (Pilsner/lager)
Pepper and salt
4 slices of mustard cheese without rind
50 g (1³/₄ oz) corn salad
1 head of chicory (endive)
2 tbsp vinaigrette

Allow the fresh cream cheese to soften and then mix it with 1 tbsp of the beer, pepper, and salt. Smear the mustard cheese with the mixture and roll the slices up tightly. Wrap the rolls in cling film and place them in a refrigerator for half an hour.

Wash and dry the corn salad, wash the chicory, remove the heart and slice into strips. Mix the vinaigrette with the remainder of the beer and toss the corn salad and chicory in the dressing.

Portion the salad between four plates, slice the cheese rolls at an angle and place these slices on the salad.

Preparation time: approx. 15 minutes (plus 30 minutes waiting time).

Suggested wine: German Riesling Kabinette from the Mosel.

Ham pouches with feta and tomato

(quick cheese starter or lunch dish)

FOR TWO

100 grams (3¹/₂ oz) Feta cheese
2 sun-dried tomatoes in oil
1 tbsp chopped basil
Pepper
2 slices of Ardennes ham sliced more thickly
2 stems of chives

Cut the Feta into cubes and blot the dried tomatoes with kitchen paper to dry them before slicing finely. Mix the Feta, tomato, basil, and ample freshly-ground pepper.

Lay out the slices of ham and spread them with the feta mixture. Make pouches of the ham and bind them with a length of chives.

Preparation time is approx. 10 minutes.

Tip: use genuine Greek Feta for this dish!

Suggested wine: Greek Robola from Cephalonia or Italian Soave Classico Superiore.

Mushrooms and cheese on toast

(quick cheese starter or lunch dish)

FOR TWO

100 grams (3¹/₂ oz) oyster mushrooms
1 shallot
1 clove of garlic
1 tbsp butter
2 tbsp fresh thyme
Pepper and salt
2 slices white bread
2 thin slices of goat's-milk cheese (Bûche)

Clean the mushrooms and slice them thinly, chop the shallot. Wipe the pan with a clove of garlic and heat the butter in it. Fry the mushrooms with 1 tbsp of thyme over a high heat for five minutes. Season the mushrooms with pepper and salt after cooking.

Toast the bread and then place the mushrooms on the toast. Place a slice of goat's-milk cheese on each piece of toast and sprinkle the remaining thyme over them. Place under a pre-heated grill to melt and brown the cheese.

Preparation time approx. 15 minutes.

Suggested wine: a young Chinon, Bourgueil, or St-Nicholas de Bourgueil from the Loire.

Mini cheese pancakes (poffertjes) with herbs

(quick cheese starter or lunch dish)

FOR TWO

200 g (7 oz) self-raising flour
Salt
I egg
100 g (3½ oz) fresh herb cheese
200–250 ml (6¾–8½ fl oz) milk
2 tbsp chopped mixed herbs
Cooking oil

Sieve the flour and add a pinch of salt to it. Blend the egg and herb cheese with 200 ml (6¾ fl oz) of milk to form a smooth mixture. Pour this into the flour and stir with a whisk or hand mixer to form a good batter. If required add additional milk.

Coat a small omelette pan with oil and fry the mini pancakes until they are golden brown. For true Dutch-style poffertjes you will need a special pan with individual forms like a bun tin.

Preparation time is approx. 20 minutes.

Suggested wine: a New Zealand Sauvignon Blanc

Fried goat's-milk cheese with apricot sauce
(starter)

FOR TWO

50 g (1³/₄ oz) dried apricots
1 tbsp balsamic vinegar
1 packet of 4 bread crumb-coated mini goat's-milk cheeses (kept chilled)
Cooking oil

Place the apricots in a glass dish and cover with water. Bring the water to the boil in a microwave oven. Allow the apricots to cool off slightly and then puree them in a blender. Bring the sauce to taste with balsamic vinegar.

Deep fry the goat's-milk cheeses until golden brown in hot oil and serve with the apricot sauce. Delicious with roast potatoes, sun-dried tomatoes, and spinach.

Preparation time is approx. 15 minutes.

Suggested wine: a French Côteaux de l'Aubance (Loire) or Viognier Vins de Pays de l'Ardêche.

Strong cheese mousse with rocket

(starter)

FOR TWO

1 sun-dried tomato in oil
1 sprig of basil
100 g (7 oz) fresh cream cheese or cottage cheese (at room temperature)
2 tbsp grated old cheese
1 tbsp lemon juice
1 tbsp olive oil
Pepper and salt
50 g (1³/₄ oz) rocket leaves

Cut the tomato into small pieces and puree it with some basil and fresh cream in a blender. Add the grated cheese to the mixture.

Combine the oil and lemon juice by beating them together in a bowl. Season to taste with salt and pepper. Add the rocket leaves to the mixture, if necessary breaking larger leaves in half.

Serve the rocket salad on two plates and then make four oval balls of the cheese mixture using two spoons and place these on the salad. Delicious with ciabatta bread.

Preparation time approx. 15 minutes.

Suggested wine: northern Italian wines such as Cortese, Arneis, Favorita, Trebbiano etc.

Pasta salad with spring cheese, yellow pepper, cherry tomatoes, and herbs

(lunch dish or starter)

FOR TWO

200 g (7 oz) penne (pasta)
Pepper and salt
100 ml (3³/₈ fl oz) olive oil
3 tbsp white wine vinegar
1 clove garlic, chopped
4 tbsp chopped mixed herbs
150 g (5³/₄ oz) spring cheese* or fresh cream cheese
1 yellow pepper
75 g (2⁵/₈ oz) cherry tomatoes

Cook the pasta in plenty of boiling salted water (with a little oil) until the penne are *al dente*.** Rinse the pasta under cold running water and leave to drain. Make a dressing with remaining oil and the vinegar by beating them together with freshly-ground pepper and salt, chopped garlic, and the herbs. Spoon the dressing over the pasta and leave it to soak in for two hours.

Cut the cheese and the yellow pepper into chunks and cut the tomatoes in half. Mix this all together with the pasta and serve as a cold salad.

Preparation time approx. 20 minutes (plus 2 hours waiting time)

Suggested wine: a dry rosé from Provence, the Rhône, or Languedoc-Roussillon (e.g. Collioure).

* Spring cheese is made with milk from the lush new spring grass. If unavailable use fresh cream cheese.
** Pasta cooked *al dente* is firm but can be bitten.

Farfalle with gorgonzola sauce

(lunch dish or starter)

FOR TWO

250 g (8⁷/₈ oz) farfalle (butterfly pasta)
Salt
1 tbsp oil
250 g (8⁷/₈ oz) Torta di Mascarpone e Gorgonzola (Magor)
10 sage leaves
Pepper
3 tbsp freshly grated Parmesan

Cook the farfalle in ample boiling water with salt and the oil until *al dente**. Drain the pasta but save the water it was cooked in.

Melt the cheese with the sage finely cut into strips in a small pan. Add the water from the pasta to create a smooth sauce. Coat the pasta with the sauce and sprinkle with parmesan and season to taste with pepper. Delicious with tomato salad.

Preparation time is approx. 15 minutes.

Suggested wine: a full-bodied Italian Chardonnay, Pinot Grigio from Trento or Alto-Adige, or a Tocai Fruilano.

* Pasta cooked *al dente* is firm but can be bitten.

Three-cheese risotto with broccoli

(main course)

FOR TWO

1 shallot
1 clove of garlic
400 g (14 oz) broccoli
approx. 450 ml (1 pt) chicken stock
40 g (1³/8 oz) butter
150 g (5¹/2 oz) risotto rice
50 ml (1¹/2 fl oz) dry white wine
25 g (⁷/8 oz) grated Gruyère cheese
30 g (1 oz) grated Pecorino cheese
30 g (1 oz) grated Parmesan cheese
Pepper

Peel and finely chop the shallot and the garlic. Clean the broccoli and remove the florets from the stalks (the stalks are not used). Bring the stock to the boil.

Melt half of the butter in a large pan with a thick base and glaze the shallot and garlic for approx. 5 minutes until golden yellow and soft. Add the risotto rice and stir the rice as it is fried until the grains are glazed. Add the wine and bring to the boil while continuing to stir.

Once the wine has been wholly absorbed add 100 ml (3³/8 fl oz) of the boiling stock to the rice and continue to stir. Once this liquid has been absorbed add further stock 100 ml (3³/8 fl oz) at a time until all the stock has been added.

Midway through the cooking time add the broccoli florets and continue to stir the risotto regularly. Cook for approx. 25 minutes until the rice is tender.

Add the different cheeses to the risotto together with the remaining butter and pepper and mix them in. Remove from the heat and leave to rest for 3 minutes.

Preparation time approx. 30 minutes.

Hint: by replacing the cheese with three different types of hard vegetarian cheese you have a delicious vegetarian dish.

Suggested wine: Italian Chianti Classico, Valpolicella Clasico Superiore, Ghemme, Rosso Piceno, Rosso Conero, or Enianto.

Kernhem cheese-rye bread terrine

(for a buffet or dessert)

FOR EIGHT

300 g (10¹/₂ oz) Kernham Classique cheese from the refrigerator (or other strong-tasting red bacteria cheese)
1¹/₂ leaves of gelatine
100 ml (3¹/₄ fl oz) dark beer (spicy)
200 g (7 oz) fresh cream cheese
Pepper and salt
400 g (14 oz) dark rye bread
8 small mini-bunches of grapes
2 ripe pears

Remove the rind from the cold cheese and cut thin slices with a cheese slice. Soak the gelatine in ample cold water. Bring the beer to the boil and dissolve the unfolded gelatine in it. Soften the fresh cream cheese in a microwave oven and mix with the beer. Season the mixture with pepper and salt. Coarsely grind or mince the bread in a mincing machine or blender/mixer.

Line a bread tin or terrine dish with cling film and coat with some of the cream cheese mixture and place in the refrigerator.

Spoon a layer of crumbled rye bread in the dish and cover with some cream cheese. Place several slices of the Kernham (or other cheese) on top and continue in this fashion until all the ingredients are used, finishing with a layer or rye bread and several spoonfuls of the cream cheese mixture. Place the dish in a refrigerator for four hours.

Turn out the terrine onto a cutting board and cut it into thin slices. Serve the cheese terrine with grapes and pear segments.

Preparation time is approx. 45 minutes (plus 12 hours waiting time).

Suggested wine: a sweet German or Austrian Riesling, Beerenauslese, or Ausbruch etc.

238

Cheese balls with port and nuts

(dessert)

FOR TWO

150 g (5¹/4 oz) fresh cream cheese
30 g (1 oz) Roquefort
1 tbsp white port
Pepper
50 g (1³/4 oz) chopped hazelnuts

Allow the cream cheese and Roquefort to come to room temperature. Blend the two types of cheese together with the port and some freshly-ground pepper in a blender and then place the mixture in a refrigerator until firm.

Form small balls of the cheese mixture and roll them in the chopped hazelnut. Portion the cheese balls between two plates. Delicious with fruit loaf.

Preparation time is approx. 15 minutes plus 30 minutes waiting time.

Suggested wine: French sweet wine, e.g. Loupiac, Ste-Croix-du-Mont, Cadillac, Cérons, Monbazillac, or Saussignac.

These cheese recipes were provided by culinair.net of The Netherlands and had previously been published in the food magazine *Smakelijk Eten*.

Recipe creation: Petra Kramp, food styling: Atie Gathier, photography: Ron Duizings, Studio: PK Culinair, Ton Borghouts, The Hague.

A final word

This encyclopedia is the result of a great deal of research and it has not been easy to distil such a body of information about cheeses from all over the world. Some countries, or their dairy industry seem to have gone to great lengths to provide information and especially illustrations while the official organisations in others appeared willing but eventually gave a rather vague impression.

I am pleased that this book is finally finished for more than one reason. In the past three years it has become clear to me that there is considerable interest in such a book in which the reader can make an exciting journey through the cheeses of the world in a simple manner. I really hope that this book can give further impulse to readers above all to discover the products of those small-scale craft-based cheesemakers in your own country and elsewhere. Try for yourself the different cheeses and other delicacies of these countries. Taste authentic craft-made cheese for yourself and you will quickly realise how much more delicious it is, but far healthier also.

Is this encyclopedia complete? In short, no. It is quite impossible in such a modest volume to describe every cheese in the world. Such a book could dedicate itself perhaps to the cheeses solely of France, Italy, and Spain.

So far as the accuracy of this book is concerned, in the two years it took to write scores of new cheeses made their appearance and others disappeared and others changed appearance. Hence such a book can never be up to date to the very minute because the world of cheese is far too vigorous and ever-changing for that. Yet this encyclopedia does provide an accurate picture of the fine and delicious cheeses that await you if you choose to explore what is out there.

Acknowledgements

The realisation of this encyclopedia was made possible with the help of a great many people who I wish to thank. In first place my parents and grandparents who imparted some of the French, Sicilian, Neapolitan, and Spanish love of good eating in my blood. Secondly I wish to thank my wife for her enormous help and patience in recent years. Without her strength and support I would never have completed this project. Also a special word of thanks for our friends Henk and Carla Dijstelbloem, cheese specialists of Oss in the Netherlands and for "good old Ton" ("c'est le bon Ton qui fair la musique"), journalist, publisher of PK Culinair, The Hague, The Netherlands.

Additional information and illustrations

- Ton Borghouts, PK Culinair, The Hague, The Netherlands
- Ron Duijzings, PK Culinair Photo Studio
- Verbakel & Seggelink, most appreciative cheese importers of The Netherlands, Hillegom, The Netherlands
- Theo & Kyrillos Aridjis, Greek importers, Utrecht, The Netherlands
- Inao Paris (Elodie Pasty), France
- Sopexa France and The Netherlands
- Syndicat Interprofessionnel du Fromage Munster/Munster Gérome, Colmar, France
- Association des Fromages d'Auvergne, Aurillac, France
- Icex, The Netherlands, Belgium and Madrid, Spain
- Vinos de Espana, The Hague
- Consorcio de los quesos de España, Madrid
- The Italian Embassy, The Hague
- ICE Nederland
- Central Marketing of Gesellschaft der Deutschen Agrarwirtschaft (CMA), Bonn
- British Cheese Board, UK
- British Embassy, The Hague
- Royal Danish Embassy, The Hague
- Mejeriforeningen, Danish Dairy Board, Denmark
- Union Suisse du Commerce de Fromage SA, Berne
- Adhésion & Associés France, France
- Adhésion & Associés Italia, Italy
- Dairy Farmers of Canada
- South Africa Dairy Foundation, Lynnwood Ridge, South Africa
- South African Embassy, The Hague
- Australian Dairy Corporation, Australia
- Richard Thomas, Australia
- Food from Sweden, Stockholm
- Bord Bía, Irish Food Board, Dusseldorf
- Irish Dairy Board, Kerrygold Germany, Krefeld

- Turkish Embassy, The Hague
- Beldis NL, IJsselstein
- Coberco Kaas, Meppel
- Laiterie Fromagerie Sèvre & Belle, Celles-sur-Belle
- Fromagerie Guilloteau, Pélussin
- Union de Sociétés Coopératives Fromagères Françaises (SCOFF), Givors,
- Laiteries H. Triballat, Rians
- Coopérative Fromagère jeune Montagne, Laguiole
- Fromagerie Ermitage, Bulgnéville
- Bongrain Export, France
- Astra-Calvé, France
- Union des Coopératives Laitières d'Isigny-Ste-Mère, Normandy
- Laiterie fromagerie Alric (Papillon), Roquefort-sur-Soulzon
- Rippoz, France
- Uniqueijo, Sao Jorge, The Azores
- Agrupamente de produtores de queijo de Azeitáo, Palmela
- Grafton Village, Vermont
- Restaurant Kohinoor of India, Arnhem

And the many friends among cheese throughout the world who helped me with information and photographs, including:

Janne Koskinen, Helsinki,
"My lad" Kevin, Australia
Michaël Tommasi, Slow-Food Provence
J-P. Dubarry, Paris
Maurice Legoy, France
Linda Freeman, culinary publications, California
Laura Werlin, journalist and author of *The New American Cheeses*, California
Bonnie Atkins, Californian Cheese, California
Lynn, New York Cheese
Marcel Lachenmann, USA

Suggested further reading

Spectrum Kaasatlas, Nancy Eekhof-Stork, 1977, Spectrum Amsterdam International

Winning ways with Cheese, The English Country Cheese Council, 1983, Purnell Publishers Ltd.

The World Encyclopedia of Cheese, Juliet Harbutt, 1998, Anness Publishing Limited, London

Steven Jenkins Cheese Primer, Steven Jenkins, 1996, Workman Publishing, New York

The Cheese Companion, Judy Ridgway, 1999, Quintet Publishing, London

Kaas en Wijn, Robert Leenaers, 1998, Kosmos/Z&K Publishers, Utrecht

Alles over Nederlandse kaas, The Dutch Dairy Bureau, Rijswijk

Dairy products from Denmark, Danish Dairy Board, Aarhus

Kennwort Käse, primer on German delicacies, C.M.A., Bonn

Het beste stukje Zwitserland, 1982, Schweizerische Käseunion AG, Bern

La Suisse Gourmande, 1992, Pro Gastronomia, Vevey

The Wine & Food of Austria, Giles MacDonogh, 1992, Mitchell Beazley Publishers, London

Catálogo de quesos de España, 1990, Ministerio de Agricultura Pesca y Alimentacion

Spain Gourmetour, The perfect match, May–August 1996, ICEX Madrid

L'Italie des fromages DOC., Un grand patrimoine, Franco Angeli, Ministero Agricultora e Foreste

A la découverte des fromages Italiens, Italie le théátre des saveurs, ICE Paris/AFIDOC.

The New American cheeses, Laura Werlin, Stewart, Tabori & Chang, New York

Index

A

Abbaye de - (Monastery cheeses)	160
Abbaye de Belloc	160
Abbaye du Mont des Cats	160
Abertam	108
Abondance AC	160
Acehuche	121, 126
Adelost	41
Affidélice au Chablis	161
Afuega'l Pitu	121
Ahuntz Gasna	163
Aisy Cendré	161
Akavi	209
Akkawi	209
Albarracín	121
Algeria	209
Alhama de Granada	122, 137
Alicante	122
Aliva ahumado	121
Aliva ahumado DO	121
Allgäuer Bergkäse	93
Allgäuer Emmental	93
Altenburger Ziegenkäse	93
American Cheddar	224
Ami du Chambertin	162
Anari	116
Añejo	122
Anevato	111
Annato	56
Anneau du Vic-Bilh	162
Ansó-Hecho	122
Anthotyro	114
Anthotyros	111
Antigoontje	85
Apérobic	176
Appenzel	99
Applewood	53
Aracena	122
Ardi Gasna	162
Ardrahan	66
Arina	76
Armada	122
Arôme	163
Arômes au vin blanc	163
Arômes aux gènes de marc	163
Arzúa	122
Asiago d'Allevo	140
Asiago DOC	139
Asiago Pressato	139
Asino	139
Asses milk	210
Australian blue-veined cheese	220
Australian Brie	220
Australian Camembert	220
Australian Cheddar	219
Australian Cheshire	219

Australian Colby	219
Australian cottage cheese	222
Australian cream cheese	222
Australian creamed cottage cheese	222
Australian double & triple cream	220
Australian Edam	220
Australian eye cheeses	219
Australian Feta	222
Australian flavoured Cheddar	219
Australian Fontina	220
Australian fresh unripened cheese	222
Australian Gloucester	219
Australian Gouda	220
Australian Haloumy	219
Australian hard grating cheese	221
Australian Havarti	220
Australian Leicester	219
Australian Mascarpone	222
Australian matured (tasty) Cheddar	219
Australian mild Cheddar	219
Australian Neufchatel	222
Australian Parmesan	221
Australian Pecorino	221
Australian Pepato	221
Australian processed Cheddar	219
Australian Provolette	219
Australian Provolone	219
Australian quark/quarg	222
Australian Raclette	222
Australian Red Leicester	219
Australian Ricotta	222
Australian Rigatino	221
Australian Romano	221
Australian semi-matured Cheddar	219
Australian Stracchino	222
Australian stretched curd	219
Australian Swiss types	220
Australian Tilsit	222
Australian vintage (extra tasty) Cheddar	219
Australian washed rind cheeses	222
Australian white mould surface ripened cheese	220
Azeitão ⚙	117
Azul	124

B

Babia y Laciana	122
Baby Edam	74
Bacteria	23
Bagnes	99
Bagòss di Bagolino	155
Baladi	209
Balaton	108
Banon	163
Barselle	84

Basing ✿	53
Basket cheese	124
Bastiaanse	76
Bath	53
Batzos	112
Bauernhandkäse	95
Bavarian Blue	97
Beaufort AC	164
Beauvoorde	85
Beenleigh Blue ✿	53
Bel Paese	140
Bel Paese	140
Bellelay	102
Bellelay	99, 102
Benasque	122
Bergader Blue	94
Bergkäse	93, 99, 104, 101, 104
Berkswell	53
Bethmale	177
Bettelmatt della Valdossola	155
Beyaz Peynir ✿	107, 115
Beyos	123, 129
Bierkäse	98
Bishop Kennedy ✿	64
Bitto DOC	140
Bjalo Salamureno Sirene	110
Blauwe Bastiaanse	73
Bleu d'Auvergne AC	164
Bleu de -	164
Bleu de Bresse	166
Bleu de Laqueuille	164
Bleu des Causses AC	166
Bleu du Haut-Jura/Bleu de Gex/Bleu de Septmoncel AC	166
Bleu du Vercors/de Sassenage AC	167
Blue Brie	97
Blue Cheshire	56
Blue Rathgore ✿	69
Blue Vinney ✿	53
Blue Wensleydale	62
Bluefort	73
Blue-veined cheeses (pates persillées)	25
Bocconcini	140
Boeren Gouda	78
Boerenjumbo	79
Boerentik	79
Bonchester	65
Bosworth ✿	54
Bosworth Leaf	54
Bouchon	162
Bougon	176
Boulette d'Avesnes	167
Boulette de Cambrai	167
Bouquet des moines	86
Boursault	167
Boursin	168
Bra DOC	140
Branzi dell'alta val Brembana	155
Bread and cheese	34
Brebiou	168
Brebis	168
Brebis des Pyrénées	168
Brick	225
Brie	93, 168
Brie artisanal de Coulommiers	169
Brie de Meaux AC	169
Brie de Melun AC	170
Brie fermier	169
Brigand	86
Brillat-Savarin	170
Brin d'Affinois	170
Brinzâ	109
Brinzâ de burduf	109
Brique -	170
Briquette -	170
Brocciu Corse/Brocciu AC	171
Bruss delle Langhe	155
Brussels cheese	86
Bruz di Murazzano	147
Bryndza	107
Brynza	209
Buelles	123
Buffalo ✿	54
Bufones	133
Bulgaria	109–110
Bureba	123
Burgos	123, 227–228
Burrata delle murge	155
Butterkäse	94
Button/Inncs ✿	54
Buxton Blue	54

C

Cabécou de Rocamadour	199
Caboc ✿	65
Cabrales	132
Cabrales DO	124
Cabreiro de Castelo Branco	118
Cáceres	124
Cacio	149
Caciocavallo Silano DOC	141
Cacioricotta Lucano	155
Caciu	148
Cádiz	124, 137
Caerphilly	63
Cairnsmore	65
Calahorra	124, 137
Cambazola	94, 97
Camel's milk	210
Camels and dromedaries	12
Camembert	94
Camembert au Calvados	173
Camembert au cidre	173
Camembert de Normandie AC	171
Camerano	124
Cancoillotte	173
Canestrato Pugliese DOC	141
Canistratu	148
Cantabria DO	124
Cantal AC	173
Cantal de caractère	174
Cantal entre-deux/doré	174
Cantal jeune/doux	174
Cantal vieux	174

Cantenaar	79
Cantonnier	223
Caprice des Dieux	174
Capricorn Goat	54
Caprini	141, 142
Capriole Banon	227
Caravane	211
Carotene	56
Carré de l'Est	174
Casale de Elva	155
Cascaval	109
Casciotta d'Urbino DOC	141
Cashel Blue 🌸	66
Casieddu di Moliterno	155
Casin	124
Casolet della Val Camonica	155
Cassoleta	124
Castellano	124
Castelmagno DOC	141
Castelo Branco	118
Cebrero/Cebreiro	125
Celtic Promise 🌸	63
Centrifuge treatment for bacteria	78
Centrifuging against bacteria	83
Cerney	54
Chabichou du Poitou AC	174
Chabichou du Poitou au lait cru, moulé à la louche	175
Chabis	175
Chablis	161
Chamois d'Or	175
Chaource AC	175
Charolais	176
Château d'Arville	86
Chaumes	176
Cheddar	54
Cheddar with port	55
Cheddar with port and stilton	55
Cheddar process	84
Cheddarisation	52
Cheese and wine	34
Cheese balls with port and nuts	239
Cheese marks	72
Cheesemaking	71
Chenna	214
Cheshire	55
Chester	94
Chevagne	86
Chèvre/Fromage de chèvre	177
Chimay	87
Chimay à la bière	87
Chimay au lait cru	87
Chimay Grand Classique	87
Chura	213
Coagulum	156
Coberco Meppel	76
Colby	225
Cold pack	225

Comté AC 177
Conches 99
Conejero 125
Coolea 66
Cooleeney 67
Coquetdale 56
Cornish Pepper 56
Cornish Yarg 56
Corsendonk 87
Corse 178
Cotherstone 56
Cotija 228
Cougar Gold 225
Coulommiers 178
Coverdale 56
Cows 13
Crandale 57
Cream cheese 226
Cream Gouda 80
Creamy Lancashire 58
Crema Bel Paese 140
Crescenza 142, 152
Croghan ⚛ 67
Crottin de Chavignol/Chavignol AC 179
Crowdie/Gruth ⚛ 65
Crowley 226
Crumbly Friesian Edam 75
Cuajada 126
Curado 130
Curd 18
Curé Nantais 179
Curworthy ⚛ 57

D

Dacca 214
Dairies 52
Damenkäse 94
Damme Brie 87
Danablu (danish blue) 46
Danbo 47
Danish Blue 46
Danish Cheddar 49
Danish cheesemaking 46
Danish Feta 47
Danish Fontina 48
Danish Mozzarella 48
Dauphin 179
Deense blue and white mould cheeses 48
Delft Blue 73
Delicatess 83
Delicatess des Saisons 83
Delicatess Mosterd (mustard) 83
Denominación de Origen Protegida 120
Derby 57
Devon Blue 57
Di alpeggio 141
Dil Peynir 115
DO 120
DOC (Denominazione di Origine Controllata) 139
Dolcelatte 142

Doolin ⚛ 67
Doppelrahm Frischkäse (double cream fresh cheese) 96
Doppelrahmstufe 93
Doruvael 74
Double Edam 74
Double Gloucester 57
Double Worcester 57
Draining 19
Dreiviertelfettstufe 93
Dreux 180
Dry Jack 226
Drying out 29
Duberki 210
Dubliner 67
Duddleswell ⚛ 57
Dunlop ⚛ 65
Duro 14
Durrus ⚛ 67
Dutch herb cheese 82
Dutch hole cheese 23, 82
Dutch sheep's-milk cheese 84

E

Edam 74, 94
Edam with cumin 75
Edam with herbs 75
Edel de Cléron 180
Edelpilzkäse 94
Edible mushroom cheese 94
Elbo 48
Elva 155
Emlett 57
Emmental 99, 105
Emmental de Savoie 180
Emmental Français/Emmental Grand Cru 180
Enzymes 17
Epoisses AC 180
Escarun di Pecora 142
Eski Kaser 116
Esrom 49
Etivaz 100
Etivaz à rebibes 100
Etorki 181
European regulations 52
Evora 118
Ewijk family 77
Exmoor Blue ⚛ 57
Explorateur 181

F

Fagottini 142
Faisselle 155, 181
Farfalle with gorgonzola sauce 236
Farmhouse Caerphilly 63
Farmhouse Cheddar 54
Farm cheese 74
Farmhouse Gouda 78
Farmhouse Jumbo 79

Farmhouse Lancashire	59	
Farmhouse Leiden with keys	84	
Fat content in cheese	71	
Fat content in dry matter	24, 72	
Fat in milk	17	
Feta	107, 112	
Fettstufe	93	
Finlandia Swiss	43	
Finn ✿	58	
Fiore Sardo DOC	142	
Five Counties	58	
Flor de Guía ✿	126	
Fogasser	129	
Fondue aux tomates	104	
Fondue de la Suisse Orientale/ Ostschweizer fondue	103	
Fondue Gruérienne	103	
Fondue of eastern Switzerland	104	
Fondue Valaisanne	103	
Fontal	49	
Fontina DOC	142	
Formaella Arachovas Parnassou	113	
Formaggio di Fossa	155	
Formai de Mut Dell'alta DOC	143	
Formaio embriago	155	
Formatge blanquet	122	
Formatge de Cassoleta	124	
Formatge de tovalló	134	
Formatge pell Florida	126	
Formatge serrat	134	
Fougerond	84	
Fougérus	182	
Fourme d'Ambert/	100	
Fourme de Montbrison AC	181	
Fourme Fribourgeois	100	
Fresh cheeses	23	
Fried goat's-milk cheese with apricot sauce	233	
Friesian Gouda	78	
Friesian Nagelkaas	76	
Frischkäse	92	
Fromage à raclette	101, 182	
Fromage bleu	164	
Fromage de Bruxelles	86	
Fromage de chèvre	159	
Fromage de Herve	88	
Fromagée du Larzac	182	
Fromages blancs	158	
Fromages fondus	159	
Fromages frais	158	
Fynbo	49	

G

Gabriel	67
Gailtaier Almkäse	105
Gaishorner Emmental Auslese	105
Galotyri	113
Gammelost	39
Gamonedo	126
Gaperon	183
Garrotxa	126, 135
Gata-Hurdes	126

Gatenkaas	23
Gaztazarra	126
Geheimratskäse	95
Geitost	39, 41
Gejtost/Gjetost	39
Genestoso	127
Genuine Loo	87
Giganti	149
Giovane	148
Girolle	102
Glarnerschabzieger	102
Glenphilly	58
Gloucester	58
Goat's-milk cheese	76, 227
Goat's-milk cheesemaking	76
Goats	14
Golden Cross	58
Golfio	129
Gomera	127
Gomser	99
Gorgonzola	142
Gorgonzola di Monte	143
Gorgonzola DOC	143
Gorgonzola dolce	142, 144
Gorgonzola naturale	144
Gorgonzola picante	143
Gorgonzola staggionato	144
Gormas	144
Gouda	77, 95
Gouda (Italian style)	80
Gouda "grass" or "May" cheese	79
Gouda with cumin	79
Goutaler	82
Goutaler	82
Gowrie	65
Graddost	41
Grana Padano DOC	144
Gratte Paille	183
Graukäse della Valle Aurina	155
Graviera Agrafon	113
Graviera Kritis	113
Graviera Naxou	113
Grazalema	127, 137
Grevéost	41
Grien tsiss	76
Grojer	107
Groyer	105
Gruyère	99, 101
Gubbeen	67

H

Halbfettstufe	93
Halloum	209
Halloumi	109, 116
Ham pouches with feta and tomato	230
Handkäse	95
Harbourne Blue ✿	58
Hard cheeses	23
Harzer Käse/Olmützer Quargel/ Mainzer Käse	95
Havarti	49
Heating	19

Heat-treated milk	57
Heidi Gruyère	220
Hereford Hop ✿	58
Herreno	126–127
Herrgardsost	41
Herve	88
Hettekaas	86
Heuvelland Grottenkaas	82
Hipi iti	218
Holland-Brabantse Gouda	78
Hollandse gatenkaas	82
Huntsman	58
Hushällsost	41

I

Iberico	128
Ibores	126, 128, 133, 135–136
Ibores DO	128
Idiazábal	126
Idiazábal DO	128
Ilves	44
Iran	210
Iraq	210
Irish Cheddar	68
Irish Vintage Cheddar	68
Isle of Mull	65
Israel	209-210

J

Jarlsberg	40
Jbane	209
Jibne	209
Jibneh	209
Jordan	210
Jubna	209
Jupneh	209
Juustoleipä	44

K

Kalathaki Lymnou	113
Karut	213
Kasar Peynir	115
Kaschgaii	210
Kaser	116
Kaseri	109
Kashkaval	107, 109, 141
Kashkawan	210
Káskaval	109
Kasseri	109, 113
Katiki Domokou	113
Keeping cheese at correct temperature	29
Kefalograviera	113
Kefalotyri	114
Kernhem	84
Kernhem cheese-rye bread terrine	238
Kerrygold	68
Kikorangi	218

Kislik	210
Kollumer	78
Kopanisti	114
Korbkäse	95
Körniger Frischkäse	96
Kotijuusto	44
Koy Peynir	115
Krut	213

L

Laban	210
Labaneh	210
Labneh	210
Labniya	210
Lactose	17
Lactoserum	151
Ladotyri Mytilinis	114
Laguiole AC	183
Lajta	108
Lanark Blue ✿	65
Lancashire	58
Landana	83
Langres AC	184
Lappi	44
Lebanon	116, 209–210
Lebbene	210
Lebbene be-zet	210
Lebnye	210
Leche del ganado	120–121
Leerdam	82
Leiden	84
León	129
Leyden	84
Liébana DO	129
Lighvan	210
Limburg	89, 95
Limburg Caves cheese	82
Limburger	89, 95
Liptoi	108
Listeriosis	16
Livarot AC	184
Llangloffan Farmhouse	64
Los Peynir	115
Lour	210
Low fat cheese	93
Low salt Gouda	79
Low-fat Gouda	79

M

Maasdam/Maasdammer	82
Maasland	79
Maasland, mature	79
Maaslander, old	79
Magor	144
Mahon DO	129
Mainzer Käse	95
Maiorchino	148
Majorero	125
Majorero DO	129

Málaga	129, 137
Mallorquín	129
Malvern ✿	59
Manchego	124, 127
Manchego DO	131
Mandur	109
Manouri	114
Manur	109
Mare and ass milk	12
Maredsous	89
Maroilles AC	185
Marzulinu	148
Mascarpone	144
Mató	131
Maturing cheese	20, 71
Maturity indication	71
Mauritanian cheese	211
Meira	210
Menallack Farmhouse ✿	59
Mendip	59
Merina branca	118
Merlijn	89
Mesclados	121
Mesost	42
Metsovone	114
Metton	173
Microfiltration	78
Mihalic Peynir ✿	116
Milk protein	17
Milleens	69
Milner	80
Milner with cumin	80
Milner extra mature	80
Milner mature	80
Mimolette	74, 186
Minas Frescal	228
Minas prensado	228
Min-Gabhar ✿	69
Mini cheese pancakes (poffertjes) with herbs	232
Molbo	50
Mon Chou	96
Monastery cheeses	85, 160
Mondseer	105
Mont d'Or AC	186
Mont St-Francis	227
Montasio DOC	145
Montbriac/Rochebaron	186
Monte Veronese DOC	146
Monterey Jack	226
Montjoux	187
Montsec	131
Morbier AC	187
Morocco	209
Mould	23
Moulis	188
Mountain cheese	93, 99, 104, 101, 104
Mozzarella	146, 147, 226
Mozzarella Affumicata	146
Mozzarella di Bufala	146
Mozzarella di Bufala Campana DOC	146
Munajuusto	44
Munster	88, 93, 95, 188
Murazzano DOC	147
Murcia	132
Murcia al vino	132
Murol	190
Murolet	190
Musciu	148
Mushrooms and cheese on toast	231
Mustard cheese rolls with fresh cream cheese and beer	229
Mysost	40
Myzithra	111, 114

N

Naboulsi	210
Napoli Contadino	80
Neufchâtel AC	191
Nisa ✿	118
Nökkelost	39, 40
Non pasteurised Gouda	78
Noord-Holland Gouda	78
North Holland Gouda	78
Nucía	132
Nuits d'Or	191

O

Oaxaca	228
Odenwälder Frühstuckskäse	96
Oka	223
Old Amsterdam	80
Old Bruges	89
Old factors cheese	75
Old Worcester	57
Olde York	59
Oldenwald breakfast cheese	96
Olivet au foin	191
Olivet cendré	191
Olmützer Quargel	95
Orienta	83
Orkney Extra Mature Cheddar	65
Orla ✿	69
Oropesa	132
Orsières	99
Orval	89
Oschtjepka	107
Ossau-Iraty AC	192
Osterkron	105
Oszczypek	107
Oud Brugge	89
Oude commissiekaas	75
Oxford Blue ✿	59

P

Paglierina di Rifreddo	155
Palmero	132
Palo cortado	129
Paneer	115
Panela	228
Panir ✿	210, 213, 214

Panire	213	Pâtes fraiches	25
Pant Ys Gawn	64	Pâtes molles à croûte fleurie	25
Parmigiano Reggiano DOC	147	Pâtes molles à croûte lavée	25
Parrano	80	Pâtes molles croûte fleurie	158
Pas de Bleu	89	Pâtes molles croûte lavée	158
Pasiego	132	Pâtes persillées	25, 159
Passendaele	90	Pâtes persillées/fromages bleus	159
Passendaele Bel Age	90	Pâtes pressées cuites	25, 159
Pasta filata	114, 139, 146–147, 149, 219, 228	Pâtes pressées non cuites	26, 159
Pasta salad with spring cheese, yellow pepper, cherry tomatoes, and herbs	235	Pavé	193
		Pavé d'Affinois	193
Pastorello	222	Pecorino	148
Paterkaas	90	Pecorino di Filiano	155

Pecorino Romano DOC	148
Pecorino Sardo DOC	148
Pecorino Siciliano DOC	148
Pecorino Toscano DOC	149
Pedroches ✿	132
Pélardon AC	194
Peñamellera	132
Penbryn ✿	64
Pencarreg ✿	64
Penicillium gorgonzolai	144
Penicillium roqueforti	200
Pérail	194
Peral	132
Père Joseph	90
Persillé	194
Pestoso	133
Petit Bayard	164
Petit Breton	194
Peyir	210
Peynir	115
Piacintinu di Enna	155
Picante da Beira Baixa	118
Pichtogalo chanion	114
Pico	118
Picodon affiné méthode Dieulefit	195
Picodon de l'Ardèche	136
Picodon de la Drôme AC	194
Picón	136
Picón DO	132
Picos de Europa	132, 136
Pido	133
Pié d'Angloys	195
Pipatu	149
Pithiviers au Foin	195
Podhalanski	107
Pont-l'Evêque AC	196
Porrua	133
Port Salut	196
Postel	91
Pouligny-St-Pierre AC	197
Pråtost	42
Pressed and heated curd cheese	25
Pressed but unheated curd cheese	26
Prima Donna	80
Primusali	148
Prince Jean	91
Privy Councillor's cheese	95
Prosdij	80
Provolone Valpadana DOC	149
Provula di Floresta	155

Q

Quark	94
Quartirolo Lombardo DOC	150
Queijinho da Tomar	120
Queijinhos Alentejo	118
Queijo Amarelo da Beira Baixa	117
Queijo da ilha	119
Queijo de Cabra Serrano Transmontano	118
Queijo de la serra	117
Queijo flamengo	117

Quenby	60
Quesaílla	133
Queso afiejo	228
Queso asadero	228
Queso blanco	228
Queso Cabrales	124
Queso de Castilblanco	134
Queso de Fuerteventura	129
Queso de Hierro	127
Queso de los altos	123
Queso de los puertos de Aliva	121
Queso de mortera	122
Queso de Nata	124
Queso de Nata de Cantabria	124
Queso de papa	228
Queso de Sajambre	129
Queso fresco	227–228, 228
Queso jalapeño	228
Queso medio Luna	228
Queso quesadilla	228
Quesu Gamonéu	126
Quesuco DO	133
Quesucos	129
Qurut	213

R

Rabaçal	118
Raclette	101, 197
Ragusano DOC	150
Rahm Frischkäse (fresh cream cheese)	
Rahmstufe	93
Reindeer	12
Raschera d'Alpeggio	151
Raschera DOC	151
Raschera tipico	151
Rässkäse	99
Reblochon (de Savoie) AC	197
Red bacteria cheeses	84
Red Cheshire	56
Red Leicester	59
Reggianito	228
Regueijao	118
Reijpenaer	81
Remoudou	91
Rennet	18
Ricotta	151
Ricotta dolce	151
Ricotta salata	151
Ridder	40
Rigotte	199
Rigotte de Condrieu	199
Risotto with three cheeses and broccoli	237
Robiola	151
Robiola bossolasco	152
Robiola caramagna	152
Robiola cocconato	152
Robiola del bek	152
Robiola delle Langhe	152
Robiola di Mondovi	152
Robiola di Roccaverano DOC	152
Rocamadour AC	199, 200

Rochebaron	186	Siberia	135
Rollot	200	Sierra Morena	135
Romadur	92, 96	Silter della Val Camonica	155
Romania	109–110, 116	Sint Jan	92
Roncal	122	Siraz	109
Roncal DO	133	Sirene	110
Roquefort AC	200	Skyr	39
Roucou	186	Smoked cheese	82
Roucoulons	201	Smoked Gouda	82
Rouy	201	Soft cheeses	23
Royalp	101, 102	Soft cheese with washed rind	25
Rubens	91	Soft cheese with white surface mould	25
		Somerset Blue	57
		Somerset Brie ✿	60
		Soumaintrain	206
		Spalen	99
		Speisequark	96
Saanen	99	Spijker	81
Saanenhof	77	Spitzkäse	95
Saffron	56	St. Andrews	65
Saganaki	114	St. Killian	69
Sage Derby	57	St-Agur	201
Saladito Valenciano	124	St-Albray	201
Salato morbido	155	St-André	202
Salers AC	205	Stangenkäse	95
Saloio	119	St-Aubin	202
Salting	19	Steinbuscher	96
Samsø	50	Ste-Maure de Touraine AC	202
San Michali	115	Steppenkäse	96
San Simón	133	St-Félicien	203
Sankt Patron	105	Stilton	60
Santarém	119	Stinking Bishop	62
Sao Jorge	119	Stirring	19
Sapsago	99, 102	St-Marcellin	203
Sardo	228	St-Morgon	203
Saudi Arabia	209	St-Nectaire	204
Sauermilchkäse	92, 210	St-Nectaire Fermier	204
Sbrinz	99, 101	St-Nectaire Laitier	204
Scamorza	146, 155	Stôckli	102
Schabzieger	99, 102	Stolwijker	78
Schichtkäse	96	St-Paulin	205
Schlosskäse	105	Stracchini	152
Schnittkäse	97	Stracchino	152
Selles-sur-Cher AC	206	Stravecchio	148
Selva	134	Stravecchione	148
Semicurado	130	Strong cheese mousse with rocket	234
Semi-hard cheeses	23	Subenhara	82
Senforte	82	Sussex Slipcote ✿	62
September cheese	79	Sveciaost	42
Ser trapistaw	107	Swaledale	62
Serac	99	Syria	209–210
Serbia	109		
Serena	135		
Serena DO	134		
Seret penir	210		
Seré	99		
Serpa ✿	119	Taleggio DOC	152
Serra da Estrela ✿	119	Taze Kaser	116
Serrat	134, 136	Teifi ✿	64
Servilleta	134	Teleme	227
Sfela	115	Telemea	110
Sheep	13	Tenerife	135
Sheep's-milk cheese	227	Tenero	140
Shropshire Blue	59	Terrincho	120

S

T

Testun	153
Tête de Moine	99, 102
Tetilla	122, 125
Tetilla DO	135
Texelaar	78
Three-cheese risotto with broccoli	237
Ticklemore	62
Tierno	130
Tiétar	135
Tilsit	99, 102
Tilsiter	93, 97
Toma Piemontese DOC	153
Tomar	120
Tomme	99, 207
Tomme de chèvre	99
Tomme de Chèvre du Pays Nantais	207
Tomme de Savoie	207
Tophat Cheddar	55
Torta del Casar ❀	136
Torta di Gorgonzola	154
Tourrée de l'Aubier	207
Trace elements	17
Tradition Salers	205
Trappist cheese	93, 97
Trappista sajt	108
Trautenfelser Edelschimmel	105
Trenta ❀	81
Trikalino	115
Tronchen	124
Tronchon DO	136
Tulum Peynir	115
Tuma	148
Tuma d'la paja	154
Tumazzu	148
Tupi	126
Tupi DO	136
Turunmaa	45
Tybo	50
Tymsboro ❀	62
Tyn Grug	64
Tyning	62
Tiroler Almkäse	105
Tiroler Bergkäse	105
Tiroler Graukäse	105

U

Ulloa	136
Ultrafiltration	78
Urbiés	136

V

Vache des Pyrénées	207
Vachelin	177
Vacherin du Haut-Doubs AC	186
Vacherin du Mont d'Or	99, 102, 186
Vacherin Fribourgeois	99, 102
Vacherinus	142
Valdeón	132
Valdeón DO	136

Valdeteja	136
Valençay AC	207
Valle Brembana DOC	143
Valle d'Aosta Fromadzo DOC	155
Valle de Arán	136
Valtellina Casera DOC	154
Västenbottenost	42
Vecchio	148
Vegetarian Gouda	81
Vera	137
Vidiago	137
Viejo	130
Viereck-Hartkäse	97
Viertelfettstufe	93
Vieux Bruges	89
Vieux Chimay	87
Vieux-Lille	208
Villalón	137
Vitamins	17
Vollfettstufe	93
Voralberger Alpkäse	105
Voralberger Bergkäse	105
Vulscombe	62

W

Water buffalo	12
Waterloo	62
Watou	92
Weinkäse	93, 97
Weiss-blau käse	97
Weisslacker	98
Wensleydale	62
Wensleydale with cranberries	63
Westlite	80
Whey cheese	111
White Cheshire	56
White May cheese	79
White Stilton	61
Wigmore	63
Wijnendale	92
Windsor Red	63
Winzerkäse	208
Wistermarschkäse	98
Wolverlei	77
Wistermarschkäse	98
Witte meikaas	79
Wrongel	18

X

Xenestoso	126
Xinomyzithra	114
Xinomyzithra Kritis	115

Y

Yaks	12
Yorkshire Blue ❀	63

Z

Zamorano DO   137
Zebu   12
Zuheros   137
Zwatit gewina   210

 = suitable for vegetarians